The Criminal Event

An Introduction to
Criminology in Canada

Third Edition

The Criminal Event

An Introduction to
Criminology in Canada

VINCENT F. SACCO
Queen's University

LESLIE W. KENNEDY
Rutgers University

NELSON

THOMSON LEARNING

Australia • Canada • Mexico • Singapore • Spain • United Kingdom • United States

NELSON

™

THOMSON LEARNING

The Criminal Event:
An Introduction to Criminology in Canada
Third Edition

by Vincent F. Sacco and
Leslie W. Kennedy

Editorial Director and Publisher:
Evelyn Veitch

Executive Editor:
Joanna Cotton

Marketing Managers:
Murray Moman/Karen Howell

Developmental Editor:
Christine Langone

Production Editor:
Julie van Veen

Production Coordinator:
Hedy Sellers

Creative Director:
Angela Cluer

Cover and Interior Design:
Katherine Strain

Cover Images:
Katherine Strain

Copy Editor:
Matthew Kudelka

Proofreader:
Allyson Latta

Composition Analyst:
Zenaida Diores

Printer:
Transcontinental

**National Library of Canada
Cataloguing in Publication Data**

Sacco, Vincent F., 1948–
     The criminal event : an
introduction to criminology in
Canada

3rd ed.
Includes bibliographical references
and index.
ISBN 0-17-616907-5

1. Criminology. 2. Crime—Canada.
I. Kennedy, Leslie W., 1951–
II. Title.

HV6025.S23 2001   364
C2001-901815-0

*Statistics Canada information is
used with the permission of the
Minister of Industry, as Minister
responsible for Statistics Canada.
Information on the availability
of the wide range of data from*

*Statistics Canada can be obtained
from Statistics Canada's Regional
Offices, its Word Wide Web site
at http://www.statcan.ca, and
its toll-free access number
1-800-263-1136.*

To
Tiia, Daniel, Katherin, and Ema
Ilona, Alexis, Andrea, and Grandparents

Table of Contents

PART TWO THEORIES OF CRIME   101

CHAPTER FOUR PSYCHOSOCIAL CONDITIONS AND CRIMINAL MOTIVATIONS   103

Preface

This third edition of *The Criminal Event* appears during a time that has witnessed a dramatic increase in the kinds of theoretical and empirical research that we have argued are so central to the development of a useful and meaningful criminology. This has in many ways made the task of revision both easier and more enjoyable than it might otherwise have been. The notion that the subject matter of criminology includes but extends well beyond the study of what offenders do has become an important organizing principle of contemporary research.

In this edition of *The Criminal Event*, as in the previous editions, we maintain our commitment to the view that criminology can be taught in an integrative fashion, with theories and data presented in a way that involves more than a simple recitation of facts. We break with conventional textbook approaches, which emphasize "buffet-style" approaches to the study of crime. Though many of these textbooks provide students with the basic tools of modern criminology, they tend to do so in a highly disjointed fashion. Too often those books are about the debates that criminologists have with each other rather than about the social realities of crime and criminality. In contrast, we use the idea of the criminal event as a central theme around which the teaching of criminology can be organized. This theme runs through our discussions of what motivates people to commit crime, of who suffers and how, and of what we should do about the problem of crime. This perspective allows us to examine the determinants of crime, as well as individual choice and opportunity, as part of a more complete explanation of criminal outcomes.

Furthermore, we believe we should look at crime in different contexts, since variations in situations and settings produce variations in the ways in which crime evolves. We have identified three domains of crime that guide our analysis of context: the family, leisure, and work. These domains include most daily behaviour and have been the main areas in the study of crime and its consequences.

Though our approach to the subject matter of criminology differs from that of other writers, we cover much of the same ground. Within the framework of the criminal event, we discuss all of the major issues to which new students of criminology need to be exposed. We discuss the dominant theories of crime, the most important empirical approaches to its study, and the many and varied research findings which inform our understanding of crime. As Richard A. Wright has said, introductory criminology books often have failed to reflect the current state of the research. We have tried not to fall into the trap of simply repeating old truths; we have sought confirmation of our points in current empirical studies.

To recap:

- Our use of an integrating theme—the criminal event—enables the reader to understand crime as more than simply a collection of loosely connected elements.
- Because it is important to study crime in different contexts, we have identified three domains of crime—family, leisure, and work—to guide our discussion of context.
- We give careful and detailed consideration to all of the major criminological theories.
- We use as much contemporary research as possible to inform our points of discussion.
- We summarize our discussions to point out how the criminal event perspective can be used in developing strategies for preventing crime.

WHAT'S NEW IN THE THIRD EDITION

In this edition, besides updating crime statistics and research studies (including new example boxes), we have added material on a number of topics. Most notably, we have elaborated our discussions of biology and crime and of the character of criminal transactions. More fundamentally, we have attempted to more clearly articulate our understanding of how the criminal event concept differs from other approaches (those which are offender-centred) that have dominated the study of crime. At all points in this revised edition, we have updated our discussions in ways that take advantage of new data, new theoretical thinking, and new examples that the real world of crime makes available to us. We believe these changes strengthen our arguments and demonstrate their continued relevance.

This edition includes an Instructor's Manual, Test Bank, Computerized Test Bank, and videos. For chapter links, quizzes and more, visit our Web site at www.criminalevent-3e.nelson.com.

ACKNOWLEDGMENTS

With this as with previous editions, we have benefited greatly from the assistance and advice of many people. We are grateful to Joanna Cotton at Nelson Thomson Learning for encouraging us to do a third edition and for her support throughout the project. A very special thank-you is owed to Julie van Veen, our production editor, whose frequent e-mails were a constant reminder that one never finishes a manuscript when one thinks one finishes a manuscript. We are also very thankful to Matthew Kudelka for his careful editing of the manuscript, and Allyson Latta for her keen eye in proofreading.

We would also like to thank our reviewers:

Gina Antonacci, Humber College

Stephen Baron, Queen's University

Larry R. Comeau, Sheridan College

Fiona M. Kay, Queen's University

Edward Thompson, University of Toronto

Vince Sacco, as always, would like to thank his friends and colleagues at Queen's University and elsewhere. Steve Baron, Roberta Hamilton, Fiona Kay, Carl Keane, Wendy Schuler, Bob Silverman, Lynn Wagar, and Elia Zureik were all helpful in their own ways (often without knowing it). Karen Hindle's attention to editorial details did much to allow us to get the manuscript in earlier than anybody thought we would. Vince is also very grateful to his current and former students—graduate and undergraduate—for their interest in and support for the kinds of approaches which this book develops. As classes get bigger, and human relations in the university become more distant, he owes an increasing debt to those students whose own passion for what they are doing continues to be an important motivator. (The "informal discussion groups" from 274 and 387 were of particular importance in this regard.) Finally, Daniel (the funniest guy he knows), Katherin (whose criticisms always teach him something), and Tiia (whose patience and understanding are limitless)—he thanks you most of all.

Les Kennedy would like to thank the staff and faculty at the School of Criminal Justice at Rutgers University, specifically Shirley Parker and Edith Laurencin, for the help in clearing time for this all-consuming job of writing. Marcus Felson has provided excellent feedback on our ideas. To all his current and former students, thanks are due for providing the intellectual stimulation to continue to follow these ideas. And, as always, thanks to his family, Ilona, Alexis, and Andrea, who fill his days with new and interesting adventures!

Part 1

Foundations

Chapter 1

What Is Criminology?
Defining and Constructing the Problem of Crime

> WHAT'S IN CHAPTER ONE

In this chapter we introduce criminology as a discipline and consider how both criminologists and the public think about crime. Modern criminology has its roots in the so-called classical and positivist schools of thought. The former derives from the eighteenth century, the latter from the nineteenth; both sets of ideas are still influential. Classical thought views offenders as rational—that is, as deterred by threats of sanctions and as responsive to social control. Positivists contend that criminal behaviour has causes outside those who perpetrate it, and must be fought by attacking those causes. We also examine how crime and criminals are portrayed in popular culture, and how these portrayals affect how Canadians think about crime. Finally, we explore the different ways that criminologists conceptualize **crime**. We contend that too many criminologists equate crime with the actions of the offender only. This last section serves as the point of departure for Chapter 2 (and the rest of the book), in which we discuss criminal events.

Crime
A behaviour that breaks the criminal law and is liable to public prosecution and punishment.

INTRODUCTION

Every day we are confronted with many different accounts of crime events in our neighbourhoods and cities, and across the country. These crimes include stabbings in back alleys; beatings carried out by gangs whose only motivation is to steal distinctive clothing from their young victims; major commercial frauds in which lending agencies fleece clients of their savings; and con games that target vulnerable people with get-rich-quick schemes. We must find ways to make sense of these crime events, which on the surface appear quite different from one another.

In this book it is our central contention that there are consistent ways for us to approach these and other crimes, ways that allow us to make sense of them and to place them in a broader context. We may not always be able to understand why people do certain things, but at very least we can search for explanations of crime by examining such factors as circumstances and offender and victim characteristics. What factors led up to the act? Who else was involved? Where did the event take place? What did the police do? We also want to know what was done after the event occurred, to deal with its consequences. What punishment was handed down to ensure that similar events would not happen again? The examples presented above at first seem to be unique social events; in fact, they share many characteristics that enable us to classify them the same way—that is, as criminal events.

In presenting an overview of explanations of crime, we will introduce the major theories of criminology as well as the research methods and data that are used to test hypotheses and to identify trends in crime. We will also present findings from the considerable research literature, with particular emphasis on crime that occurs at home, during leisure, and at work, and during the times when and places where most crimes occur. Because explanations of crime heavily influence views on how society should respond to it, it is important to understand what the current program responses are and how they can be brought into line to deal more effectively with crime.

The discipline of criminology has gained in stature and credibility over the years. It has also developed strong traditions, many of which are complementary, as will be seen. Next we look at criminology as a discipline, as it is practised in Canada and other countries. After this we will review the various factors that influence the study of crime.

NTL

5

Chapter 1: What Is Criminology?
Defining and Constructing the
Problem of Crime

WHAT IS CRIMINOLOGY?

THE INTELLECTUAL ORIGINS OF CRIMINOLOGY

The "founder" of criminology was an Italian philosopher named Cesare Beccaria, who wrote in the late 1700s about the need to account for the psychological reality of the offender. The state, he contended, needs to use the fear of pain to control behaviour. Beccaria called for reform of the repressive and barbaric laws of the eighteenth century, an era when justice was administered in arbitrary and abusive ways. The offender's standing in the community had a direct impact on the treatment he or she could expect from the courts; justice in this sense was relative rather than absolute.

According to Beccaria, the degree of punishment should be sufficient to outweigh the pleasure derived from the criminal act (Martin, Mutchnick, and Austin, 1990: 8). Beccaria's views, and those of Jeremy Bentham after him, heavily influenced modern thinking about deterrence and punishment. According to this **classical school** of thought, the "rational man" would act to avoid punishment. Thus it was important that laws be clear about both how one should act and what the costs of deviating from this lawful behaviour would be (Bohm, 1997).

Beccaria is better described as a social reformer than as a criminologist in the modern sense of the term. He was more interested in changes that would make the criminal justice system effective and fair than he was in explaining the causes of crime. Still, implicit in Beccaria's view was a model of what offenders are like and why they offend. For Beccaria, the offender's behaviour could be understood in terms of "**hedonism**." In short, he saw the offender as a kind of rational calculator seeking to maximize pleasure and minimize pain. It follows that a person commits crime when the pleasure promised by the offence outweighs the pain that the law threatens.

The classical model of "rational man" led to a view that the law could be used as an instrument of control. This assumed, however, that men and women were not only free to act but also equal in their ability to do so. In the late 1800s Cesare Lombroso began to question this assumption. In direct opposition to Beccaria's assumption that people have free will, Lombroso believed that human behaviour was *determined*. For Lombroso, individuals responded to their surroundings in predetermined ways, and some were born with behavioural deficiencies that led to criminality. In other words, heredity

Classical school
A school that views the offender as a "rational person" who would be deterred only by the threat of sanction.

Hedonism, principle of
The principle that the seeking of pleasure and avoidance of pain are the ultimate aims and motivating forces of human action.

Atavism
The theory that offenders are less likely to conform to the demands of contemporary social life because they are related to a more primitive evolutionary condition.

Positivist school
The philosophical position, developed by Auguste Comte, that scientific knowledge can come only from direct observation, experimentation, and provision of quantitative data (e.g., finding the cause of crime within the criminal).

was a principal cause of criminal tendencies (Martin, Mutchnick, and Austin, 1990: 29). These assumptions led Lombroso to argue that "criminal types" existed.

For Lombroso, one important type was the "atavistic criminal." **Atavism** suggests a throwback to an earlier period in human evolution. In other words, Lombroso's atavistic criminals were less likely to conform to the demands of contemporary social life because they reflected a more primitive human condition. Lombroso believed that the physical signs of atavism could be described and measured scientifically. Born criminals not only acted in a particular way but *looked* a particular way. The atavistic criminal often had ears of unusual size, fleshy lips, pouches in the cheeks, and a head of unusual size and shape (Vold, Bernard, and Snipes, 1998). Lombroso was not suggesting that these physical characteristics directly caused criminal behaviour; his point was that they were indicators that the person was more likely to behave criminally.

Lombroso is important not because of his specific theories, but because of how he approached the problem of crime generally. Unlike the classical writers who preceded him, he did not see crime as a product of free will; instead, he belonged to the **positivist school**, which considered crime in terms of causes and effects.

The legacies of classical and positivist thought are alive and well in modern-day criminology. That being said, they have taken researchers in somewhat different directions. As we will see in Chapter 4, positivist theories encourage us to consider the factors that push or pull people into criminal conduct. In contrast, the classical legacy is linked to theories that emphasize the factors constraining people from developing or acting on criminal motivations. As we will discuss in Chapter 5, when these constraints are weak, people have more freedom to do as they please—which sometimes means behaving criminally. As you will soon see, these ideas are not necessarily contradictory.

For all their differences, the various theories that fall within these two schools of thought share a fixation on criminality rather than on crime. That is, they focus on the offender rather than on the situations and broader social contexts within which offenders act.

WHAT DOES IT MEAN?

CLASSICAL VERSUS POSITIVIST

Classical criminology views the offender as rational—that is, as deterred by the threat of legal sanction and responsive to social control. Positivists contend that criminal behaviour has causes outside those who perpetrate it, and must be fought by attacking those causes.

7

Chapter 1: What Is Criminology?
Defining and Constructing the
Problem of Crime

THE MODERN STUDY OF CRIMINOLOGY

Modern criminology draws on a number of different disciplines. In Canada and elsewhere, it is "guided by the view that criminology is not a discipline but a field of study that is shaped by the insights and perspectives of many different social and even natural sciences" (Gartner, 2000). Criminologists attempt to understand not only the motivations of the offender but also the circumstances leading up to the act and its consequences for the victim(s), for others in the community, and for society at large. Criminologists are also asked to suggest how we should respond to crime (e.g., Should policing strategies be changed? Should crime prevention programs be developed?). Finally, criminologists monitor how changes in the laws and their interpretation affect how people behave in society and, in turn, how agents of social control respond to this behaviour.

Because criminology is an interdisciplinary field, people with quite different types of training are involved in the study of crime. Criminologists can be historians, psychologists, political scientists, economists, or legal scholars. Generally, however, when it is taught outside criminology and criminal justice departments, criminology is treated as a subdiscipline of sociology. Sociology has become the most important home of criminological training in North America because sociologists tend to be more involved than other researchers in the study of social problems. Also, the major figures in the teaching of criminology have been sociologists by training; this fact is then reflected in the courses that are offered. In contrast, European criminologists are more often found in law schools, which gives criminological research a more legal orientation on that continent.

Canadians have been doing research in criminology for a long time. Criminologists in this country are found mainly in sociology and criminology departments. The interests of Canadian researchers cover the entire range of topics in criminology. Examples are homicide (Silverman and Kennedy, 1993), violence against women (Johnson, 1996), corporate crime (Snider, 1993), and organized crime (Beare, 1996). In this book we draw on both Canadian and international research. Criminology as a field of study has been growing most strongly in the United States, spurred by federal funding in the 1970s and 1980s in response to social disorder in American cities. More recently, the U.S. government has generously funded studies of drug-related crime. Even so, U.S. federal funding for criminological research is low relative to the amounts committed to other areas, such as medical and biophysical research. This, even

WHAT IS CRIMINOLOGY?

CRIMINOLOGY

Taking an interdisciplinary approach, criminologists attempt to understand (a) the factors that prompt or fail to inhibit criminal motivation, (b) the circumstances leading up to the act, and (c) the consequences of the act for the victim(s), for others in the community, and for society at large. Criminologists are also asked to suggest how we should respond to crime. Finally, criminologists monitor how changes in the laws and their interpretation affect how people behave in society and, in turn, how agents of social control respond to this behaviour.

though criminological research is often expensive. We are thinking in particular of large-scale victimization surveys and longitudinal studies of offenders.

There is a great deal of interest in the study of crime in countries outside North America. For example, many countries have conducted large-scale victimization surveys. In Britain, the British Crime Survey (Kershaw et al., 2000) has been used heavily to develop policing policy, community crime prevention programs, and offender programs. Again, we will draw on such work in this book.

Our presentation will be heavily influenced by recent thinking in criminology—thinking that strongly emphasizes the routine nature of crime and maintains that individual lifestyles bring offenders and victims together in time and space to create crime opportunities. The crime that results creates consequences for all parties concerned, as a result of either police intervention or the actions of third parties.

THE PUBLIC'S INTEREST IN CRIMINAL EVENTS

Before we examine how criminologists think about and try to understand crime, we first consider the images of crime and criminals that come to us through television, films, and other forms of popular culture. Most of us embark on the study of crime with some strong—and faulty—preconceptions, which originate in images derived from popular culture.

CRIME NEWS

THE INTEREST IN CRIME NEWS

While there are differences across media types and across communities with respect to the amount of coverage that crime receives (Liska and Baccaglini, 1990), generally speaking crime is widely reported by all popular news media (Sacco, 1995). Why is this? The simple answer is that audiences are interested in such stories: crime news "sells" (Gordon and Heath, 1981). Some readers/viewers perceive crime news as an important source of "facts"; others are caught up in the dramatic and sometimes lurid nature of crime news.

NTL

9
Chapter 1: What Is Criminology?
Defining and Constructing the
Problem of Crime

Katz (1987) contends that the public's fascination with crime news has little to do with a search for the truth about crime or with the dramatic qualities of crime reporting. Rather, he maintains, crime news allows audience members to work out their own positions on moral questions of a general yet also personal nature. For example, many crime stories deal with the competence or insensitivity of offenders. As Katz (1987: 50) expresses it, we read accounts of "ingenious, vicious, and audacious crimes of deception that trick the close scrutiny of diligent customs inspectors, of the most bloody murders, of big heists in broad daylight." Stories such as these demonstrate to the audience the nature and limits of human competence and human sensitivity. They interest the audience because the dilemmas of assessing personal competence and of maintaining one's own moral sensibility are routinely encountered in daily life. For Katz (1987: 72), reading crime news is a "ritual moral exercise [and as such] appears to serve a purpose similar to the morning shower, routine physical exercise and shaving."

THE CONTENT OF CRIME NEWS

Studies on the content of crime news have yielded interesting findings (Howitt, 1998). *First,* there seems to be little relationship between the amount of *crime news* and the amount of *crime* (as measured, for instance, in official statistics). In other words, objectively measured trends in crime do not correspond closely with trends in the amount of crime news (Garofalo, 1981a; Katz, 1987). *Second,* the amount of attention the media give to crime depends on the type of offence. Violent, relatively rare crimes such as homicide are emphasized, whereas property crimes, white-collar offences, and other nonviolent, frequently occurring crimes are underreported (Chermak, 1998; Randall, Lee-Sammons, and Hagner, 1988). *Third,* crime news exaggerates the proportion of offences that result in arrest (Sacco and Fair, 1988; Skogan and Maxfield, 1981); that is, the media portray the police as far more effective than they really are. *Fourth,* the media focus their attention on the early stages of criminal justice processing (detection and arrest); the later stages of legal processing are largely ignored (Hans, 1990).

Also, media coverage is notable not only for what it includes but also for what it excludes. Crime reporting is often criticized for ignoring the relationship between crime and broad social conditions. Humphries (1981) suggests that news reports associate criminal violence with youth, maleness, and minority membership and ignore how labour markets and related institutions have historically shaped employment opportunities and the size and composition of the pool of people vulnerable to arrest. This tendency to portray crime as perpetrated mainly by pathological individuals precludes alternative explanations. For instance, a report about a single mother accused or convicted of child abuse may describe her as "disturbed" and ignore the following questions: "Was the mother receiving welfare or was she unemployed? Was the child attending a day-care program or receiving any other social services? Had the mother been a victim of child abuse?" (Gorelick, 1989: 423).

The biased nature of crime reporting is obvious in Voumvakis and Ericson's 1984 study of newspaper accounts of attacks against women. The accounts covered in this study offered explanations for the "crime wave," but did so by emphasizing (a) how the victims' actions placed them at risk, (b) the need for a more coercive—and presumably more effective—response from the criminal justice system, and (c) the pathology of offenders. Voumvakis and Ericson maintained that these terms of reference, although not necessarily unreasonable, were restrictive in that they ruled out alternative interpretations, especially ones that would have linked crimes against women to more general patterns of gender inequality. Reporting that emphasizes the need for more police, for more punishment, and for more vigilance by women does not allow for a discussion of broader programs of social reform. More recently, Stone (1993) examined how the Toronto media were treating the topic of violence against women; she found that feminist perspectives were generally absent from such reports.

THE SOURCES OF CRIME NEWS

Studies of news production practices emphasize how judgments of "newsworthiness" come to be applied to categories of events (Chibnall, 1977; Fishman, 1978). These judgments reflect how journalists perceive their society, the work they are engaged in, and the audiences they serve. For several reasons, criminal events—especially violent ones—conform closely to the professional values of journalists (Ericson, Baranek, and Chan, 1987).

First, such incidents have spatial and temporal characteristics that lend themselves easily to news production routines. Murders, thefts, and sexual assaults are discrete events. They are also "short term"—that is, they happen between one newspaper edition and the next, or one newscast and the next. *Second*, reports of criminal events are easily understood by audiences and so require little in the way of background information. Also, because there is an almost limitless supply of crime news, the number of crime-related stories can be expanded or reduced depending on the needs of media decision makers

NTL

11
Chapter 1: What Is Criminology?
Defining and Constructing the
Problem of Crime

and on the amount of space or time that must be filled on any given day (Warr, 1991). *Third*, many crimes lend themselves to a dramatic narrative form that features the exploits of clearly defined "good guys" and "bad guys" (Ericson, 1991).

News organizations rely heavily on a continuous flow of crime news. As a result, they have developed well-defined relationships with those they perceive as reliable and credible suppliers of that news (Gordon and Heath, 1981). The police are the main source of crime news; the "police wire," the press release, the news conference, and the beat reporter provide the link between the world of crime and the news media (Ericson, Baranek, and Chan, 1987). Because the police can supply a steady stream of stories that are "entertaining, dramatic, amusing and titillating" (Ericson, 1991: 207), journalists implicitly adopt a police perspective on the problem of crime (Fishman, 1981).

The relationship between police and journalists is mutually beneficial (Katz, 1987). Journalists are allowed regular access to a valued news commodity; also, they gain credibility, authority, and objectivity when they refer to the police as the official spokespeople on crime. At the same time, the police are able to present themselves as experts on crime and as "owners" of the problem of crime.

All of this helps explain why interpersonal violent crimes such as homicide and robbery receive greater coverage than crimes by or against businesses (Ericson, 1991). The established source–journalist relationships that exist with respect to "common" crimes generally do not exist in the case of business crimes. Furthermore, stories about business crime are often judged as less newsworthy because they tend to be more complex, less dramatic, and more difficult to personalize (Randall, Lee-Sammons, and Hagner, 1988).

CRIME DRAMA

Crime drama has always been important to television. From *Dragnet, The Untouchables,* and *Racket Squad* to *Law and Order* and *The Practice,* every decade has witnessed countless lawyers, police detectives, and private investigators engaged in the prime-time pursuit of law and order. Crime drama conforms closely to television's stylistic and commercial requirements (Beckett and Sasson, 2000; Sumser, 1996). These programs rely heavily on suspense and violent action, and provide a format in which both can be maximized (Sparks, 1992). As crimes are investigated, and as wrongdoers are pursued and brought to justice, opportunities abound for car chases, fistfights, and gunplay.

The essentially escapist nature of television crime drama is well recognized. No one really expects crime dramas to provide a realistic portrait of crime and criminals. The images have more to do with the needs of the medium than with a desire to accurately map reality (Beckett and Sasson, 2000). Still, it is worth noting that crime in television drama, like crime in the news, tends to be disproportionately violent (Lichter et al., 1994). Also, television criminals are generally older than their real-life counterparts—closer to the age of the audience. Real-life offenders are often poor; on television they are more likely to be affluent. In crime dramas, any association between crime and minority group membership tends to be downplayed, in order to avoid alienating a significant segment of the viewing audience (which would clearly not be in the best interests of a commercial medium). In sum, television criminals are typically "white materialists, motivated by greed and lasciviousness" (Newman, 1990: 263).

The distinction between television news and television drama is less clear than it once was (Fishman and Cavender, 1998; Tunnell, 1998; Welch, 2000). Programs such as *America's Most Wanted* and *Cops,* and the many shows that make use of amateur video to tell crime stories, combine traditional news documentary techniques with the familiar narrative style of dramatic television. These program formats (sometimes labelled "infotainment" or "reality television") have proliferated because they are popular with audiences and relatively inexpensive to produce (Kooistra and Mahoney, 1999). Crime, like other social problems, continues to be a source of both entertainment and income in the mass media (Gusfield, 1989).

TALKING ABOUT CRIME

People do more than read crime news and watch crime shows on television; they also talk about crime (Sasson, 1995). Unfortunately, social scientists seem less interested in the two-way conversations we have with each other than in the (largely) one-way conversations that the mass media have with their audiences. A major study of reactions to crime in three major American cities found that people cited their friends and neighbours, rather than the mass media, as their principal sources of information about local crime conditions (Skogan and Maxfield, 1981). That being said, talk about crime often focuses on events that have received heavy media play. Media coverage of serial killings, child abductions, and crimes committed by or against celebrities is likely to generate considerable public discussion. Much talk also centres on crime in the local environment. Residents of high-crime neighbourhoods

NTL

13
Chapter 1: What Is Criminology?
Defining and Constructing the
Problem of Crime

tend to talk more about crime (Skogan and Maxfield, 1981); they are also more likely to be personally acquainted with crime victims and thus to have more stories to tell about crime and its consequences.

In their study on fear of crime among the elderly, Kennedy and Silverman (1985) reported the surprising finding that respondents who expressed high levels of fear also had higher levels of contact with family members. The continuous cautions that the elderly (especially those living on their own) received from their families actually may have exacerbated their fears.

CRIME IN RUMOUR AND LEGEND

Sometimes talk about crime seems to bear only a tenuous relationship to reality. In 1956, news spread throughout Taipei that a number of children had been slashed with what seemed to be razor blades (Jacobs, 1965). In another famous episode in 1944, many residents of Mattoon, Illinois, were said to be the victims of a "phantom anaesthetist" who entered their homes and sprayed them with a paralyzing gas (Johnson, 1945). In 1969, the story spread through the city of Orléans, France, that Jewish dress-shop owners were kidnapping young women and selling them into the "white slave trade" (Morin, 1971). More recently, stories have arisen in many North American communities about the threat posed to children by Halloween sadists, who poison or otherwise contaminate the "treats" they dispense to unsuspecting children (Best, 1990).

There was no evidence to corroborate any of these stories. Their fanciful quality suggests a close kinship with the sociological concept of "rumour" (Rosnow, 1988; Rosnow and Fine, 1976). Like all rumours, they represented forms of **improvised news** in that they expressed anxieties and uncertainties about some aspect of social life (Shibutani, 1966). For example, Best (1990) contends that the spread of stories about Halloween sadists during the 1970s was a response to three forms of social strain that characterized the period. The *first* was increasing public concern over the vulnerability of children to child abuse and other victimizing experiences. The *second* was the general increase in the fear of crime and in the threats posed to personal safety by anonymous strangers. The *third* was an increasing mistrust of people outside of one's group. Best (1990: 143) characterized the Halloween sadist as a symbolic expression of these three anxieties: "The sadist, like other dangers, attacks children—society's most vulnerable members; the sadist, like the stereotypical criminal, is an anonymous, unprovoked assailant; and the sadist, like other strangers, should be met with suspicion rather than trust."

Improvised news
Similar to rumour; expresses anxieties and uncertainties about some aspect of social life.

Urban legend
Captivating and plausible fictional oral narratives that are widely regarded as true stories.

Folklorists use the term **urban legend** to characterize many of the crime stories that travel along interpersonal channels of communication (Brunvand, 1981, 1984, 1986, 1989). Brunvand (1984: ix) describes these legends as "highly captivating and plausible, but mainly fictional oral narratives that are widely told as true stories." Urban legends are widely circulated; typically they deal with attempted abductions in shopping malls or amusement parks, psychopaths who terrorize baby-sitters, the contamination of children's "lick and stick" tattoos with hallucinogenic drugs, and criminally insane killers who stalk couples on "lover's lane." While these stories vary in their details from place to place and over time, their moral substance has remarkable durability.

Wachs (1988) contends that crime folklore has considerable entertainment value, in that the stories, whether told or heard, provide opportunities for dramatic and often humorous release. She further characterizes these stories as "cautionary tales" that advise listeners of the dangers of urban life and the need for constant vigilance.

Some urban legends are more newsworthy than others. Stories about bicycle thieves generally have less currency than stories about killers on the loose. While talk about corporate and white-collar criminals seems to be rare, it does exist (Kapferer, 1989). In recent years, for instance, stories have circulated that some major businesses are under the control of satanic cults (Brunvand, 1984) or are wilfully contaminating food products (Kapferer, 1989). In some inner-city African-American communities, rumours circulate which suggest that certain tobacco companies and fast-food outlets are run by genocidal, racist organizations (Pipes, 1997; Turner, 1993).

Sometimes stories have very real consequences even after they have been exposed as hoaxes. In the summer of 1993 a media scare erupted over the "discovery" of hypodermic needles in Pepsi cans. All aspects of Pepsi's operations were scrutinized to determine how this could have happened. After much bad publicity, Pepsi was able to demonstrate that it was virtually impossible to insert a needle into a can during the high-speed canning processes employed in its plants. The story was later exposed as a series of hoaxes, but not before serious damage had been done to Pepsi's image. Concerns have been raised not only about the serious consequences of such hoaxes but also about the media's role in sounding the alarm and perpetuating public doubts about a product.

NTL

15

Chapter 1: What Is Criminology?
Defining and Constructing the
Problem of Crime

BOX 1.1

The Fiend under the Car

Many of the urban legends we transmit through our conversations (and increasingly via the Internet) concern the actions of violent strangers. One such story, which began to circulate widely in the mid-1990s, focused on "teenage punks" or "gangsters" who, it was said, hid beneath cars parked in supposedly safe places, like suburban shopping malls. According to the most popular forms of the story, the offender struck when the passenger was standing next to the car, opening the door. At that point he slashed the victim's ankles with a knife. When the victim bent over in pain or shock, she was robbed or raped by the offender. Several aspects of this story should be noted:

- The victim was typically female, and the offender was typically male.
- Robbery was commonly regarded as the motive for the crime, but sometimes it was claimed that the attack was part of a gang initiation.
- The colour of the offender was only rarely specified. When it was specified, the offender was said to be black.
- While such crimes have been attributed to many different places, no verifiable incidents have been discovered.

The popularity of this story may reflect its value as a cautionary tale about the dangers that lurk even in those places in the urban (and suburban) environment where we expect to feel safe. The tale also has parallels with stories that many adults heard as children about murderous fiends or mythical monsters hiding under their beds.

Source: www.snopes.com

CRIME MYTHS

Much of what we see on television or hear during late-night storytelling sessions can be described as **crime myths** (Kappeler, Blumberg, and Potter, 2000)—that is, distorted and misleading information that is nevertheless accepted as fact. For instance, many people believe these crime myths:

- The elderly are more likely to be victimized than any other group in society.
- Most crime is violent.
- Serial killers account for a substantial number of murders each year.
- Rates of victimization have risen dramatically in recent years.
- The risk of wife assault increases substantially on Super Bowl Sunday.

Yet according to the best social scientific evidence, none of these statements is true.

Crime myths
Distorted and misleading information that nevertheless is accepted as fact.

According to Kappeler and colleagues (2000), crime myths serve several important social functions. *First*, they help us organize our views about crime and the criminal justice system by providing a ready-made framework that clearly identifies criminals, victims, and crimefighters. *Second*, these myths support and maintain established views about crime. *Third*, they help us fill the gaps in our knowledge that social science has not yet filled, or cannot fill. *Fourth*, they provide an emotional outlet for our responses to crime and help establish channels for transforming emotions into action.

Because crime myths are so pervasive and so durable, they sometimes damage our objectivity. Marcus Felson (1998) contends that 10 myths—that is, fallacies derived from popular culture—obscure our understanding of the empirical realities of crime:

The dramatic fallacy The media's emphasis on strange and violent crimes that are shrouded in mystery leads us to believe that such incidents are typical. Felson points out that most crime is not very dramatic at all. Property crime is far more common than violent crime. Furthermore, most of the violent crime that does occur is "minor" (i.e., it involves minor injuries or no injuries). Homicide, in contrast, is statistically rare.

The cops and courts fallacy There is a tendency in the media to exaggerate the justice system's role in producing and preventing crime. Felson suggests that the frequency and distribution of crime have more to do with the social organization of everyday life than with the practices of the police or the courts.

The not-me fallacy The crudely drawn portraits of offenders in many television shows and films lead us to believe that offenders are fundamentally different from the rest of us. However, many people who do not think of themselves as criminals have certainly committed criminal acts. Also, our own tendency to obey the law may have less to do with our innate goodness than with the absence of temptation to offend.

The innocent youth fallacy We tend to think of youth as a time of innocence, and the media support the view that offenders are likely to be middle-aged. However, all of the available research indicates that for most common types of crime, adolescence and young adulthood are high-risk ages for both offending and being victimized.

The ingenuity fallacy The media often encourage us to think that the typical offender is a criminal genius (as, for example, in the films about the fictional serial killer Hannibal Lector). Felson points out that in fact most crime

NTL

17

Chapter 1: What Is Criminology?
Defining and Constructing the
Problem of Crime

requires little planning or intelligence. The most common types of crime are quickly and easily committed, and the offenders who commit them are unskilled.

The organizational crime fallacy   Organized and white-collar crime exist. However, Felson reminds us that most crime is not organized. Moreover, crime organizations that do exist tend to be loose and informal rather than rigid. Presentations in films of well-structured hierarchical criminal syndicates are highly exaggerated versions of the reality.

The juvenile gang fallacy   Juvenile gangs figure prominently in media treatments of crime. However, gangs are less well structured and less "corporate" than the media often lead us to believe.

The pestilence fallacy   When we look for causes of social phenomena, we tend to focus on factors that are morally equivalent to the phenomenon in question. In other words, we tend to believe that "bad" things have "bad" causes and "good" things have "good" causes. By implication, we tend to seek the causes of a social problem (such as crime) in other social problems (such as poverty). However, this logic discourages us from asking some interesting questions. For instance, why does a prosperous country such as the United States have such a high rate of property crime? Why did crime rates in Canada and the United States climb so dramatically between the mid-1960s and mid-1970s, a period of economic growth? Questions like this should encourage us to uncouple judgments about morality from judgments about the usefulness of our explanations.

The agenda fallacy   People with a political or social agenda often link that agenda to conclusions about the causes or prevention of crime. Anti–day-care advocates may claim that children in daycare are more likely to grow up to be offenders. Pro-gun advocates may claim that firearm ownership is a powerful crime deterrent. Too often, claims like this are made in the absence of empirical evidence. So it is important to disentangle our understanding of crime from the political agendas of those who speak to us through the media.

The morality fallacy   This is a special case of the agenda fallacy; it blames high or rising crime rates on moral decline. Felson contends that such a view is not logical. High murder rates in the United States do not mean that Americans prize murder or that they are trained to behave in murderous ways.

In the chapters that follow, the gap separating cultural myth from empirical reality will become more and more apparent.

BOX 1.2

The Mythology of Random Violence

A central concern of many contemporary crime myths is the theme of random violence. Urban legends, media portrayals, and political rhetoric about "new" categories of crime such as "home invasion," "car jacking," and "serial murder" reinforce the public's view that random violence—in many different forms—has become a significant social problem. But what exactly is random violence? And how accurate are the claims made about it in popular culture? An informative answer to questions like these is provided by sociologist Joel Best in *Random Violence: How We Talk about New Crimes and Victims* (1999).

According to Best, the concern about random violence reflects three assumptions: that such violence is *patternless*, that it is *pointless*, and that it is *on the rise*. Best contends that all three assumptions are highly questionable.

- *Patternless*. If by the term *random* we mean without pattern, then clearly violence is not random. Based on the social scientific evidence, it is completely incorrect to assume that all members of this society face an equal risk of becoming crime victims. The research in fact tells us that risks vary dramatically by age, by gender, by social class, and by a range of lifestyle indicators. Based on the horror stories we read in the mass media, we might think that we are all equally likely to be murdered. Actually, the evidence shows that young, socially disadvantaged males are far more likely to be killed than other Canadians.
- *Pointless*. The violent crimes we read about in the newspaper often seem senseless. Why would one youth beat up another youth over a pair of gym shoes? And why would a child "out of the blue" attack his classmates with a gun? But whether an act is pointless is very much a matter of perspective. Very often, violent offenders believe that they had valid reasons for doing what they did. They often say they were "angry" or "tired of being pushed around." Of course, we may not see these as valid reasons, and we may claim that their acts were pointless. But this circular reasoning implies that the acts were pointless by definition. The participants may have seen their actions as very sensible.
- *On the rise*. A big part of the concern about random violence is that it is becoming more common. Indeed, many people believe that crime rates are climbing even though the statistical evidence reveals strong trends in the opposite direction. Moreover, claims about whether violence is getting worse or getting better assume that some point of historical reference exists against which comparisons can be made. For example, rates of many kinds of crime are higher now than they were in the 1950s but lower now than they were a few years ago. In short, glib overall statements about how random violence may be spiralling out of control are surely exaggerated.

NTL

19
Chapter 1: What Is Criminology?
Defining and Constructing the
Problem of Crime

CONCEPTUALIZING CRIME

Criminology, like all of the social (and other) sciences, is built on three foundations: theory, research, and conceptualization. *Theories* attempt to explain the relationships between categories of phenomena. *Research* refers to the studies that criminologists conduct in the "real world" to test their theories or to generate new ones. The nature of criminological theory and research is a central issue in later chapters of this book. *Concepts* are general terms that are used for classifying objects, persons, relationships, or events. In other words, concepts are the linguistic categories that we use to classify those aspects of social or physical reality that interest us. A central concept in the field of criminology is, of course, crime. In day-to-day conversation we use this term in a very casual manner; in the context of this book, it is important for us to look more closely and more precisely at it. What do criminologists mean by it? What acts and behaviours does crime include? What does it exclude?

This is an extremely important matter, because how we conceptualize crime dictates the questions we ask about it. Below we focus on three conceptualizations: crime as *legal construct*, crime as *normative violation,* and crime as *social control*. While these differ from one another in some important ways, they share a tendency to define crime in offender-centred terms.

CRIME AS LAWBREAKING

The dominant way of thinking about crime is in legal terms. Thus, **crime** is conceptualized as a behaviour that breaks the law and is liable to public prosecution and punishment. In this conceptual scheme, crime is defined relative to the concept of law. Thus, the law may be understood as a form of social control that evaluates the moral nature of the behaviour in question. When we describe an act as criminal, we imply that the act is disvalued. It is a form of wrongdoing that "good people" should avoid at the risk of punishment. One of the major functions of the law is to deter people from engaging in the behaviour that it prohibits. The law comprises a set of written rules that are supported by state authority and accompanied by a standardized schedule of penalties.

Those who conceptualize crime in legal terms find it useful to distinguish between crime *mala in se* and crime *mala prohibita*. This distinction alerts us to the fact that not all

---

WHAT IS IT?

CRIME

In legal terms, crime is defined as behaviour that breaks the law and is liable to public prosecution and punishment. A criminal intention (*mens rea*) without the action (*actus reus*) is not a crime.

Mala in se
Crimes that are perceived historically and cross-culturally as wrong.

Mala prohibita
Crimes that are condemned through prohibition.

Actus reus
The mere physical criminal act.

Mens rea
The wilful quality of a criminal act.

crimes resonate to the same degree with popular morality. Crimes *mala in se* are crimes that are seen as wrong in and of themselves. They are acts that most people would see as wrong even if they were not against the law, and that have been widely condemned both historically and cross-culturally. Murder, robbery, and other predatory crimes are examples of crimes *mala in se*. In contrast, some types of behaviours are not as widely or as consistently condemned. Crimes *mala prohibita* are acts that are wrong not in and of themselves but by prohibition. Alcohol consumption and certain sexual activities, for instance, are viewed as criminal only in some societies and only at some points in history.

Brantingham, Mu, and Verma (1995) note that although Canada has over 40,000 different federal and provincial statutes and municipal bylaws, only those which are defined by federal law are technically crimes. The principal piece of Canadian criminal law is the Criminal Code, a federal piece of legislation that includes most but not all of the categories of offending we normally think of as crimes.

CONTEXT

The fact that someone behaves in a way that *seems* to be inconsistent with the requirements of the law does not mean that he or she has committed a crime. To be criminal in a legal sense, an act must be intentional (Boyd, 2000). The mere physical act—known legally as the **actus reus**—is not enough. There must also be a wilful quality to the act—what the law refers to as **mens rea**. Moreover, to be criminal, an act must be committed in the absence of a legally recognized defence or justification (Boyd, 2000). For example, while the law defines assaultive behaviour as a crime, a particular assaultive act may not be criminal if it was accidental (rather than intentional), or was committed in self-defence (and therefore legally justifiable).

INDIVIDUAL ACCOUNTABILITY

All criminal law derives from a model of behaviour that accounts for individual psychology. Individuals must employ judgment in controlling their acts so that accidents do not occur. A criminal intention (*mens rea*) without the action (*actus reus*) is not a crime. Since intent is part of the definition of crime, prosecutors must establish such purpose in the perpetrator. They sometimes try to do this by constructing the motive; however, establishing a motive does not establish guilt. Intent and action together are required to obtain a criminal conviction.

NTL

21

Chapter 1: What Is Criminology?
Defining and Constructing the
Problem of Crime

Courts can also define the criteria used in judging guilt. In some situations, individuals commit acts that they don't have the power to prevent. These cases are covered by a judgment of competence, which may be restricted because of age, duress, self-defence, or insanity. With respect to age, all criminal behaviours of youths are handled not in the criminal justice system, but rather in the **juvenile** system. In Canada, children under 12 cannot be held responsible for their actions in the criminal sense. Children from 12 to 17 are held culpable for their actions but are judged separately from adults through the *Young Offenders Act* (YOA). The law thus recognizes that though young people must be held responsible for their actions, age is a relevant factor in determining how responsibility is to be assigned.

The *Juvenile Delinquents Act*, which the YOA replaced, was based on a philosophy of *parens patiae* —that is, the state, acting as a kind of "superparent," and was given wide latitude in dealing with children. The YOA makes the rights and responsibilities of youth much more central issues (Corrado and Markwart, 1996).

Individuals operating under **duress** can claim that they did not intend to commit a crime and therefore are not guilty. For this defence to succeed, the accused must prove that some unlawful constraint or influence was used to force him or her to commit an act that he or she otherwise would not have committed (Rush, 1994). Duress is often difficult to prove. The degree of force used must be commensurate with the degree of harm the individual perceived was being directed his or her way. Duress is never a defence against murder.

SELF-DEFENCE

Self-defence involves actions taken to protect oneself or one's property, involving reasonable force, in the face of a threat. These cases are not always straightforward, and our view of self-defence is evolving. Originally, the doctrine of self-defence held that the danger must be immediate and severe in order for criminal actions to be justified. More recently, in delineating situations in which self-defence claims may be made, the law has begun to recognize issues such as the power differential between the victim and the offender, and/or the presence of a long-term pattern of abuse and the fear that might be associated with it. An example of this is the "battered woman syndrome." A battered woman who killed her abuser may claim self-defence when she had reasonable cause to think that her life was in danger (regardless of whether she had actually been physically abused in the immediate incident). The Supreme Court of Canada has accepted the argument of self-defence in these cases.

Juvenile
In Canada, anyone under 12 cannot be responsible for their own actions in the criminal sense. Children age 12 to 17 are held culpable for their actions but are held separate from adults when their criminal responsibilities are assessed.

Duress defence
Some unlawful constraint of influence used to force an individual to commit an act that he or she otherwise would not have committed.

Self-defence
Actions taken to protect oneself or one's property, involving reasonable force, in the face of a threat.

INSANITY

It is up to the defence to prove a state of insanity; the prosecution is not required to prove sanity. In effect, this restricts the extent to which an individual can claim that a limited capacity to form intent resulted from mental breakdown.

LEGAL AND SOCIAL CONTROLS

The legal system plays an important role in managing criminal events. Legal definitions of crime may appear to be immutable—that is, determined by clear-cut rules of evidence in establishing guilt or innocence—but in reality, they are not. Legal responses are often heavily influenced by circumstances, public tolerance, and judicial discretion. The police and the courts apply the law not only to prevent crime and punish criminals but also to reduce social conflict. Any study of crime needs to account for behaviour that is disorderly or dangerous but not yet unlawful. Alternative or informal legal responses set the outside limits of criminality by redefining the criminal justice system's responses to misbehaviour.

The law is only one form of social control (Black, 1976). Social life is also regulated by informal expectations about how people should and should not behave. Whether we call these expectations etiquette, professionalism, or simply good taste, people evaluate the morality of each other's behaviour and respond accordingly in a variety of ways. Gossip, ridicule, and ostracism are all forms of social control, and involve fewer formal social processes than do legal forms. When actions are classified as crimes, much more is implied than a mere condemnation of the behaviour. When we call an act a crime we are implying that the problem will be processed in a particular way and that specific state agencies will assume responsibility for solving it. In other words, to label a particular deed a crime is to assign "ownership" of the problem at hand to the police, the courts, and other criminal justice agencies (Gilsinan, 1990).

If a problem is defined as one that involves an uninformed public acting on the basis of incomplete or incorrect information, experts in education might be expected to provide a solution. If a problem is defined as one that results from some medical condition, mental or physical health professionals will dominate efforts to solve it. When behaviour is deemed criminal, the issue will likely be surrendered to law enforcement and crime prevention specialists. Clearly, these alternative approaches have dramatically different consequences. As Gusfield (1989) notes, it makes a real difference whether we see social problems as involving people who are troubled or people who are troublesome.

NTL

23

Chapter 1: What Is Criminology?
Defining and Constructing the
Problem of Crime

BOX 1.3

The Insanity Defence in Canada

For a variety of understandable reasons, the insanity defence is often the focus of considerable controversy.

For instance, in 1999 a Winnipeg man named Robert Chaulk was charged with the New Year's Eve slaying of two of his neighbours. Chaulk had been the central figure in an earlier Supreme Court ruling that widened the definition of criminal insanity to include those who are unable to recognize the moral depravity of their crimes.

In June 1987, Chaulk and a co-accused were convicted of first-degree murder in the stabbing and beating death of an 83-year-old Winnipeg man named George Haywood. During their trial, defence psychiatrists had argued that the pair suffered from a rare condition called "folie à deux." The term implies that the offenders had experienced a joint psychotic episode. However, the jurors found the two guilty, and they were sentenced to life with no chance of parole for 25 years.

However, in 1990 the Supreme Court of Canada ordered a new trial after re-examining the Criminal Code "moral-wrong test." The Court found that an individual can claim insanity not only if he or she fails to understand that a criminal act is legally wrong but also if he or she cannot comprehend the degree to which the act is morally wrong. In a retrial, the jurors found the two defendants not guilty by reason of insanity.

Chaulk received two life sentences for the New Year's Eve 1999 killings, but the case did much to focus attention on the legal meaning of insanity. Many critics of the justice system question how great a role psychiatric testimony should play in legal proceedings.

Sources: D. Roberts, "Insanity Rulings Blasted after Killings in Winnipeg," *Globe and Mail*, January 5, 1999: A1, A7; "Man Gets Two Life Sentences in Killings," *Globe and Mail*, December 4, 1999: A2. Used by permission.

CRIME, POLITICS, AND THE LAW

Where do the criminal laws come from in the first place? Two answers to this question have been advanced (Grattet, Jenness, and Curry, 1998; Kueneman, 2000). The first is that laws arise from a social consensus about morality and about the need to respond to particular types of events in particular ways. The second is that reactions to crime have more to do with power, conflict, and inequality than with social consensus.

At a very broad level, these approaches differ with respect to how they perceive the role of social interests (Bockman, 1991). According to consensus theorists, society's members have many interests in common, and their reactions to crime serve these collective interests. Laws are written and enforced to meet the needs of the majority. Deviation from these laws is generally accepted as reason for punishment. Conflict theorists, for their part, contend that in a complex society, different social groups may pursue different interests, and how well they succeed at this depends on how powerful they are. In this sense, reactions to crime reflect particular class, cultural, or other social interests rather than broader collective interests.

THE CONSENSUS VIEW

In the study of law, the concept of social consensus is meant to alert us to the apparently broad-based agreement in society regarding what kinds of acts are serious crimes warranting direct and immediate intervention, and what kinds are not. **Consensus theory** is associated with a number of important scholars (Durkheim, 1964; Parsons, 1951; Pound, 1943). It suggests that even in a complex, highly differentiated society like our own, people who differ from one another in terms of gender, age, ethnicity, and social class are likely to agree on certain basic moral standards.

Punishment is directed toward a commonly agreed-on set of behaviours that offend social mores. We punish murderers more severely than we punish other criminals because of the general social consensus that murder is among the most serious infractions a person can commit. By passing laws, we "criminalize" behaviours that are widely understood as threatening to our shared values. We attach the most severe penalties to those crimes which offend most deeply our sense of collective morality.

Consistent with this view, a large body of public opinion research indicates that by and large, our legal responses to crime reflect widespread social sentiments (Goff and Nason-Clark, 1989; Johnson and Sigler, 2000; Miethe, 1982; Warr, 1989).

The consensus position has attracted much criticism. Opponents of this view have argued that it oversimplifies the complex relationships among groups pursuing different interests with varying levels of resources. In measuring consensus in public opinion surveys, we confront the question of where the consensus came from in the first place. It is one thing to argue that consensus spontaneously

Consensus theory
Theory proposing that laws and punishment be enforced in order to maintain the collective interests shared by members of society.

WHAT DOES IT MEAN?

CONSENSUS VERSUS CONFLICT

Social consensus is meant to alert us to the apparent broad-based agreement in society regarding what kinds of acts are serious crimes and deserving of direct and immediate intervention, and what types are not. Conflict approaches contend that responses to crime must be seen as part of a larger struggle between groups attempting to use the law, or legal control, in the pursuit of their own interests.

NTL

25

Chapter 1: What Is Criminology?
Defining and Constructing the
Problem of Crime

BOX 1.4

Don't Some Laws Reflect Consensus?

The view that laws emerge out of and reflect special interests seems to be contradicted by the commonsense observation that at least some laws seem to reflect the interests of everyone in society. For example, laws against murder, robbery, and sexual assault would seem to be in the interest of everyone, not just those who have the most power.

However, the late British sociologist Steven Box (1981) argued that it is not really correct to say that the law prohibits murder, sexual assault, and robbery. Rather, it prohibits certain types of these behaviours, and at the same time does not prohibit behaviours committed by more powerful people that are equally or even more destructive.

With respect to murder, for instance, Box wrote:

> The criminal code defines only some types of killing as murder; it excludes, for example, deaths which result from negligence such as employers' failure to maintain safe working conditions in factories or mines ... or deaths which result from government agencies' giving environmental health risks a low priority ... or death resulting from drug manufacturers' failure to conduct adequate research on new chemical compounds before conducting aggressive marketing campaigns. [Therefore] criminal laws against murder, rape, robbery and assault do protect us all, but they do not protect the less powerful from being killed, sexually exploited, deprived of their property, or physically or psychologically damaged through the greed, apathy, negligence and the accountability of the relatively more powerful (48–9).

emerges from the collective will of the population. It is quite another to suggest that consensus results from the fact that some individuals have a vested interest in reacting to criminal events in a particular way and are able to convince the rest of the population that their world view is the right one. In either case, we might find that public opinion data reveal widespread agreement on the relative seriousness of different crimes.

CONFLICT, POWER, AND THE LAW

In contrast to the consensus view, **conflict theory** asserts that even where a consensus exists regarding what constitutes a serious crime and what does not, we must take into consideration the source of the consensus. Moreover, it

Conflict theory
Theory that argues that in a complex society, social groups may pursue different interests, and the achievement of success depends on how powerful they are. Responses to crime are interpreted as part of a larger struggle among groups that attempt to use law, or legal control, in pursuit of their own interests.

is incorrect to maintain that this consensus is a spontaneous product of group life. As one critic of the consensus position has noted:

> Laws do not simply appear miraculously on our law books and do not reflect "society's" values. Instead, the acts and people we call "criminal" and our concern with crime at any given time reflect the activity of groups in this society seeking legal support for economic, ideological and status interest (Sheley, 1991: 39).

From this standpoint, definitions of crime must be seen as part of a larger struggle among groups attempting to use the law, or legal control, in the pursuit of their own interests.

IDENTIFYING COMPETING SOCIAL GROUPS

There is little agreement among scholars as to what constitutes competing groups. Marxian scholars locate attempts to control the mechanisms for reacting to crime in the conflicts between social classes (Chambliss, 1986; Reiman, 1998). For these theorists, class conflict is a central feature of capitalist societies. The powerful economic classes, which own property and industries, seek to expand and consolidate their control of the less powerful classes, which must sell their labour to the capitalist class in order to survive. The legal machinery provides one important means by which they can do so (Schissel, 1992).

Marxian scholars also encourage us to recognize that industries that pollute the environment and victimize consumers are generally treated less harshly than street criminals who, say, rob convenience stores (Michalowski and Bohlander, 1976). This is because the criminalization and aggressive prosecution of these actions by industries would not be consistent with capitalist interests. Marxians argue that the average person might well agree that the cold-blooded killer of a convenience store night clerk should be treated more harshly than the CEO of a corporation that sells defective—and potentially dangerous or even lethal—products, but this does not demonstrate evidence of a spontaneous consensus about what types of crimes are more serious. It merely demonstrates how powerful interests are able to manipulate the consciousness of the members of a capitalist society.

Other proponents of the conflict position favour a model of group relations that is more diffuse than the one embraced by the Marxians. For them, laws and other aspects of the legal machinery reflect interests other than class

NTL

27
Chapter 1: What Is Criminology?
Defining and Constructing the
Problem of Crime

ones (Bernard, 1981; Gusfield, 1963; Jenkins, 1992; Turk, 1976). Conflicts arise between cultural, lifestyle, and ethnic groups, and the factors propelling groups to use the legal machinery in the service of their interests are often diverse. The conflicts that social groups are involved in are not always fought on a level playing field. Groups vary in their access to the resources that allow them to influence social outcomes. The machinery of legal control can be thought of as one of these resources. Groups may wish to see laws passed in order to have their values officially recognized by society; or they may wish to use the law to control a group that they believe threatens their values or social position.

PEACEMAKING

Quinney and Wildeman (1991) offer a perspective on conflict theory that emphasizes peace and social justice. They argue that many of the dilemmas and contradictions in mainstream ("bourgeois") criminology in the United States at the end of the twentieth century are the result of a theoretical chaos in the field. As they see it, this chaos stems from the persistence of certain popular beliefs that dominate thinking about crime. As originally outlined by Pepinsky and Jesilow (1984), these include the following:

- Crime is increasing.
- Most crime is committed by the poor.
- Some groups are more law-abiding than others.
- White-collar crime is nonviolent.
- Regulatory agencies prevent white-collar crime.
- Rich and poor people are equal before the law.
- Drug addiction causes crime.
- Laws make people behave themselves.

According to Quinney and Wildeman (1991), these beliefs betray a blindness to society's fundamental inequalities. In American society, the state has the power to control punishment, and as a direct result, certain groups are treated unfairly by the criminal justice system. In this respect, criminalization is a means of imposing violence on the **underclass**.

Quinney and Wildeman encourage us to consider alternative ways of responding to social ills, and to consider as well the broader factors that generate crime, which include social and economic disadvantage. They advocate a criminology of **peacemaking**; this would involve reducing punishment and imprisonment and promoting programs that encourage treatment, rehabilita-

Underclass
A class of society that almost exclusively inhabits segregated, disadvantaged neighbourhoods.

Peacemaking
A process that involves reducing punishment/imprisonment and promoting programs that encourage treatment, rehabilitation, alternatives to incarceration, mediation, and enhanced social justice.

tion, alternatives to prisons, mediation, and enhanced social justice. Peacemaking's nonviolent approach to crime reduction includes strategies of problem-oriented policing in which the emphasis is on *preventing* crime rather than *reacting to* crime in a punitive way (Quinney and Wildeman, 1991: 107).

FEMINIST APPROACHES

The idea of peacemaking has found its way into feminist approaches to criminology (Simpson, 1989). In the **feminist** view, felicity and harmony are regarded as the highest values, and much emphasis is placed on the themes of caring, sharing, nurturing, and loving. According to Harris (1991):

> This contrasts sharply [with] the orientation that values power and control above all else. Where the central goal is power, power conceived as "power over" or control, people and things are not viewed as ends in themselves but as instruments for the furtherance of power. Hierarchical institutions and structures are established both to clarify power rankings and to maintain them. The resulting stratifications create levels of superiority and inferiority, which carry differential status, legitimacy, and access to resources and other benefits. Such divisions and exclusions engender resentment and revolt in various forms, which then are used to justify greater control (88).

A major part of the feminist effort, Harris suggests, involves attempts to identify and confront characteristics and values that are not conducive to the full realization of human potential. Feminists also reject negative values that are used to justify stereotyping and that work to support the groups in power (Daly and Maher, 1998). Consistent with the ideas offered in the criminology of peacemaking, the feminist view proposes that the emphasis on control (which is epitomized in incarceration) be replaced by an emphasis on strategies that address the serious disharmony in society. The potential for crime and violence can be reduced by undermining social inequalities and enhancing social interaction (Boritch, 1997; van Wormer and Bartollos, 2000).

BATTERED WOMEN AND CRIME

The feminist reinterpretation of social control is consistent with the fact that in the legal landscape, more and more claimants are not only representing certain groups as victims but also negotiating to have offenders considered in a

Feminist
A theoretical orientation that critically assesses power relationships in society particularly as those relationships relate to gender inequality.

NTL

29
Chapter 1: What Is Criminology?
Defining and Constructing the
Problem of Crime

different light. A similar trend can be seen with respect to the cases of women who kill their husbands after suffering long-term physical abuse. What has confounded the courts in dealing with these cases is that often there is no evidence of self-defence at the time of the murder and, in many instances, the crime actually seems to have been premeditated. Advocates contend that women charged with such crimes should not be judged solely on the evidence gathered on the scene. Rather, adjudication of the act should include consideration of the pattern of abuse that preceded it.

> ## WHAT DOES IT MEAN?
>
> ### BATTERED WOMAN SYNDROME
> This syndrome is characterized by a sense of helplessness. Women come to believe that they cannot leave an abusive relationship, and that they cannot act effectively to reduce the violence.

As stated earlier, the courts have come to accept **battered woman syndrome** as a defence. This syndrome is characterized by a sense of helplessness: as a result of ongoing violence, women come to believe that they can neither leave the abusive relationship nor act effectively to reduce the physical abuse; thus, violence is their only recourse. Striking back when the abuser is asleep or otherwise vulnerable makes the act seem premeditated.

Battered woman syndrome The sense of helplessness felt by women who come to believe that they can neither leave an abusive relationship nor effectively act to reduce the violence.

Until quite recently, women who killed their abusive partners in such circumstances were routinely convicted of manslaughter or murder and often were sentenced to long prison terms. But in the late 1970s and early 1980s, the courts began to allow expert witness testimony regarding the battered woman syndrome and how it was possible for the experience of long-term abuse to have imparted a sense of imminent personal danger (generally required in a self-defence plea) in a woman who killed an abusive partner (Gillespie, 1989). In many other nations, battered woman syndrome is still not recognized as a special justification for homicide. However, in North America expert witness testimony is allowed in such cases, and this testimony influences court verdicts.

THE FOCUS ON OFFENDERS

Legal conceptualizations of crime, whether they are rooted in consensus visions or in conflict ones, are much more concerned with crime or criminal behaviour than they are with actual criminal events (Gould, 1989). In other words, when it comes to deciding what a crime is or whether a crime has occurred, the law focuses on what offenders *do* rather than on other event elements. From a legal standpoint, crime is largely synonymous with the actions of the offender. By implication, when criminologists resort to legal conceptualizations, they are encouraging us to think about crime as merely something that offenders do. This is a rather narrow vision of crime. If crimes are equivalent to offenders' actions, the only interesting questions appear to be those relating to those actions. This discourages us from asking other questions—relating, for instance, to the roles of victims and bystanders—that may be equally important.

OTHER CONCEPTUALIZATIONS

Many social scientists have argued that legal conceptualizations of crime are too limited, and have suggested alternative ways of thinking about crime. One early critic, the sociologist Thorsten Sellin (1938), maintained that the use of legal definitions to delimit the subject matter of criminology violated a fundamental criterion of scientific inquiry. According to Sellin, the scientist must be free to use his or her own terms in attempting to understand any phenomenon, including crime. Legal definitions surrender the boundaries of the field of criminology to politicians and legislators. Moreover, Sellin maintained, because laws reflect diverse administrative needs, the acts that the law defines as criminal often have very little in common. Smoking marijuana, homicide, "disturbing the peace," and sexual assault differ from one another in a variety of ways. If the criminologist wants to understand what causes crime, Sellin argued, the effort will be stymied by the heterogeneous nature of the subject matter.

Sellin's solution was to reconceptualize crime in ways that made more sense, sociologically speaking. According to him, instead of thinking about the subject matter of criminology as "acts that violate the law," it was more helpful to conceptualize the field as the study of violations of **norms** of conduct. Norms of conduct are widely shared cultural rules about which people feel strongly. For Sellin, acts that violated these rules shared an important characteristic: they defied broadly held expectations of what constituted appropriate conduct. Thus, in the present era homicide and sexual assault violate conduct norms (so defined), but smoking marijuana and disturbing the peace do not. While this conceptualization may be less comprehensive than the legal definition, Sellin believed that it was more useful since it only included acts that had important behavioural similarities.

A very different way of conceptualizing crime has been advanced by sociologist Donald Black. In a 1983 paper, Black argued that much of what the justice system regards as crime is understood as something quite the opposite by those whom it labels as offenders. From the offender's perspective, crime often has a moral basis. According to Black, many kinds of offending are best con-

Norms
Rules that govern social activities and define social roles, role relations, and standards of appropriate conduct.

NTL

31
Chapter 1: What Is Criminology?
Defining and Constructing the
Problem of Crime

ceptualized as forms of **social control**. Thus, for Black, crime is one of the means by which people respond to the behaviours of others that they define as inappropriate.

Seen in this way, assaults, vandalism, and even murder can be understood as quests for justice (Agnew, 1990; Katz, 1987; Lee, 2000). This position recognizes that those who are judged to be offenders often feel victimized by those against whom they offend. Studies of homicide have shown that the eventual victim is often the first party to have brandished a weapon or threatened deadly force (Luckenbill, 1977; Wolfgang, 1958). Similarly in many cases of assault, offenders may feel that they are merely responding to verbal or physical transgressions on the part of others (Felson, Baccaglini, and Ribner, 1985; Luckenbill, 1984). A wife who shoots her husband after years or decades of abuse may question a justice system that categorizes her as the offender and the husband as the victim. Such examples, Black maintains, encourage us to recognize that social control is behind many different kinds of crime and that there is real social scientific value to be derived from thinking about crime as a form of social control.

CONCEPTUAL LIMITATIONS

On the subject of defining crime, Robert Bursik and Harold Grasmick have written:

> Unlike some other substantive areas examined within the social sciences, one of the most problematic issues in the area of criminology actually involves defining the behavior that we study. While this may seem to be a curious state of affairs to an outside observer, some very tricky conceptual and theoretical problems arise in this seemingly simple task (1993: 19).

The alternative conceptualizations offered by Sellin, Black, and others remind us that the central subject matter of criminology can be defined in a number of different ways. Conceptualizations are not right or wrong; they are merely more or less useful. Obviously, thinking about crime as a violation of law, a violation of conduct norms, and a form of social control are three different ways of defining the subject matter. That being said, all three conceptualizations share an important feature: they are offender-centred. In other words, they conceptualize crime as the act of the offender. As we will see in later chapters, there is another and potentially more useful view: that crime is primarily an event.

Social control
The regulatory institutions of society—especially the law enforcement and judicial systems—and how they operate, encompassing rule enforcement at all levels.

SUMMARY

Contemporary criminology draws on a variety of techniques and perspectives. As a field of study, it has its roots in the intellectual traditions of the eighteenth and nineteenth centuries—traditions that are still influential. The first approach, classicism, views offenders as rational beings who weigh the benefits of criminal activity against the costs of apprehension. The second approach, positivism, looks at offenders' behaviour as something determined by their constitution and/or social and economic conditions.

Most of us approach the study of crime with many preconceptions, which we develop mainly through the images we confront in popular culture. Films, television, newspapers, and informal storytelling sessions often focus on tales of crime and violence. These images originate in the media's need to entertain mass audiences, and often bear little relationship to what criminologists learn from more careful studies of the phenomenon of crime. In later chapters we will regularly question the understandings of crime that popular culture underwrites.

In this chapter, we also discussed the conceptualization of crime—that is, what the term is intended to mean when used in the context of criminological discussion. Most commonly, crime is understood as an act that violates the law. However, other conceptualizations of crime are possible—for example, it is a violation of conduct norms, or a form of social control. That being said, the overarching trend in contemporary criminology is to conceptualize crime in offender-centred terms. In other words, however we define crime, we implicitly define it as something an offender *does*—as an act an offender commits. In the remainder of this book, we adopt an alternative position. Instead of treating crime as an *act* that an offender commits, we treat it as an *event* in which others are involved aside from the offender. In the next chapter we consider the character and the implications of crime-as-event.

QUESTIONS FOR REVIEW AND DISCUSSION

1. What is the difference between an action in which there is no intent to harm and an action in which an individual has this intent?
2. How well do you think consensus arguments explain the laws against pornography?

NTL

33
Chapter 1: What Is Criminology?
Defining and Constructing the
Problem of Crime

3. Should people who have psychological problems always be excused for their crimes? If not, why not?

4. In what ways do your family and friends talk about crime? How does this influence your sense of how much crime there is? How does their discussion of crime compare with what you read or hear through the media?

5. Is news reporting of crime accurate? Discuss the factors that may create distortions relating to the extent and incidence of crime.

INFOTRAC COLLEGE EDITION

Explore InfoTrac College Edition, your online university library, which includes hundreds of popular and scholarly journals in which you can find articles related to the topics in this chapter. Visit InfoTrac through your Web browser (**www.infotrac-college.com**), or through this book's Web site (**www.criminalevent-3e.nelson.com**).

WHAT'S ON THE WEB?

For chapter links and quizzes, check out the accompanying Web site at **www.criminalevent-3e.nelson.com**.

Chapter 2

The Criminal Event

WHAT'S IN CHAPTER TWO

In this chapter we introduce the concept of the "criminal event," and explain how crime takes place through the convergence of motivated offenders with victims and various third parties. We also discuss the three stages of criminal events: precursors, transactions, and aftermath. *Precursors* relate to the way the law defines acceptable behaviour in society and to how people in the community define morality. Precursors also include the various factors that bring offenders and victims together. *Transactions* are the exchanges that take place during the event, as well as its situational context. Key considerations here include the offender's behaviour, the role of the victim, and the effects that third parties—including the police—have on the event. The *aftermath* refers to the consequences of the crime, including the harm to the victim, the punishment of the offender, and the public reactions to crime.

INTRODUCTION

In this chapter we provide a framework for organizing our integrated approach to the analysis of crime and crime control. This framework emphasizes the study of crime as **criminal events** (Brantingham and Brantingham, 1993; Gould, 1989; Meier, Kennedy, and Sacco, 2001). As we have already pointed out, throughout most of the history of criminology, researchers have tried to understand crime largely in terms of the actions of criminal offenders (Meier et al., 2001; Miethe and Meier, 1994). The simple implication of this approach is that a crime represents little more than the expression of the will of a person who is motivated to behave criminally. If this view is valid, the task

Criminal event
Comprises its precursors, including the locational and situational factors that bring people together in time and space; the event itself, including how the interactions among participants define the outcomes of their actions; and the aftermath of the event, including the reporting to the police, their response, the harm done, and the redress required, and the long-term consequences of the event in terms of public reactions and the changing of laws.

of the criminologist is to try to explain why some people behave criminally, while the task of the police and other criminal justice agencies is to prevent offenders from behaving criminally or to capture and reform them after they have done so.

Although we cannot hope to understand crime in society without reference to the lawbreaker, it is also true—as noted earlier—that there is much more to crime than the offender. In many cases, crimes also involve victims who resist their victimization and in so doing affect the course of action (Kleck and Sayles, 1990; Webb and Marshall, 1989; Ziegenhagen and Brosnan, 1985). Furthermore, crimes often involve bystanders and witnesses, whose presence can deter an offender or whose apparent tacit approval of the offender's actions can facilitate the commission of the crime (Shotland and Goodstein, 1984). Bystanders or victims may also summon the police, whose appearance at the scene may affect the response of offenders.

The criminal event cannot be separated from the physical and social settings in which it occurs (Brantingham and Brantingham, 1993; Miethe and Meier, 1994). Many forms of crime are intricately linked to the routine activities in which both victims and offenders engage, and to the places in which these activities occur (Sherman, Gartin, and Buerger, 1989). More generally, criminal events involve the public, whose response to perceived increases in crime levels results in pressure on police to pursue more aggressively some categories of offenders. On an even broader scale, crimes involve the actions of lawmakers and the social groups to whom they are responsive. The concept of the criminal event encourages us to conceptualize crime in terms that encompass but also extend beyond the study of offenders. In other words, rather than being *individual* events, crimes are *social* events (Gould, 1989; Meier, Kennedy, and Sacco, 2001).

CRIMES AS SOCIAL EVENTS

To characterize crimes as "events" is to recognize them as incidents that occur at particular times and in particular places. Like any other type of social event—a dinner party, a corporate board meeting, a car accident—criminal events are more likely to happen in specific circumstances and to involve specific types of people. This conceptualization of crime runs counter to our tendency to think about criminal events as merely the by-product of chance. We speak of the crime victim as having been "unlucky." We maintain that crimes

BOX 2.1

The Diverse Character of Criminal Events

Case One

I left my brother to look after the kids, but he left shortly after I did. When I got home in the morning, my mom was crazy, she was yelling that she was going to send my kids to the welfare, she is always saying that. She said that I was an unfit mother. She started hitting me in the face. I went and got one of my knives and I stabbed her. I didn't mean to hurt my mom (cited in Van Brunschot, 2000: 143).

Case Two

My brother, Carl, had his first experience with cocaine when he was 17 and a junior in high school. One of his friends had some cocaine in his locker at school and asked if he wanted to try it. They did it in the parking lot. Carl had agreed because the guy was a friend and he wanted to see what it was like. He didn't do it again until a year later when the same friend offered him some more. He said he enjoyed the first experience but could not explain why it had taken a year before he did it again (cited in Henry and Eaton, 1999: 119).

Case Three

Sometime late on the 5th or early the next morning, Vilem Luft stabbed his wife, Bohumila, to death in their Kitchener home. He next took a rifle and shot his daughter and their three sons. Then he shot himself (Wood, 2000: 35).

Case Four

[Transamerica] employees exploited a flaw in the technology fund's pricing mechanism—a flaw public officials were not aware of, company officials said. The daily closing value of the fund was set at 10 a.m. eastern time, to coincide with the closing of markets in Luxembourg rather than in Toronto. Employees knew whether the fund would increase or decrease in value the next day based on the Nasdaq performance. For example, if the units in the fund were priced at $10 on a Tuesday morning and the Nasdaq fell 5 percent that day, employees sold units at $10, knowing the unit price would be lower on Wednesday. Other policy holders would absorb the loss, because they would pay $10 for a unit that was destined to fall. Transamerica officials said the employees breached the company's code of conduct governing personal trading because they put their own interests ahead of those of the company's clients (Howlett, 2000).

occur because some people are "in the wrong place at the wrong time." If such events are accidents, however, they are *systematic* accidents (Felson, 1987). Like many other surprises in life, criminal events are made more or less likely by the choices people make about how and where they spend their time, energy, and money.

The term *event* also suggests an *episodic* quality. Criminal events, like all forms of social events, have a beginning and an end. This is not to deny that the participants in the event may have had a prior association or—in the case of a homicide, for instance—that some form of conflict may have predated the event (Luckenbill, 1977). It *is* to suggest, however, that the criminal event has its own dimensions, which are both related to and distinct from what went on before it. In a similar way, we can speak of the aftermath of criminal events, in which other social processes are set in motion. Much of the daily business of the criminal justice system is relevant in this respect. Offenders are accused and tried, court dispositions are carried out, and victims must learn to cope with the pain of victimization (Miller et al., 1996). Also, members of the public who learn about criminal events through mass media reports or conversations with neighbours may become more concerned about their personal safety or about the crime problem and its effect on society (Chiricos, Pagett, and Gertz, 2000).

The *social* character of criminal events derives from the fact that they involve interactions between people. If the event has several offenders, these offenders interact with one another as well as with victims, and bystanders (if any). In turn, the police interact with these participants and others. Even an act of vandalism involving a lone youthful offender and an unoccupied school building has social dimensions. A sticker on the door advising that the property is patrolled by security guards may encourage the offender to weigh the risks associated with the offence. Conversely, a run-down building with broken windows may be read by the offender as announcing that no one cares about the appearance of the property (Kelling and Coles, 1996). In either case, the offender reads the signs and—using past experience as a guide—interprets them, and then acts accordingly. The vandalism itself may be intended as a message to other youths or to unpopular teachers.

In this way, the behaviour of each participant in the criminal event intersects with and influences the behaviour of other participants. This interaction does much to shape the course of the event, and to determine the stages through which it proceeds and the extent to which it will be judged as serious. In order to fully appreciate the complexity of criminal events, we must understand their behavioural and situational elements (Birkbeck and LaFree, 1993). A consideration of the principal participants in these events provides a useful starting point.

BOX 2.2
Stranger Homicide Events

In all probability, stranger homicides frighten the public more than any other type of event. Data collected by the Canadian Centre for Justice Statistics suggest that the "typical" homicide departs in some significant ways from the popular stereotype (Janhevich, 1999). According to the statistics compiled by policing agencies:

- Strangers commit a minority of homicides in Canada. In 1996, for instance, 14 percent of all homicides involved strangers.
- Stranger homicides are more likely to involve males. Overall, two out of three homicide victims are male, as are about nine out of ten offenders. With stranger homicides, over eight in ten victims are male, as are virtually all offenders.
- Most stranger homicides occur outside the home. Around one-quarter of stranger homicides occurred in a home setting. In contrast, most nonstranger homicides occur in the home.
- Strangers are less likely to use firearms in homicides. Firearm use is greatest when the offender and the victim were acquainted with each other (30 percent). Firearms are used in about 23 percent of events involving strangers.
- Assaults and robberies are the most common precipitating crime in a stranger homicide. Overall, about half of such homicides involve another offence (as compared to about one-quarter of homicides involving nonstrangers). The most common precipitating offences were robberies, assaults, and sexual assaults. Break and enter was involved in about 4 percent of stranger homicides.

Source: Janhevich, 1999.

OFFENDERS

OFFENDER CHARACTERISTICS

Criminological research indicates that particular social characteristics are associated with a higher likelihood of offender involvement in criminal events. For most offences, offenders tend to be young, disadvantaged males. The relationship between age and offender status has been well documented (Gottfredson and Hirschi, 1990; Hartnagel, 2000a). Involvement in offending is highest among those in late adolescence and early adulthood. Property crime offending peaks at a somewhat earlier age than does violent offending (Flowers, 1989). Property crime arrests peak at age 16, and then drop by half by age 20; violent offending reaches a peak at around age 18 (U.S. Department of Justice, 1988). Crimes such as embezzlement, fraud, and gambling do not conform to this general trend: they are characterized by higher levels of involvement somewhat later in the life cycle (Steffensmeier and Allan, 1995).

Offender status is also strongly related to gender (Boritch, 1997; Miethe and McCorkle, 1998; Tremblay, 2000) (see Table 2.1). Data collected from Canadian policing agencies in 1999 revealed that 86 percent of all adult offenders and 75 percent of all youth offenders (between ages 12 and 17) who were charged with violent crimes were males (Tremblay, 2000). Seventy-eight percent of adults and of youth charged with property crimes were also male (see Table 2.2). While the rate at which women are arrested has increased somewhat over the past 30 years, the offending rates of males continue to be higher than those of females in virtually every category of crime. Also note-worthy is that most of the increase in women's offences during this period related to property crime; the violent crime offence rates for females have remained fairly steady (Boritch, 1997: 30). Although recent evidence indicates that the gender gap in offending has been closing, much of the rhetoric about the "new female criminal" has overstated the case. The narrowing of the gender gap has occurred mainly with respect to nonviolent property crime, for which the gender differential has always been less extreme than for violent crime (Boritch, 1997: 37; Hartnagel, 2000). For most types of criminal events, offending is still very much a male activity.

For many "common" varieties of crime, such as assault, burglary, robbery, and homicide, offending is associated with social and economic disadvantage (Miethe and McCorkle, 1998). This finding emerges most clearly when the most serious forms of crime are examined (Harris, 1991). Arrest data reveal that offenders tend to be unemployed, temporarily employed, or employed in part-time, unskilled, or semiskilled jobs (Flowers, 1989). Offending is also associated with minority group membership. This last association has been extensively documented with respect to African Americans in the United States and Native people in Canada (Sampson, 1985; Silverman and Nielsen, 1992; Wood and Griffiths, 2000). Corporate crimes suggest a departure from this pattern, in that offenders involved in such crimes tend to be "predomi-nantly well-educated people with good jobs" (Snider, 1992: 320).

An emphasis on the social and demographic characteristics of individual offenders should not deflect attention from the fact that offending very often has collective dimensions. For example, most delinquent acts are committed in groups rather than by individuals (Osgood et al., 1996; Tanner, 2001; Venkatesh, 1997). Criminal events involving corporate offending or organized

TABLE 2.1

PROFILE OF INCARCERATED OFFENDER POPULATIONS IN CANADA, 1998–1999

	Male		Female	
	Number of Offenders 12,532	%	Number of Offenders 305	%
Profile				
Age 20–34	6,100	49	170	56
Serving a first penitentiary sentence	6,489	52	210	69
Length of sentence				
Under three years	2,241	18	99	32
Three to six years	3,832	31	103	34
Six to ten years	2,066	16	31	10
Ten years or more	1,866	15	20	7
Life or indeterminate	2,527	20	52	17

Aboriginal Inmates

	Number 2,203	%
Age 20–34	1,325	60
Serving a first penitentiary sentence	1,184	59
Length of sentence		
Under three years	469	21
Three to six years	783	36
Six to ten years	343	16
Ten years or more	231	10
Life or indeterminate	377	17

Source: Solicitor General of Canada, *Basic Facts about Corrections, 1999 Edition.* Ottawa: Public Works and Government Services Canada.

crime may involve several complex levels of organization (Gordon, 2000; Snider, 1992). Offender organization strongly affects the course of criminal events.

TABLE 2.2

ADULTS (18+) CHARGED, BY GENDER
(SELECTED OFFENCES, %), 1999

Offence Type	Male	Female
Homicide	91	9
Attempted murder	87	13
Assaults	84	16
Sexual assaults	98	2
Other sexual offences	97	3
Abduction	60	40
Robbery	91	9
Violent crime—total	**86**	**14**
Break and enter	94	6
Motor vehicle theft	93	7
Fraud	71	29
Theft over $5,000	78	22
Theft under $5,000	70	30
Property crime—total	**78**	**22**
Mischief	88	12
Arson	82	18
Prostitution	47	53
Offensive weapons	89	11
Criminal code—total	**82**	**18**
Impaired driving	89	11
Cannabis offences	87	13
Cocaine offences	82	18
Other drug offences	83	17

Source: S. Tremblay (2000), "Crime Statistics in Canada 1999," Statistics Canada, *Juristat*, Catalogue No. 85-002, Volume 20, Number 5: 20. Used by permission of Statistics Canada.

BOX 2.3

Risk Factors, Gender, and Delinquency

Researchers interested in the study of offending behaviour have sought to determine the factors that place individuals at higher risk of criminal activity. For example, Linda Simourd and Donald Andrews (2000) attempted to identify risk factors with respect to juvenile misbehaviour. In particular, they were interested in whether the factors that seem to put youth at risk of delinquency differ between the genders. In other words, is a factor such as associating with antisocial peers indicative of a high risk of delinquent involvement for males *and* females? The authors used a technique called meta-analysis to review the results of a large number of studies done over 30 years. The major findings of their analysis included the following:

- The general risk factors that were important for female youths were also important for male youths. In addition, no particular risk factor was important for a particular gender.
- In descending order, the most important risk factors for male and female youths were antisocial attitudes and peers, temperament or misconduct problems, educational difficulties, poor parent–child relations, and minor personality variables (e.g., empathy, moral reasoning).
- In contrast, lower social class, family structure or parental problems, and personal distress were not strongly related to delinquency.
- When various sample and study characteristics were taken into account, the general pattern of results was unchanged.

OFFENDER PERCEPTIONS

When asked to explain their actions, offenders typically offer two types of accounts: excuses and justifications (Scott and Lyman, 1968). With an **excuse**, an individual admits that a given act was wrong but denies responsibility for it. With a **justification**, on the other hand, an individual accepts responsibility for the act but denies its immorality. These accounts provide distinct interpretations of offenders, their victims, and their offences.

A study of convicted rapists found that though offenders admitted their offences, they denied that they were to blame for what had happened (Scully and Marolla, 1984). By offering excuses relating to the use of drugs, alcohol, or persistent "emotional problems," they attempted to deflect blame from themselves. In a similar way, police who used excessive force against suspects explained away their actions as a natural outcome of the strong emotions that arise in police work (Hunt, 1985). White-collar offenders tend to argue that they committed their crimes out of ignorance or an inattention to detail and, furthermore, that their actions must be considered in the context of an otherwise law-abiding life. Even contract killers may offer rationalizations for the

Excuse
Denial of responsibility for an acknowledged wrongful act.

Justification
Accepting responsibility for the act while denying the immorality of the act.

HOW DO THEY DIFFER?

EXCUSES VERSUS JUSTIFICATIONS

An excuse admits that a given act is wrong but denies responsibility for the act. A justification, on the other hand, accepts responsibility for the act but denies its immorality.

murders they are paid to commit. According to Levi (1981), organized-crime hit men often claim that if they hadn't shot someone (i.e., fulfilled their "contract"), someone would have shot them.

Offenders may even claim that their crime had positive effects. For example, white-collar criminals may argue that their actions saved a failing business and thereby preserved jobs. They may also favourably compare their offences with those of "real" criminals such as robbers and rapists (Benson, 1985). People who are guilty of workplace theft or income tax evasion often defend their actions by arguing that "everyone does it" and "the only real crime is getting caught."

Offenders' accounts may also make reference to the culpability of victims. A rapist may contend that the victim seduced him or that she said no but really meant yes (Scully and Marolla, 1984). These justifications do not deny the accusation, but they do deny the moral and legal interpretations that others attach to the behaviour. In cases of police violence, some types of people are defined by the police as legitimate targets of physical force because they are known "cop haters" or troublemakers (Hunt, 1985).

Offenders' accounts often reflect pervasive cultural beliefs. For instance, a rapist's excuses and justifications will borrow from more general sexist beliefs in the blameworthiness of sexual assault victims. Also, the cultural environment and the historical period partly determine the degree to which an offender's account is plausible. In the late twentieth century, people tend to reject demonic possession as an excuse for crime, yet such accounts would have been accepted in an earlier period. For another example, the "culture" of large bureaucracies currently allows white-collar offenders to deny personal responsibility for their actions (Benson, 1985), yet public sentiment is beginning to hold these individuals accountable (Snider, 1992).

Offender accounts also alert us to the fact that we apply the label of "offender" with only relative certainty. Most of us are unequivocal in our judgment of the man who hides in the bushes and sexually assaults a woman who happens by. Until recently, however, we have been reluctant to apply the label "rapist" to a man who behaved violently toward a woman he knows well. Many people believe that a husband who assaults his wife has somehow committed a less serious act than has a stranger who assaults another stranger (Bograd, 1988).

Our judgments about the suitability of an offender label may be further complicated by the social context in which the offending occurs. A homicide that results from a heated argument between drunken patrons of a bar may not seem as clear-cut as one that occurs in a more sedate environment. When we draw attention to the relationship between offender labels and offender characteristics, to the victim–offender relationship, or to the social setting, we are suggesting that the study of the offender is inseparable from the study of other dimensions of the criminal event.

It is worth noting that not only offenders but also their family members offer excuses and justifications for criminal conduct. Hazel May (1999) conducted in-depth interviews with people related to offenders who had been convicted of murder. Offenders' relatives, she found, like offenders themselves, need to understand murder as something other than "the purposeful act of an 'evil' person" (May, 1999: 503).

VICTIMS

"VICTIMLESS" CRIMES

For many types of criminal events, it is useful to recognize a victim role. Victims include people whose purses are stolen, whose homes are broken into, or who are murdered in the course of the event. For other event categories, such as drug use and gambling offences, victims cannot be said to exist in any direct and immediate way, although many would argue that it is incorrect to consider such offences **victimless crimes** (Schur, 1965; Meier and Geis, 1997).

Victimless crimes
Criminal events in which a victim does not exist in any direct and immediate way. Examples: gambling or abusing drugs by personal choice.

The issue of whether the law should be applied to victimless crimes revolves around the idea of harm. While there is widespread support for legalizing various forms of vice, great concern persists as to the potential negative effects of doing so. The prevailing view is that vice is not victimless and needs to be regulated through criminal law.

Those who propose removing the legal sanctions associated with victimless crimes argue that policing these acts represents an overreach of the law and that consenting adults should have the freedom to partake in certain activities. Furthermore, criminalization tends to affect only the disadvantaged and others who cannot pursue these activities in private (Wagner, 1997). Advocates of legalization also argue that many of the problems associated with victimless crimes would be eliminated if these behaviours were permitted in regulated (but legal) environments. From their perspective, it is not the behaviour itself but rather the fact that it has been driven underground that gives rise to the surrounding criminal subcultures.

VICTIM CHARACTERISTICS

Canadian General Social Survey (GSS)
A large Canadian national survey that periodically has as a focus criminal victimization, crime prevention behaviour, and perceptions of crime.

Surveys of direct victims of crime demonstrate that involvement in criminal events as a victim, like involvement as an offender, is not a random matter. In fact, many of the social characteristics associated with offending are also associated with victimization. For one thing, like offenders, victims of crime tend to be young. According to a 1999 national study of victimization risk, the **Canadian General Social Survey (GSS)**, the highest rates of both violent and property (theft) crimes were experienced by people between 15 and 24. The overall rate of personal crime for young people was about 15 times the rate for those over 65 (see Table 2.3). This overall finding regarding age differences in victimization risk is consistent with those of similar surveys done in the United States and elsewhere (Kennedy and Sacco, 1998). Despite much talk about a crime wave against the elderly, people over 65 are the least likely to be victims of crime (Fattah and Sacco, 1989). In fact, the 1999 GSS results indicate that rates of victimization for those 65 or older are lower than for any other age group.

Surveys of crime victims also show that gender differences vary by type of crime. For instance, the 1999 GSS revealed that while males experienced a robbery rate of 12 per 1,000, women suffered a rate about half that—7 per 1,000. Regarding assault, males had a rate of 92 per 1,000, females 70 per 1,000. With respect to sexual assault, the rate for men was 8 per 1,000, for women 33 per 1,000 (Besserer and Trainor, 2000). Note that several researchers question whether surveys such as the GSS accurately portray the levels of women's victimization—an issue we will return to in the next chapter.

The link between social disadvantage and victimization is less clear-cut, as it varies by the type of event (Cohen, Kluegel, and Land, 1981; Miethe and McCorkle, 1998). Regarding serious crimes of violence, studies generally support the conclusion that poor people and ethnic minorities are more likely to become victims of crime (Mirrlees-Black et al., 1998, Zawitz et al., 1993). In Canada, Aboriginal people account for 2 or 3 percent of the population but 15 percent of murder victims (Silverman and Kennedy, 1993: 220). Our ability to describe relationships involving crime and ethnicity is impaired by the fact that data on the relationship between ethnicity and crime are not routinely collected in Canada except in cases of homicide.

TABLE 2.3

PERSONAL VICTIMIZATION RATES PER 1,000 POPULATION, BY VICTIM CHARACTERISTICS, AGE 15+, CANADA, 1999

Characteristics	Rate
Overall Rate of Victimization	186
Sex	
Male	183
Female	189
Evenings out (per month)	
Less than 10 evening activities	75
10–19 activities	128
20–29 activities	186
30+ activities	305
Residence	
Urban	199
Rural	138
Age	
15–24	405
25–34	262
35-44	170
45-54	128
55-64	64
65+	27
Marital status	
Married	104
Common law	245
Single	347
Separated or divorced	276
Widowed or widower	69
Household Income	
0–14,999	254
15,000–29,999	194
30,000–39,999	174
40,000–59,999	199
60,000+	193

Source: Sandra Besserer and Catherine Trainor (2000), Criminal Victimization, 1999, *Juristat*, 20(10): 19. Used by permission of Statistics Canada.

TABLE 2.4

HOUSEHOLD VICTIMIZATION RATES PER 1,000 HOUSEHOLDS BY HOUSEHOLD INCOME, CANADA, 1999

Income Level	Total Household Crime	Break and Enter	Motor Vehicle Theft	Theft Household Property	Vandalism
0–14,999	183	53	27	57	46
15,000–29,999	220	52	36	67	65
30,000–39,999	245	50	43	79	73
40,000–59,999	247	50	51	73	72
60,000+	279	58	60	75	86

Source: Sandra Besserer and Catherine Trainor (2000), Criminal Victimization, 1999, *Juristat*, 20(10): 22. Used by permission of Statistics Canada.

With respect to some forms of household theft, and personal theft that does not involve contact between the offender and the victim, the risks of victimization are greater for higher-income groups (Laub, 1990; Sacco and Johnson, 1990). Table 2.4 shows the data from the national survey of crime victims undertaken by Statistics Canada in 1999; it reveals that in general, the risks of various forms of household victimization increase with household income.

VICTIM PERCEPTIONS

Like offenders, victims may be reluctant to define events in which they are involved as crimes. In some situations a crime—even while it is under way— may involve ambiguous or unfamiliar elements that are not readily understood as criminal victimization. A study of mugging victims reported that many of those who were victimized did not immediately define the event as a predatory crime; some even thought the mugger was a neighbour in search of assistance or someone playing a joke (Lejeune and Alex, 1973).

Willingness to label an event a crime generally depends on the degree of coherence between the victim's definition of a "typical crime" and the characteristics of the event in question (Greenberg, Ruback, and Westcott, 1984). However, some crimes are inherently more ambiguous than others. With many forms of sexual victimization, the event may be very difficult for the victim to label. One study found that women who were sexually assaulted did not define the act as rape unless sexual intercourse was involved (Scheppele and Bart, 1983). Crime definitions are generally less ambiguous when the event's illegality is obvious (Agnew, 1985b).

The issue of family violence provides an especially vivid illustration of the importance of victim definition processes. It has been well documented that women are reluctant to label as criminal or abusive the violence that occurs in an intimate relationship (Johnson, 1996). As with sexual assault, Western culture until recently strongly tended to blame women for their victimization in domestic relationships. Women who remain in abusive relationships may be labelled "sick" or "masochistic," or accused of "bringing it on themselves." If they attempt to flee the abuse or confront the abuser, they often find that few supports are available (Johnson, 2000). Moreover, these actions may increase rather than reduce the risk of future victimization. As parents, in-laws, and neighbours choose sides, many blame the victim for breaking up the family; they may even suggest that if she really loves her children she should "made the best of it." All of this discourages the woman from viewing herself as a victim. Acknowledging that one's mate is an abuser is the first and hardest step in reevaluating and changing one's life circumstances and may well bring on violent retaliation by the abusive partner. A denial of the violent character of the victimization and the victimizer may result in the abused partner tolerating conditions that an outsider would think intolerable (Ferraro and Johnson, 1983).

BYSTANDERS AND WITNESSES

Criminal events often involve others aside from offenders and victims. In many events, **bystanders** are more than passive spectators. By their mere presence they may deter an offender from committing a crime, or prevent an incident from escalating. Conversely, they may facilitate the offender's actions. For example, a young male who is insulted by someone in the presence of his peers may be inclined to respond aggressively.

Bystanders may also call the police or offer to act as witnesses. What bystanders do, if anything, depends on several factors. For example, their actions may be influenced by their view of or relationship to the victim and/or offender (Steffensmeier and Steffensmeier, 1977), by their assessment of the personal costs associated with intervention, and by their confidence in their ability to intervene (Shotland and Goodstein, 1984).

Bystanders
Criminal event participants whose presence may affect the course of action even though they are not centrally involved in the event as offenders or victims.

Bystanders are also affected by what they perceive to be transpiring between victim and offender. According to Shotland and Straw (1976), bystanders are less likely to intervene in a violent assault perpetrated by a man against a woman if they perceive them to be married rather than strangers. Davis (1991) suggests that when people witness adults physically abusing children in public, their reluctance to intervene in a "private matter" outweighs their concern for the child's welfare.

From the perspective of bystanders, criminal events are often ambiguous. We do not expect to witness a crime, and we may be so engrossed in our own activities that an event may be well under way before it comes to our attention (Hartman et al., 1972). By the time we make sense of the event and think of a response, it may be too late. The presence of several bystanders tends to reduce the likelihood that any one bystander will assist a victim, especially if the bystanders are strangers to one another and do not share a common cultural frame of reference (Shotland, 1976). One bystander among many is required to accept only part of the responsibility for not acting; he or she may rationalize that somebody else would take action if something were seriously wrong.

THE POLICE AND CRIME

When an event comes to their attention, the police may invoke a wide array of discretionary powers (e.g., collecting evidence, investigating the claims of the victims, and arresting the offender or offenders). In short, the police have the power to "certify" an event as a crime by assessing the match between the event as they understand it and their working knowledge of what the law disallows.

How do the police become involved in situations that they might designate as crimes? It is worth emphasizing here the distinction between proactive and reactive policing. Black (1970) notes that with **proactive policing**, the police become involved when their own investigative or patrol activities bring to their attention events that may be designated as crimes. Only about 10 percent of the time do the police become involved as a result of proactive policing. In contrast, with **reactive policing** the police become involved in criminal events when asked to do so by a member of the public. So it is important to understand the circumstances in which citizens request police intervention.

Proactive policing
Police involvement in incidents as a result of their own investigative or patrol activities, which bring to their attention events that may be designated as crimes.

Reactive policing
The police become involved in criminal events when asked to do so by a member of the public.

REACTIVE POLICING

Most crimes that come to the attention of the police are reported by the crime victims themselves. According to many surveys, people who reported crimes to the police were most likely to say they did so because they hoped to recover stolen property, because "the offence was a crime," or because they wished to avoid being further victimized by the offender. The 1999 GSS found that many victimizations are not reported to law enforcement agencies. Sexual assault is the crime least likely to be reported: police officers were not informed of 78 percent of sexual assaults; in contrast, only 61 percent of nonsexual assaults went unreported. The criminal event most likely to be reported in 1992 was break-and-enter: 62 percent of these incidents were reported (Besserer and Trainor, 2000).

The most common reasons given for not reporting criminal victimization were that the victim did not consider the incident important enough to report and that the victim felt that the police could not do anything about it.

Victims may choose not to report because they perceive that the crime was of a personal or private nature. For example, rates of reporting for stranger-perpetrated crimes are generally slightly higher than those for crimes perpetrated by someone known to the victim (Gartner and Macmillan, 2000). Sometimes victims are themselves involved in criminal activity at the time of the incident and are therefore reluctant to invite a police investigation (Block, 1974). Other times, they do not report crimes because they have at their disposal other means of dealing with the situation (Kennedy, 1988). For example, a teenage boy who has been assaulted by a peer may be more likely to seek retaliation through personal action than through police intervention.

Members of some demographic groups are somewhat more likely than members of other groups to report crime to the police, although differences in this regard are not especially strong (Gottfredson and Gottfredson, 1988). For example, crimes involving female or elderly victims are more likely to be reported, other factors held constant. Perhaps this is because many women and many elderly have fewer alternative resources at their disposal for dealing with victimization and its consequences (Fattah and Sacco, 1989; Skogan, 1976). People who view the criminal justice system negatively may be more

WHAT DOES IT MEAN?

PROACTIVE VERSUS REACTIVE POLICING

In proactive policing, the police become involved in incidents as a result of their own investigative or patrol activities, which bring to their attention events that may be designated as crimes. In reactive policing, the police become involved in criminal events when requested to do so by a member of the public.

hesitant to contact the police; however, this seems to be a minor factor (Block, 1974; Gottfredson and Gottfredson, 1988).

Available data indicate that reporting decisions are strongly influenced by the characteristics of the criminal event itself. The more serious the event, the more probable that it will be reported to the police. Thus, incidents that involve physical injury, significant property loss, or the use of a weapon, or that occur in or near the victim's residence, are more likely than incidents without these characteristics to be brought to the attention of the police (Block, 1974; Gottfredson and Gottfredson, 1988; Skogan, 1977).

These findings are consistent with the view that people report crimes to the police when there is good reason to do so, and don't when the costs of reporting outweigh any potential benefits. For victims of sexual assault or wife abuse, fear of retaliation and concerns about stigmatization or mistreatment by police may negate the advantages associated with reporting. In general, the reporting of crime is best viewed as a rational decision-making process that takes into account the crime, the offender, the victim's resources, and the perceived limitations of the police.

PROACTIVE POLICING

As the police engage in routine patrol work, they may encounter individuals or situations they define as criminal. Proactive policing is not in any sense a random or arbitrary process. Rather, it is heavily influenced by police priorities, prevailing community concerns, available police resources, and the styles and traditions that characterize police work in given areas (Desroches, 1991). This is exemplified in the modern-day commitment by most Canadian police agencies to community-based or problem-oriented policing (see Chapter 11). Ericson (1982) reports that police officers who are engaged in patrol activities use cues that structure their proactive work. For example, their attention may be attracted by individuals who appear in particular places at particular times of the day. Conversely, events that could be defined as crimes are not labelled as such because the police choose not to stop and question a suspect.

The line between reactive and proactive police mobilization is often unclear (Ericson, 1982). Citizens may decide to mobilize the police reactively as a result of police-sponsored crime prevention campaigns that encourage them to do so. Conversely, widespread public concern about specific crime problems may influence police to adopt a proactive mobilization strategy. Desroches (1991) reported on a police investigation of sexual behaviour in public washrooms, known as "tearooms." Evidence was gathered through police surveillance techniques, which suggests a proactive police stance on the problem. However, Desroches indicates that this police involvement was largely a response to requests from citizens or businesses for more aggressive enforcement.

POLICE INVOLVEMENT IN DEFINING CRIMINAL EVENTS

The type of mobilization—that is, proactive or reactive—does not indicate how the police will intervene in a particular event. Officers' actions depend on a variety of factors, including the characteristics of the incident, the behaviour of the participants, and the nature of the requests being made of the police (Gottfredson and Gottfredson, 1988; Mastrofski et al., 2000).

Police tend to respond most emphatically (i.e., treat officially) to events that they perceive as conforming to legal definitions of serious crimes (Black, 1970; Gottfredson and Gottfredson, 1988; Gove, Hughes, and Geerken, 1985). Also of importance in determining police response is the relationship between the victim and the offender. According to Black (1970), the more distant the relationship between victim and offender, the more likely the police are to regard the incident as criminal. This observation is consistent with the often cited tendency of police officers to process crimes "unofficially" when the disputants are family members (Bell, 1987).

The characteristics of victims and offenders influence police decisions. In an American study of police responses to interpersonal violence, Smith (1987) found that police officers are less likely to employ legal solutions in situations that involve African-American or female victims. In contrast, Boritch (1992) reports that the criminal justice system deals more harshly with female offenders than male offenders—especially when the former deviate from accepted standards of femininity. Violence between males is more likely to result in arrest than is violence between a male and a female, which tends to be resolved through less formal means, such as the physical separation of the disputants. Police decision making is also influenced by the demeanour and preferences of the event participants (Smith, 1987). Police are more likely to label an event as a crime when the complainant is deferential to them or requests that they take official action (Black, 1970; Gove, Hughes, and Geerken, 1985).

Increasingly, police discretion in especially sensitive areas—such as family violence—is being removed. In most jurisdictions police officers are now

Mandatory charge rule
Legal or procedural regulation that requires the police, in domestic violence cases, to make an arrest when they have physical evidence suggesting that an assault has taken place.

required, through a **mandatory charge rule,** to make an arrest when they have physical evidence that an assault has taken place, even if the victim is reluctant for them to do so (Johnson, 1996). This practice was established in part as a response to the finding (Sherman and Berk, 1984) that arrest is the most effective way to deter violence among intimates and that mediative techniques do not curtail repeat offences.

Some observers contend that removing police discretion reduces the chances that police bias will influence decisions about the seriousness of certain violent acts. Others argue that it deprives the police of the opportunity to defuse situations before they become dangerous. Arrest may actually increase the likelihood of violence in domestic situations (Sherman, 1992). It has also been argued that bringing individuals into an overburdened court system that is ill equipped to handle their problems merely creates new problems.

Some critics of mandatory charging contend that this policy disempowers some women instead of empowering them (Loseke, 1989). For example, a woman who does not want her husband arrested, but only wants the police to talk to him, may be reluctant to call the police if arrest is the inevitable outcome. Similarly, some women of colour maintain that because their husbands cannot always expect fair and equitable treatment from the police, they are reluctant to report incidents of marital violence. In situations like this, the removal of discretion may act against women's interests.

THE SETTING OF CRIMINAL EVENTS

THE SOCIAL SETTING

To suggest that a relationship exists between criminal events and the places in which these events occur is to imply that location involves something more than happenstance. In other words, place matters. Something about particular types of locations increases—or decreases—the likelihood that criminal events will unfold. Any attempt to investigate these issues is plagued by the fact that particular types of places are intricately linked to particular types of activities. People who live in the centre of a major city may structure their activities differently from those who live on the suburban fringe. Those of us who do not live in the downtown core may occasionally journey there in search of "excitement," but for rest and relaxation we head for the countryside. We shop at malls, drink in taverns, perform occupational tasks at work, and read or study at the library. We might ask why some of these places host more criminal events than others. Is it because certain types of people tend to be attracted to these settings? Does the physical character of a place make criminal events more or less likely? Are the activities associated with a particular setting more or less likely to lead to criminal events? We discuss these issues in greater detail in later chapters. It is useful at this point to review some of the empirical evidence about the locations of criminal events.

THE COMMUNITY SETTING

According to data collected by police and survey researchers, rates of many types of crimes tend to be higher in urban centres than in rural areas (Brantingham and Brantingham, 1984; Felson, 1998; Fischer, 1995). The 1999 GSS revealed significant differences between urban and rural areas in rates of certain violent crimes. For example, the assault rate was 85 per 1,000 for urban dwellers but 65 per 1,000 for rural residents, and the robbery rate was 11 per 1,000 for urban dwellers and too low to calculate for rural residents. In contrast, rates for sexual assault did not substantially differ by area of residence: urban residents were sexually assaulted at a rate of 21 per 1,000, and rural residents at a rate of 18 per 1,000. Total household victimization also differed by location. Urban residents reported having their households victimized at a rate of 232 per 1,000 households; for rural residents the rate was only 164 per 1,000 households (Besserer and Trainor, 2000).

In urban centres, crime rates vary across neighbourhoods (Bursik and Grasmick, 1993). Research into the factors that characterize high-crime neighbourhoods sometimes produces conflicting evidence (Brantingham and Brantingham, 1984); that being said, the data generally indicate that these areas are likely to be poor and densely populated and to have transient populations.

Even in cities or neighbourhoods characterized by high crime rates, most locations are crime-free. For example, while we may think of subway stations as dangerous places, Normandeau (1987) found that most subway stations in Montreal had relatively low rates of crime, with only a few stations accounting for most of the crimes in the system. This point is more generally illustrated in Sherman, Gartin, and Buerger's study (1989) of the locations of requests for police assistance in the city of Minneapolis over a one-year period. This study revealed that a handful of "hot spots" accounted for the majority of service calls; specifically, only 3 percent of the locations in the city (addresses or street intersections) accounted for 50 percent of the 323,979 calls. With respect to predatory crimes, robberies occurred at 2.2 percent of these locations, rapes at 1.2 percent, and automobile thefts at 2.7 percent.

THE PHYSICAL SETTING

Data from the 1999 GSS found that 50 percent of victimization incidents that respondents described to interviewers took place in or around the home of the

---

BOX 2.4

Provincial Differences in Crime Rates

Crime rates vary from province to province. While the pattern is not perfect, there is a general tendency for rates of both violent and personal crime to increase from east to west.

Figure 2.1

Crime Rates, Canada and the Provinces, 1999: Property Crime

[1]Data for St. John's were not available for 1999 and have been estimated based on the 1998 data.

Source: S. Tremblay, 2000. "Crime Statistics in Canada, 1999." *Juristat* 20(5): 6. Used by permission of Statistics Canada.

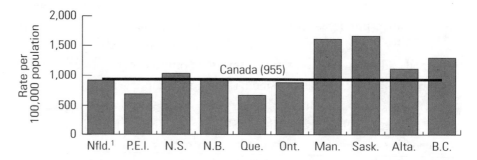

Figure 2.2

Crime Rates, Canada and the Provinces, 1999: Violent Crime

Source: S. Tremblay, 2000. "Crime Statistics in Canada, 1999." *Juristat* 20(5): 8. Used by permission of Statistics Canada.

victim or some other private residence (Besserer and Trainor, 2000). A further 29 percent took place in a commercial setting or public place, such as a restaurant, school, or shopping mall; 23 percent took place in a "public place" such as a parking lot or a street.

What are the characteristics of the locations of criminal events? With respect to some types of crimes, important factors are the physical design of places and the existence (or not) of **defensible space** (Newman, 1972; Taylor and Harrell, 1996). In the case of a property crime, settings that offer concealment in the form of poor street lighting, large bushes or shrubs, or hidden alleyways may make a target more attractive to an offender. Similarly, a convenience store located near a vacant field may be more vulnerable to robbery than one located on a busy city street (Sherman, Gartin, and Buerger, 1989).

Defensible space
The physical design of a place that may deter or attract an offender.

In a somewhat different way, patterns of family violence may be related to some elements of physical design. Violence between husbands and wives typically occurs in private settings. An examination of cases reported to 164 policing agencies in Canada found that 88 percent of incidents occur in the home (Bunge, 2000a). This pattern held whether the accused was a current spouse or a former spouse. The growth of single-family homes not shared with boarders, lodgers, or servants—coupled with the widespread cultural understanding that the home is a private setting closed to neighbours, friends, or even other family members, except by invitation—helps ensure the concealment of such violence (Gelles and Straus, 1988). Within the home, not all locations are equally risky. According to Gelles and Straus (1988), violence occurs most often in the kitchen, followed by the living room and the bedroom, although the latter place tends to be the setting for the most violent confrontations:

A fight that erupts in the bedroom, in the early morning, constrains both parties. It is too late to stalk out of the home to a bar and too late to run to a friend or a family member. The bed and the bedroom offer no protection and there are precious few places to flee or take cover (Gelles and Straus, 1988: 94).

In contrast, the bathroom is relatively free of spousal violence, in part because such rooms are small, have locks, and are understood to be places of individual privacy.

TEMPORAL SETTING

Criminal events are more likely to occur in particular places; they are also more likely to occur at particular times (Cohen and Felson, 1979; Bursik and Grasmick, 1993). In other words, crime is no more randomly distributed in time than it is in space. Data collected by Canadian policing agencies in 1993 showed that incidents of assault were most likely to occur between 9 p.m. and 3 a.m. (Canadian Centre for Justice Statistics, 1993). Clermont's analysis (1996) of the crime of robbery found that this offence was also more likely to occur at night. Miethe and McCorkle (1998) contend that evenings and weekends are the peak times for most violent and property crimes. They suggest that this is because darkness brings with it certain other social conditions. At night there tend to be fewer people out and about who can provide each other (and each other's property) with adequate protection. The night also provides greater anonymity, and greater cover for crime commission. Also, people are more likely to engage in drug and alcohol consumption in the evening and on weekends, and this may render both potential offenders and potential victims more susceptible to engagement in criminal events.

Criminal events are also unevenly distributed over the calendar year. For instance, Clermont's study of robbery found that financial institutions were most likely to be robbed in the month of January, and that individuals and residences are more vulnerable during the summer months. In one way, it should not surprise us that criminal events have a temporal structure. Our jobs, our families, and our social commitments greatly influence how we spend our time (Felson, 1998). Moreover, within a given society there is a pattern to people's occupational, family, and leisure commitments. This is why we find ourselves in rush hours on weekday afternoons and on crowded beaches on summer weekends. The temporal structure of our daily activities reflects the rhythms and tempos of social life, and these rhythms and tempos influence not only where but also when the principal players in criminal events find each other.

Criminologists are especially interested in the long-term trends in crime levels. Figure 2.3 shows that crime rates peaked in the early 1990s and have been falling ever since. In 1999 the rate of crime nationally dropped for the eighth consecutive year. However, while the rate in 1999 was roughly equal to the rate in 1979, it was also over 60 percent higher than the rate in 1949. Explaining why crime rates rise (Cohen and Felson, 1979) and fall (Kennedy and Veitch, 1997) when they do, and as sharply as they do, is a major task of criminology.

Figure 2.3
Crime Rate by Type of Offence, Canada, 1962–99

Source: S. Tremblay, 2000. "Crime Statistics in Canada, 1999." *Juristat*, 20(5): 4. Used by permission of Statistics Canada.

SOCIAL DOMAINS

Social domains can be thought of as major spheres of life in which we invest most of our time and energy. In Chapters 8, 9, and 10 we focus on the three most important social domains: the family and household, leisure, and work. Each domain is distinguished by particular locations and patterns of activity (Lynch, 1987). People differ with respect to the amount of time they spend in each of these domains. For the elderly retired person, the social domain of the household may be of greatest importance. Children spend much of their time at home, but during the teenage years, involvement in this social domain declines and involvement increases in the workplace and in leisure activities outside the home.

Social domains differ in terms of their private or public character (Fischer, 1981). The household is the most private of settings, and the people we encounter there are generally better known to us than those we encounter at work or at leisure outside the home. While we tend to think of private domains as safer places than public domains, concern is increasing about the prevalence of criminal actions that were once seen as private acts. The definition of privacy is changing, and so are the ways in which the law and the police treat privacy. Criminal events that once went undetected in the "privacy" of

Social domains
Major spheres of life in which we spend most of our time and energy.

the home are now more likely to attract public attention and police action. Private affairs in the business setting are also attracting more attention; awareness is increasing of the need to prosecute white-collar criminals whose socioeconomic status once put them beyond the reach of the law.

The distinctions we make among social domains may not apply equally to all individuals. Some people work at home; others restrict their leisure activities to the household; still others perceive the workplace as a leisure setting— a chance to gossip with co-workers. Despite these complications, the identification of distinct social domains helps us clarify differences in patterns of criminal events.

The social activities that occur in these social domains, the people we encounter in them, and the relationships we have with those people strongly influence the kinds of criminal events that take place in a given social domain, as well as reactions to them. According to a number of victim surveys, people who report that they often go to bars in the evening also report higher rates of victimization (Felson, 1998). Police data and observations of barroom behaviour suggest that taverns are the site of a disproportionate amount of crime (Engs and Hanson, 1994; Roncek and Pravatiner, 1989).

Many types of criminal events develop in leisure settings. Much juvenile crime—including drug use, vandalism, and fighting—resembles leisure pursuits (Agnew and Peterson, 1989). Also, juvenile crime is most likely to occur when youths are engaged in unsupervised peer activities such as "hanging out" (Kennedy and Baron, 1993; Osgood et al., 1996). Many forms of sexual assault, especially "date rape," occur in leisure environments rather than in more structured environments (DeKeseredy and Kelly, 1993; Johnson, 1996). Similarly, homicides are most likely to occur when the participants are engaged in recreational pursuits in informal settings (Luckenbill, 1977).

Other types of criminal events are more closely related to nonleisure activities. For the organized criminal, crime is a form of work. For the white-collar or corporate criminal, the offending behaviour may simply be an extension of his or her legitimate business practices. Often, there is a direct relationship between a person's job and the risk of criminal victimization (Block, Felson, and Block, 1984; Kennedy and Sacco, 1998). For example, people who handle money, who work in an environment that is open to the public, or who travel from one worksite to another are especially vulnerable to many forms of victimization (Collins, Cox, and Langan, 1987; Mayhew, Elliott, and Dowds, 1989). Partly for these reasons, taxi drivers, police officers, and nurses experience relatively high rates of violence (Block, Felson, and

Block, 1984). In still other cases, an *absence* of activity is related to the occurrence of criminal events. With respect to breaking and entering, for instance, households that are unoccupied for long periods of time are at greater risk of victimization than are households that have higher and more regular occupancy rates (Cohen and Cantor, 1981; Cromwell, Olson, and Avary, 1991; Waller and Okihiro, 1978).

STUDYING THE CRIMINAL EVENT

When studying **criminal events**, it is important to develop explanations that move beyond the motivations of offenders and the responses of victims. A more comprehensive view considers the **precursors** of the event (e.g., the locational and situational factors that bring people together in time and space); the **transactions** (which tell us how the participants' actions defined the outcomes of the event); and the **aftermath** (including the report to the police, their response, the harm done and the redress required, and the long-term consequences of the event in terms of public reactions and the changing of laws). Figure 2.4 shows a model of the criminal event and its key components.

Precursors
Situational factors that bring people together in time and space.

Transactions
The interactions between individuals that have led to the outcome of a crime.

Aftermath
Events that occur after the committed crime.

PRECURSORS

As criminologists, we are interested in more than just the motivation of the offender and the actions of the victim that led up to the criminal act. These elements come together in a transaction that increases the likelihood that a crime will take place. Once we understand that criminal events derive from predisposing conditions, it is easier for us to separate the social behaviour that is criminogenic (i.e., that breeds crime) from that which does not. Studying the precursors of criminal events also allows us to see that behaviour that is defined or that evolves into criminality in one situation may not have the same consequences in other situations. The relationship between participants, the interpretation of the harmfulness of the acts, the anticipated responses to certain behaviour, the nature of the location—all may or may not combine to create a criminal outcome.

HOW DO WE DEFINE IT?

THE CRIMINAL EVENT

The criminal event consists of its precursors, including the locational and situational factors that bring people together in time and space; the transaction, including how the interactions among participants define the outcomes of their actions; and the aftermath of the event, including the reporting to the police, their response, the harm done and the redress required, and the long-term consequences of the event in terms of public reactions and the changing of laws.

In determining the precursors of crime, we must reconstruct criminal events using information that may have been distorted by faulty memories, rationalizations, and so on. But it is exactly this process that the courts use to establish guilt or innocence. In order to reflect legal as well as social reality, criminologists must incorporate a similar process in their approaches to crime.

TRANSACTIONS

In studying transactions, we are assessing the circumstances, incidence, and frequency of certain types of crimes. As we will see in Chapter 3, different data sources (e.g., uniform crime reports, victim surveys, self-report studies) tell us

Figure 2.4
Model of the Criminal Event

about different aspects of the event, or at least provide different perspectives on such events.

We are interested in the particular groups that are affected by different types of crime. In this context we are able to examine changes in offender behaviour and in the extent of victimization. We are especially interested in viewing the criminal event not in isolation but rather as it relates to social events and to other criminal events. Discerning trends in these events helps us understand the extent to which we need to respond to them. We also want to understand how trends in crime patterns coincide with shifts in social and economic conditions, resources for policing, and so on. The explanations that these types of analysis provide throw light on the vulnerability of certain groups to social change, and on the extent to which legal intervention can work to deter or alter criminal behaviour.

Earlier, we discussed the problems associated with defining (or not defining) certain events as criminal. Victims may not immediately appreciate that they have been victimized; offenders may rationalize their behaviour as something other than criminal. The strict definition of criminality derives from the actions of the police, who certify criminality by enacting legal process—that is, by either naming an event as criminal or arresting an offender.

What about the events that do not come to the attention of the police but that we could nevertheless define as criminal? This question has important implications for how we define criminal events, and for the processes by which the police target certain victims or offenders. Clearly, criminal events are dynamic not only in terms of their responsiveness to interactional factors in the environment but also in terms of the claims that are made about them by interested parties. These claims are constantly changing in response to changing political and cultural values.

THE AFTERMATH

The extent to which we can develop an integrated perspective depends heavily on the types of crime information to which we have access. We are concerned not only with the actual event but also with the reactions by the police, victims, and others. As we will see, a robbery, rape, fraud, or illegal drug deal can generate "a series of ripples emanating from the crime scene to many individuals, places and situations" (Ramos, 1998: 291). In considering the aftermath of an event, we are interested in the degree to which the victim has been harmed and in the resources needed to aid in his or her recovery. We are also concerned with whether the offender feels that he or she can repeat the offence with impunity. With respect to punishment, has there been sufficient certainty, severity, or celerity to deter a repeat occurrence? Questions like this frame a great deal of the discussion about how we are managing our crime problems. Lending focus to this debate are the responses to different types of crime. We need to understand that our responses to criminality are strongly affected by the reasons we assign for its occurrence. Moreover, our responses will influence the types of crime that we will experience in the future.

SUMMARY

A criminal event is a social event. Like all other social events, it has a beginning and an end. Criminal events are social in that they involve interactions among people. The nature and form of this interaction shape the course of the event, determine the stages through which it proceeds, and define how serious it is judged to be in terms of harm done. Many different types of actors are involved in these events.

The most obvious participant is the offender. Offenders tend to be young, disadvantaged males. At the same time, we are witnessing a growth in family violence; the typical offender in a family crime is an older and better-off male. Also, more and more women are committing property crimes.

Much attention has been directed at trying to understand the motivations, as well as the group pressures, that influence the behaviour of criminals. The study of offender perceptions provides an important source of information about the pressures that direct individuals to behave in certain ways. Offenders may choose to deal with their blameworthiness by rationalizing their crimes.

Victims of crime, like offenders, tend to be young and male. That being said, other groups are heavily victimized in particular types of crime. Sexual assault and family violence are disproportionately directed against women. The nature of victims and their relationship to offenders, then, is very much a function of the type of event that has occurred and is governed by location and circumstance. Like offenders, victims may redefine the event as harmless, or at least not criminal. Victim definitions can be very important in influencing the actions taken by criminal justice agencies in criminal events.

Bystanders and witnesses also play a role in defining and interpreting the social events that become crimes. They may defuse a violent situation, or they may actually promote violence through their actions. While bystanders can be helpful in clarifying what actually occurred during a criminal event, their accounts often prove to be inaccurate.

The police play a major role in criminal events. They have the power to certify an event as a crime by assessing the match between the event as they have come to understand it and their knowledge of what the law disallows. In reactive policing, the police respond to reports from citizens, who may be either victims or bystanders. In proactive policing, certain groups or communities are targeted for police attention as a way of preventing criminal events.

With respect to intervention, the police are heavily influenced by their perceptions of what they can do to reduce crime. Police use a great deal of discretion in their work—discretion that can be used negatively to discriminate against certain groups. Police discretion in family violence cases is increasingly being removed.

The police operate by administering the law. Although they enjoy some discretion in applying it, the legal structure has clear expectations relating to the personal behaviour of "civilians" and the response by the police to the breaking of these expectations. Law is a form of social control that defines individual actions on the basis of socially acceptable standards. Criminal events are social events, and as such are governed by both societal and legal tenets. Some forms of control are socially based. Gossip, ridicule, and ostracism may combine with legal threats to discourage individuals from acting in a criminal manner.

One other important aspect of criminal events is the conditions under which they occur. The different social dimensions of people's lives invite different types of behaviour and offer circumstances that may or may not give rise to criminal events. A comprehensive view of the criminal event must consider three key components: precursors of the crime, the transaction itself, and the aftermath.

Criminal events are complicated. In this chapter we have discussed their basic dimensions, and in so doing have raised questions about who participates in these events, when and where they occur, and why they elicit particular forms of societal reaction. In order to understand a criminal event, we need to understand how each of its elements combines and interacts with the others. For example, we cannot address the issue of sexual assault by reducing the problem to a single question: Why do some men commit sexual assaults? Instead, we need to put this question in an appropriate context that also asks why some women are more likely than others to be victimized by sexual assault, when and where such assaults are most likely to occur, and why police, lawmakers, and members of the public think about sexual assault the way they do.

QUESTIONS FOR REVIEW AND DISCUSSION

1. How do offenders see their actions relative to their victims and to the situations in which they find themselves?
2. What do we mean when we say that crime is a social event that takes place in time and space?
3. What role does the legal system play at each stage of the criminal event? Is it always the same agency that deals with the precursors, the transaction, and the aftermath?
4. When does a social event become a criminal event?
5. What does it mean when we say that a criminal event takes on the character of a transaction?

INFOTRAC COLLEGE EDITION

Explore InfoTrac College Edition, your online university library, which includes hundreds of popular and scholarly journals in which you can find articles related to the topics in this chapter. Visit InfoTrac through your Web browser (**www.infotrac-college.com**), or through this book's Web site (**www.criminalevent-3e.nelson.com**).

WHAT'S ON THE WEB?

For chapter links and quizzes, check out the accompanying Web site at **www.criminalevent-3e.nelson.com**.

Chapter 3
Researching Criminal Events

WHAT'S IN CHAPTER THREE

In this chapter we discuss the major types of information about crime to which criminologists have access. We describe these data sources and evaluate their usefulness. We begin by addressing two very general types of crime information: observations and reports. We then discuss specific sources of crime data, including police, victim, and offender reports. We conclude with a discussion of crime rates.

INTRODUCTION

A central concern of modern criminology—and a focus of several of the chapters in this book—is to explain the form, content, and distribution of criminal events. To this end, we need to address several important questions: Why do particular types of events occur? When and where do they occur? Why do they unfold the way they do? Why are some people more likely than others to be involved in events, as offenders or victims? In this chapter we take up a related issue: How are the questions raised by criminological theory to be answered?

In assessing the validity of dominant explanations of criminal events, criminologists do not rely on idle speculation. Rather, they seek to determine the extent to which these explanations are consistent with the empirical evidence that describes these events. In other words, they have more confidence in a given theory if it is able to organize and make sense of the "facts of crime" as revealed by research data. This means, of course, that we need to concern ourselves with the quality of crime data. We begin by addressing two very general types of crime information: observations and reports.

OBSERVING CRIME

DIRECT OBSERVATION IN NATURALISTIC SETTINGS

At first glance, the study of criminal events might seem a relatively straight-forward matter. If researchers wish to investigate criminal events, why do they not just position themselves so as to observe these events directly?

Observation can be accomplished in several ways. The researcher can covertly observe a setting in which criminal events are known to occur with some frequency; *or* attempt to gain access to police or private security surveil-lance videotapes in order to monitor the action in a high-crime setting; *or* associate with people who engage in offending behaviour in order to observe their actions and the actions of those with whom they interact; *or* obtain per-mission from the local police to join patrol officers for tours of duty on city streets (Ericson, 1982; Ferraro, 1989).

> ### HOW ARE THEY USED?
>
> ### OBSERVATIONS VS. REPORTS
>
> Without question, most criminological research proceeds through the use of reports rather than observations.

Such methods of learning about crime events seem to have an obvious advantage, in that they allow researchers direct access to the types of information in which they are inter-ested. But they also have serious limitations. *First*, they may not be very efficient, because statistically speaking, crimes are relatively rare events. Even if one conscientiously observes a high-crime setting, criminal events will occur only infrequently. Similarly, when one associates with chronic offenders, it becomes obvious that much of their time is spent in crime-free activity. Thus, researchers would have to expend a considerable amount of time and energy to amass a sufficient number of observations to allow something meaningful to be said about offenders or offending.

Second, criminal behaviour is usually secretive behaviour. Those who are engaged in such conduct generally do whatever they can to ensure that observers (including criminologists) do not have as good a view as they might like.

Third, observation methods raise ethical issues. We should be concerned about the legal and moral obligations of the researcher who observes a crime in progress. We also should be leery of modes of data collection that involve researchers covertly observing people who are going about their business, or misrepresenting themselves to people who take them into their confidence.

Fourth and finally, the data yielded by **direct observation** are limited with respect to the types of questions they can answer. Direct observation may allow us to observe criminal events, but it does not necessarily tell us much about why the events occur where they do, or why some people are more likely than others to be participants. For example, the systematic observation of a high-crime subway platform might provide an opportunity to witness a number of minor thefts or assaults. However, these observations will not tell us how this subway platform differs from others where the crime rate is much lower. Similarly, observations (by whatever means) of juvenile misconduct tell us very little about why some juveniles engage in law-violating behaviour while others do not. And while police ride-alongs increase the researcher's exposure to particular types of events, they do so in a way that is subject to many limitations. As we have mentioned in previous chapters, the police generally become involved in criminal events after being called in by civilians. Thus, while police ride-alongs may do much to increase our understanding of the role of police in criminal events, they tell us little about what happened before police assistance was sought.

In sum, observation alone generally does not tell us much about how offenders, victims, and other event participants perceive their own actions and the actions of others. We cannot glean from observation why the offenders act the way they do, how they perceive their victims, why they are willing to risk punishment, and what they believe the rewards of their actions to be. Through observation, answers to questions like these can only be inferred.

EXPERIMENTAL OBSERVATION

A second observational approach involves experimentation. Instead of waiting for things to happen, the researcher interested in exploring some aspects of criminal events arranges for them to happen. **Experimental observation** allows for controlled observation of behaviour. Also, by varying experimental conditions, researchers can study the relationship between different conditions and event outcomes.

In one well-known experimental study, Shotland and Straw (1976) intended to shed light on how bystanders respond when a man attacks a woman. Subjects in the experiment were told that they were taking part in an "attitude study." Each subject was directed to a separate room, where a questionnaire was to be completed. Shortly after beginning work, the subject heard a loud verbal argument between a man and a woman in the hallway. After

Direct observation
A technique in which an investigator attempts to develop a theory through exploration, or confirm hypotheses through direct participation in and observation of the community or other social grouping being studied.

Experimental observation
An experimental method, often conducted in laboratories, in which the experimenter creates the conditions necessary for observation rather than searching for naturally occurring situations.

approximately 15 seconds of heated discussion, the man physically attacked the woman, violently shaking her while she struggled, resisting and screaming. The screams were loud, piercing shrieks, interspersed with pleas to "get away from me" (Shotland and Straw, 1976: 991). What the experimental subjects did not know was that the assailant and the victim were drama students who were confederates of the researchers. Shotland and Straw's study revealed that subjects were more likely to intervene when they believed that the attack involved strangers rather than a married couple.

Tracy and Fox (1989) designed an experiment investigating automobile insurance fraud, a type of white-collar crime that does not often come to the attention of law enforcement officials. The researchers were interested in discovering whether auto repair shops tend to give higher estimates for body work on insured vehicles. To investigate this, drivers who were confederates of the researchers presented assigned cars to randomly selected body shops across the state of Massachusetts. The analysis, which took the amount of damage and several other variables into account, revealed that on average, estimates for insured vehicles were 32.5 percent higher than estimates for uninsured vehicles—a difference that the researcher concluded was unrelated to the extent of the damage, the sex of the driver, or the location of the body shop.

The experimental approach has also characterized much of the research into the effect of violence in the media on behaviour (Howitt, 1998). In several classic experiments, the researchers were able to observe aggressive behaviour in children after they had watched a film or cartoon that contained significant violent imagery. Critics of such research charge that because the experimental situations are artificial, they tell us very little about real-life criminals (Surette, 1992). The essence of this charge is that there is a huge difference between the violence willingly carried out in an experiment—when it is encouraged and does no real harm to anyone—and the types of criminal violence that concern the criminal justice system and so many members of the public.

As these examples illustrate, experiments may provide a valuable means for answering some types of questions about criminal events. Still, this method presents some major problems, and its use by criminologists has been limited. Most of the experimental work that has been done has not focused on what many consider to be the vital roles in criminal events: offender and victim. Instead, as in the case of the Shotland and Straw study, experiments have been used to study the reactions of witnesses or bystanders to contrived situations (Farrington et al., 1993; Frinell, Dahlstrom, and Johnson, 1980; Shotland and Goodstein, 1984).

Experiments that seek to entice people into criminal conduct or that feign the victimization of unsuspecting experimental subjects pose obvious ethical dilemmas. In some circumstances, experiments like these place not only the study subjects but also the researchers at risk of physical or emotional harm.

REPORTING CRIME

THE CRIME FUNNEL

The data used most often by criminologists interested in the study of criminal events come not from direct observation but from the reports of those who have direct knowledge of those events—principally the police, victims, and offenders. Criminal justice agencies aside from the police (e.g., courts and prisons) can also be important sources of information about criminal events. After all, these agencies are in the "crime business" and keep records of people who are arrested, cases that go to trial, and the number of people incarcerated.

If our interest centres on the criminal event, the data made available by the various criminal agencies differ in terms of their value. In part this is because different agencies have different needs and therefore do not all collect the same type of information. Of equal importance is the fact that criminal justice agencies are connected to one another in a "volume-reducing system" (Reiss, 1986). In other words, there is a high level of attrition as cases travel through the various stages of the criminal justice system. Not all criminal events that come to the attention of the police result in an arrest, not all arrests result in a trial, and not all trials result in a conviction. Some writers have described this attrition process as a **crime funnel** (Silverman, Teevan, and Sacco, 2000). For example, according to government estimates (Canada, 1982), in the early 1980s:

Crime funnel
A "volume-reducing system," meaning that there is a high level of attrition as cases travel through various stages of the criminal justice system.

- about 60 percent of all break-and-enter incidents were reported to the police;

- 10 percent of all break-and-enter incidents eventually resulted in someone being charged with the crime (17 percent of all of those reported to the police); *and*

- 5.8 percent of all break-and-enter incidents resulted in a conviction (60 percent of those incidents that resulted in a charge).

Dutton (1987) argued that as cases of wife assault move through the criminal justice system, a "winnowing process" occurs. He found that the probability of wife assault being detected by the justice system was about 6.5 percent. Once detected, the probability of arrest was about 21.2 percent. In other words, offenders in cases of wife assault had only a 0.38 percent chance of being punished by the courts.

POLICE REPORTS

For the purpose of studying criminal events, the data contained in police records are quantitatively and qualitatively superior to those maintained by the courts and correctional agencies. In a quantitative sense, police data encompass a larger number of criminal events. In a qualitative sense, police data are not directly subject to the various sorting procedures whereby cases may later be processed out of the system in a nonrandom manner.

Police crime data are based on criminal events about which the police have knowledge. You will recall, however, that any measure of "crimes known to the police" cannot be expected to be synonymous with all crimes that occur, because many crimes—especially less serious ones—are not reported to the police. Data discussed in previous chapters indicate that as much as 50 percent of the crime reported by victims to survey interviewers is not reported to the police. You will also recall that proactive policing results in the discovery of relatively few crimes. Thus, the types and number of crimes about which the police have knowledge depend mainly on the reporting behaviour of members of the public.

Furthermore, not all criminal events that come to the attention of the police become part of the official record. In Edmonton, Kennedy and Veitch (1997) found that the huge number of calls (both 911 and complaint line) to the police was leading to congestion in the communication centre. In 1991 the number of calls to that centre, including both 911 (serious injury accidents, alarms, and in-progress criminal occurrences) and the complaint line (non-emergency), peaked at 485,309. Over 100,000 of these callers hung up before getting a response, as it was taking 81 seconds on average to answer a non-emergency call. Kennedy and Veitch suggest that the actual number of crime occurrences may have been higher than reported, as complainants grew frustrated because they couldn't get through to the communication centre and simply stopped trying to report these crimes. The Edmonton Police Service changed its phone system, mainly by directing complaints to four new divisional stations and twelve community stations. By 1994 the average speed of answer of calls had been reduced to 55 seconds, and the number of abandoned calls to 50,000.

Getting through to the police does not guarantee that a crime will be recorded. When a citizen calls the police to report a crime, it does not necessarily follow that a car will be dispatched or that any subsequent action will be taken (Gilsinan, 1989). Even when the police do show up at the scene, they may decide to treat the matter unofficially or as something other than a crime.

Some event characteristics increase the likelihood that a crime will be recorded (Gove, Hughes, and Geerken, 1985). Events with elements that suggest a high degree of legal seriousness are more likely to be recorded as crimes (Gottfredson and Gottfredson, 1988). Also, when strong physical evidence or compelling testimony indicates that a crime has occurred, the event is more likely to enter the official record. An event is also more likely to be treated as a crime when the person who makes the complaint to the police urges that official action be taken (Black, 1971; Mastrofski et al., 2000).

Recording rates reflect not only the characteristics of the event but also the characteristics of the policing agency. Specifically, highly professional police departments are more likely to officially record crimes (Gove, Hughes, and Geerken, 1985), in part because these departments tend to make greater use of crime data in developing departmental priorities and deploying resources. Highly professional departments also rely more heavily on existing official records in the processing of citizen complaints, because there is a stronger incentive at all departmental levels to "write up" a larger number of police–citizen interactions (Skogan, 1977).

The descriptions of events that are officially labelled as crimes by the investigating officer often undergo significant changes as they move through the internal bureaucracy of the police department. As information travels from the line officer through the communications section to the records division, offences may be shifted from one category to another, downgraded, or ignored (Skogan, 1977). In sum, the amount of crime recorded by the police department is affected by the internal organization of the department and by the bureaucratic procedures by which information is processed (McClearly, Nienstedt, and Erven, 1982).

The Canadian Centre for Justice Statistics (CCJS) (1990) attempted to determine the extent to which differences between Edmonton and Calgary crime levels could be accounted for by differences in record-keeping practices. Edmonton has always had a higher crime rate than Calgary—a difference that has never been adequately explained by social and demographic factors usually associated with higher crime rates (e.g., high unemployment, interprovincial migration). The CCJS study found that data "leakage" in the stages between the original call to the policing agency and the processing of information in the records section was greater in Calgary than in Edmonton. In Calgary, about 80 percent of cases reached the records section, compared to about 94 percent in Edmonton. To some degree, then, Edmonton's higher crime rate in the late 1980s was attributable to differences in how agency data were collected.

THE UNIFORM CRIME REPORTING SYSTEM

Uniform crime reporting system (UCR)
The UCR is a survey collated by Statistics Canada based on crime reports from police departments nationwide. The information is available to the government, criminologists, politicians, and the mass media.

In Canada and the United States, crime data gathered by the police are collected and processed as part of what is known as a **uniform crime reporting system (UCR)**. Canada's UCR was developed through the joint efforts of Statistics Canada and the Canadian Association of Chiefs of Police, and has been operating since 1962. Its stated objective is to provide police departments with a consistent set of procedures for collecting information relevant to crimes that come to the attention of the police.

In simple terms, the UCR is a survey. Police departments across the country report crime information in a standardized format to the federal statistical agency (Statistics Canada), which collates that information and makes it available to interested data users, including government departments, criminologists, politicians, and the mass media. Since 1982 the Canadian Centre for Justice Statistics—a division of Statistics Canada—has been responsible for collecting information from police departments, which regularly respond to the survey.

There are really two UCR surveys (Grainger, 1996; Tremblay, 2000). One is the original UCR survey (UCR 1), which collects "aggregate" information from police departments on a monthly basis. For the past several years, however, a revised UCR survey (UCR 2) has been carried out, with the goal of

WHAT IS IT?

UNIFORM CRIME REPORTS

In Canada and the United States, crime data gathered by the police are collected and processed as part of a uniform crime reporting system (UCR). The UCR's stated objective is to provide police departments with a consistent set of procedures for collecting information relevant to crimes that come to the attention of the police.

correcting deficiencies in the original survey (Silverman, Teevan, and Sacco, 2000). These deficiencies included the following:

1. UCR 1 counting rules stipulated that offences that were completed and offences that were merely attempted were to be counted in the same category (an exception was made for the offence of homicide). In terms of the amount of harm done, there is usually a substantial difference between completed crimes and attempted crimes. When completions and attempts are aggregated, these differences are obscured.

2. When more than one legal violation occurred in the context of a single event, UCR 1 stipulated that only the most serious act be counted. "Most serious" in this context generally meant the offence carrying the longest maximum sentence under the Criminal Code. In situations where an offender committed several crimes in the context of a single event, this rule undercounted the number of crimes.

3. UCR 1 required that personal crimes be counted differently from property crimes. For personal crimes, only one crime per victim was counted; for property crimes, one crime was counted for each "separate and distinct incident." For example, in an incident where several privately owned vehicles parked in one block were spray-painted with what seemed to have been the same spray can, it was concluded that one incident occurred and thus one offence (of wilful damage) was recorded.

More basic problems with UCR 1 related to the *types* of data it collected and the *form* in which it presented them. UCR 1 restricted itself to relatively few types of data. These included the type of offence (as defined by the Criminal Code), the number of offences reported, and the number of offences that were "unfounded." Offences are unfounded when, on the basis of a preliminary investigation, it is judged that the crime reported as having occurred did not occur. With UCR 1, the number of "unfounded" crimes was subtracted from the number of crimes reported to yield a count of "actual offences."

UCR 1 also reported limited information about the persons charged with the offence (i.e., sex, and whether they are adults or young offenders), and the "clearance status" of the incident. **Clearance status** refers to a judgment made by the police as to whether they can identify at least one of the offenders involved in the offence. If this person is formally charged with the crime, the offence is "cleared by charge." However, if circumstances do not allow a charge to be made, the police count the incident as "cleared otherwise." This might

Clearance status
A judgment made by the police based on identification of at least one of the offenders involved in an offence.

happen, for instance, if a victim refuses to sign a complaint, or if the offender dies before he or she can be charged.

Problems like this undermined UCR 1's quality and limited its usefulness. In response, in 1988 the CCJS and the police community began to phase in UCR 2 (Grainger, 1996). The major difference between the two systems is that UCR 2 is "incident-based," whereas UCR 1 is an aggregate survey. An incident-based system is considered much more useful and much more flexible than an aggregate survey (Maxfield, 1999). It collects data relating to offenders, victims, and criminal events and compiles them on an incident-by-incident basis rather than as summaries. As a result, the various kinds of information collected by the police can be linked together in the context of particular incidents or criminal events.

UCR 2 also collects more detailed information about the characteristics of accused persons. Also, unlike UCR 1, it gathers data about the victims of violent crime. This information not only describes the basic social characteristics of offenders and victims (such as gender and age), but also their relationship and their use of alcohol or drugs (Grainger, 1996).

As of 1999, UCR 2 data were being collected from 164 policing services in seven provinces. This represented 46 percent of the national volume of police data (Tremblay, 2000).

Because of these changes, UCR data will be much more informative. Many of the problems that plagued the earlier system will be minimized. Most importantly, because the kinds of information collected by the survey have been expanded and because the system is incident-based, it will be possible to use UCR data to consider a wide array of questions that could not be addressed previously. These include questions about the characteristics of victims of crime, the location of criminal events, the differences between stranger and intimate violence, and the relationship between weapon use and level of injury.

While UCR 2 will greatly enhance the quality of police data about criminal events, it leaves unaddressed many other questions about those crimes which never come to the attention of the police in the first place.

VICTIM REPORTS

Victim reports/surveys
Large-scale studies that ask individuals about their experience with crime.

Reports from victims of crime are a second major source of information about criminal events. In **victim reports/surveys**, victims may be asked to describe what transpired during the event, how they reacted, whether the police were summoned, and what costs—physical or psychological—they may have sustained as a result of the incident. Data from victims of crime are usu-

BOX 3.1

Race and Crime Statistics

Should the UCR include information on the racial or ethnic characteristics of offenders (and victims)? At present, these data are not being compiled by Canadian policing agencies. This contrasts with the practice in some other countries, such as the United States.

Criminologist Scott Wortley (1999) has summarized the issues relevant to this controversial topic. According to Wortley, the arguments against collecting race–crime statistics have three major components:

1. UCR data largely reflect crimes that victims (and others) decide to report to the police. Where people are more likely to report crimes involving minority offenders, the minority population will be overrepresented in the crime statistics.

2. Race is not easily measured. To use "skin colour" as a measure of race is to include, for instance, white people from Russia and from England in the same category, and thus to blur important cultural differences.

3. Race–crime statistics, if they show (accurately or inaccurately) that some racial groups are more likely to offend than others, could be used to support racist beliefs and policies.

On the other hand, Wortley argues, those who support the collection of race–crime statistics maintain the following:

1. Data on the racial character of offenders are necessary if we are to be able to detect racism in the criminal justice system.

2. Race–crime statistics can be used to invalidate biological explanations of crime.

3. A ban on race–crime data would not prevent or even hinder the discussion of racist ideas.

What then is to be done? Depending on one's point of view, there are some options to consider. A first option would be a total ban on the collection of race–crime data. A second would be to collect these data at all stages of criminal justice processing. A third would be to collect information on race and crime but to restrict access to it and to the uses it can be put to. A "middle ground" solution, according to Wortley, would be to ban the routine collection of race–crime data but to allow the relationship to be investigated through "special studies."

Source: "A Northern Taboo: Research on Race, Crime and Criminal Justice in Canada." *Canadian Journal of Criminology.* April 1999. Vol. 261–74. Used by permission.

ally collected in the context of victimization surveys. These are large-scale studies that ask randomly sampled members of some larger population about their experiences with crime. To date, several major victimization surveys have been conducted in Canada. The first, the Canadian Urban Victimization Survey (CUVS), was undertaken in 1982 in seven major Canadian urban areas

(Solicitor General, 1983). A second major study, the Violence Against Women Survey (VAWS), was undertaken in 1993. There are no current plans to repeat this study (Johnson, 2000; Johnson and Sacco, 1995). Three other studies have been undertaken as part of the Canadian General Social Survey (GSS). These national surveys were conducted in 1988 (Sacco and Johnson, 1990), 1993 (Gartner and Doob, 1994), and 1999 (Besserer and Trainor, 2000). The plan is to continue to conduct the GSS victimization survey regularly, at roughly five-year intervals. Canada has also participated in the International Crime Victimization Surveys (see Box 3.2).

Because criminal victimization is a statistically rare event, a large number of interviews must be conducted if such surveys are to yield a sufficient number of cases for analysis. The CUVS gathered data from roughly 60,000 urban Canadians; the 1999 GSS employed a sample of about 26,000. Because of these large sample sizes, victimization surveys are very expensive (Strike, 1995).

To improve the efficiency of the undertaking, it is common in victimization research to conduct interviews by telephone. When this approach is taken, researchers often use sampling procedures to generate a sample of telephone numbers to be called. These procedures restrict data collection to households with working telephones. This may not be as serious a bias as it might at first appear: households without telephones account for less than 2 percent of the target population (Besserer and Trainor, 2000).

BOX 3.2

The Victimization Survey in International Context

In 1996, Canada participated in the International Crime Victimization Survey for the third time. This survey, which is co-ordinated by the Ministry of Justice in the Netherlands and the UN Interregional Crime and Justice Research Institute, is intended to provide comparable information on victimization in several different countries around the world.

A standard questionnaire is used to gather the information in each country, and similar techniques are used to conduct the survey. Usually 1,000 or 2,000 people are interviewed in each country. Respondents are asked about the occurrence of 11 different crimes for the five-year period preceding the interview. The 11 crimes are robbery; sexual assault; assault; theft of personal property; burglary; attempted burglary; theft of car, van, or truck; theft from car; vandalism to car/van or truck; theft of motorcycle/moped or scooter; and theft of bicycle. The following graph shows the victimization rates for the participating nations:

BOX 3.2 (continued)

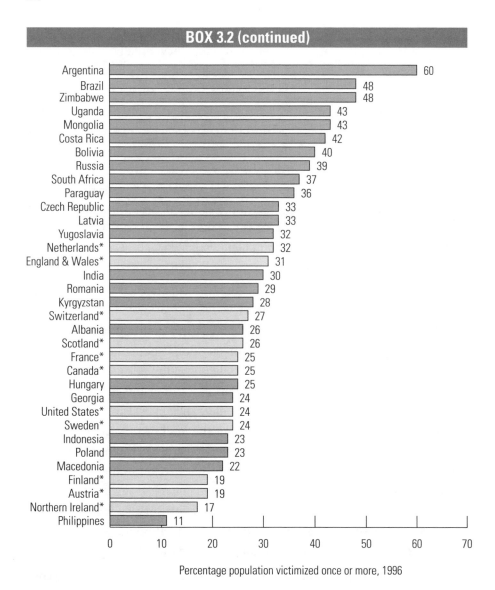

Percentage population victimized once or more, 1996

Figure 3.1
Victimization Rates, 1996

*The 11 western industrialized countries are shown in light-coloured bars.

Source: International Crime Victimization Survey, 1996. Used by permission of Statistics Canada.

In the typical victimization survey, respondents are asked about a range of crimes against the person (e.g., sexual assault, assault, robbery, personal theft) and against property (e.g., break and enter, theft of household property,

WHAT ARE THEY?

VICTIMIZATION SURVEYS

Victimization surveys are large-scale studies that ask randomly sampled members of some larger population about their experiences with crime.

vandalism). Since these studies focus explicitly on victimization, they usually restrict themselves to the study of crimes involving a direct victim. Special topic surveys, such as the VAWS, may even further restrict the range of victimization experiences about which respondents are asked.

Victimization interviews usually have two parts. First, all respondents (whether they have been victims of crime or not) are asked questions from a "screening questionnaire." Some questions gather basic information on the gender, age, and other social and demographic characteristics of the respondents; others ask respondents about their fear of crime or their attitudes toward the criminal justice system. More importantly, the screening questionnaire is used to identify those respondents who experienced one or more of the types of victimization that are of interest to the researchers.

Respondents are asked whether they have been victimized. Those who say yes are usually asked a detailed series of questions about the victimization incident. Questions of this type make up the second major part of the interview. Victims may be asked questions about the location and circumstances of the crime or their relationship to the offender. They may also be asked about the financial losses they sustained or about the level of physical injury they suffered. Information may also be gathered regarding whether the victim reported the crime to the police or took any other action in the aftermath of the victimization episode.

As valuable as they are, data from victimization surveys, like UCR data, have been subject to criticisms relating to their methodology (Miethe and Meier, 1994; Skogan, 1986). Chief among these are the following:

- Certain crimes are thought to be undercounted (e.g., domestic violence offences).
- Undercounting may result because people forget things that happened to them—a phenomenon especially likely if the crime was a relatively minor one or—perhaps worse—if the individual is especially accustomed to being victimized.
- People may forget or misrepresent the time frame of their experiences and report crimes that are actually outside the time reference of the study. This inflates incidence rates.
- Respondents may lie to please the interviewer (i.e., respondents may fabricate crimes in order to provide data).

BOX 3.3

GSS (1999) Property Victimization Screen Questions

B1.   The next few questions ask about some things which may have happened to you during the past 12 months. Please include acts committed by both family and non-family members. During the past 12 months, did anyone deliberately damage or destroy any property belonging to you or anyone in your household (such as a window or a fence)?

B2.   [Excluding those incidents already mentioned,] during the past 12 months + did anyone take or try to take something from you by force or threat of force?

B3.   [Other than the incidents already mentioned,] did anyone illegally break into or attempt to break into your residence or any other building on your property?

B4A. [Other than the incidents already mentioned,] was anything of yours stolen during the past 12 months from the things usually kept outside your home, such as yard furniture?

B4B. [Other than the incidents already mentioned,] was anything of yours stolen during the past 12 months from your place of work, from school or from a public place, such as a restaurant?

B4C. [Other than the incidents already mentioned,] was anything of yours stolen during the past 12 months from a hotel, vacation home, cottage, car, truck or while traveling?

B5.   During the past 12 months, did you or anyone in your household have a motor vehicle such as a car, truck, motorcycle, etc?

B6A. [Other than incidents already mentioned,] did anyone steal or try to steal one of these vehicles or a part of one of them, such as a battery, hubcap or radio?

B6B. [Other than the incidents already mentioned,] did anyone deliberately damage one of these vehicles, such as slashing tires?

B7.   [Excluding the incidents already mentioned,] during the past 12 months, did anyone steal or try to steal anything else that belonged to you?
   (a) [Excluding the incidents already mentioned,] were you attacked by anyone at all?
   (a) [Other than the incidents already mentioned,] did anyone threaten to hit or attack you, or threaten you with a weapon?

Source: Canadian General Social Survey, 1999, Statistics Canada, Family, Household and Social Statistics Division. Used by permission of Statistics Canada.

Those who believe that vicitmization surveys are valuable offer several reasons. *First*, because victimization surveys collect information directly from victims of crime, they can tell us about crimes that have not been reported to the police. Thus, they provide a more valid estimate of the actual crime rate (Fattah, 1991).

Second, because victimization surveys use samples drawn from the general population, data are collected from both victims and nonvictims over a given period. This allows researchers to compare the two groups and to analyze which social and demographic groups face the greatest risks of victimization, and how these risks are affected by particular kinds of behaviours such as drinking alcohol and living alone. These data can help us develop theoretical models linking victim involvement in criminal events to factors of this type (Hindelang, Gottfredson, and Garofalo, 1978; Miethe and Meier, 1994).

Third and finally, victimization surveys enable us to investigate the consequences of victimization and the ways that victims cope with these consequences.

OFFENDER REPORTS

Interviews with offenders can give us important insights into their behaviour, attitudes, and motivations. We can learn why they commit certain types of offences, how they feel about their victims, and how they assess their risk of being apprehended by the criminal justice system (Junger-Tas and Marshall, 1999).

REPORTS FROM KNOWN OFFENDERS

Offender reports

Data gathered from a sample of known offenders, such as prison inmates.

Perhaps the most obvious form of **offender report** makes use of data gathered from a sample of known offenders such as prison inmates or those who have been convicted of an offence and are awaiting sentence (Baunach, 1990). Surveys of this type can shed light on a range of subjects, including the use of weapons by offenders (Wright and Rossi, 1986) and the characteristics of offenders' victims (Innes and Greenfeld, 1990). Understanding these things gives us useful insights into how offenders regard their own actions and those of other event participants.

One major concern with surveys of known offenders relates to the generalizability of the findings (Flowers, 1989). Many offenders are not captured, and many of those who are captured are not convicted or sentenced. As a result, what we learn in interviews with convicted offenders may not be representative of the larger offender population.

ETHNOGRAPHIC RESEARCH

Ethnographic research

Studies in which the researcher attempts to directly observe and interact with the people being studied in a naturally occurring context.

Ethnographic research is another means for gathering information from known offenders. As a research strategy, ethnography moves beyond the use of structured interviews; the researcher attempts not only to speak with but also to directly observe and interact with the people being studied (Wright and Bennett, 1990). The researcher gathers offender accounts by informally participating in and developing some intimate knowledge of the social world of the offender (Fleisher, 1995).

This approach rests on the assumption that formal interviews with offenders yield very limited research data. Researchers often find it difficult to gain access to members of "outlaw" motorcycle gangs (Wolf, 1991), organized crime groups, and professional thieves through conventional means (Ianni and Reuss-Ianni, 1972; Wolf, 1991). However, if researchers are able to cultivate informal relationships with offenders, they may be able to penetrate their social worlds and thereby learn much that would be invisible to outside researchers. Ethnographic studies of street gangs (Baron, 1997; Kennedy and Baron, 1993), violent criminals (Fleisher, 1995), and male prostitutes (Calhoun and Weaver, 1996) have provided insights that could not have been gleaned from police statistics or victim surveys. Chambliss (1975), a proponent of this method of urban ethnography, contends that the data on organized crime, professional theft, and other presumably difficult-to-study events are much more available than we usually think. "All we really have to do is get out of our offices and onto the streets. The data are there; the problem is that too often the sociologist is not" (39).

SELF-REPORT STUDIES

Self-report studies predate victimization surveys, having become popular in the 1950s and 1960s. Like victimization surveys, **self-report studies** gather data from the members of some large population. However, instead of being asked about their involvement as victims in criminal events, respondents are asked about their involvement as offenders. Like victimization surveys, self-report studies are intended to uncover crimes that have not been reported to the police (as well as to elucidate those that have). Also like victimization surveys, self-report studies allow the sample to be broken up into respondents who have and who have not been involved in criminal events over a specified

Self-report studies
Respondents' reports about their involvement as offenders.

period. This enables the researcher to compare offenders and nonoffenders in terms of social and lifestyle characteristics that might be useful in testing explanations of criminality.

Self-report research has most often been used in the study of juvenile crime, although there is nothing in the approach that prevents it from being applied to adult crime (Maxfield, Weiler, and Widom, 2000) or to "nontradi-

WHAT IS IT?

SELF-REPORT STUDY

Instead of being asked about their involvement in criminal events as victims, respondents are asked about their involvement as offenders. Like victimization surveys, self-report studies are intended to uncover crimes that have not been reported to the police (as well as to elucidate those that have).

BOX 3.4

Self-Reported Crime among Criminologists

Mathew Robinson and Barbara Zaitzow (1999) attempted to use the self-report method to determine the degree to which "crime experts" commit crimes. The study was conducted through a mail survey of a sample of members of the American Society of Criminology. Anonymous questionnaires were sent to a random sample of 1,500 members of the ASC. Respondents were asked if they had engaged in a variety of criminal offences "ever" and "within the past 12 months." In all, 522 surveys were returned. Major findings of the study included the following:

1. Not surprisingly, more respondents admitted having engaged in the less serious crimes about which they were asked. For example, 92 percent and 88 percent reported driving above the speed limit "ever" and in the previous 12 months respectively.
2. Fifty-five percent admitted to committing theft "ever"; however, only 7 percent admitted to having done so in the previous 12 months.
3. A rather large percentage of respondents admitted committing a violent offence. Thirty-six percent reported that they had verbally threatened another person "ever," and 15 percent indicated that they had done so in the past six months. Twenty-five percent said that they had "physically attacked another person" "ever," and 2 percent had done so in the previous six months.
4. Two-thirds of the respondents (66 percent) reported that they had driven under the influence of drugs or alcohol at some point in their lives, and another 35 percent indicated that they had done so in the previous six months.
5. The only sexual offence that more than 10 percent of the respondents admitted that they had committed was adultery (defined as "sexual relations with a person not your spouse"). Twenty-three percent reported "ever" having done so, and 16 percent reported having done so in the previous year.
6. Nearly one in five (19 percent) admitted to committing tax fraud at some point, and 7 percent admitted to having done so in the previous year.

tional" offences such as computer crime (Sacco and Zureik, 1990). The emphasis on juveniles has largely been a matter of convenience: juveniles, in the context of the school classroom, represent a captive audience for the researcher (Chilton, 1991). Once a sample of respondents has been selected, the data about self-reported delinquency are collected in one of two ways (O'Brien, 1985). Some researchers use a questionnaire that includes a checklist of delinquent acts. Subjects are asked to indicate whether they have committed each of the acts and, if so, how often over a given period. Alternatively, researchers may ask respondents about their delinquent conduct in face-to-face interviews (Teevan and Dryburgh, 2000). Each approach has its advantages. Questionnaires make it easier to ensure the respondent's anonymity. Interviews, however, allow for more detailed questioning about the circumstances surrounding the delinquent conduct (Gold, 1970).

THE LIMITATIONS OF CRIME REPORTS

Much of what we know about criminal events is based on the reports provided by offenders, victims, and the police. In addressing the limitations of these data, two issues require consideration: the type of event that is captured by each method of data collection, and the perspective brought to bear on those events that are captured.

WHAT TYPE OF EVENT?

Each of the methods we have discussed in this section is somewhat restricted in terms of the kinds of criminal events it illuminates. Victimization surveys usually ask respondents only about those events that have a direct and immediate victim. Because they are household surveys, they tend to exclude crimes that victimize businesses or the wider community (e.g., vandalism of public property). Victimization surveys also exclude victims to whom access is limited, including children, the homeless, and residents of psychiatric or other institutions (Weis, 1989).

Self-report studies have been used mainly to obtain information about the "common delinquencies" of youth. They have been criticized for excluding the more serious but less common types of delinquency (e.g., extreme forms of violence), while emphasizing nonserious forms of behaviour (e.g., "cutting classes," "disobeying parents") (Gove, Hughes, and Geerken, 1985; Junger-Tas and Marshall, 1999). When students in criminology classes are asked to demonstrate with a show of hands whether they have committed any of the "crimes" listed in the self-report questionnaires, a large number always respond in the affirmative. Even political leaders have admitted to experimenting with marijuana as youths. A loose interpretation of these data can make it seem that everyone is a criminal. More realistically, these data do support the idea that criminal offending (even of the more serious variety) is far more common than official statistics would lead us to believe. By implication, distinctions between "offenders" and "everyone else" are made only with great difficulty (Felson, 1998; Gabor, 1994).

The police reports that form the basis of the UCR are in some ways the most comprehensive data source. Unlike victimization surveys, the UCR includes crimes without direct victims, as well as crimes committed against businesses, the community, and those individuals who are unlikely to appear in surveys (Biderman and Lynch, 1991). A limitation of the UCR system is that the data it collects are based only on crimes the police know about.

WHOSE PERSPECTIVE?

The issue of perspective is central to any attempt to make proper use of crime report data. Each method offers a limited perspective, since it elicits information from only some types of event participants. As we saw in Chapter 2, event participants' understanding of criminal events may differ quite markedly. We expect, therefore, that their reports will reflect these differences.

Victimization data rely on victims' perceptions of criminal events. As such, their quality is subject to whatever distortions—intentional or not—characterize these perceptions. Also, respondents' reports are subject to many compromises. For example, respondents may fail to disclose experiences in which the researcher is interested (Skogan, 1986). If someone is victimized during the course of an illegal activity, he or she may not want to tell the researcher about it. If the event is of minor significance, it may be forgotten by the time of the interview; this may be a particular problem when the reference period about which the respondent is asked is very long. The opposite problem involves **telescoping** (Gaskell, Wright, and O'Muircheartaigh, 2000). In such cases, crimes the victim regards as significant life events may be reported as having occurred during the reference period, when in fact they actually occurred earlier. Telescoping is most likely to be a problem in the study of serious violent crimes.

Telescoping
Reporting a crime as occurring during the reference period when it actually occurred at an earlier time.

WHAT DOES IT MEAN?

TELESCOPING

Crimes that the victim regards as significant life events may be brought forward in time so that the respondent reports them as having occurred during the reference period when they actually occurred at an earlier point in time. Telescoping is most likely to be a problem in the study of serious violent crimes.

In many cases of serious victimization, the victim may be reluctant to report the event to a researcher—for instance, in cases of family violence or sexual assault when the victim feels ashamed or embarrassed or believes that reporting the event may put him or her at risk (Johnson, 1996).

Victims' perspectives are limited in other ways. If respondents cannot or do not define an event as a crime, they are unlikely to tell a researcher about it (Block and Block, 1984). In some situations, people may be victimized but not realize it; many forms of fraud are intended to have precisely this outcome. Similarly, if a purse is stolen but the victim believes that she has lost it, she will not report it to a researcher who asks her a question about theft. Much of the criminal harm that is perpetrated by corporations and governments is not readily apparent, even to those who are directly affected; as a result, victims may have no idea that they have been victimized (Walklate, 1989).

Respondents are also likely to differ in their views as to what level of violation constitutes a crime (Gove, Hughes, and Geerken, 1985). For instance, some studies show that highly educated people are more likely to report being the victim of an assault. This finding is most reasonably interpreted in terms of class differences in the definition of injury or in the willingness to tolerate violence, rather than in terms of the greater threats of criminal violence faced by more highly educated respondents (Skogan, 1990a).

Self-report studies allow us to understand criminal events from the perspective of the offender. Yet the offenders who have the most to hide may be the least willing to participate in the research (O'Brien, 1985). Moreover, some offenders may exaggerate their wrongdoings (perhaps as a show of bravado), while others may be reluctant to admit to involvement in criminal activity (Wright and Bennett, 1990). When the latter do report, they may be more willing to admit to trivial rather than serious offences (Jupp, 1989).

Regarding the UCR system, the organizational perspective of policing agencies determines the rules for collecting data. Administrative and political pressures may dictate that certain kinds of criminal events (e.g., impaired driving) be policed more stringently than others (e.g., "soft" drug use) (Jackson, 1990; O'Brien, 1985; Schneider and Wiersema, 1990). Police practices, public tolerance for particular kinds of behaviour, and the needs of the agency for particular kinds of data all influence the ways in which data are collected (Savitz, 1978).

Reiss (1986) contends that the perspective implicit in police data offers a distinct advantage over self-report and victimization data. The latter two data sources reflect the views of highly self-interested parties; in contrast, police data allow for a more balanced picture. Police reports of criminal events are based on a wider variety of information sources, including victims, offenders, bystanders, and witnesses. Also, police data usually are collected closer in time to the actual event than is the case with victim and offender surveys. As a result, police data are less likely to be influenced by the selective effects of memory.

In a similar vein, Gove, Hughes, and Geerken (1985) suggest that compared to other data sources, official statistics provide more rigorous criteria for defining criminal events. They argue that victimization surveys give us only the victim's perspective, which is insufficient in determining whether a crime has in fact occurred. In order to make this judgment, we also need to know the offender's intention, the circumstances surrounding the event, and the condition of the victim.

Criminal events that are recorded in official statistics have passed through two filters. *First*, they have been judged sufficiently serious to be worth reporting to the police. *Second*, they have been certified by the police as serious events deserving of criminal justice intervention. According to Gove, Hughes, and Geerken (1985), the reports contained in the UCR provide a good indicator of "the extent to which citizens feel injured, frightened, and financially hurt by a criminal act" (489). However, we should not conclude from this that discrepancies between police and other forms of data should be resolved in favour of the former. Police records, like other official records, are not always accurate. Too often they are "misplaced, haphazard, and/or incomplete" (Fleury et al., 1998).

These different perspectives have very important implications for how criminal events are understood. For example, if an individual gets into a fistfight with a drinking buddy, that event might be understood differently within the context of different data collection systems. If the individual is asked in a victimization survey whether anyone has hit him or threatened to hit him, and he responds honestly, he is likely to be counted as a victim. If he is asked in a self-report survey whether he has hit anyone, and he answers honestly, he is likely to be counted as an offender. If the police are summoned, they may, because of the circumstances and the relationship between the parties, screen the event out so that it never enters the official record.

We do not necessarily expect reports from different event participants to tell us the same things. Victimization surveys and UCR data may disagree because they employ different criteria in determining the types of events that are to be included (Blumstein, Cohen, and Rosenfeld, 1992; Gove, Hughes, and Geerken, 1985; Menard and Covey, 1988; O'Brien, 1986). Thus, if researchers undertook a victimization survey in a given community and then compared the survey rates with the UCR rates for that same community, several sources of variation would be apparent. The UCR measures would encompass crimes committed against businesses, institutionalized people, and individuals who do not have a permanent residence; the victim survey would probably omit such crimes. The UCR rates would include crimes committed within the policing jurisdiction, irrespective of victims' place of residence. Thus, the UCR might include crimes committed against tourists who were visiting the community, as well as crimes against commuters who work in the community but live elsewhere. In contrast, the victimization study, because it usually involves a household survey, would restrict attention to crimes committed against community residents, whether or not the crime occurred in the local community or elsewhere.

Similarly, the descriptions of offenders that emerge from police reports of crimes serious enough to have passed through citizen and police filters cannot be expected to concur with offender profiles that emerge from self-report studies that focus on nonserious delinquency (Loeber, Farrington, and Waschbusch, 1998).

For decades, criminologists have been intensely debating the relative value of specific crime measures. Clearly, no single data source can answer all of the questions we have about crime events (Jackson, 1990; Menard and Covey, 1988). Because our data sources tell us different things, it does not really make sense to think about one data source as *better* than another. Later chapters will rely extensively on data derived from a variety of sources, and it will be important for us to approach these data cautiously and critically. The following discussion of women's victimization illustrates this point well.

MEASURING WOMEN'S VICTIMIZATION

Do men or women face the greatest risk of criminal victimization? The answer depends on which crimes we focus attention on, and on which data sources we use. According to the 1998 UCR 2, 51 percent of victims of assault were women, and so were 92 percent of victims of sexual assault. But at the same time, 70 percent of adult homicide victims were men, and so were 56 percent of adult victims of robbery (Tremblay, 1999).

The 1999 GSS indicates that while the rates for robbery are much higher for men than for women (12 incidents per 1,000 versus 7 per 1,000), the rates for theft of personal property and assault are largely comparable (80 incidents per 1,000 women, and 71 incidents per 1,000 men). Regarding sexual assault, the rate for women is four times the rate for men (33 incidents per 1,000 versus 8 per 1,000).

Findings like these strongly influence how the public agenda is formulated; they also tend to legitimize some social problem "claimsmakers" at the expense of others. Feminist social critics who attempt to raise public awareness of the problem of crime against women are often opposed by those who claim that women's fear of victimization is an irrational reaction to a world that threatens men more than it does women (Fekete, 1994). For their part, some feminist researchers have generated research findings that offer estimates of female victimization that are wildly at odds with the data yielded by more traditional measures (Gilbert, 1997).

PATTERNS OF FEMALE VICTIMIZATION

All of this points to a need to understand the patterns of female victimization revealed by police data and victimization surveys. The logical starting point in such an exercise is to determine areas of agreement across methodological approaches to women's victimization. Two such patterns are consistently reported by the advocates of both traditional and more critical research approaches (Boritch, 1997; Gartner and McCarthy, 1996; Tjaden and Thoennes, 1998a). The first pattern is that women are more likely than men to be victimized by people they know or with whom they have some ongoing relationship. The second (which is related) is that women have a greater tendency than men to be victimized in private (most notably the home) rather than public settings.

These patterns are easy to detect as they relate to the crime of homicide. Women are more likely than men to be murdered in the home, and are more likely to be murdered by a relative. In 1999, 71 individuals in Canada were killed by a current or ex-spouse. Eighty percent of these victims were women. Seventeen other women were killed by a current or ex-boyfriend, whereas only three men were killed by a current or ex-girlfriend (CCJS, 2000).

DOMESTIC AND SEXUAL ASSAULT

The two types of assault we associate most closely with the victimization of women—domestic assault and sexual assault—also illustrate the private and intimate character of female victimization. To understand why official data and victimization surveys portray female victimization as they do, we need to consider how well these measure crimes that are committed in private places and that involve offenders and victims who are intimately related.

As already noted, many women who are abused in the context of marital relationships do not define what is happening to them as criminal (Johnson, 1996). Several cultural factors encourage these women to view such incidents as normal and to blame themselves for the violence (Ferraro and Johnson, 1983). Even the fact that a woman phones the police to report an attack by a spouse does not necessarily mean that she defines the event in criminal terms; her action may have less to do with "reporting a crime" than with trying to obtain immediate assistance in order to prevent injury. And even if women do define such events as crimes, they may choose not to phone the police for a variety of reasons (Kantor and Straus, 1987). They may perceive that taking such action places them at greater risk, or they may be concerned that the police or other criminal justice agents will not take them seriously.

The appearance of the police at the scene of a domestic violence incident does not always mean that the event will be counted as a crime. If there is no clear evidence of physical harm, the police may engage in mediation—that is, attempt to cool the parties down, listen to their respective accounts, or issue stern warnings (Bell, 1987; Kantor and Straus, 1987). The victim may be given information or advice or referrals, instead of being treated like a complainant in a criminal matter.

In many domestic disputes, the police view the law as a means for dealing with the disorderly situation rather than as a means for addressing the problem of wife assault (Gondolf and McFerron, 1989). As a result, often no legal action is taken because the situation is not seen as warranting a legal response. Even situations that do involve a legal resolution do not necessarily require that official note be taken of the fact that a woman has been victimized. O'Grady (1989) discovered that in Newfoundland, many instances of domestic violence were legally recorded not as assaults but as "weapons" or "drunk and disorderly in the home" offences.

As we pointed out in Chapter 1, many jurisdictions have attempted to reduce the use of police discretion in the handling of domestic assaults by passing laws that make arrest mandatory in these situations. However, these laws do not completely prevent the police from engaging in discretionary decision making. In one jurisdiction, police arrested an abuser in only 18 percent of the cases in which arrest was possible, despite the existence of a presumptive arrest law (Ferraro, 1989).

Victims of sexual assault, like victims of domestic violence, may be reluctant to apply a criminal label if the offender is an acquaintance. Using U.S. national victimization data, Lizotte (1985) reported that the factors that make a strong case for prosecution are closely related to women's reporting decisions. Women are less likely to report an incident to the police when they are unmarried, when the offender is not a stranger, and when the offender has a right to be in the location in which the offence occurred. Thus, the UCR measures sexual assaults for which the legal evidence is relatively clear but which are not necessarily typical of women's sexual victimization.

Though it is often claimed that victimization surveys broaden the search for incidents of women's victimization, these surveys also clearly exclude many types of events. Most notably, they undercount crimes that involve intimates—precisely the types of crimes that disproportionately victimize women. Moreover, victimization surveys usually ignore victimization in the form of obscene phone calls, exhibitionism, and sexual harassment in the workplace (Gillespie and Leffler, 1987; Hanmer and Saunders, 1984; Junger, 1987; Stanko, 1985).

The Canadian VAWS survey represents one of the most ambitious and sophisticated attempts ever made to investigate the problem of violence against women (Johnson, 1996; Johnson and Sacco, 1995). As the survey included only female respondents, it does not allow us to compare directly the experiences of men and women. But it does represent an attempt to focus on the specific problem of male violence against women in a way that takes into account the limitations that have hampered many previous efforts.

A total of 12,300 women aged 18 and older in all 10 provinces were interviewed for VAWS. Respondents were selected using random-digit dialling techniques and were interviewed over the telephone. The survey methodology reflected extensive consultations with government officials, academics, and women's groups directly involved in the problem of violence against women. Careful testing of survey questions, multiple measures, selection and training of interviewers, and lifetime victimization rates were all incorporated into the design of the survey (Johnson, 2000). The survey design was especially sensitive to the ethical and safety problems that could be created if those being interviewed might still be living with their victimizers. The survey yielded a wealth of valuable data and has become the model for similar surveys in the United States and elsewhere (Tjaden and Thoennes, 1998a).

Obviously, claims that women experience low rates of crime must be assessed with extreme caution. This is not because the research is done crudely or carelessly, but because all research approaches have limitations.

CRIME RATES

The form in which we most often encounter reports of criminal events is the crime rate—a widely used measure in criminology. Although journalists and politicians, among others, often issue declarations about rates of crime, we are seldom encouraged to think critically about what crime rate measures really are.

THE NATURE OF CRIME RATES

What are **crime rates**? As defined by Nettler (1984), "a rate compares events during a specified time against some base of other events, conditions or people. It takes the form $(m/P)k$, where m is a measure of some occurrence, P is a population count (or tally of some other condition of interest), and k is a constant" (47).

As this definition suggests, computing crime rates is fairly straightforward. First we develop some estimate of the numerator (m)—that is, some count of criminal events. We have already discussed the major forms of such counts—crimes recorded by the police or reported in victimization surveys or self-report studies. Next we select a measure of the denominator (P). This is generally thought of as a measure of the population that is exposed to the events, or is at risk of being involved in the events, as offenders or victims. The number we obtain when we divide the number of criminal events (m) by the measure of exposure or risk (P) is multiplied by some constant (k), so that the rate can be expressed per k units of exposure. The selection of the constant is largely arbitrary, but rates are traditionally expressed per 1,000 or per 100,000 units of exposure.

Crime rate
Measures that calculate the amount of crime relative to the occurrence of some count of events, conditions, or people.

BOX 3.5

Calculating Crime Rates

To calculate a crime rate, we require three quantities. The first is a count of the number of crimes. In the expression $(m/P)k$, this is the quantity m. Based on data collected in the 1999 UCR, it has been estimated that in 1999 there were 2,494,762 Criminal Code violations.

Next we need a measure of the population that could have been involved in these crimes as victims or offenders. In the expression $(m/P)k$, the measure of the at-risk population is P. Based on census data, we estimate the 1999 population of Canadians to be 30,491,294.

Finally, in the expression $(m/P)k$, we need a constant, k, which will allow us to express the number of crimes that occur per k members of the population.
Putting all of the above together, we can calculate the rate of Criminal Code violations per 100,000 Canadians as follows:

$$\frac{2,494,764}{30,491,294} \times 100,000 = 8,182 \text{ incidents per 100,000 Canadians}$$

SOME USES OF CRIME RATES

As criminologists, we make extensive use of crime rates when investigating criminal event patterns. By analyzing these rates, we can assess the value of particular theoretical arguments as to how and why these events occur. Crime rates are also used by noncriminologists for a variety of other purposes. One of the most popular is as a "social barometer" that indexes the quality of life (Bottomley and Pease, 1986). Just as the GNP is employed as an indicator of our collective economic well-being, crime rates are often read as indicators of our social well-being (Waller, 1982).

At a personal level, we may factor information about crime rates into our decisions about whether we will buy a home in a particular neighbourhood, vacation in a particular place, or allow our children to attend a particular school.

CRIME RATES AS MEASURES OF RISK

Usually we are interested in crime rate measures to the extent they are measures of risk. When we are told that "the rate of violence is much higher in the United States than in Canada," we are being led to believe that when differences in population sizes are taken into account, the risk of becoming a victim of violence is much greater south of the border than north of it. Similarly, when we are told that the neighbourhood to which we are thinking of moving has a much higher crime rate than the neighbourhood in which we currently live, we may want to reconsider our decision.

How adequate are crime rates as measures of risk? The answer to this question depends on how much confidence we have in the numbers that are used in calculating the crime rate. We have already discussed the many problems that confound our tallies of criminal events (that is, the numerator m of the crime rate equation). However, we also should be concerned about crime rate denominators (P).

In selecting a crime rate denominator, the usual practice is to use the total population residing within the jurisdiction in which the count of events has taken place. Such measures are usually referred to as **crude crime rates** because they provide only a very general assessment of the level of risk (Silverman, Teevan, and Sacco, 2000). They do not take into account the demographic characteristics of the population, or the empirical fact that different segments of the population are involved in criminal events with different levels of frequency. This problem is sometimes countered through

Crude crime rate

Crime rate measures which employ as a denominator the total population in some jurisdiction and thus which take no account of the demographic structure of the population.

BOX 3.6

Crime Rates as News

How do crime rates and other crime statistics become news? Vincent Sacco (2000) attempted to answer this question by examining news reports about crime statistics that appeared in the English-language print media during the calendar years 1993 and 1994. This investigation was organized around two broad issues.

The first concerned the means by which crime statistics become part of the news flow. To whose statistics are journalists attentive, and what are the "news hooks" on which stories featuring rates, trends, and percentages hang? The analysis of press coverage revealed that crime stats become news in basically three ways:

- Most commonly, through a "data release" in the form of a press conference, the release of a new study, or the periodic release of data by some state agency.
- Through some form of "debunking"—that is, journalists (or those whom they cite) call into question what earlier statistics are leading audiences to believe.
- Through the use of statistical information as "background" with respect to some more substantive theme.

The second major issue addressed by the study involved the steps journalists took to turn "dry" and "boring" statistics into news. The analysis found that there was considerable journalistic energy invested in efforts to present statistics in ways that emphasized humour, drama, and the public interest.

Crime rates also are used to assess the effectiveness of community-based crime prevention programs such as Neighbourhood Watch and Operation Identification, as well as a large number of other criminal justice interventions (Gabor, 1990b). As well, changes in crime rates are often used to evaluate the quality of police services.

Claims-making activities often include organized efforts to produce and publicize crime rate data that "document" the issues to which the claims-makers wish to draw attention (Best, 2001; Gilbert, 1997). According to Gilbert (1997), these efforts "embody less an effort at scientific understanding than an attempt to persuade the public that a problem is vastly larger than is commonly recognized" (63). Best (1988) and Hotaling and Finkelhor (1990) have written about how "advocacy numbers" have been used in defining the problem of missing children. They suggest that "guesstimates" of the number of children abducted by strangers have greatly overestimated the prevalence of the problem. Best maintains that the use of crime data for political purposes generally proceeds from three basic assumptions: big numbers are better than small numbers; official numbers are better than unofficial numbers; and big official numbers are best of all. As a result, data collection agencies, official or otherwise, may experience more pressure to keep numbers high than to keep them accurate (Reuter, 1984a).

Crime rates provide us with an important means for comparing crime incidence across jurisdictions and across groups. In this context, they have been offered as a way of measuring individual risk of crime victimization.

Age-specific
The crime risk for a certain age group.

the use of a denominator that better reflects the population at risk. When **age-specific crime rates** are calculated, the base number may include only people between 18 and 24. However, the difficulties inherent in determining a number that accurately reflects particular subpopulations sometimes leaves such rates open to charges of inaccuracy.

HOW DO THEY DIFFER?

CRUDE VERSUS AGE-SPECIFIC CRIME RATES

In selecting a crime rate denominator, the usual practice is to use the total population residing within the jurisdiction in which the count of events has taken place. Such measures are usually referred to as "crude" crime rates. Age-specific crime rates use a denominator that better reflects the population at risk, such as individuals 18 to 24.

Nonetheless, we can reasonably argue that a more refined measure would take into account the differential risks faced by distinct segments of the population. Thus, since most of the crimes counted in crime and victimization rates involve young males, it may make more sense to standardize the level of risk in terms of the proportion of young males in the population rather than in terms of the total population. This is because a shift in the size of this segment of the population will more strongly affect the overall crime rate than will shifts in other segments of the population, such as elderly women.

Not only the demographic composition but also the location of communities may be relevant to an understanding of crime rates (Gibbs and Erikson, 1976; Stafford and Gibbs, 1980). The concept of **ecological position** refers to geographic and economic relationships that link the community for which the rate is being calculated, to nearby communities.

Ecological position
Incorporates geographic and economic relationships within a community in the analyses of crime rates.

Ecological analyses help explain how two communities can have populations of similar size and demographic composition but differing crime rates. Say, for example, that Community A is a considerable distance from neighbouring communities so that the residents of those other communities do not commute to Community A, either for employment or for recreational purposes. In other words, the members of the neighbouring communities are not regularly available as offenders or victims in Community A. When the official crime rate of Community A is calculated in terms of the population residing within Community A, most of the at-risk population will be taken into account.

Say that in contrast, Community B is a "central city" within a larger metropolitan area. Members of neighbouring communities travel to and spend most of their working days in Community B. As well, residents of these satellite communities regularly shop or attend cultural events in the central city. When the residents of the satellite communities commit crimes or are victimized as they visit Community B, these crimes are counted in the official crime rate of the central city. However, because these individuals are not residents of Community B, they are not counted in the denominator. If we fail to account for the differences in the ecological positions of Communities A and B, we may be at a loss to explain why the latter community has a generally higher crime rate.

The CCJS study (1990) that we mentioned earlier in this chapter suggests that some of the variation in the crime rates of Edmonton and Calgary may be attributable to differences in ecological position. Calgary has no significant suburban population; in contrast, around 100,000 people live in the suburbs surrounding Edmonton. When the rates for the two communities were recalculated on the basis of the metropolitan area rather than on the basis of city populations, the total Criminal Code rate for Edmonton was 8.2 percent lower, while the corresponding decrease in Calgary was only 0.43 percent.

At a more basic level, it is reasonable for us to ask whether population measures are adequate indicators of risk in the calculation of crime rates. Population measures suggest how many people expose themselves to risks (of offending or victimization), but they do not tell us *how frequently* they expose themselves. Populations differ not only with respect to demographic structure but also with respect to members' potential for victimization. For example, communities in which people regularly spend a great deal of time engaged in evening activities outside the home may have very different rates for some types of crimes than communities in which most people stay at home most of the time. The risky lifestyles that characterize the former communities make their members more vulnerable to victimization (Baron, 1997; Kennedy and Forde, 1990).

Many sociologists are now contending that we need to measure risk more directly (Balkin, 1979; Fattah and Sacco, 1989; Stafford and Galle, 1984). For instance, the elderly may have lower rates of victimization because they expose themselves less often to the risk of victimization; if their victimization rates were to be adjusted in this light, they might more closely approximate those of younger people (Lindquist and Duke, 1982). Efforts to examine such hypotheses have had only limited success (Clarke et al., 1985; Fattah and Sacco, 1989). Before we can investigate these issues comprehensively, we will need to considerably refine our definition of "exposure."

SUMMARY

Research data are indispensable to our understanding of criminal events. They allow us to test theoretical ideas; they help us chart the dimensions of criminal events for policy purposes; and they provide us with indicators of the quality of life. Data about criminal events can be derived from many different sources, but tend to be generated by one of two basic investigative strategies: observation and reports.

Criminal events can be directly observed in naturalistic settings or in the context of field or laboratory experimentation. Much can be learned about criminal events by waiting for them to happen (as in field studies) or by making them happen (as in experiments), but most contemporary research depends on information revealed by reports about crime.

The reports used most widely are generated by those who are most active in criminal events: police, victims, and offenders. UCR data, which are collected by the police, describe a wide range of crimes and provide a continuous national record. Recent revisions to the UCR survey are likely to increase the value of UCR reports for both academic and policy purposes. The major limitation of UCR data relates to the fact that any police-based information system can tell us only about crimes that come to the attention of the police in the first place. Crimes that the police do not learn about—and there are a significant number of them—are not included in the UCR system.

Surveys of victims and offenders are intended to illuminate those crimes which are not recorded by the police. These surveys provide valuable information; they are also subject to all of the problems that characterize all surveys. Victims and offenders are not always as accessible as we would like them to be, and we cannot always be sure that they will not—intentionally or not—distort the truth in response to questions about their involvement in criminal events.

The problems associated with these major sources of crime data—police, victim, and offender reports—do not suggest a lack of knowledge or awareness on the part of those who collect the data. Rather, they alert us to the fact that any attempt to investigate complex social phenomena is fraught with inherent difficulties. The ways in which crime data construct our statistical images of crimes against women illustrate this fact.

No single data source is likely to answer all of our questions about criminal events. The major data sources tell us quite different things, because they capture different types of events and bring different perspectives to bear on those events. So it is unproductive to engage in endless debates about the superiority of one data source over another. The usefulness of any data source depends heavily on how well it helps us address particular questions.

We should not dismiss crime data just because our data sources are flawed and less comprehensive than we would like. If we use them wisely, we can learn a great deal from crime data. Even when we know that our data are problematic, we often know *how* they are problematic. The errors that characterize our efforts at data collection are often systematic rather than random; when we know the sources and consequences of these systematic errors, data are more valuable than they might otherwise be.

QUESTIONS FOR REVIEW AND DISCUSSION

1. How useful are crime rates as a measure of our "quality of life"?
2. UCR crime data often figure prominently in press reports of crime trends. What does the informed news consumer need to know about these rates?
3. What types of data collection problems do victimization studies and offender self-report studies share?
4. What are some of the more important ethical problems confronting researchers in criminology?
5. Why is it too simplistic to claim that victimization surveys and self-report studies of offending are "better" than UCR reports?
6. Do the major forms of crime measurement support or dispute the popular notion that there are "lies, damned lies, and statistics"?

INFOTRAC COLLEGE EDITION

Explore InfoTrac College Edition, your online university library, which includes hundreds of popular and scholarly journals in which you can find articles related to the topics in this chapter. Visit InfoTrac through your Web browser (**www.infotrac-college.com**), or through this book's Web site (**www.criminalevent-3e.nelson.com**).

WHAT'S ON THE WEB?

For chapter links and quizzes, check out the accompanying Web site at **www.criminalevent-3e.nelson.com**.

Part 2

Theories of Crime

Chapter 4

Psychosocial Conditions and Criminal Motivations

WHAT'S IN CHAPTER FOUR

In this chapter we begin our review of the theories that have been used to explain crime. We focus on attempts to answer this question: Why are some people more inclined than others to behave in ways that violate the law? To this end, we examine the sources of offender motivation, including physiological and psychological deficiencies, troublesome social conditions, and the offender's commitment to cultural beliefs that condone criminal conduct.

INTRODUCTION

What are criminological theories, and why do we need them? In day-to-day conversation we tend to use terms such as *theory* and *theoretical* to describe things that may be interesting but are certainly irrelevant, unimportant, or impractical. We often dismiss what someone tells us with the retort, "That may be true in theory, but it doesn't have much to do with reality!" Students of criminology need to recognize that far from being irrelevant, theories can be extremely useful and practical analytical tools.

Criminological theories can be understood as generalized explanations of criminal phenomena (Bohm, 1997). They provide potential answers to questions about why crimes occur, why some types of people are more likely than others to be involved in crimes (as offenders or as victims), why crimes are more likely to occur in certain places and at certain times, and why agencies of social control respond to crime as they do.

> ### WHAT ARE THEY?
>
> #### CRIMINOLOGICAL THEORIES
>
> Theories provide us with answers to questions about why crimes occur, why some types of people are more likely than others to be involved in crimes as offenders or as victims, why crimes are more likely to occur in certain places and at certain times, and why agencies of social control respond to crime as they do.

Criminological theories
Generalized explanations of why, how, and with what consequences crimes occur.

Criminologists are not alone in seeking answers to these questions. Angry newspaper editorials offer seemingly reasonable accounts of why crime rates are rising. On any given Sunday morning, television preachers explain crime and associated problems in terms of evil forces at large in the world. Crime victims may ask what they did that led to their victimization. Though not always recognized as such, these accounts of why and how crimes occur represent a kind of theoretical thinking. However, we expect more from criminological theories than from the many "folk theories" that are part of our conventional wisdom.

First, **criminological theories**—at least of the type discussed in this book—are intended as general explanations rather than specific ones. Put another way, such theories are usually not interested in why one particular offender committed a particular crime; rather, they try to explain the patterns that characterize criminal phenomena in general. For example, we want our theories to tell us why males are more likely than females to commit a violent offence, why the chances of victimization are reduced as people grow older, why big cities have higher rates of some kinds of crime than small towns, or why crime rates shot up in the 1960s.

Second, we expect our theories to be consistent with—and help make sense out of—the *facts* of crime as revealed to us by research. The gross facts of crime, as we currently understand them, are often consistent with a variety of different theoretical perspectives. As a result, the evidence sometimes seems to support, at least partially, apparently competing views. For example, why do we find higher rates of many types of theft in bigger cities? Some sociologists have argued that large cities undermine the social controls that might discourage people from stealing (Wirth, 1938). Others have suggested that bigger cities are more likely to be home to the kinds of people (e.g., young, unmarried males) who tend to steal no matter where they live (Gans, 1962). Alternatively, we might argue that the city provides a setting that accommodates an elaborate network of thieves, targets, and fences and thereby turns theft into a profitable and enduring activity (Fischer, 1975; 1995).

On the surface, each of these theories of crime and urban life seems equally viable, since each is consistent with the general patterns of empirical data. This suggests that in order to assess the relative value of these theories, we need more detailed empirical knowledge about the relationship between crime and urban settings. As empirical data accumulate, we would hope to discover that one of the theoretical positions better accounts for the patterns we are observing.

This brings us to a *third* requirement of criminological theories: like all scientific theories, they must be falsifiable. That is, they must be stated in terms that allow us to test them, so that we can discover which theories provide false accounts of the phenomena we are observing. A theory that cannot be rejected no matter what we discover is of little use to us.

Criminological theories are not intellectual abstractions without real-life implications. On the contrary, they are often highly practical, especially when we use them as guides in our efforts to deal with crime as a social problem. Obviously, how we understand the causes of a problem has important consequences for what actions we take to resolve it.

The field of criminology has never been short of theories about crime. To the uninitiated, the choice of explanations can be bewildering: theories often seem to contradict or at least compete with one another. Our review focuses on several types of theoretical questions. The first question concerns the behaviour of offenders, discussed in this chapter and in Chapter 5. Why are some people more inclined than others to behave in ways that violate the law?

In Chapter 6 we turn to another type of theoretical question. How do we understand the situations that allow offenders to act on their propensities? As we will see, an emphasis on situations and opportunities complements the more traditional motivational theories of crime. In Chapter 7 we examine theoretical explanations of what occurs in the aftermath of crime.

EXPLAINING OFFENDER BEHAVIOUR

For many theorists, there is one simple question: Why do offenders do what they do? Traditionally, criminologists have offered two general answers to this question. Criminal behaviour can be understood as the product of unique factors that "motivate" lawbreaking. This approach derives from the positivist school of thought and seeks to discover the causes of criminal conduct. Alternatively, criminal behaviour can be understood as the product of "behavioural choices" that are freely and rationally made. This approach derives from the classical school of thought and considers it misguided to search for causes of criminal behaviour (causes referring to those factors that drive people to act in particular ways).

These perspectives differ in terms of the prominence they attach to the role of "will" in human affairs. Theories that derive from the classical school conceptualize criminal behaviour as wilful and purposeful. Theories that derive from the positivist school perceive will as a less significant characteristic of criminal behaviour, and seek instead to understand how social and other factors compel—or at least encourage—criminal conduct. This chapter deals with theories that reflect the positivist tradition; theories that reflect the classical tradition are discussed in the next chapter.

Three broad subthemes can be identified. The first views criminal motivation as resulting from deficiencies in the offender's physiological or psychological makeup. The second views offenders as a product of troublesome social conditions that propel them toward crime. The third views motivation as arising from the offender's commitment to cultural beliefs that condone criminal conduct.

BIOCRIMINOLOGICAL EXPLANATIONS OF CRIMINAL MOTIVATION

As we noted in Chapter 1, modern scientific criminology is rooted in the work of the nineteenth-century biological positivist Cesare Lombroso and his students. Lombroso was interested in trying to understand how physical characteristics and evolutionary anomalies could explain why some people acted in ways that were prohibited by law. In the 1930s, interest began to shift away from the study of biological causation and toward the study of social causation. Almost from the start, criminology seems to have treated biological explanations with considerable suspicion (Wright and Miller, 1998: 14).

Recently, however, there has been a resurgence of interest in biological accounts of criminal offending. To a considerable degree, this reflects a growing tendency to view criminology as an "interdisciplinary" field. This development has been spurred by the publication of a large number of reviews and analyses of published research. These reviews and analyses have helped make the findings of biological research on crime more accessible to scholars who have not received biological training (Wright and Miller, 1998)(see Box 4.1).

The more recent biological theories differ from earlier ones in a number of ways (Cullen and Agnew, 1999; White and Hanes, 2000). *First*, as will become clear, they focus on a range of biological factors including genetic inheritance, and on a range of environmental factors including diet and birth complications. *Second*, they do not argue that biological factors lead directly to crime; rather, they tend to argue that biological factors affect those developmental processes that result in conformity. *Third*, they usually argue that the impact of biological factors is mediated by the social environment. In other words, biology "interacts" with the social environment.

BOX 4.1

Biology and Crime

A useful summary of much of the empirical research on the relationship between biological factors and crime has been provided by Patricia A. Brennan, Sarnoff A. Mednick, and Jan Volavka (1995). Their review of a large number of studies reaches the following conclusions:

On Genetics

"Criminal behavior in parents increases the likelihood of nonviolent crime in the offspring. The relationship is due, in part, to genetic transmission of criminogenic characteristics. This genetic effect is stronger for females and is especially important for recidivistic crime."

On Perinatal Factors

"Delivery complications are associated with juvenile and adult violent crime. The effect of delivery complications on crime is stronger in more unstable families."

On Neuropsychological and Neurological Factors

"Frontal lobe dysfunction has been found to be associated with adult violent crime. Left hemisphere front-temporal dysfunction is related to a wide variety of antisocial outcomes."

On Neurochemical Factors

"Reduced cerebrospinal fluid 5-hydroxyindoleacetic acid (a metabolite of serotonin) levels have been found in individuals exhibiting impulsive aggression, especially those with a history of alcohol abuse."

On Psychophysiology

"Antisocial individuals evidence reliably reduced levels of autonomic reactiveness and poor conditioning of autonomic responses. Prospective studies reveal a relationship between EEG slow alpha activity in childhood and arrests for property crime in adulthood."

On Biosocial Interactions

"Biosocial factors have been found to be especially likely to predict criminal outcome when combined with adverse social environments."

GENETICS

In recent years there has been a renewed interest in the influence of **genetics** and physiology on the creation of criminal offenders. This school of thought argues that certain individuals are more likely to commit crimes due to faulty genetic programming (Mednick, Moffitt, and Stack, 1987).

Genetics
In criminology, a field of study that attempts to determine how certain presocial factors such as family ties and blood relations influence criminal outcomes (often in conjunction with environmental factors).

The genetic approach has been taken in an effort to determine the importance of family ties or blood relations to individual deportment. It is argued that violent crime, in particular, can be explained in terms of genetics. For instance, individuals with intimate family ties offer the same protection from harm as do animals to their blood connections. In contrast, individuals with less intimate ties (e.g., adopted children) are more likely to be subject to violence from nonblood relations (e.g., stepparents)(see Daly and Wilson, 1988).

Ellis (1982) conducted a review of genetic explanations of crime. Genes influence behaviour through the nervous system. Humans may be so similar genetically that we cannot explain differences in behaviour by genetic variation; forces outside the individual must count for more. So how do nature (genes) and nurture (environment) influence human behaviour, and criminality in particular? The debate on this question is old and heated. The effects of the two have been studied in four different ways: general pedigree studies; twin studies; karyotype studies; and adoption studies.

DO THEY EXIST?

CRIME GENES

Until we can improve our methods, we have no real scientific basis for arguing for (or against) the existence of a "crime gene."

General pedigree studies

A nonexperimental approach to the study of intergenerational transmission of genetically predisposed behaviour between related individuals.

Twin studies

A nonexperimental study designed to research and compare criminal predispositions between dizygotic and monozygotic twins.

As Ellis (1982) explains, **general pedigree studies** involve establishing the extent to which people who are related also behave similarly. This approach is nonexperimental, because it is difficult to control the effects of common genetic background versus environmental influences. Parents share both genetic and environmental factors with their children; it follows that if both parents and children are criminal, it is likely because of these shared factors rather than some environmental factor they do not share. The evidence shows that 30 to 45 percent of individuals with criminal records had one or more parents with criminal records. But knowing about "crime in the family" does not really make it easier for us to use genetics in explaining criminality. This is because it is almost impossible to detach family biology from environmental factors (including family socialization)(Curran and Renzetti, 2001).

The second type of nonexperimental design is the **twin study**. According to Ellis (1982), this design allows us to compare the two types of twinning that occur in humans. Most often, twins are the result of two ova fertilized by two separate sperm. These dizygotic (DZ) twins share 50 percent of genetic programming. In contrast, if a single fertilized ovum splits very early in its development, monozygotic (MZ) twins who share 100 percent of genetic programming are formed. A key concept in twin studies is the notion of "concordance." Concordance is a quantitative measure of the degree to which the observed behaviour or trait of one twin matches that of the other (Akers, 1994). Of central interest for our purpose is the degree of concordance regarding criminal behaviour.

Twin studies show a higher level of concordance between MZ twins in their criminality than between DZ twins. This has led some researchers to conclude that genetic commonalities are the key contributory factors (Katz and Chambliss, 1995). However, because of the strong similarity in their appearance, MZ twins elicit common responses from others more so than do DZ twins. This similarity in treatment—a factor in the socialization of MZ twins—may be more important in guiding behaviour than the fact that they share genetic programming. Twin studies also seem to show that the inherited factors associated with crime are more powerful among women than among men (Hodgins, 2000). Like other genetic studies, twin studies are characterized by a large number of methodological problems—for instance, wide variation in the ways in which criminality is defined and in the methods according to which zyosity is determined (Curran and Renzetti, 2001).

The third type of study discussed by Ellis (1982) involves genetic karyotypes. **Karyotype studies** compare the size, shape, and number of specific chromosomes in individuals. Some researchers report that in criminal males, the Y chromosome has a higher than expected probability of being larger. Also, research shows that some offenders have an unusual number of chromosomes—that is, a number other than the 23 pairs typical in humans. XYY karyotype males are rare among the criminal population, but they are still more likely to be encountered there. The research in this area suffers from small samples and inconclusive explanations. The correlations that exist are not readily interpreted as causative factors.

A related idea that has attracted the attention of the mass media, the public, and some academics is the premenstrual syndrome (PMS) hypothesis. Like the XYY argument, the PMS argument derives from the idea that the origins of crime and violence can somehow be found in gender-based genetic differences (Katz and Chambliss, 1995). Explanations attributing causal significance to PMS imply that women—like men—may do things the law disallows because of hormonal imbalances. However, as with the XYY argument, the attention paid to PMS theory probably outstrips whatever explanatory value the idea may have. Many feminists contend that the PMS hypothesis lends a scientific gloss to the old stereotype that women are emotional prisoners of their biology.

Karyotype studies
These claim that an individual's chromosomes—that is, their size, shape, and number—are a causal factor in criminality.

Adoption studies
The behavioural comparison of near-birth adoptees to their genetic and their adoptive parents.

The fourth design is based on **adoption studies**. As Ellis (1982) points out, we can contrast the behaviour of near-birth adoptees (people adopted by nonrelatives shortly after birth) with that of both their genetic and their adoptive parents. If the behaviour is due to genetics, adoptees should more closely resemble their genetic parents (whom they have never seen) than their adoptive parents. Of course, identical twins would be ideal for such studies, but it is unusual for such twins to be separated, so research of this type is rare (Coleman and Norris, 2000). Still, properly executed adoption studies offer a powerful experimental design for isolating the influences of genetic factors from the influences of socialization and other environmental effects. For example, if some individuals exhibit criminal tendencies that are consistent with their birth parents but not with their adoptive parents, it is assumed that this behaviour is due to genetic programming.

In the research to date, the efficacy of using *genotypes*—that is, genetic makeups—to identify likely candidates for criminal behaviour is not very well established. The most credible research is provided by adoption studies; these have in fact reported fairly low rates of concordance between the offending patterns of identical twins who were separated at birth and raised with different families (Mednick, Moffitt, and Stack, 1987). Adoption studies offer little evidence that genetic differences explain differences in criminality.

Walters and White (1989: 478) summarized the problems of genetic-based research as follows:

> Genetic factors are undoubtedly correlated with various measures of criminality, but the large number of methodological flaws and limitations in the research should make one cautious in drawing any causal inferences at this point in time. Our review leads us to the inevitable conclusion that current genetic research on crime has been poorly designed, ambiguously reported, and exceedingly inadequate in addressing the relevant issues.

Crime gene
The sociobiological perspective that certain genes may be linked to criminality.

Until these deficiencies are addressed, there is no real scientific basis for arguing for (or against) the existence of a **crime gene.**

CONSTITUTION

Constitutional structure
Predispositions toward crime are claimed to be expressed by biological factors, such as phenotypes or body types, and psychological propensities.

Biological approaches have also focused on the **constitutional structure** (i.e., the body types and psychological propensities) of offenders. After reviewing research by Garofalo (1914) on Italian convicts and studies by Sheldon (1949) on incarcerated juveniles, Wilson and Herrnstein (1985) concluded that certain physiological similarities can be detected among offenders. For example, short, muscular young males are more likely than others to appear in prison populations. According to Wilson and Herrnstein (1985: 103), "The biological factors whose traces we see in faces, physiques, and correlation with behaviour of parents and siblings are predispositions towards crime that are expressed as psychological traits and activated by circumstance."

The difficulty with the constitutional approach is that knowing about **body type** doesn't tell us much about a person's propensity to act criminally; it merely tells us (and only if we believe the research) that some inmates happen to be short and muscular. Moreover, body typing ignores the fact that one of the most popular activities in men's prisons is weightlifting. It also fails to consider the fact that in a violent encounter, the less muscular combatant will tend to lose the contest and end up in the hospital, while the more muscular participant will emerge as the victor and end up in prison. Furthermore, this approach doesn't address other important factors related to crime, including the circumstances in which a motivated offender comes to participate in criminal activity.

In defending the constitutional approach to criminality, Wilson and Herrnstein (1985) borrowed from classical criminology to argue that crime is a rational act based on a calculation of potential gain versus loss. Through this process, individuals weigh the probabilities that they will succeed or fail in their endeavours. Individuals may discount potential costs through a process whereby immediate gratification becomes the paramount concern. This choice is not really a free choice, however, as it is predetermined by poor socialization and constitutional deficiencies. The short time horizons possessed by individuals with these deficiencies distort how they make their decisions about benefits and costs. These individuals will tend to involve themselves in criminal activity for short-term gain. According to Wilson and Herrnstein, they represent criminal types who need to be isolated and subjected to high levels of deterrence. Thus, the state's role is to set up contingencies that will reduce the benefits and increase the costs of misbehaviour.

The deterministic nature of constitutional theories firmly establishes them in a positivistic framework that maintains there is little offenders can do to change their propensities to act criminally. From this perspective, we need to reduce the likelihood of criminal activity by isolating individuals who are likely to be problem offenders.

Body type

In order to determine the relationship between physique and criminality, Sheldon categorized ("somatotyped") three basic types of body build—endomorphic, ectomorphic, and mesomorphic—that are associated with a particular type of temperament.

BOX 4.2

Body Type and Criminal Behaviour

In a famous study, William Sheldon (1949) tried to determine the relationship between physique and the tendency to engage in criminal behaviour. Sheldon used a method called *somatotyping* to categorize three basic types of body build—endomorphic, ectomorphic, and mesomorphic. Each of these, he argued, was associated with a particular type of temperament.

As pictured in Figure 4.1, the body types represent extreme forms. Most individuals are a combination of all three types.

Having compared a sample of known delinquents with a control group of students, Sheldon concluded that delinquents were more likely to have mesomorphic physiques and the accompanying temperament, which emphasized risk-taking, adventure, and an interest in physical activity.

Figure 4.1

Sheldon's Somatotypes in Relation to Physique and Temperament

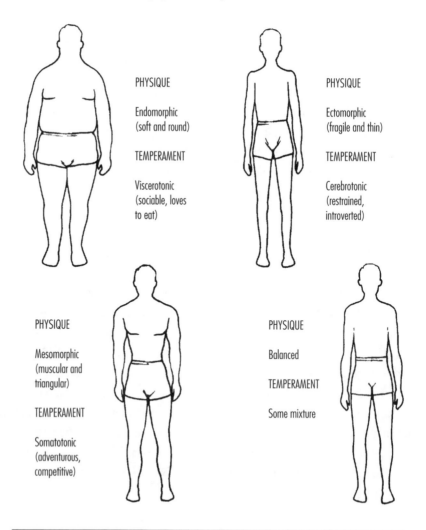

PHYSIQUE

Endomorphic
(soft and round)

TEMPERAMENT

Viscerotonic
(sociable, loves
to eat)

PHYSIQUE

Ectomorphic
(fragile and thin)

TEMPERAMENT

Cerebrotonic
(restrained,
introverted)

PHYSIQUE

Mesomorphic
(muscular and
triangular)

TEMPERAMENT

Somatotonic
(adventurous,
competitive)

PHYSIQUE

Balanced

TEMPERAMENT

Some mixture

Source: Curt R. Bartol, *Criminal Behaviour: A Psychosocial Approach*, 3rd Ed. (Englewood Cliffs, NJ: Prentice-Hall, 1991).

DIET

Some researchers are interested in the degree to which **diet** can affect behaviour. Strong scientific evidence supports the idea that certain individuals are more prone to hyperactivity or aggressive behaviour following a sudden intake of sugar (hypoglycemia) (Dorfman, 1984). In a famous case, a San Francisco city supervisor attributed his 1978 murder of the mayor and a fellow supervisor to his diet of Twinkies and other "junk food." His lawyers were able to use what has come to be known as the **Twinkie defence** to convince a jury that their client suffered from "diminished mental capacity" and was therefore not guilty of murder.

Some researchers contend that food allergies—for instance, to milk, eggs, or chocolate—can lead to aggressive or violent behaviour (Wright and Miller, 1998). The idea that diet can be a major cause of violence seems questionable; that being said, it is clear that a change of diet can have a dramatic effect on the behaviour of prisoners. In a study of detention homes in California, it was established that when the diet of 276 juveniles was revised—mostly by reducing sugar intake—antisocial behaviour declined by 48 percent, incidents of theft by 77 percent, incidents of assault by 82 percent, and refusal to obey orders by 55 percent (Kinderlehrer, 1983: 143). Similar results were obtained when supplies of orange juice were increased—a finding that has led some researchers to attribute the former negative behaviours not to excessive sugar content but rather to vitamin and nutrient deficiencies in prisoners' diets (Dorfman, 1984).

The focus on nutrients has led to research on the relationship between **trace element** patterns and a predisposition to violence. One study compared 24 pairs of violent and nonviolent brothers; a second study matched 96 violent males of mixed age and background with 96 nonviolent males who served as a control group. The research revealed that the violent subjects fell into two groups: type As, who tested high in copper and low in sodium and potassium and who were episodically violent, and type Bs, who were the reverse and who displayed consistently antisocial behaviour. As the type A pattern tends to fade with age, parole boards could use hair analysis (a procedure for tracking trace elements) to predict, on the basis of the mineral content in the subject's body, when episodic violence will likely cease (Dorfman, 1984: 46).

Diet
The concept that the behaviour of certain individuals can be affected by their diet.

Twinkie defence
When a defendant experiences diminished mental capacity and is therefore not guilty of criminal behaviour due to an overconsumption of junk food.

WHAT IS IT?

THE TWINKIE DEFENCE

The argument that due to the overconsumption of junk food, a defendant experienced "diminished mental capacity" and is therefore not guilty of criminal behaviour.

Trace elements
Mineral content in the subject's body determines episodic violence or antisocial behaviour.

The applicability of these findings to offenders outside institutions is impossible to determine. They do provide some interesting suggestions as to how lifestyle—especially diet—influences our actions. They do not tell us much about what situations elicit violence, or about what social factors (e.g., early childhood socialization, peer pressure, or fear of stigmatization) may play a role in deterring it.

The ingestion of substances other than food has attracted a great deal of attention in criminological analyses. Drugs, including alcohol, are present in many criminal events. The criminality that surrounds the illicit sale and purchase of drugs makes their use of interest to us. As with dietary factors, it is unclear how important drugs are explaining criminality. Their presence in criminal situations may be related to but not central to explanations of criminality. Many people use (and abuse) alcohol without becoming violent and attacking other people. Yet as evidenced by the many bar fights that occur, alcohol sometimes seems to fuel violent attacks.

Explanations based on genetics, constitution, and diet can be summed up this way: if one accepts that crime is a cultural and social concept, defined through custom and law, it seems unlikely that such a thing as a "criminal type" or a "crime gene" exists whereby behaviour is preprogrammed to deviate from this social construct—or, indeed, that certain people with particular body types or diet will generally offend. These explanations, while interesting, seem to be more useful for describing the conditions of incarcerated offenders and assisting in controlling their behaviour than for predicting the likelihood of criminality in the first place.

INTELLIGENCE AND CRIME

NEUROPSYCHOLOGICAL THEORY

IQ
A measure of intelligence derived from standardized testing procedures that compare individuals' mental and chronological ages.

There has been an upsurge in interest in the relationship between **IQ** and behaviour (see Murray and Herrnstein, 1994). It has long been recognized in criminological research that a correlation exists between IQ and delinquency. According to one well known expert:

After sex and age, the single most firmly established psychological fact about the population of offenders is that the distribution of their IQ scores differs from that of the population at large. Instead of averaging 100, as the general population does, offenders average about eight points lower (Herrnstein, 1995: 49).

What remains in doubt is the meaning of the "weak to moderate negative correlation between IQ (intelligence quotient) and delinquent behavior" (Akers, 1994: 77). Some researchers contend that the relationship between IQ and crime may be indirect—that IQ affects school performance and delinquency results from these problems in school (Hirschi and Hindelang, 1977). Moffitt, Lynam, and Silva (1994) argue that one way to approach this issue is to look beyond IQ by applying **neuropsychological theory,** according to which people with identical IQ scores can have very different patterns of mental strengths and weaknesses. Moffitt and colleagues claim that IQ offers limited information about which of these strengths or weaknesses influences behaviour. The IQ test compresses an aggregate measure of abilities (notably verbal skills and spatial perception) into a single composite indicator of performance. Most neuropsychological test batteries include a standard IQ test, which measures verbal and spatial functions very accurately, but they also add more tests to cover functions such as memory, motor skills, and mental self-control. A battery of neuropsychological tests can reveal, for instance, that children with identical low IQ scores may be suffering from different and relatively isolated problems such as impulsive judgment, weak language processing, poor memory, or inability to match visual information with motor actions. Each type of deficit could be more accurate than the overall IQ in predicting delinquency, but each would contribute to delinquency through a unique theoretical causal chain (Moffitt et al., 1994: 279).

Neuropsychological theory
The theory that people with identical IQ scores can have very different patterns of mental strengths and weaknesses (e.g., verbal skill, spatial perception) that can influence behaviour.

LEARNING DISABILITIES

Culliver and Sigler (1991) provide an extensive review of the relationship between learning disabilities and juvenile delinquency. **Learning disabilities** are defined as problems faced by children and youths with dyslexia, dysgraphia, aphasia, perceptual and motor deficits, poor intersensory integration, and minimal brain dysfunction. Although these disabilities are often difficult to detect, it is strongly believed that they are directly related to delinquent behaviour in youths.

Culliver and Sigler report that five hypotheses have been used to study this relationship:

Learning disabilities
Difficulties faced by children and youths with dyslexia, dysgraphia, aphasia, perceptual and motor deficits, poor sensory integration, or minimal brain dysfunction.

- The **school failure hypothesis** argues that academic failure results from learning disabilities and that this failure becomes self-perpetuating. As a result of their frustration, students become more aggressive, and are in turn labelled as troublesome. Through rejection from teachers and

School failure hypothesis
The theory that self-perpetuating academic failure resulting from learning disabilities causes frustration and aggressive behaviour.

Susceptibility hypothesis
The theory that learning disabled students have unique characteristics, such as impulsiveness and irritability, and thus are more likely to become delinquent.

Differential arrest hypothesis
The theory that learning disabled children are more likely to be apprehended by the police since they are less likely to conceal their activities.

Differential adjudication hypothesis
The theory that delinquents with learning disabilities who are arrested and charged are more likely to be convicted of crimes due to their inability to cope with the process of criminal justice adjudication.

Differential disposition hypothesis
The theory that learning disabled delinquents have a higher chance of receiving harsher sentences than other delinquents.

administrators, these youths withdraw from mainstream activities and become involved in inappropriate behaviour and, ultimately, delinquency.

- The **susceptibility hypothesis** contends that learning disabled students have unique characteristics, such as impulsiveness, inability to anticipate future consequences, and irritability. In acting out their feelings, they are more likely to become delinquent.

- The **differential arrest hypothesis** posits that learning disabled students are more likely to be apprehended by police because they are less able to conceal their activities than are their non-learning disabled peers. This hypothesis also suggests that learning disabled students cannot effectively interact with police because of their abrasiveness and poor social perception and are therefore more likely to be arrested.

- The **differential adjudication hypothesis** argues that delinquents with learning disabilities who are arrested and charged are more likely to be convicted of crimes due to their inability to cope with the process of criminal justice adjudication. "Moreover, learning disabled students are unable to vindicate their feelings and concerns regarding the criminal charges" (Culliver and Sigler, 1991: 125).

- Finally, according to the **differential disposition hypothesis**, learning disabled delinquents face a higher chance of receiving harsher sentences than do non-learning disabled delinquents.

Culliver and Sigler report that while the potential link between learning disabilities and delinquency has generated much interest, research results "tend to create more confusion and uncertainty than fact upon which sound theories can be built and effective programs developed" (1991: 125). This same conclusion is reached by Cornwall and Bawden (1992) in their assessment of the link between reading disabilities and aggression. As Skaret and Wilgosh (1989) state, the problems with the research should lead us to deal with the effects of learning disabilities on delinquency in a different way. Instead of struggling to provide definitive findings supporting a causal relationship, perhaps we should pay attention to the fact that adolescents with learning disabilities seem to be at relatively high risk for delinquency. "Sound remedial education practices, including counselling and other support systems will improve academic achievement and social skills, and *may, possibly*, lead to some reduced delinquent behaviour" (Skaret and Wilgosh, 1989: 121). This is the same prescription offered by Moffitt, Lynam, and Silva (1994) in their conclusions about the remedial effects of using psychoneurological testing in assessing propensity toward delinquency.

PSYCHOPATHOLOGY

For the most heinous crimes, such as sexually motivated murders and serial murders, we often apply the label of **psychopath** to the perpetrator.

Psychopaths are often described as aggressive, insensitive, charismatic, irresponsible, intelligent, dangerous, hedonistic, narcissistic, and antisocial. They are perceived as superb manipulators, and as capable of pretending to possess "normal" human emotions even while remorselessly carrying out their personal agendas. They are outwardly normal but are famously unable to maintain long-term commitments to people or programs.

It is believed that psychopaths are more dangerous than other criminals, and that they behave criminally consistently over their lifetime. It has been argued that psychopathy results from a number of environmental causes; it has also been argued that biological factors play a role in producing psychopathy. For example, Hodgins (2000: 225) states that there is indeed evidence that a genetic factor contributes to psychopathy. Because of differences in their autonomic nervous systems, psychopaths may be less responsive to incoming stimuli that would normally produce a fear reaction. If it is correct that psychopaths possess a nervous system that dampens stimulation, they may be suffering from a kind of "stimulation hunger" that causes them to seek out stimulation even while simultaneously failing to learn from the aversive conditioning to which they are subjected (Katz and Chambliss, 1995). Jeffery (1990: 364) suggests that we look at psychopaths in terms of how the nervous system functions in times of threat. As Jeffery points out, psychopaths do not become anxious or fearful in the presence of punishment or danger because their autonomic nervous systems are not aroused by danger. Also, because psychopaths are unable to anticipate the consequences of their actions, they make little attempt to avoid punishment or pain.

According to Hickey (1991), the term *psychopath* is used to describe a wide range of individuals who have been determined by societal and medical standards to possess antisocial qualities and characteristics. Hickey adds that the label of psychopath is used interchangeably with that of **sociopath**. Furthermore, because the term is so general, the psychopath "often turns out to be exactly what we want him or her to be" (1991: 50). In other words, the concept of the psychopathic personality is so broad that it could apply to almost anyone who breaks the law (Akers, 1994). Psychopathic characteristics such as irresponsibility, untruthfulness, and a lack of guilt associated with antisocial conduct are just as discernable in successful corporate executives,

Psychopathy
A sociopathic disorder characterized by lack of moral development and the inability to show loyalty to others.

Psychopathology
Study of abnormal behaviour.

Sociopathy
Antisocial personality disorder involving a marked lack of ethical or moral development.

athletes, and even national leaders as they are in criminals. Not surprisingly, estimates of the number of psychopaths in the population vary wildly, from 10 percent to 80 percent depending on the definition of psychopath being employed.

For criminological researchers, the dilemma in all of this is that psychopaths can hide their symptoms while leading "normal" lives. We only learn about their tendencies after they act out their antisocial fantasies. Often it takes some time to uncover these individuals' acts, as shown by the long crime sprees of serial murderers. Paul Bernardo and his wife Karla Homolka were convicted in the 1990s for the torture-murder of two Ontario schoolgirls; they were regarded by many of their neighbours as normal members of the community.

SOCIAL CONDITIONS AND CRIMINAL MOTIVATION

It has been argued that people's social circumstances can make it difficult for them to be law-abiding. Criminal behaviour can thus be understood as the means people resort to in attempting to deal with the problems and frustrations they encounter in their lives.

From this perspective, many types of crime and delinquency can be understood as forms of "problem solving" (Brezina, 2000). That is, individuals commit crimes in order to adapt to conditions and situations that threaten them in some way. Criminals are not sick, and are not the victims of faulty genes; rather, they are rational actors whose behaviour is goal-oriented. This perspective encourages us to understand that crime often has a real appeal for the offender.

FRUSTRATED AMBITIONS

People who aspire to goals they cannot realistically attain may feel pressure to behave criminally. This pressure is most likely to be felt by those who occupy disadvantaged positions in the social structure. Perhaps the best-known version of this argument was articulated in the late 1930s by the sociologist Robert Merton, who was trying to explain how particular forms of social organization create the strains that lead to nonconformity.

Using American society as an example, Merton (1938) argued that if everyone is encouraged to pursue material success, those who do not have access to legitimate means for achieving that success will be frustrated by their lack of opportunity. Those at the bottom of the social hierarchy—the poor, ethnic minorities, recent immigrants—do not have easy access to inheritance, quality education, or other means for realizing the American Dream. Since success is still important to them, they must find ways to adjust to the social strain society places on them. These adjustments may often involve criminal conduct.

BOX 4.3

Merton's Paradigm of Deviant Behaviour

Robert Merton (1938) argued that nonconformist behaviour results when people are encouraged to pursue cultural goals that prevailing social arrangements do not allow them to achieve. These individuals may have internalized these goals, but they also lack legitimate means for achieving them. As a consequence, they must adjust their behaviour to accommodate the gap between the goals and the means. Merton identified five adaptations in the goals–means relationship.

1. *Conformity*. Individuals who make this adaptation accept as legitimate both the goals and the means for achieving them. This is the adaptation most people make.
2. *Innovation*. Innovation involves accepting the goals but rejecting the means of goal attainment. For example, a person who embezzles accepts material gain as a legitimate goal but rejects the culturally prescribed means for achieving it.
3. *Ritualism*. This adaptation involves accepting the means for achieving the goal but rejecting the goal itself. Individuals who engage in ritualism simply "go through the motions" without coming any closer to the goals they supposedly seek.
4. *Retreatism*. Here, both means and goals are rejected. At least in terms of what the culture prescribes, those who opt for this adaptation can be described as dropouts.
5. *Rebellion*. Like retreatism, this form of adaptation involves rejecting both goals and means. Rebellion differs from retreatism in that it involves substituting other goals as well as other means by which they might be achieved.

Merton presented his five adaptations in schematic form as follows (where + means accept and − means reject).

	Goal	Means
Conformity	+	+
Innovation	+	−
Ritualism	−	+
Retreatism	−	−
Rebellion	−	−
	(+)	(+)

Anomie theory
Theory that says anomie occurs when cultural norms and goals break down.

In his **anomie theory**, Merton proposed that frustration and alienation develop when individuals who aspire to society's economic goals (including upward social mobility) lack access to the means for achieving those goals. That is, a gap exists between expectations and opportunity. In responding to the anomie that develops due to this gap, they adapt in certain ways. One such adaptation involves resorting to crime to achieve conventional goals such as wealth. Blau and Blau (1982) argued that it is not absolute but relative deprivation that results in frustration and a sense of personal injustice; this in turn leads to criminal activity.

Consider the gangster Al Capone. Arguably, the goals to which he aspired did not differ significantly from the goals pursued by "legitimate" business-people. Capone sought wealth, power, and celebrity. He differed from conventional entrepreneurs with respect to the means he employed to achieve these objectives, but not with respect to the objectives themselves. Seen in this way, the behaviour of gangsters, thieves, and other goal-oriented criminals is best understood as the product not of a pathological personality but of social arrangements that create a gulf between what people aspire to and what is actually available to them.

STATUS DEPRIVATION

Several years after Merton published his work, Albert Cohen followed a similar line in his investigation of gang delinquency among working-class juveniles. In Cohen's view (1955), much juvenile crime was rooted in the problems experienced by disadvantaged youths. These youth aspired to middle-class status, but were often judged inadequate by a school system that dispensed status rewards on the basis of middle-class criteria. In other words, children from the working class typically found that their socialization experiences had not prepared them to compete effectively for status in the classroom; as a result, they came up short when they were assessed by the school's **middle-class measuring rod**. According to Cohen, working-class youths often felt frustrated and inadequate when they confronted middle-class expectations regarding punctuality, neatness, and the need to postpone gratification.

Middle-class measuring rod
The middle-class ethic, which people use to compare and determine their status, that prescribes an obligation to strive, by dint of rational, ascetic, self-disciplined, and independent activity, to achieve worldly success.

Middle-class youths may reject the source of their problem—namely, the middle-class value system of the school. In this way, delin-

WHAT DOES IT MEAN?

MIDDLE-CLASS MEASURING ROD

Working-class youth may feel frustrated and inadequate when they confront middle-class expectations regarding punctuality, neatness, and the need to postpone gratification.

quent subcultures emerge through "a process of adaptations by youth to what they perceive as blocked access to middle-class status" (Vowell and May, 2000: 45). Delinquency may signal such a rejection, especially if it celebrates standards that run directly counter to those of middle-class society. Delinquency that seems intended to offend members of conventional society rather than to achieve some specific goal may serve this purpose. Cohen found that much delinquency has an "in your face" quality precisely because it is meant to signify a rejection of middle-class values. According to Tanner (2001: 63), aggressive and destructive delinquency often appears senseless to others, but to the delinquents themselves "it is a powerful way of hitting back at a system that has done them no favours."

STRAIN AND DELINQUENCY

Richard Cloward and Lloyd Ohlin (Cloward, 1959; Cloward and Ohlin, 1960) borrowed heavily from Robert Merton to demonstrate that a comprehensive theory of delinquency must explain not only why juveniles engage in delinquency but also why they engage in some types of delinquency and not others. Like Merton, they argued that the motivation to delinquency can be located in the discrepancy between the goals to which lower-class youths aspire and the means available to achieve them. Cloward and Ohlin were also influenced by Merton's view that not everyone in society finds the **legitimate means** to conventional ends equally available. For some people, the legitimate means of obtaining success goals, such as education or a good job, are out of reach; it is precisely this lack of legitimate opportunity that creates the pressure to deviate in the first place.

> **Legitimate means**
> Widely accepted routes of achieving cultural goals through institutions.

However, Cloward and Ohlin extended Merton's theory by arguing that it is important to recognize that illegitimate means are also structured. Opportunities to be criminal are no more evenly dispersed in society than are legitimate means to achieve success goals. Building on this logic, Cloward and Ohlin theorized that the kind of delinquent a youth becomes depends on the kinds of opportunities he or she has to be delinquent.

Cloward and Ohlin (1960) used the term **illegitimate means** to encompass two major aspects of the delinquent opportunity structure. The *first* is the opportunity to learn a delinquent role. As Sutherland (1947) noted, learning how to be delinquent and why it is acceptable to be delinquent are necessary precursors to being delinquent. The *second* is the opportunity to actually play a delinquent role. An individual can become a member of a drug network or

> **Illegitimate means**
> Two aspects of the delinquent opportunity structure: opportunity to learn and to play the delinquent role.

stolen-car ring only if such organizations exist in his or her social environment. For Cloward and Ohlin, then, a central theoretical problem was to understand how particular types of community organizations make particular types of delinquent opportunity structures possible. Their analysis identified three forms of delinquent opportunity structures, each of which was associated with particular types of social conditions.

The first form, the **criminal pattern**, is characterized by a rational delinquency oriented toward the pursuit of monetary objectives. The prime examples of this are organized theft and the sale of drugs or other illicit goods or services. Delinquency of this type is most likely to emerge in lower-class neighbourhoods where a stable adult criminal world exists and where the criminal and conformist sectors of the community are highly integrated. When such integration exists, the "cop on the beat" is willing to look the other way and the "honest" storekeeper is occasionally willing to fence stolen goods. The presence of a stable adult criminal world provides a structure for recruitment and upward mobility for juveniles who perceive criminality as a possible career.

Neighbourhoods that give rise to the criminal pattern can be described as socially organized; we expect a different pattern to emerge in neighbourhoods that are socially disorganized. Socially disorganized slums lack a stable adult criminal world and thus an established criminal structure. This situation can be doubly frustrating for neighbourhood youths who have already encountered the disparity between legitimate goals and legitimate opportunities. Moreover, as Shaw and McKay (1942) pointed out, these areas lack the social controls that might contain the behavioural manifestations of this frustration. For these reasons, Cloward and Ohlin discerned in socially disorganized areas a **conflict pattern** of delinquency. The conflict pattern is characterized by gangs who express their frustration by fighting over contested neighbourhood turf.

Finally, Cloward and Ohlin maintained, it is unwise to assume that everyone who engages in criminal or conflict opportunities will be successful. We are not all cut out to be drug dealers or gang warriors. Cloward and Ohlin used the term *double-failures* to describe people who are unable to succeed through either legitimate or illegitimate means. Double-failures tend to become involved in a **retreatist pattern** in which delinquency is organized around the consumption of drugs.

Criminal pattern

A rational delinquency oriented toward the pursuit of monetary objectives, exemplified by organized theft and the sale of illicit goods or services.

Conflict pattern

A pattern that occurs in socially disorganized neighbourhoods, where youth often experience the disparity between legitimate goals and legitimate opportunities, and this leads to aggressive behaviour.

Retreatist pattern

Pattern exhibited by people who are unable to succeed through either legitimate or illegitimate means (double-failures), and who resort to delinquency organized around the consumption of drugs.

RECENT VERSIONS OF THE STRAIN ARGUMENT

A GENERAL STRAIN THEORY

Strain theory is no longer a dominant view in criminology; however, interest in it has been reviving recently (Menard, 1995). For instance, Agnew (1992) has proposed a **general strain theory**, which extends the logic of the argument well beyond what was originally proposed by Merton. According to Agnew, strain theory focuses on negative relationships with others. In negative relationships, individuals are not treated the way they would like to be treated; such relationships promote anger, fear, and frustration, which may lead to delinquency.

With specific reference to juvenile offending, Agnew argues that there are three main types of strain. The *first* type results when we believe that others are preventing us or threatening to prevent us from achieving what we want to achieve. This type is most familiar because it is very similar to the type of strain described by Merton. The *second* type of strain results when we believe that others have removed or are threatening to remove what we already possess and what we value. This might include the loss of a boyfriend/girlfriend, a move out of one's neighbourhood, or the death of a parent. The *third* type of strain results when our relationships with others cause us to experience negative life events. This type might include negative relationships with teachers, abuse by parents, or bullying by peers.

As individuals attempt to cope with the negative emotions that these relationships cause them to experience, they may explore delinquent solutions. Depending on the type of strain being experienced, drug use may be a means of escape, violence may be a way to get even, theft may allow the acquisition of material goods that are not otherwise available. Several tests of the revised general strain theory have provided empirical support for the argument and helped us understand better how strain and delinquency are related (Brezina, 1996; Paternoster and Mazzerole, 1994). Agnew and White (1992) found that the various types of strain have a significant impact on delinquency and that the effects are most visible among adolescents who lack self-efficacy and who have delinquent friends. More recent tests have suggested that the processes linking diverse types of strain to delinquent outcomes may be even more complicated. For instance, Paul Mazerolle and his colleagues found that the motivating influence of strain may vary from one type of crime to another (Mazerolle et al., 2000). These researchers analyzed data collected from a sample of high school–aged youth, and found that strain seems to have a direct effect on violence; however, its effect on other types of delinquency

Strain theory
The theory that the constant emphasis on success in society and its possible attainment consistently contradicts the actual opportunity facing people—especially at the bottom of society, where the greatest amount of crime occurs.

General strain theory
A focus on negative relationships between people that promote anger, fear, and frustration, which may lead to delinquency.

BOX 4.4

An Example of Strain and Crime

The general strain theory argues that social relationships cause crime in part by causing stressful circumstances, which youths then attempt to avoid. An especially vivid example of this is found in a study by Bernard Schissel and Karl Fedec (1999) of juvenile prostitution. The authors used social service data from Saskatoon and Regina on 400 young offenders to investigate, among other things, the relationship between an abusive childhood and involvement in the youth sex trade.

Their results show clearly that youth become involved in prostitution at least in part because their early lives were characterized by abuse and neglect. For both Aboriginal and non-Aboriginal youth, greater levels of childhood physical abuse are associated with greater involvement in prostitution. Also, youth who were victims of sexual abuse are more likely to be involved in the sex trade.

It is not as clear exactly how sexual abuse results in prostitution. Several explanations can be suggested. Schissel and Fedec cautiously argue that abuse tends to damage young people's self-esteem and psychological skills; this in turn reduces the likelihood of educational or other conventional forms of success. Importantly, the authors also show just how dangerous the sex trade is for young prostitutes, both physically and sexually. They conclude:

> The social policy implications that emanate from research such as this are clear. Young prostitutes develop and live in contexts of constant danger. Without caring intervention, the risk that these youths run, probably unparalleled anywhere else in society, will shorten their lives. Given that their supposed criminality is not one of choice but of coercion and victimization, an immediate, non-legalistic, non-condemnatory intervention strategy is crucial, not only for the integrity of a society that so far has failed to stop adult predators of children and youth (1999: 51).

(e.g., drug use) depends on the presence of other factors such as relations with deviant peers.

CRIME AND THE AMERICAN DREAM

Even more recently, Messner and Rosenfeld (1997) have elaborated on Merton's argument to explain why the United States has such high rates of serious crime relative to other industrialized nations. Like Merton, they suggest that the root of the problem is the "American Dream," which they define as a commitment to the goal of material success that everyone in society pursues in conditions of open, individual competition. As a result of widespread allegiance to the American Dream, many people adopt an "anything goes" mentality as they chase their personal goals.

According to Messner and Rosenfeld, the problems created by the American Dream are magnified because the economy and the lessons that it teaches dominate other social institutions, such as the family and the school. They note, for instance, how family activities and routines are required to conform to the schedules and rewards of the labour market, and that despite much rhetoric about "family values," it is the homeowner and not the homemaker who is admired and respected. In a similar way, the school is not a setting that produces model citizens but one that teaches competition for grades as students prepare for labour force participation.

This institutional balance of power, they argue, has two important consequences. *First*, it allows the competitive and individualistic message of the American Dream to diffuse to other settings. *Second*, because the lessons of the economy override the lessons taught in other institutional environments, the social control that we expect the school or the family to exert over criminal behaviour is undermined. Both conditions are conducive to high rates of crime. Canadian studies of crime have suggested that Canadian society is able to protect those who fall out of the race for the "dream," through social assistance programs and strong community support—although with changes in government policies, these programs and supports may be falling away (Papadopoulos, 1997). The increasing strength of the competition model in Canadian society may lead us to parallel the American experience in promoting individual success; as a result, elements of the strain evident in parts of the American population may appear in Canada as well. What this means for Canadian crime rates remains unclear.

CULTURE AND CRIMINAL MOTIVATION

Another important approach locates the origins of criminal motivation in the cultural worlds to which offenders have been exposed. The cultural milieu in which we are socialized provides us with our ideas of right and wrong, moral and immoral, appropriate and inappropriate. When our socialization is successful, we internalize these views and try to behave in ways that conform to the cultural standards we have learned. It follows that if we are exposed to beliefs and ideas that support behaviour the law defines as criminal, we may be more likely to behave like criminals.

Like strain theories, cultural accounts of crime present a "normalized" picture of the offender. In other words, offenders are not necessarily pathological; they merely have learned a particular set of cultural lessons. Their behaviour is normal within a particular cultural context.

DIFFERENTIAL ASSOCIATION

Differential association
The theory that criminal behaviour is learned in the process of interaction with intimate groups.

Cultural approaches focus not only on norm violation as criminal behaviour but also on criminal behaviour that is normative (Alarid, Burton and Cullen, 2000). One of the pioneers of this perspective was Edwin Sutherland, who in the 1930s proposed a cultural theory of crime that he called the **theory of differential association**. Against the prevailing wisdom of his day, Sutherland (1947) maintained that crime is a learned behaviour. In the process of interacting with others whose own views support criminal conduct, one person can learn to be criminal just as another can learn to be a mechanic, a stamp collector, or a lover of classical music. According to Sutherland, the differential rate at which people associate with the carriers of criminal values determines the differential rate at which they engage in criminal conduct.

For Sutherland, differential association involves two important types of learning. *First*, one must learn the actual techniques of crime commission. Sometimes these techniques are very simple and do not differ markedly from law-abiding behaviour. For example, stealing a car when the owner has left the keys inside is not so different from driving one's own car. Other times, specialized skills are required—for instance, stealing a locked car when the keys have not been left inside.

Sutherland emphasized that knowledge or technical skills alone are insufficient to explain criminal behaviour. Everyone has some idea of how to commit a wide variety of crimes. Yet although most of us could figure out how to murder or assault someone, we refrain from committing such acts. So *second*, aside from technical knowledge, one must have exposure to the "specific direction of motives, drives, rationalizations and attitudes" (Sutherland, 1947: 6). Stated differently, to behave criminally, one must learn that crime is an acceptable type of behaviour.

Consistent with the principles of the theory of differential association, Desroches (1995) found that half of the bank robbers he studied became involved in that type of crime as a result of their association with other offenders. Typically, they learned this skill from more experienced criminals who convinced them that bank robbery is both fast and easy. Through this process of differential association, they learned not only how to rob banks but also how to justify the crime and to view it as a low-risk offence.

BOX 4.5

The Tenets of Differential Association Theory

Edwin Sutherland was one of the few criminologists to formulate a theory in terms of an interrelated set of propositions. The following statements, from Traub and Little (1980), refer to the process by which a particular person comes to engage in criminal behaviour:

1. *Criminal behaviour is learned.* Negatively, this means that criminal behaviour is not inherited as such.
2. *Criminal behaviour is learned in interaction with other people in a process of communication.* This communication is mainly verbal, but also includes gestures.
3. *Most learning of criminal behaviour occurs within intimate personal groups.* Negatively, this means that the impersonal agencies of communication, such as movies and newspapers, play a relatively unimportant role in the genesis of criminal behaviour.
4. *When criminal behaviour is learned, this learning includes (a) techniques of committing the crime, which are sometimes very complicated, sometimes very simple; and (b) the specific direction of motives, drives, rationalizations, and attitudes.*
5. *The specific direction of motives and drives is learned from definitions of the legal codes.* In some societies an individual is surrounded by people who invariably define the legal codes as rules to be observed; in other societies he or she is surrounded by people whose definitions are favourable to the violation of legal codes.
6. *A person becomes delinquent because of an excess of definitions favourable to violation of law over definitions unfavourable to violation of law.* This is the principle of differential association. It refers to both criminal and anticriminal associations and has to do with counteracting forces. When people become criminal, they do so because of contact with criminal patterns and also because of isolation from anticriminal patterns.
7. *The process of learning criminal behaviour by association with criminal and anticriminal patterns involves all of the mechanisms involved in any other learning.* Negatively, this means that the learning of criminal behaviour is not restricted to the process of imitation. A person who is seduced, for instance, learns criminal behaviour by association, but this process would not ordinarily be described as imitation.
8. *Though criminal behaviour is an expression of general needs and values, it is not explained by those general needs and values, since noncriminal behaviour is an expression of the same needs and values.* Thieves generally steal in order to secure money, but likewise honest labourers work in order to secure money. The attempts by many scholars to explain criminal behaviour by general drives and values—such as the happiness principle, striving for social status, the money motive, or frustration—have been futile and must continue to be so, since they explain lawful behaviour as completely as they explain criminal behaviour.

All of this suggests that cultural knowledge and beliefs exist that promote criminality; however, only a few of us are offered sustained exposure to that knowledge or those beliefs. Sutherland's approach has been especially helpful in explaining why normally law-abiding individuals commit crimes at work. According to Sutherland (1961), white-collar crime occurs because people have learned how to commit it and because they have learned from others that it is acceptable.

SUBCULTURAL EXPLANATIONS OF CRIMINAL MOTIVATIONS

In complex, highly differentiated societies like our own, cultural "pockets" exist in which groups of people are engaged in intensive interaction and confront common problems or share common interests. It is in this sense that we speak of subcultures of rap music fans, marathon runners, or the police. Participants in these worlds are also participants in the larger culture shared by the rest of us; in that sense, these **subcultures** are both part of and distinguishable from the larger culture. It can be argued that subcultural involvement promotes criminal behaviour when the subcultural values in question are inconsistent with the conformist values enshrined in law.

Subculture
A group of people in a dominant culture with different values, evident in their expression of deviant behaviour.

Thorsten Sellin (1938) suggested that the high rates of crime among immigrant groups can be understood with reference to the culture conflict that ethnic subcultures encounter. His view acknowledged that when people migrate from one country to another, they carry with them considerable cultural baggage. We recognize this fact when we visit a restaurant in Little Italy or attend a cultural festival in Chinatown. This cultural baggage often also includes ways of acting that, although not considered criminal in the country of origin, are defined as such in the host country. By way of illustration, Sellin (1938) tells the story of a Sicilian father in New Jersey who "killed the 16-year-old seducer of his daughter, expressing surprise at his arrest since he had merely defended his family honour in a traditional way" (68).

Like Sellin, anthropologist Walter Miller (1958) attempted to understand how the cultural values of a particular group can increase the likelihood of criminal conduct. Miller studied lower-class life in a large eastern American city in an effort to identify the distinct character of lower-class culture. He was especially interested in how this subculture related to the delinquencies of lower-class male youths. He argued that life among the lower class was organized around six **focal concerns**:

Focal concerns
Concerns around which life in the lower class is organized: trouble, toughness, smartness, excitement, fate, and autonomy.

BOX 4.6

Crime and Culture

Many theories of crime encourage the view that crime rates are higher among recent immigrants. For instance, Thorsten Sellins's theory of culture conflict (1938) focused on the criminogenic character of the conflict between immigrant and host cultures. In a similar way, strain theories suggest that the social and economic problems faced by new immigrants may put them in conflict with the law. Moreover, it is part of the "popular wisdom" about crime that those who are new to Canada are a bigger source of trouble than those who were born here.

To what extent are these beliefs supported by the empirical evidence? Robert M. Gordon and Jacquelyn Nelson (2000) reviewed existing studies and analyzed data from the province of British Columbia. They concluded that contrary to popular belief, people from non-Aboriginal, visible ethnic minorities are significantly underrepresented in the federal correctional system and in the youth and adult correctional systems of British Columbia. In fact, there were only about half as many immigrants as one might expect, given their numbers in the general population.

In explaining this pattern, the authors highlighted the nature of recent immigration. British Columbia attracts a large number of Asian immigrants each year, and many of them, for various reasons, are finding it easier to adjust than the ones who arrived before them. One of the biggest differences is financial: more recent Asian immigrants are bringing legitimate financial resources with them. Many of them are investors, retired people, or entrepreneurs.

As the authors point out, these findings complicate our understanding of the relationship between immigration, culture, and crime; they also demand that we critically reexamine the theories that attempt to link these concepts.

1. *Trouble.* Life is a series of troublesome episodes: trouble with the police, with the welfare officer, with one's neighbours, and so on.
2. *Toughness.* "Machismo" is widely prized in lower-class areas as an interactional style.
3. *Smartness.* This refers not to intellectual ability, but rather to the ability to live by one's wits.
4. *Excitement.* Life is best described as boring and monotonous, and punctuated occasionally by thrill-seeking behaviour. Excitement might include bouts of drinking or fighting.
5. *Fate.* Life is largely seen in terms of good luck and bad luck.
6. *Autonomy.* There is a general desire to be free of the control of police, landlords, welfare workers, and others who might seek to regulate life.

WHAT DOES IT MEAN?

SUBCULTURE OF VIOLENCE

A powerful cultural emphasis on social honour and on the need to save face when a threat to one's honour arises in a public setting means that a derogatory remark made about one's character may be seen as sufficient reason to engage in physical battle. To argue that violence, in this sense, is subcultural is to argue that it is "normative."

Subculture of violence
A subculture in which disproportionate rates of criminal violence are the product of a group's commitment to subcultural values and norms that condone violence as an acceptable means of resolving interpersonal conflict.

For Miller, these focal concerns were problematic in themselves because they suggested a value orientation at odds with the legal code. People who live their lives in terms of these focal concerns are likely, sooner or later, to end up in trouble with the law. For Miller, the problem was aggravated by the fact that the slum areas he was investigating were conducive to the emergence of juvenile gangs. In these gangs, he suggested, the focal concerns of the lower class were exaggerated as youths attempted to model what they understood to be adult behaviour. The result was a kind of overconformity to a value scheme that promoted behaviour likely to invite legal sanction.

Other theorists have applied similar logic to explain patterns of homicide and assault. Noting that much interpersonal violence is concentrated socially (e.g., among young members of the urban underclass) or regionally (e.g., in the American South), they argue that offenders (and often their victims) may behave as they do because they are immersed in a **subculture of violence** (Felson et al., 1994; Rice and Goldman, 1994; Wolfgang and Ferracuti, 1967). This subcultural orientation, it is argued, requires that some kinds of transgressions be resolved in a violent fashion.

Much assaultive violence seems to originate in what many would consider minor or trivial altercations. An exchange that begins with a stare, a jostle, or an insult may end with one of the parties seriously injured or dead. Subcultural theorists maintain that patterns like this only make sense when we recognize the underlying powerful cultural emphasis on social honour and the need to save face. Given this emphasis, a derogatory remark made in a public setting may be enough to provoke physical retaliation.

To argue that violence, in this sense, is subcultural is to argue that it is normative. In other words, the physical defence of one's honour is not merely what one *can* do but what one *must* do to retain the respect of other participants in the culture. Because the violence is normative, the person who behaves violently is unlikely to feel shame or embarrassment for doing so.

In the context of the subculture-of-violence argument, it is the particular cultural interpretation given to an affront to character—not the affront per se—that is the source of the violence. Precisely because cultural environments differ, a sneer is less likely to provoke trouble in a university faculty club than it is in a lower-class bar.

A weakness of the subcultural approach is that it tends to infer rather than identify independently the differences between subcultural values and subcultural behaviours. Hagan (1985) argues that there is little empirical evidence to suggest that groups adhere to deviant subcultures in which violence is considered integral to the group's functioning. The violence is more likely to be a consequence of situational factors such as opportunity and circumstance rather than a specific group goal.

IS MAINSTREAM CULTURE CRIMINOGENIC?

Subcultural arguments generally proceed from the assumption that it is useful to distinguish between a subculture that somehow promotes criminality and a conformist mainstream culture (i.e., the one reflected in criminal law). Yet not all theorists who have examined the relationship between crime and culture share this assumption. Some contend that the "conformist" culture may itself promote criminal behaviour.

For instance, it can be argued that violence against women is greatly encouraged by broad patterns of cultural belief. According to many feminist writers, sexual assault and wife abuse have less to do with the subcultural orientation of a deviant minority than with pervasive cultural representations of women in the entertainment and advertising media. When slasher movies, television dramas, and sexually explicit, over-the-counter magazines and videos portray women as willing or deserving victims of violence, it is not surprising that the message is picked up and acted on by some in society.

In a similar vein, Coleman (1987) argues that the behaviour of white-collar and corporate criminals is in many ways promoted by a **culture of competition** that defines wealth and success as the central goals of human action. He asserts that criminal action in the support of either profit margins and bottom lines or personal success clearly reflects the influence of pervasive cultural beliefs. "[The] fear of failure is the inevitable correlate of the demand for success, and together they provide a set of powerful symbolic structures that are central to the motivation of economic behaviour" (Coleman, 1987: 417).

One of the most influential statements concerning the relationship between criminal behaviour and mainstream culture was provided by David Matza and Gresham Sykes (1961). Their analysis of juvenile delinquency led them to conclude that much youthful crime is better said to reflect **subterranean values** than subcultural values. Subterranean values are not (as subcultural values are) part of the belief system of some identifiable criminal

Culture of competition
A cultural atmosphere in which crime is promoted by competition that defines wealth and success as central goals of human activity.

Subterranean values
Values that are held by many in society, although they may conflict with other cherished values.

minority. Rather, they are values that are held by many in society, although they may be in conflict with other cherished values. The concept of the subterranean value has never really been fully developed, and only rarely has it been investigated empirically (Hagan et al., 1998).

Matza and Sykes suggested that although many researchers have identified values such as "disdain for work" and "search for kicks and thrills" as subcultural values of delinquency, considerable evidence indicates that these value orientations are much more widely held. Middle-class conformists and juvenile delinquents may express their disdain for work or search for kicks in very different ways, but the value orientations held by both groups seem to have much in common. Anyone who has seen *Natural Born Killers, Hannibal,* or similar blockbuster movies would be hard-pressed to make the case that violence does not have a wide cultural appeal.

According to Matza and Sykes (1957), the rules of conventional society are rarely as inflexible as subcultural theories make them out to be. In fact, those who learn the lessons of mainstream culture understand that although criminal behaviour is *usually* wrong, it is not *always* wrong. Conventional morality prohibits us from acting criminally, but it also provides us with reasons why it is sometimes all right to do so. Matza and Sykes term these culturally derived justifications of criminal conduct techniques of **neutralization** and argue that in a very real way, they make offending possible.

Neutralization theory
The view that delinquents often use linguistic constructions (i.e., excuses or rationalizations) to reduce the guilt resulting from their delinquent behaviour.

Matza and Sykes (1957) identified five neutralization techniques used by juvenile offenders. *First,* offenders deny responsibility and contend that their crimes resulted not from ill will but from circumstances and conditions beyond their control. *Second,* they deny injury and claim that the crime did not harm others. *Third,* they deny the victim, accepting responsibility for their actions and acknowledging the harmful consequences but also suggesting that the victims were to blame for what happened to them. *Fourth,* they condemn the condemners and argue against the negative evaluations that others make of them. *Fifth,* they appeal to higher loyalties and maintain that their actions were necessary in order to meet obligations to family and peers.

The central point of the neutralization argument is that knowledge of neutralization techniques precedes and makes possible involvement in criminal activity. In other words, people are able to break the law because they define the law as irrelevant to their own behaviour. People acquire knowledge of neutralization techniques as they gain knowledge of the cultural environment to which they are exposed. As a result of this process, they come to view criminal acts as acceptable, and this gives them the freedom to commit such acts. Once vandalism is redefined as a "harmless prank," assault as "getting even," and theft as "borrowing," there is a loosening of the moral inhibitions that might normally prohibit these behaviours.

Later research has not provided unequivocal support for Matza and Sykes's claim that neutralization precedes rather than follows involvement in crime (Agnew and Peters, 1986; Hamlin, 1988). Most studies have found that those who use neutralization techniques are more likely to engage in crime and deviance, but this correlation tends to be weak (Costello, 2000). Some researchers have tried to account for the complexities of neutralization processes by arguing that neutralization is a "hardening process" (Minor, 1981). In other words, over time, criminal behaviour and techniques of neutralization become mutually reinforcing; attempts at neutralization both precede and follow criminal involvement. As a result, the commitment to both the behaviour and the cultural definition of the behaviour intensifies. Thus, the employee who steals at work may define the pilfering as a legitimate substitute for unpaid overtime or, alternatively, as a harmless activity (given that the costs are covered by insurance). The resulting behaviour may reinforce itself over time as the commitment to the act and to the morality of stealing develop in a mutually supportive fashion.

WHAT DOES IT MEAN?

TECHNIQUES OF NEUTRALIZATION

First, through *denial of responsibility*, offenders express their belief that their crimes resulted not from ill will but rather from circumstances and conditions beyond their control. Second, through *denial of injury*, offenders reject any claim that the crime resulted in harm to others. Third, through *denial of the victim*, offenders accept responsibility for their actions and acknowledge the harmful consequences, but suggest that the victims were to blame for what happened to them. Fourth, offenders argue back at the negative evaluations others make of them by *condemning the condemners*. Fifth, by *appealing to higher loyalties*, they maintain that their actions were necessary in order to meet obligations to family and peers.

SUMMARY

What causes some people to behave criminally? This question reflects the influence of the positivist school of criminology, which views criminal behaviour as the product of causal forces working within or upon the offender. Sociobiologists have argued that some individuals are genetically programmed in such a way that they are more likely to commit crimes. Wilson and Herrnstein claim that one can detect certain physiological similarities among offenders. In their view, offenders' constitutional deficiencies lead them to discount the costs of crime through a process whereby immediate gratification becomes a paramount concern. This discounting can also be the result of physiological episodes brought about by problems with diet, drugs, alcohol, and so on.

A strong and consistent sociological tradition in criminology emphasizes social conditions as a major influence on motivations to offend. This perspective views criminal behaviour as the means by which some people attempt to deal with the frustrations they face in day-to-day life. The frustrated ambitions of individuals who aspire to achieve legitimate success but who lack the means to do so result in anomie, which can lead to criminal innovation.

According to Merton, criminogenic conditions reside in the gap between ambition and legitimate means, as dominant **cultural goals** both inspire and frustrate members of society (Cernkovich, Giordano, and Ruddolph, 2000). This gap can widen as a result of the economic deprivation resulting from unemployment, especially for young people. Most crime is committed by individuals in the lower socioeconomic groups, and prisons are most likely to be filled with individuals from these groups. Some criminologists have argued, however, that this is the case not necessarily because these groups are more delinquent, but rather because they are easy targets for the police, who expend more effort on street crime than they do on white-collar crime.

The focus on frustration has led criminologists to look at gang delinquency among working-class juveniles. According to Cohen, much juvenile crime is rooted in the difficulties experienced by disadvantaged youths who aspire to middle-class status but are judged inadequate by a school system that assigns status rewards on the basis of middle-class criteria. Rejection of this value system may signal delinquency.

According to cultural theorists, the criminogenic conditions that influence individual behaviour emerge from the milieu in which offenders operate (Alarid, Burton, and Cullen, 2000). There is not necessarily anything pathological about offenders; they may merely have learned a particular set of cultural lessons in how to act criminally. Their behaviour, then, is normal within their particular cultural context, and explicable given that they have been thrust outside the normal operations of society. The same process that ostracizes offenders also strengthens the bonds among insiders, as sanctions are applied against norm violators.

So it is possible to look at criminals as outsiders who are punished for failing to conform with the explicit norms of the dominant culture. It is also possible to look on certain criminal behaviour as normative. Sutherland's differential association theory proposes that crime is learned behaviour. For Sutherland, the differential rates at which criminals associate with the carriers

Cultural goals
Legitimate objectives held by all or by diversely located members of society.

of criminal values determine the differential rates at which they engage in criminal conduct. This perspective allows us to account for the fact that certain cultural insiders, while adhering to the law in their personal lives, commit crimes in the context of their working lives.

The idea that there may be more than one set of values in society raises the possibility that mainstream culture is itself criminogenic. Matza and Sykes contend that those who learn the lessons of mainstream culture learn that criminal behaviour is usually wrong, but not always. Some acts can be rationalized or neutralized with explanations that find their basis in the tenets of mainstream society.

QUESTIONS FOR REVIEW AND DISCUSSION

1. What types of diet are more likely to make people criminal? Is the link between poor diet and criminality a direct one?
2. Can you think of exceptions to the body-typing predictions for some crimes that are not likely to be committed by people with particular body shapes?
3. Why do you think we pay so much attention to explanations of violent behaviour that emphasize "psychopathology"?
4. How is crime learned from others?
5. Why do individuals need to neutralize their feelings about the victims of their crimes?

INFOTRAC COLLEGE EDITION

Explore InfoTrac College Edition, your online university library, which includes hundreds of popular and scholarly journals in which you can find articles related to the topics in this chapter. Visit InfoTrac through your Web browser (**www.infotrac-college.com**), or through this book's Web site (**www.criminalevent-3e.nelson.com**).

WHAT'S ON THE WEB?

For chapter links and quizzes, check out the accompanying Web site at **www.criminalevent-3e.nelson.com**.

Chapter 5

Offending, Social Control, and the Law

WHAT'S IN CHAPTER FIVE

In this chapter we examine how informal and formal social controls influence criminal offending. Offenders may not require a distinct or unique motivation to commit crime. Rather, people may offend when social pressures that could have prevented them from doing so are weak or absent. These pressures can arise from the social bonds to others that restrict illegal behaviour. This control may extend beyond family and friends to the community. It is here, through informal sanctions such as shame and guilt, and through the deterrence that develops through the application of the law, that individuals are precluded from criminal behaviour.

INTRODUCTION

The theories discussed in the previous chapter seem to suggest that since criminal behaviour has unique characteristics, it requires unique motivations. However, in putting so much energy into determining the unique cultural and social arrangements driving crime, motivational theories risk losing sight of a basic question: Is motivation sufficient or necessary to explain offending? Just because individuals are moved or inclined to behave in particular ways, does this mean they will? Motivational theories assume that it is the propensity, desire, or willingness to offend that separates offenders from nonoffenders.

Many theorists argue that the motivation to behave criminally is probably much more widespread than actual criminal behaviour (Agnew, 1993). We can all think of times when lying, cheating, or stealing might have been the most effective way of achieving our goals. According to critics of motivational theories, what separates the offender from the nonoffender has less to do with the presence of motivation and more to do with the ability or willingness to act on this motivation. This position acknowledges that we are not always free to act in ways consistent with our motivations.

In this chapter we consider how informal and formal social controls influence criminal offending. The underlying significance of these perspectives is that criminal behaviour may not require a distinct or unique criminal motivation. Instead, people may offend when the social pressures that would prevent them from doing so are weak or absent. Thus, criminal behaviour is not so much the product of criminogenic forces as it is a rational choice made by individuals who feel no constraints about engaging in it. The emphasis on rationality, choice, and control reflects the legacy of the classical school of thought.

SOCIAL TIES AND CONFORMITY

SOCIAL CONTROLS AND THE INDIVIDUAL

Informal social control
Casual methods of coercion employed by community members to maintain conformity.

It has been argued that **informal social controls,** in the form of relationships that people share with others who support and promote the values of conformity, are an important source of social control. Many theorists contend, for instance, that strong social ties between juveniles and their (conformist) teachers, parents, and peers discourage involvement in delinquency. Thus, strong ties to parents make possible effective adult monitoring and supervision of juvenile leisure activity (Alarid, Burton, and Cullen, 2000; Gottfredson and Hirschi, 1990; Wells and Rankin, 1988, 1991). Parent–child relationships characterized by caring, trust, and intimate communication offer support to adolescents who may be contemplating delinquent reactions to the problems that face them (Patterson and Dishion, 1985).

CONTAINMENT THEORY

Containment theory
Theory, based on control theory, that youth are insulated from delinquency by inner and outer containments that constrain non-conformist behaviour.

The criminologist Walter Reckless (1967) developed **containment theory** to try to explain how even in areas characterized by high rates of delinquency, many youths seem to be so law-abiding. Like many of the theorists discussed in the previous chapter, Reckless recognized that many factors can "pull" and "push" people into crime—for example, they can be pulled into crime by the attraction of what they see as "easy money," or pushed by the frustration resulting from blocked opportunity. However, what interested Reckless most was the fact that many more youths seemed to experience these motivational pushes and pulls than engaged in delinquent conduct.

BOX 5.1

Depression and Delinquency

What role do psychological conditions play in the development of delinquency? One answer to this question stresses the relevance of social bonds. A research project undertaken as part of a much larger study of crime and delinquency in the city of Chicago (called the Project of Human Development in Chicago Neighbourhoods) investigated this question by interviewing almost 800 adolescent girls (Obeidallah and Earls, 1999). The researchers found that mildly to moderately depressed girls may be at risk of engaging in delinquency. More specifically, the researchers found the following:

- Although 40 percent of nondepressed girls engaged in property crimes, 68 percent of girls who were mildly to moderately depressed did so. Furthermore, 42 percent of girls who were not depressed engaged in crimes against other persons, compared to 82 percent of mildly to moderately depressed girls.
- Fifty-seven percent of mildly to moderately depressed girls engaged in higher levels of aggressive behaviour, compared to only 13 percent of those who were not depressed.

All of this suggests that depressed adolescents tend to lack self-esteem and to drift toward delinquent peers. However, one interpretation stresses the role of social control factors:

> Some research suggests antisocial youth have weakened attachments to prosocial institutions. Because depression promotes a lack of interest and difficulty in concentrating, youth may withdraw from prosocial activities and institutions (e.g. schools, athletics), thus attenuating their attachment to these institutions and increasing their likelihood of engaging in antisocial behaviors (Obeidallah and Earls, 1999: 3).

Using the logic of **control theory**, Reckless reasoned that youth are insulated from delinquency by "**inner**" and "**outer**" **containments** that constrain nonconformist behaviour. *Outer containments* are those aspects of the individual's social environment which help ensure that delinquent behaviour does not occur. Most importantly, these include relationships with family members and with members of other primary groups. These groups set standards for individuals, teach and reinforce appropriate conduct, and provide a sense of belonging. *Inner containments* are those elements which are part of the individual's psychic makeup; for Reckless, these containments were the more important of the two. Inner containments are the products of effective socialization and the successful internalization of rules of acceptable behaviour. Reckless concluded that the most important element of inner containment is

Control theory
A group of theories which proceed from the assumption that criminal behaviour emerges in the absence of controls (internal or external) that might check or contain it.

Inner containments
The products of effective socialization and the successful internalization of rules regarding acceptable behaviour.

Outer containments
Aspects of the individual's social environment (e.g., primary groups) that help ensure that delinquent behaviour does not occur.

self-concept. A "good" self-concept implies an ability to tolerate frustration, a strong sense of responsibility, and a clear orientation toward future goals. Most importantly, the containment value of self-concept implies an ability to think of oneself as a "law-abiding person." Such a view of self can be an effective buffer against pressures to deviate.

WHAT ARE THEY?

INNER AND OUTER CONTAINMENTS

Inner containments represent the products of effective socialization and the successful internalization of rules of acceptable behaviour. Outer containments are those aspects of the individual's social environment that help ensure that delinquent behaviour does not occur.

Bond, theory of the
Theory that strong social bonds insulate youths against the delinquent environment.

Social bond
In social control theory, the strength and quality of the relationships that link potential offenders to conformist others and that serve to insulate them from criminal influences.

Attachment
The degree to which children are sensitive to the expectations of parents or teachers.

Commitment
The size of the investment of time and energy that a youth has made to a conventional activity, such as getting good grades.

Involvement
Participation in the world of conformity so that little time is left for delinquency.

Belief
The degree to which youths believe that the conformist values of parents and teachers are worthy of respect.

THEORY OF THE BOND

The most influential statement of the relationship between social ties and social control is Travis Hirschi's **theory of the bond.** Hirschi (1969) argued that the causes of juvenile delinquency are not located in some type of unique delinquent motivation, but rather in the weakness of the **social bond** linking delinquent adolescents to the world of conformist others. Weak bonds allow individuals to formulate behavioural intentions that reflect narrow self-interest. Lying, cheating, and stealing are often the outcome.

According to Hirschi, the bond to conformist society has four distinct strands. The first strand, **attachment**, refers to the degree to which children are sensitive to the expectations of parents and teachers. When children are sensitive to expectations, they must take the potential reactions of conformist others into account when contemplating delinquency. When youths care about the views of their parents and teachers, they define delinquency as a less attractive option.

The second strand, **commitment**, refers to the amount of time and energy youths invest in conventional activities such as obtaining good grades. The more juveniles invest in such things, the less likely they are to engage in behaviours that jeopardize them.

The third strand, **involvement**, refers to participation in the world of conformity—jobs to be done, projects to be undertaken, goals to be achieved, and deadlines to be met. In short, involvement in the world of conformity leaves little time for involvement in delinquency. This reminds us of the adage that "idle hands are the devil's workshop."

The fourth strand is **belief**. Hirschi diverges from subcultural theorists in that he does not believe that delinquents are committed to a set of distinctly delinquent values. Rather, they vary in the extent to which they believe that the conformist values of parents, teachers, and others are worthy of respect.

Strong social bonds—defined by Hirschi as high levels of attachment, commitment, involvement, and belief—insulate youths against delinquent involvement. To explain why some youths are delinquent while others are not, we must focus on the weakness of delinquents' bonds rather than on the factors that motivate them to behave in criminal fashion.

GENERAL THEORY OF CRIME

More recently, in collaboration with Michael R. Gottfredson (1990), Hirschi has proposed a **general theory of crime** that is applicable to all forms of crime, including white-collar and organized crime. Unlike some theorists, these two argue that there is no need to offer distinct explanations for distinct types of criminal conduct. This is because despite their differences, many types of crime can be defined as "acts of force or fraud undertaken in pursuit of self-interest" (1990: 15). They also suggest that the acts we call crimes share many common elements:

- They provide immediate gratification of desires.
- They are exciting, risky, or thrilling.
- They provide few or meager long-term benefits.
- They require little skill or planning.
- They result in pain or discomfort for the victim.

In short, they argue, crime as a type of activity appeals to people who are impulsive, short-sighted, physical, risk-taking, and nonverbal. They use the term *low self-control* to describe this propensity and maintain that people who are attracted to crime will also be attracted to other, analogous activities, such as drinking and driving (Keane, Maxim, and Teevan, 1996) and drug use (Sorenson and Brownfield, 1995).

What are the sources of low self-control? For Gottfredson and Hirschi, it originates in child rearing. Child rearing that is effective in discouraging delinquency requires that parents monitor their child's activity, recognize deviant behaviour when it occurs, and punish such behaviour when it does occur. Low self-control results when this process goes awry. Parents may not care what their children do, and even if they are concerned, they may be unable to supervise their children effectively or to punish the offending behaviour.

WHAT DOES IT INCLUDE?

THE THEORY OF THE BOND

The first strand, *attachment*, refers to the degree to which children are sensitive to the expectations of parents and teachers. *Commitment*, the second strand, refers to the amount of time and energy youths invest in conventional activities such as obtaining good grades. The third strand, *involvement*, refers to their degree of participation in the world of conformity. The fourth strand, *belief*, refers to the degree to which youths believe that the conformist values of parents, teachers, and others are worthy of respect.

General theory of crime
The theory that criminal activity appeals to people who are impulsive, short-sighted, physical, risk-taking, nonverbal, and, most importantly, have low self-control.

For Gottfredson and Hirschi, low self-control is the key cause of criminality (Arneklev, Grasmick, and Bursik, 1999; Piquero, MacIntosh, and Hickman, 2000). As such, it explains why some people rather than others are likely to behave in a criminal fashion. However, they also recognize the need to distinguish between criminality as a propensity and crime as a social event. Crimes occur when individuals with low self-control encounter situations and opportunities that are conducive to offending.

Since the publication of the general theory of crime, a number of studies have been undertaken to assess its central argument. Several of these studies report results consistent with the theory (Burton et al., 1998; Keane, Maxim, and Teevan, 1996; Pratt and Cullen, 2000; Sorenson and Brownfield, 1995); others are more critical. Some writers have argued that although the theory is valuable, it must be used in conjunction with other theoretical arguments that emphasize the importance of criminal opportunity (LaGrange and Silverman, 1999; Longshore, 1998; Longshore and Turner, 1998), social learning (Pratt and Cullen, 2000), or external social control (Nakhaie, Silverman, and LaGrange, 2000).

POWER CONTROL THEORY

Power control theory
The theory that due to differential control (i.e., girls are subject to greater control than boys) within the patriarchal family, males have a higher propensity to engage in risk taking and delinquent behaviour.

Power control theory, which was developed by John Hagan, A.R. Gillis, and John Simpson (Hagan, 1989; Hagan, Gillis, and Simpson, 1979, 1987, 1988), provides another example of how family relationships permit or discourage delinquency. Of central interest to these researchers is the fact that males are much more delinquent than females. Hagan, Gillis, and Simpson try to explain this fact in terms of the family's differential ability to control male and female children.

Consistent with the general social control argument, power control theory argues that social control is stratified within the family setting (Tibbets and Herz, 1996). In traditional patriarchal families, which accept a cultural claim to male dominance, girls are subject to greater control than boys. Also, mothers are assigned greater responsibility for controlling dependent children. This position has two important implications. *First*, the informal social control processes in which family members are involved affect female more than male family members. Mothers are more likely to be the subjects and daughters are more likely to be the objects of this control. *Second*, as a result of these differences, male children are considerably freer than female children to engage in a wide range of risk-taking behaviour, some of which involves delinquency.

The power control argument assumes that we must situate family relations of control in the broader context of economic and occupational stratification. Thus, parents who have more authority and more autonomy in the workplace are less likely to be strict disciplinarians at home. Moreover, these parents are more likely to encourage entrepreneurial forms of risk-taking among their children. In this way, relations of authority in the workplace are mirrored in parent–child relations.

A recent revision to power control theory tries to account more precisely for how parents—and especially mothers—affect the delinquency of their children (McCarthy, Hagan, and Woodward, 1999). In particular, it argues that in less patriarchal homes, mothers may be more likely to exert somewhat greater control over their sons. For instance, they may encourage their sons to reject the cultural claims to male dominance and risk taking that promote delinquent conduct. At the same time, they may control their daughters less and thereby encourage female risk taking and, it follows, greater delinquency. Because family control relations reflect occupational and economic conditions, it can be expected that changes in the gendered nature of workplace authority will have important implications for changes in the gendered character of delinquency (Uggen, 2000).

INTERACTIONAL THEORY

Terence Thornberry (1987) and colleagues (Thornberry et al., 1991) have proposed an **interactional theory of delinquency** that shares, at its core, the assumptions of control theory. However, Thornberry attempts to link the logic of control theory to the insights derived from arguments stressing the role of cultural learning and peer influence. Like Hirschi, Thornberry argues that adolescents are at risk of engaging in delinquent behaviour when they have low levels of attachment to parents, of commitment to school, and of belief in conventional institutions and people. However, Thornberry emphasizes that the weakness of the ties to conventional others does not make delinquency inevitable, although it does make it more likely.

Furthermore, Thornberry argues, it is too simplistic to assume—as many theorists seem to do—that social ties to the world of conformity are unchanging. On the contrary, they may strengthen or weaken over time in response to changing circumstances. Most notably, while weak social bonds to parents or teachers may make delinquency possible, delinquency that has already occurred may further affect these relationships. Consider the example of a youth whose weak bond to her parents contributes to her engagement in

Interactional theory of delinquency
The theory that ties to conventional others, which, if weak, increase the likelihood of delinquent behaviour, can be strengthened over time in response to changing circumstances.

delinquent activities. When the parents learn about the delinquency, they may react by rejecting her or by subjecting her to severe punishment. These reactions may further undermine the relationship between daughter and parents, thus making delinquency even more possible. In terms of illuminating the criminal event, the real strength of Thornberry's argument is that it attempts to come to terms with the dynamic and fluid character of criminality.

LIFE COURSE PERSPECTIVE

Another version of social control that pays explicit attention to change over time is the **life course perspective** formulated by Robert Sampson and John Laub (1990; Laub and Sampson, 1993). Life course explanations differ markedly from explanations such as the general theory of crime discussed earlier. Explanations such as the general theory assume that perhaps one particular factor, such as low self-control, exerts rather constant effects on crime over the life cycle; in contrast, life course arguments seek to understand how and why different factors matter at different times (Bartusch et al., 1997; Paternoster and Brame, 1997).

Sampson and Laub tried to reconcile two contradictory sets of research findings. One body of research indicates that adult criminality is strongly influenced by patterns of childhood behaviour (Wilson and Herrnstein, 1985). This research suggests that people embark on criminal paths long before adulthood, so the characteristics of adults' social roles (such as unemployment) are largely irrelevant as causes of crime. Yet another body of research indicates that changes in people's lives (like getting or losing a job, or getting married, or having children) affect the likelihood of involvement in crime. According to Sampson and Laub, most criminologists focus their attention on the study of teenagers, and as a result little research has been done regarding whether the propensity to commit crime changes or remains stable over the life course.

Sampson and Laub's life course perspective makes an important distinction between "trajectories" and "transitions." **Trajectories** are the pathways on which people are located and the directions in which their lives seem to be moving. **Transitions** are specific life events—such as a first job or a marriage or the birth of a child—that may or may not alter those trajectories. For example, a juvenile who is actively involved with delinquent peers, who lives in an abusive home, and who is failing at school may be on a criminal trajectory. However, suppose that in his late teens he begins a romantic relationship with someone who is nurturing and supportive, and the two decide to get

---

Life course perspective
Adult criminality is strongly influenced by patterns of childhood behaviour, and changes in people's lives affect the likelihood of involvement in crime.

Trajectories
In the life course perspective, these describe the directions in which lives seem to be moving.

Transitions
In the life course perspective, specific events that may or may not alter trajectories.

married and raise a family. As he develops a deep commitment to the relationship and begins to plan for and think about the future, his involvement in crime diminishes. In the life course framework, the marriage is a transition that alters his criminal trajectory.

For Sampson and Laub, trajectories change when transitions alter the nature and number of social bonds that help ensure conformity. However, it is not simply the occurrence of particular life events that brings these changes about. Rather, it is the "social investment" in the institutional relationship that dictates the importance of informal social control.

Sociologist Mark Warr (1998) argues that life course transitions involve much more than changes in the amount and types of informal social control. Major life changes such as moving to a new residence or starting a new job strongly affect relationships with delinquent peers. Warr suggests that marriage often replaces involvement with criminal peers with "preoccupation with one's spouse and family of procreation" (1998: 209). He concludes that life course theory must take greater account of delinquent "peer careers" in explaining why criminal involvement changes over the life course.

The interpretative value of the life course perspective extends beyond the level of individuals. For instance, Macmillan (1995) has used life course theory to explain increases in Canadian rates of property crime over the past several decades. Over this time, he argues, young people were more likely to leave their parental homes earlier, to marry later, and to wait longer for parenthood. With respect to life course theory, the implication is that young people—especially young males—were less likely to make those transitions that would have connected them to networks of informal social control. Possibly, this led to an increase in the pool of potential criminal offenders. Macmillan's analysis suggests that changes in crime rates may be related to structural changes in the life course.

SOCIAL CONTROLS AND THE COMMUNITY

Other theorists have considered the roles played by informal social control at the level of the neighbourhood or local community. According to Wirth (1938), the larger, the more densely populated, and the more heterogeneous the community, the more accentuated are the characteristics associated with urbanism, including isolation and social breakdown. Urbanism brings together individuals who have no sentimental or emotional ties to one another. From this emerges a spirit of competition, self-aggrandizement, and exploitation. To counteract this spirit, society reverts to **formal social controls**.

Formal social control
Conventional methods of technology and physical coercion, such as the police force, used to maintain social order.

People who are in frequent social contact with strangers and acquaintances develop a reserve toward one another. The strong family and friendship
ties that are necessary for intimate communities disappear in cities; the result
is higher levels of alienation, anomie, and delinquency. As a result, says Wirth,
crime rates in urban areas are higher than those in rural areas, where informal
social controls between intimates still operate.

Some urban neighbourhoods are more successful than others at constraining the delinquent inclinations of youths. Clifford Shaw and Henry
McKay (1942), two sociologists associated with the University of Chicago,
wanted to understand why some parts of their city had consistently high rates
of crime, delinquency, and other social problems. It intrigued them that
rates of delinquency remained high and steady even in neighbourhoods where
the "turnover" of residents was rapid and so were changes in the ethnic and
demographic mix. They associated urban variations in rates of crime with the
social context of urban areas rather than with the specific characteristics of the
populations who lived in them.

Shaw and McKay found that high-crime areas are characterized by a high
degree of **social disorganization**—that is, the residents of these areas were
unable to achieve common values or solve their common problems
(Kornhauser, 1978). They argued that areas characterized by high levels of
social disorganization tend to be economically disadvantaged, to have high
rates of population turnover, and to be racially and ethnically diverse. In such
areas the informal social controls that might constrain delinquency are ineffective. As predicted by Wirth (1938), local friendship networks are less likely
to develop, and levels of participation in formal or voluntary organizations are
low. As a result, adults in these communities may be ineffective in their
attempts to supervise and control teenage peer groups that are likely to
become involved in delinquency (Sampson and Groves, 1989).

The logic of the social disorganization argument is manifested in the
many forms of crime prevention that attempt to develop a sense of community in high-crime neighbourhoods. Neighbourhood Watch and similar programs seek to increase levels of interaction among residents; at the same time
they encourage neighbours to develop a sense of responsibility for one
another.

After a long period of dormancy, interest in social disorganization theory
is surging (Peterson, Krivo, and Harris, 2000; Sampson, Raudenbush, and
Earls, 1997; Veysey and Messner, 1999). In an important restatement of this
perspective, Bursik and Grasmick (1993; Bursik, 1999) distinguish three types

Social disorganization
Long-term, widespread deterioration of social order and control
in a population.

of social controls; all three are less effective in areas characterized by high levels of social disorganization. "Private" controls are associated with family and friends and with other groups with which individuals are intimately linked. "Parochial" controls are somewhat broader and are exerted by local schools, stores, churches, and voluntary organizations. "Public" or external controls relate to the local community's ability to mobilize sources of control that originate beyond its boundaries. Local communities are not equally successful in their attempts to get urban bureaucracies to allocate funds to neighbourhood projects and to get the police to take neighbourhood problems seriously.

Bursik and Grasmick contend that when these controls are operating, they discourage crime by discouraging both criminal motivation and the opportunities for crime. They also note that these controls do not appear instantaneously; rather, they develop slowly over time as residents associate with one another and establish relationships. Factors that contribute to neighbourhood instability undermine the processes that lead to effective community controls, and thus make higher rates of crime and delinquency more likely.

Social disorganization theories, both older and newer ones, are usually perceived as relating specifically to city life. But they may be more general than this. For example, Osgood and Chambers (2000) found that in several American states, rates of juvenile arrests for violent crime in rural areas and small towns were related to such "urban" variables as residential instability, family disruption, and ethnic heterogeneity. Also, there is no theoretical basis for the idea that primary, parochial, and public controls have less to do with rural life than with life in major urban areas.

THE POWER OF LAW: THE DETERRENCE DOCTRINE

SPECIFIC AND GENERAL DETERRENCE

Laws threaten penalties for their violation. **Deterrence** theories are concerned with how these threats are communicated to potential offenders. The belief that legal deterrence is a valuable mechanism of crime control continues to dominate criminal justice philosophy and practice (Maxwell and Gray, 2000). Deterrence theories attempt to determine whether the threat of penalties decreases the likelihood of offending. **Specific or special deterrence** refers to how individuals are deterred, through **punishment**, from offending or reoffending. Suppose you break into a house, are apprehended, and then are

Deterrence
Theory of prevention in which the threat of punishment or retribution is expected to forestall some act from occurring.

Specific/special deterrence
The ways in which individuals are deterred from offending or reoffending by receiving punishment.

Punishment
Confinement, restriction of activities, infliction of pain, and other measures taken for retribution, to enforce compliance, or to bring about behavioural changes.

BOX 5.2

Provincial Differences in Crime Rates

Criminologists have long noted that in general, crime rates in Canada increase from east to west. Timothy F. Hartnagel (1997) investigated this by analyzing provincial crime rates against several other variables (percentage of population urban, percentage low income, police per capita, age composition of the population, provincial migration rates) for three different time periods (1962, 1972, 1982). He found that migration was by far the most important factor affecting provincial variations in crime rates. He concluded that higher provincial rates of migration weaken the structure of social relations. The consequence may be a decline in the power of informal social control and an increase in rates of crime. Property and violent crime rates for the provinces and territories for 1999 are presented below.

Provincial Rates of Violent and Property Crime, Canada, 1999, Rates per 100,000

	Violent crime	Property crime
Newfoundland	925	2,705
Prince Edward Island	685	2,984
Nova Scotia	986	4,013
New Brunswick	956	2,984
Quebec	666	3,722
Ontario	852	3,574
Manitoba	1,572	5,084
Saskatchewan	1,589	5,754
Alberta	1,061	4,781
British Columbia	1,284	6,761
Yukon	3,173	7,221
Northwest Territories	4,908	5,711
Inuvik	5,241	4,349

Source: Sylvain Tremblay, 2000, "Crime Statistics in Canada, 1999." *Juristat*, 20(5): 17. Used by permission of Statistics Canada.

General deterrence
The ways in which individuals, on seeing offenders receiving punishment, will be deterred from breaking the law themselves.

Severity
With reference to deterrence, the perceived or actual seriousness of the penalty for a legal infraction.

sentenced to prison for a period of time. If the prison term discourages you from committing another such crime, we can say that it is a specific or special deterrent. According to the principle of **general deterrence**, individuals are deterred from breaking the law when they watch others who have done so receive punishment. Thus, friends who watch you receive punishment for breaking the law will desist from breaking and entering.

Deterrence of any kind has three properties. The first is the **severity** of the penalty. Does the law threaten prison, or only a fine? Are offenders likely to be sentenced if they are caught, or are they likely to be released with a warning? The Criminal Code states clearly the punishment attached to each crime, and sentencing guidelines are set for judges to apply in the cases that come before them.

It is assumed that all individuals in society are aware of the law's prescriptions about punishment and are deterred in direct proportion to the escalating threat of this punishment. So it should be widely understood that the most severe punishments are reserved for the most serious crimes. Sentencing guidelines at the provincial and federal levels change fairly often; presumably this reflects changes in society's sense of the seriousness of various offences.

> ### WHAT DOES IT MEAN?
>
> #### SPECIFIC VERSUS GENERAL DETERRENCE
> Specific deterrence refers to how individuals are deterred from offending or reoffending by receiving punishment. With general deterrence, individuals who see offenders receiving punishment will be deterred from breaking the law themselves.

The second property of legal threats is the **certainty** of punishment. Regardless of what the law threatens, how likely is it that the offender will be apprehended and sentenced? Many research studies have found that with respect to deterrence, certainty is a more important factor than severity. In other words, a high likelihood of being punished is more important than being punished in a specified manner.

Certainty
With reference to deterrence, the likelihood (perceived or objectively measurable) that an offender will be apprehended or punished.

As we saw in earlier chapters, most of the crimes that are known to the police were brought to their attention by the public. For various reasons, however, many crimes go unreported. Furthermore, many crimes that *are* reported remain unsolved. In both situations, the offender "gets away" with the crime. The rational offender calculates the certainty of risk and then acts on this calculation. When risk of apprehension and conviction is high, the crime is less likely to occur.

The third property of legal threats is the **celerity (swiftness)** of punishment (Clark, 1988). When justice is delayed, the perception may arise either that the punishment is unfair or that it will have a diminished impact on the offender. Concerns have been raised that delays in the justice process may unfairly stigmatize individuals who are in fact innocent. Court backlogs that lead to trial delays of a year or more have led some to argue that cases should be dismissed without guilt or innocence being determined. The message conveyed by such dismissals would be that the criminal justice system is incapable of handling cases swiftly. This would cast doubt on the system's ability to handle them at all.

Celerity
With reference to deterrence, the swiftness (perceived or objectively measurable) with which an offender is apprehended or punished.

Mark Stafford and Mark Warr (1993) have questioned the distinction most researchers make between general and specific deterrence. In their view, the distinction is false. To assume that general deterrence is effective is to assume that those who form the audience have no direct knowledge of the punishment in question. Yet some of those who learn about the punishment of others have committed the same kind of act for which the punishment is being meted out, although they themselves did not get caught. In other words, they have experience with "avoiding punishment." Similarly, in the case of specific deterrence, it is usually assumed that the punishment the individual experiences will affect the likelihood of subsequent offending. At the same time, the individual who is being punished may have knowledge of others who committed similar acts and didn't get caught. Thus, Stafford and Warr maintain, the distinction that is usually made between general and specific deterrence rests on a number of simplifying assumptions that distort empirical realities. They suggest that instead of speaking of general and specific deterrent effects, it makes more sense to speak of indirect and direct experience with punishment and punishment avoidance. An empirical test of this view with respect to the deterrence of drinking and driving found that offending decisions are indeed affected by both personal and vicarious experiences, and that such decisions are also influenced by knowledge about both punishment and punishment avoidance (Piquero and Paternoster, 1998).

LEGAL VERSUS INFORMAL SANCTIONS

Some researchers suggest that in emphasizing the importance of penalty characteristics, deterrence theories have adopted too narrow a view of how legal threats discourage crime. Williams and Hawkins (1986) assert that the deterrent effects of legal sanctions may be supplemented by at least three other types of sanctions: commitment costs, attachment costs, and stigma of arrest.

Commitment costs refer to the possibility that arrest may jeopardize people's investments in some legitimate activity. The greater a person's investment in some conformist line of activity, the more he or she will be discouraged from offending. Commitment costs include concerns about education prospects and future employment. **Attachment costs** refer to the costs associated with the loss of valued relationships with friends and family members. The belief that arrest will weaken these ties may make arrest a fearsome prospect. The **stigma of arrest** refers to the belief that apprehension by the police may harm one's reputation. It is important to distinguish this fear that

Commitment costs
The possibility that arrest may jeopardize people's investments in some legitimate activity.

Attachment costs
The costs associated with the loss of weakened ties that may make an arrest a fearsome prospect.

Stigma of arrest
The belief that apprehension by the police may harm one's reputation.

others will learn about one's arrest from the fear that they will learn that one has committed the act. Williams and Hawkins point out that generally, less stigma is associated with driving while impaired than with being arrested for this crime. In the case of homicide, however, the stigma associated with arrest may not be much greater than the stigma associated with the commission of the act. Williams and Hawkins contend that attachment costs, commitment costs, and the stigma of arrest are forms of informal social control that are activated by formal controls, and so should be viewed as part of the deterrence process.

An illustration of how this mix of legal and informal sanctions can work is provided by research on how arrest contributes to the reduction of repeat wife assault. Donald Dutton and his colleagues (1992) examined data from Vancouver and Alberta that compared results from a general population sample with those from a group of arrested and convicted wife assaulters who were undergoing treatment in court-mandated programs. Respondents were asked to express their views on the likelihood (certainty) of specific legal and social sanctions, assuming they were to assault their wives. They were also asked to judge the severity of the punishment that would follow such an assault. Police arrest was among the legal sanctions offered. The social sanctions included police being called, the partner leaving the relationship, disapproval of friends and family, and loss of self-respect.

The arrested assaulters were more certain than those in the general samples that an arrest would occur if an assault took place. Interestingly, the general and treatment samples had similar responses to the question relating to the loss of self-respect. In terms of severity of punishment, the two samples were high with respect to all factors. Thus, deterrence seems to be a function not only of the arrest but also of the social consequences of the arrest.

To test this theory further, responses that assaulters gave before they entered the treatment program were compared with those they gave at the end of the treatment about a year later. There was an increase in the perceived severity of arrest and conviction; this was accompanied by a substantial increase in the perceived severity of losing one's partner or facing social disapproval.

Disclosure of these events, which are often kept private, can be a first step toward generating informal sanctions from friends and family toward the assaultive male and an empowering support network for the victim. Because arrest makes disclosure more likely, that informal side effect of arrest could serve to reduce recidivism (Dutton et al., 1992: 124).

Here we have a case of legal sanction (arrest) and informal sanction (social disapproval) working together to increase deterrence.

Arguments about the deterrent properties of legal sanctions do not assume that potential offenders are accurately informed about the risks they face. How accurate their perceptions are is itself an excellent question (Henshel and Silverman, 1975). We suggest that in terms of whether an individual will offend, what the law actually threatens is less significant than what people *believe* the law threatens.

SITUATIONAL DETERRENCE

Criminologist Maurice Cusson (1993) has criticized deterrence theory and research for failing to address the specific character of the situations in which crimes occur. A typical research project might ask respondents how likely it is that they would be apprehended if they attempted to steal a car. Too often, however, the context of the automobile theft is not specified. Obviously, how risky one perceives car theft to be depends greatly on the specific circumstances in which the theft is attempted. Study respondents will make certain private assumptions in order to provide an answer to the researcher's question; thus, the answers may have little to do with the actual assessment of risks that an individual makes in any specific situation.

Cusson notes also that when researchers ask survey subjects to calmly assess the risks of apprehension, they are ignoring the emotional character of the deterrence process. Deterrence, he argues, is not about the cold and rational calculation of risks but about fear. A burglar who breaks into a house may rationally believe that the chances of getting caught are low, but may still panic when he hears a noise. Fear can override rational calculation and make the deterrence process look quite different in reality than it appears in theory. For these reasons, Cusson suggests that we must consider deterrence as a situational factor. **Situational deterrence** emphasizes how the offender's fear of apprehension is related to the specific circumstances of the criminal event.

According to Cusson, potential offenders face two types of danger in the pre-criminal situation. The first type is immediate: a robber worries that the victim may fight back or be armed; a burglar worries that a barking dog may bite. The second type of danger has to do with subsequent harm relating

Situational deterrence
The ways in which the offender's fear of apprehension are related to the specific circumstances of the criminal event.

to some element in the pre-criminal situation. A television monitor in the convenience store about to be robbed does not threaten the robber directly, but it may eventually if it leads to the robber's apprehension.

Cusson notes that the risks facing offenders before and during the commission of the offence do not guarantee that the offender will be deterred. Offenders differ in terms of the level of courage they can muster in partic- ular situations and also in terms of their ability to manage the fear they do experience. Also, some crimes—such as joyriding and van- dalism—may be attractive precisely because they have an element of danger.

WHAT IS IT?

SITUATIONAL DETERRENCE

Situational deterrence emphasizes how the offender's fear of apprehension is related to the specific circumstances of the criminal event.

Cusson's analysis forces us to recognize that deterrence effects are not embodied solely in abstract legal threats; they are also found in the risks that offenders understand themselves to be facing in the settings in which criminal events actually occur.

AMBIVALENCE ABOUT CRIME AND DETERRENCE STRATEGIES

Deterrence arguments figure quite prominently in many public policy debates. Despite the perception that there is widespread consensus on the need to crack down on crime, public attitudes toward crime and its preven- tion suggest a strong degree of ambivalence, which has many sources. *First*, Canadians are concerned that the law is not being adequately enforced (Currie, 1985). Also, they feel that the law generally reflects their values (Tyler, 1990), and they obey the law because they believe it to be right. At the same time, they are critical of how justice is presently being dispensed. Many believe that the law favours the rich and the powerful and that the legal process is too slow. The system as a whole is seen as ineffective in deterring serious crime, especially in terms of the punishment that is administered (Brillon, 1985; Baron and Hartnagel, 1996).

Yet there is no consensus in the research literature regarding the effective- ness of punishment in reducing criminal behaviour. Cook (1977) reviewed the literature on deterrent effects (including the impact of capital punishment on violent crime) and concluded that there is little persuasive evidence that deterrence works or even exists. This undermines proposals for strict punish- ment regimens, especially if they are contrary to our views of what is humane and just.

Second, as Braithwaite (1989) points out, confusion has developed over what is perceived as a conflict between crime control and respect for civil liberties. Some express concern that too much informal social control impedes individual freedom—neighbours spying on neighbours can be a real threat to personal privacy. However, punishment delivered by formal agents is ineffective unless it is combined with informal social sanctions (i.e., shaming). When the risk of arrest is perceived as low and the severity of punishment is minimal, individuals can still be prevented from committing crimes by the stigmatizing reactions of others.

Third, there is a lack of consensus over the usefulness of incarceration (Miller and Anderson, 1986). At the same time, we are uncomfortable with leaving reintegration to communities. Few communities are ready to receive criminals as they begin their transition to "normal" life. In fact, some communities are actively blocking the return of released offenders, especially those who were imprisoned for sex crimes. Offenders need to be reintegrated into society and kept from reoffending, but few communities are doing much to take this job over from formal agencies.

Fourth, Canadians are ambivalent about crime because they are in awe of it. The reality of violent crimes is usually horrific, yet in the media such crimes are presented as titillating, thrilling, and addictive. It is no easy task to promote prosocial behaviour in a society in which criminals are often depicted as folk heroes (Phelps, 1983). The **folk hero syndrome** may be on the decline (see Skipper, 1985); that being said, there still exists in our society a residual belief that criminals should be admired for resisting convention.

Folk hero syndrome
A residual belief that the criminal should be admired for expressing some degree of resistance to convention.

RATIONAL CHOICE THEORIES

Rational choice theories
These focus on the offenders' actions and decisions as they are based on perceived benefits rather than on precipitating or psychological factors.

Like deterrence theories, rational choice theories have their roots in the classical tradition. However, **rational choice theories** take a somewhat broader perspective than deterrence theories. They recognize the role that legal threats play in deterring offending, but also argue that other factors—such as the potential gains that might be derived from the commission of crimes and the ease with which they can be committed—are also important.

The increasing popularity of rational choice theories can be seen at least in part as a product of the dissatisfaction of many criminologists with more traditional motivational theories (Fattah, 1993). Theories that emphasize strain or cultural learning, for instance, are seen as creating false distinctions between criminal and noncriminal activity. Rational choice theories argue that both types of behaviour are oriented toward the same kinds of ends (e.g., money, self-gratification); therefore, criminal behaviour may not require a unique motivation (Cornish and Clarke, 1986). Also, traditional motivational theories really only explain why some people may be predisposed to commit crimes—not why or how crimes are committed. Because crimes are events that occur in specific places at specific times, motivational theories can be faulted for not paying enough attention to the situational context of criminal events.

BOX 5.3

Selling Tobacco to Minors: A Rational Choice?

William O'Grady, Mark Asbridge, and Tom Abernathy (2000) investigated the willingness of Ontario merchants to sell tobacco products to young people in violation of the law. The data they examined came from 439 "compliance checks." These checks, which are undertaken by local health units, involve sending trained youth volunteers to randomly selected retailers with the express purpose of attempting to buy cigarettes. The researchers examined the effects of several types of variables on the decisions of merchants to violate the law. These variables included the level of enforcement reported by the local health unit, the type of business (e.g., restaurant, gas station), whether the outlet was in a rural or urban area, and whether the local area was a tobacco-producing area. However, the most important effects were associated with situational variables, including the tendency of merchants to comply with other tobacco laws (e.g., checking ID of the youth), time of the sales event, and the age and gender of the youth volunteers. The authors of the study concluded that the results were consistent with rational choice theories of offending:

> This rational choice explanation, however, places a strong emphasis on the situational factors involved with illegal events. Decision makers' assessment of the costs and benefits of their actions during the offense affect the choices involved in selling cigarettes to minors … It is therefore unlikely that much planning or weighing of risks is involved a priori on behalf of merchants. Rather an important cognitive risk assessment occurs at the point when a merchant is confronted with the opportunity to sell tobacco to a young person. This explains why the age (older youth) and gender (females—who generally mature earlier than males) composition of the youth teams were so important for explaining the likelihood of an illegal sale. These findings support the assumption that, if they have reason to believe that a youth "appears" to be of legal age to purchase tobacco, the merchants are more likely to supply a product (O'Grady, Asbridge, and Abernathy, 2000: 14).

Rational choice theories focus on offenders' actions based on perceived benefits rather than on precipitating social or psychological factors (Clarke and Felson, 1993; Nagin and Paternoster, 1993). As offenders seek benefits and attempt to avoid losses, they make decisions and choices that can be understood as reflecting rational thought. Rational choice theorists argue that instead of considering which broad social factors (strain or cultural values) influence offending behaviour, we should really be studying how offenders make decisions. To this end, two broad types of decisions invite our attention.

COMMITTING A CRIME

How do burglars decide on their targets? How do they decide which specific house to break into? How do they decide what to do if they see a window sticker indicating that the home is protected by an alarm system? The answers to questions like these allow rational choice theorists to develop an understanding of criminal events and of the role that offenders play in those events (Tunnell, 1992). Unlike traditional motivation theories, rational choice theory is interested in the situational character of crime (Birkbeck and LaFree, 1993).

Rational choice theories do not assume that offenders operate in a purely rational fashion. Rather, it is assumed that offenders usually proceed from a "limited rationality." In other words, they may inaccurately perceive the benefits of committing particular crimes; they may lack the time to weigh the possible outcomes; or they may have access to only limited information with which to make their decisions.

Rational choice theorists contend that because specific situational factors are important and because offender decision making varies across situations, it makes little sense to develop a generic theory of crime. The choices involved in robbing a convenience store are very different from the ones involved in stealing a car or defrauding a bank (Clarke, 1992).

THE CRIMINAL CAREER

Criminal career

A way of thinking about the sequential stages of criminal involvement over the offender's life course.

The other major issue of interest to rational choice theorists relates to the **criminal career**. How do offenders decide to get involved in crime? How and when do they decide to give up a life of crime? The notion that crime can be a career is widely shared both inside and outside of criminological literature. The true-crime section of any bookstore usually carries several titles that detail the exploits of the "professional thief," "professional robber," or "contract killer." These books let us peek into a world of crime that—at least superficially—seems to be organized in ways that reflect the occupational structure of the "legitimate" working world. In some fundamental sense, these offenders view crime as their job. They have acquired the technical skills they need to perform this job, and they derive their livelihood mainly from successful job performance. Just how superficial are comparisons between crime and legitimate work? Does it make sense to conceptualize criminal involvement in career terms?

THE CONCEPT OF CAREER

A useful place to begin this discussion is with a brief consideration of the concept of "career." A career is "the sequence of movements from one position to another in an occupational system made by any individual who works in that system" (Becker, 1963: 24). This definition is consistent with popular usage. We think of a work career as beginning at some specific point in time and continuing until death, retirement, or a voluntary or forced career change. Over

---

BOX 5.4

Robbers and Robbery

Robbery is probably the type of violent crime that most people associate with the "career criminal." Thomas Gabor of the University of Ottawa and Andre Normandeau of the University of Montreal undertook a major study of robbery, mainly in the area of Montreal and Quebec City (Gabor and Normandeau, 1989). Part of this study involved detailed interviews with 39 convicted robbers, all but one of whom were serving sentences in the Montreal area. The study revealed the following:

- The offenders were male, and most were under 30, had no more than a high school education, and came from a blue-collar background.
- The self-reported criminality was far in excess of that reported in their files.
- The offenders were motivated to rob by the fact that robbery is a fast and direct way to obtain money relative to the less lucrative and more complicated acts of break-and-enter and fraud.
- Unemployment, the need for drugs, and criminal associates were among the precipitating factors.
- Most of the subjects began their careers committing other crimes, such as auto theft or break-and-enter, before advancing to robbery.
- Early success at armed robbery allowed them to gain confidence and to develop and refine their "professional skills."
- As they aged, several offenders experienced increasing fear of prison—a change motivated in part by their negative experiences during previous periods of incarceration and by the knowledge that successive sentences were likely to be longer.

the course of the career, we can identify movement through various stages (which, in the context of formal organizations, we call promotions). Each stage brings with it new responsibilities and additional rewards and provides the individual with the skills, knowledge, and experience he or she needs to advance to successive stages.

Success in a career depends on several "career contingencies." For instance, the occupational system may allow for little career advancement, or the individual may lack the training that would allow movement beyond a certain level. Contingencies include any factors on which career success depends. Within the setting of a business or other organizational bureaucracy, a useful metaphor is a high-rise building. Each floor represents a career stage, and the career itself may be understood as the elevator that carries people upward or, in unfortunate cases, downward. Clearly, the career concept has more general applicability. Think of your college or university career as having begun when you started your post-secondary education. As your career takes you through several well-defined stages, your success will be judged in large part by the grades you receive. However, your success will also depend on career contingencies such as the types of examinations used to judge performance, the restrictions placed on program enrolment, and your abilities as a student.

How valuable is the career concept in the study of crime? Although there is a long history of research and theory that attempts to link the study of offending to the study of careers (Luckenbill and Best, 1981;Letkemann, 1973; Miller, 1978), criminologists debate whether this is a worthwhile exercise. Some criminologists maintain that the career concept is useful in understanding offenders' relative involvement in criminal activity. From this perspective, every offender can be said to have a criminal career. The use of the term *career* in this context does not necessarily mean that crime provides the offender's main source of livelihood. An individual who commits only one crime early in adolescence may have a short career in contrast to those who engage in serious crime throughout their lives. A focus on criminal careers encourages us to ask why offenders' careers develop as they do. The "criminal career" is not a theory in and of itself; that being said, it is a useful way of organizing what we know about crime.

The career concept encourages us to ask questions we would not otherwise have asked (Ayers et al., 1999; Blumstein, Cohen, and Farrington, 1988a, 1988b; Maxwell and Maxwell, 2000). What factors encourage movement into a criminal career? At what age do criminals start their careers? What degree of "productivity" constitutes a successful criminal career? How many crimes do offenders commit during their careers, and what affects their success? Finally, how and why do offenders end their criminal careers?

Advocates of the career concept contend that for theoretical reasons, it is important to distinguish questions about onset (i.e., when criminals start) from questions about frequency and desistance (i.e., when criminals end), since factors which affect one aspect of the career may be unrelated to those which affect another (Blumstein, Cohen, and Farrington, 1988a). For instance, some of the apparently confusing findings about the relationship between crime and unemployment may become more comprehensible if we recognize that unemployment may not be related to onset, productivity, and desistance in the same ways. For example, the level of unemployment may not be expected to affect the onset of criminal careers, which people typically begin in their teenage years—that is, before they are even eligible to enter the adult labour force. After a criminal career begins, the availability of legitimate work may affect the timing of desistance. An individual may abandon a criminal career if offered more profitable legitimate work. Conversely, most people end their criminal careers before middle age, but desistance may be delayed if the rate of unemployment decreases the likelihood of securing a legitimate job. In general, the career concept suggests that it may be misguided to try to find simple and direct links between familiar criminogenic concepts and rates of crime. Factors such as employment may affect different career aspects in different ways; and a factor that is important at one point of a career may have no causal significance at a later point.

THE CAREER CRIMINAL

Perhaps the most interesting findings to emerge from the research on criminal careers are those relating to "career criminals"—that is, offenders who commit crimes at very high rates. The extreme differences in the rates at which individuals offend were first documented in a cohort study undertaken by Wolfgang, Figlio, and Sellin (1972). These researchers examined the offending patterns of all males born in Philadelphia in 1945 for the period up to their eighteenth birthdays in 1963. The study identified 627 career criminals who, while they constituted only 6 percent of the original cohort and 18 percent of the delinquents, were responsible for more than half of all the crimes engaged in by cohort members. More importantly, perhaps, these career criminals were responsible for 71 percent of the murders, 73 percent of the rapes, and 82 percent of the robberies.

WHAT ARE THEY?

CAREER CRIMINALS

Career criminals are offenders who commit crimes at a very high rate.

Later studies support the view that a small number of offenders account for a large number of crimes. A longitudinal study in England, known as the Cambridge Study of Delinquent Development, found that about 6 percent of a sample of 411 boys accounted for about 50 percent of all criminal convictions (Farrington, 1989). In a study by the Rand Corporation of offenders in California, Michigan, and Texas prisons, the most active 10 percent of convicted robbers reported committing at least 58 robberies per year, while the most active 10 percent of burglars reported committing 187 or more burglaries per year (Chaiken and Chaiken, 1982).

Contrary to what we might expect, this same research also shows that offenders whose careers are characterized by high rates of offending seldom specialize in only one type of crime (Visher, 1991); rather, they tend to commit a variety of violent and property crimes (Kempf, 1987). The research into career criminals also shows that there is general stability in levels of offence seriousness over the course of a career. It does not appear, for instance, that the longer offenders offend, the more likely they are to move from one type of crime to another type that requires more technical skill or knowledge.

These findings have led some criminologists to be highly critical of the career approach to offending. Gottfredson and Hirschi (1986, 1988, 1990) question whether there is anything of value to be learned from examining criminal careers. The concept of a career, they argue, usually assumes some notion of specialization and career progress; the available evidence undermines the validity of such assumptions.

Gottfredson and Hirschi also contend that it is fruitless to search for unique factors to explain desistance from criminal careers, since all offenders—whatever offences they engage in, and whatever the rates at which they engage in them—become less productive as they age. To argue that different factors explain different career elements is also misleading, according to Gottfredson and Hirschi, since most of the factors in which career researchers are interested (such as unemployment) are only weakly related to crime. For these authors, the tendency to engage in crime is highly stable for all offenders and is related to low self-control.

In a somewhat different way, Luckenbill and Best (1981) also question the value of the career concept as a way of understanding crime and other types of nonconformity. They maintain that the analogy between legitimate and deviant careers is very limited, in large part because legitimate careers must be understood in the context of organizational settings whereas criminal careers emerge in much less structured settings. Criminal careers are not formed in response to institutional requirements that "spell out the career's positions, pathways for mobility, and rewards, while authorities enforce these rules and ensure the career's security" (1981: 197). Those who are involved in deviant careers are not able to draw on such institutional resources. They also risk the possibility of social control sanctions and exploitation by deviant associates, and their rewards from deviance are uncertain. Luckenbill and Best (1981) express the differences between legitimate and deviant careers as follows:

> Riding escalators between floors may be an effective metaphor for respectable organizational careers, but it fails to capture the character of deviant careers. A more appropriate image is a walk in the woods. Here some people take the pathways marked by their predecessors, while others strike out on their own. Some walk slowly, exploring before moving further, but others run, caught up in the action. Some have a destination in mind and proceed purposefully; others view the trip as an experience and enjoy it for its own sake. Even those intent on reaching a destination may stray from the path; they may try a shortcut or they may lose sight of a familiar landmark, get lost and find it necessary to backtrack. Without a rigid organizational structure, deviant careers can develop in many different ways (201).

Though the debate about the value of the career approach to understanding criminality is unresolved (Dechenes, 1990; Gibbons, 1988; Greenberg, 1992; Langan, 1983), comparisons between the legitimate and the illegitimate worlds of work can be strongly illuminating with respect to particular types of crime. One such type, "enterprise crime," is discussed in Chapter 10.

SUMMARY

Critics of motivation theories argue that many people contemplate breaking the law but do not. Formal and informal social controls may block them from acting in rational but criminal ways. Hirschi argues that delinquency emerges when controls diminish through the weakening of the social bonds that link adolescents to conformist others. Strong social bonds, which are based on high levels of attachment, commitment, involvement, and belief, and which are built into the socialization that individuals experience at home and at school, insulate youths from delinquent involvement. These bonds are subject to pressure from changes in the ways in which families function. They are also influenced by the degree of social disorganization experienced in communities, disorganization that can lead to weakening social ties and increased levels of criminality.

The purpose of deterrence strategies is to communicate to individuals the threat that punishment will follow delinquent acts. Deterrence does not result if the law is not imposed in a quick, certain, and severe way. But deterrence depends on many factors, including the fear of punishment, the perception of risk, and so on. It has been suggested that what the law actually threatens is less relevant to the decision to offend than what people *believe* it threatens. Perceptions of deterrence are also affected by widespread public doubts regarding the likelihood and efficacy of punishment.

Some criminals make rational choices to involve themselves in crime— that is, they weigh the benefits of crime involvement against the costs of apprehension. This may mean that certain individuals are more likely to live a life of crime. Career criminals follow a path toward heavy involvement in crime, even when they have not actually made a deliberate choice of crime as a career. There is evidence that a small number of individuals commit a disproportionate amount of crime.

QUESTIONS FOR REVIEW AND DISCUSSION

1. What factors do you think strengthen the social bonds between parents and children? What weakens those bonds?
2. How effective are various legal and informal sanctions in deterring crime? Is the threat of jail the only form of punishment that is effective in stopping crime?
3. If crime is so profitable, why don't we all commit crimes?
4. If most crime is committed by a small number of people, why can't we simply focus on that small group and make sure they are constrained from acting in criminal ways?
5. What is likely to stop a "career criminal" from continuing his or her life of crime?

INFOTRAC COLLEGE EDITION

Explore InfoTrac College Edition, your online university library, which includes hundreds of popular and scholarly journals in which you can find articles related to the topics in this chapter. Visit InfoTrac through your Web browser (**www.infotrac-college.com**), or through this book's Web site (**www.criminalevent-3e.nelson.com**).

WHAT'S ON THE WEB?

For chapter links and quizzes, check out the accompanying Web site at **www.criminalevent-3e.nelson.com**.

Chapter 6

Opportunities, Lifestyles, and Situations

WHAT'S IN CHAPTER SIX

In this chapter we focus on the role that opportunities, lifestyles, and situations play in the commission of crimes. Some criminologists have argued that to understand why crimes occur, we need to study not only offenders but also the opportunities that come their way. These opportunities can be said to emerge from the lifestyles and "routine activities" of potential victims. "Risky lifestyles" may promote higher levels of victimization. Also, we need to understand that it is possible to think about crimes not just narrowly as a product of offender motivation, but also more broadly as a product of victim–offender interaction. This transactional character of criminal events has been described in a variety of ways.

INTRODUCTION

The fact that offenders are ready and willing to engage in criminal conduct—because of their personalities, or backgrounds, or views of the law—does not in and of itself explain how criminal events occur. Potential offenders must also encounter opportunities that allow them to pursue their criminal inclinations. This is equally true of other events: an inclination to learn the saxophone, go to graduate school, or become a skydiver does not ensure that these things will happen. In such cases, as in the case of criminal events, it is useful to consider how opportunities allow individuals to act on their inclinations. It is important, as well, that we understand precisely what happens when offenders and opportunities meet. How do offenders offend, and how are victims victimized? In this chapter we consider how contemporary criminologists theorize about these and related questions.

We are strongly concerned in this chapter with the study of actual and potential crime victims. A criminal event perspective encourages us to recognize that in many situations victims are as important to the occurrence of crime as offenders. Often, crimes happen not only because offenders are present and behave in particular ways, but also because victims are present and behave in particular ways. The study of criminal offenders is, as we have seen, at least several centuries old; criminological interest in the study of victims is much more recent. It was really only in the 1960s and 1970s that scholars, building on the pioneering work of earlier writers, began to move the study of crime victims to the centre of criminological analysis (Anttila, 1974; Fattah, 1976; Kennedy and Sacco, 1998).

At least three factors account for the emergence of "victimology" as a field of study. *First,* some of the most important theoretical ideas in offender-centred criminology—such as Merton's strain theory, Sutherland's differential association theory, and social disorganization theory—were developed in the 1930s. After three decades or so of theoretical testing, in the 1960s and 1970s some criminologists began to question the utility of these accounts and to search for more novel approaches to the problem of crime. Several theoretical developments during this period, such as labelling theory and conflict theory, reflect this widespread desire to inject new life into the criminological enterprise. In a similar way, many criminologists became more and more interested in how an emphasis on the role played by victims might reorient the analysis of crime.

Second, in the 1970s the first major advances were made in the development of victimization surveys. In the United States, for instance, the National Crime Survey began to make available on a regular basis vast amounts of data about the nature, causes, and consequences of criminal victimization. This encouraged researchers to ask and answer empirical questions about why some people rather than others become victims of crime, and about the role played by victims in victimization processes.

Third, in the 1960s, Canada—and to an even greater extent the United States—experienced a dramatic rise in levels of predatory crime (Cohen and Felson, 1979). The increase in victimization levels gave birth to a powerful victims' movement that demanded governments take seriously the pain, suffering, and rights of crime victims (Weed, 1995). Governments were compelled to respond to the demands of victim organizations; this made social scientific knowledge about crime victims especially timely.

In the past few decades the study of crime victims has revolved essentially around two key issues. The first has to do with "victimization opportunity." In short, we ask why some people are more at risk of victimization than others, and how relative risk is affected by what people do. The second issue relates to the notion of "victim–offender interaction." In this respect we seek to discover how the actions of victims combine with the actions of offenders to produce criminal outcomes. This chapter considers both issues.

OPPORTUNITY THEORIES AND VICTIMIZATION

LIFESTYLE EXPOSURE

Cloward and Ohlin's analysis of criminal behaviour (see Chapter 4) extended the range of relevant theoretical questions beyond the search for motivational factors. Their theory alerts us to this cogent fact: it is not enough to understand why some people are motivated to break the law (since answers to this question generally do not explain why some laws and not others end up being broken); it is also necessary to understand how criminal inclinations are channelled by opportunities to be criminal.

Since the late 1970s the study of criminal opportunities has been dominated by researchers interested in victimization events. Their explanations, which are known as **lifestyle exposure** or **routine activities theories**, focus on how spatial and temporal variations in crime are related to variations in the opportunities to commit crime.

The lifestyle exposure theory of criminal victimization was developed by Michael Hindelang, Michael Gottfredson, and James Garofalo in their 1978 book *Victims of Personal Crime*. Their theory, which is grounded in the data of victimization surveys, seeks to explain what it is about being male, young, single, or poor that increases the chances of being victimized.

The linchpin of their argument is the concept of lifestyle. In general terms, *lifestyle* refers to the patterned ways in which people distribute their time and energies across a range of activities. We have no trouble recognizing that the lifestyle of a teenage male differs markedly from that of an elderly female. These differences relate to how and where one spends one's time, with whom one associates, and what types of leisure pursuits one enjoys. These lifestyle differences are not merely a matter of personal choice; they also reflect the social roles one is required to play and the various types of social constraints to which one is subject.

Lifestyle exposure theory
Focuses on patterned ways in which people with certain demographic characteristics distribute their time and energies across a range of activities, and their relation with the risk of victimization by motivated offenders.

BOX 6. 1

Location of Personal Victimization Incidents

Not all locations are equally risky with respect to criminal victimization. Data from the 1999 Canadian General Social Survey (GSS) allow us to examine how criminal incidents are distributed across social locations.

	Theft personal property	Sexual assault	Robbery	Assault
Inside victim's home	8%	13%	–%	10%
Around victim's home	21	–	–	10
Another private residence	4	19	–	6
Commercial place/ public institution	45	46	20	46
Street/other public place	22	12	50	28
Don't know/ not stated	–	8	–	–

–Number is zero or too small to be estimated reliably.

Source: Sandra Besserer and Catherine Trainor (2000), "Criminal Victimization in Canada, 1999," *Juristat*, 20(10): 9. Used by permission of Statistics Canada.

Where and how people spend their time is related to their risk of victimization. Engaging in evening activities outside the home increases an individual's chances of becoming a crime victim (although it is evident that the home is also a location of a fair amount of violent crime). Research also suggests that crimes are more likely to occur in some places and in the course of some activities than in others. This is illustrated by the data presented in Box 6.1.

Hindelang, Gottfredson, and Garofalo (1978: 251–64) offer the following eight propositions about victimization. These summarize the link between lifestyle and key demographic variables such as age, sex, marital status, family income, and race:

1. The more time individuals spend in public places (especially at night), the more likely they are to be victimized.
2. Certain lifestyles make it more likely that individuals will frequent public places.
3. Individuals tend to interact with people who share their lifestyle.

4. The probability that an individual will be a victim increases with the extent to which he or she and the offender belong to the same demographic category.

5. The proportion of time that an individual spends in places where there are many nonfamily members varies according to lifestyle.

6. The chance that an individual will be the victim of crime (especially theft) increases with the amount of time he or she spends with nonfamily members.

7. Lifestyle differences are related to the ability of individuals to isolate themselves from those with offender characteristics.

8. Lifestyle variations influence the convenience, desirability, and ease of victimizing individuals.

According to this argument, rates of personal victimization are relatively high for young minority males because these individuals tend to associate with people who are likely to offend (i.e., with other young minority males) and because they tend to frequent places (e.g., bars) where offending often occurs. In contrast, elderly females are likely to associate with other elderly females (whose level of offending is very low) and to avoid high-risk settings. In a sense, lifestyles structure victimization opportunities. In explaining empirical variations in levels of personal crime, Hindelang and colleagues contend that these opportunity structures, not offender motivation, are a central theoretical issue.

ROUTINE ACTIVITIES

Cohen and Felson (1979) note that traditional motivational theories in criminology are unable to explain why rates of many crimes increased so dramatically in Western nations in the postwar period. Many criminological theories (e.g., those emphasizing explanatory factors such as poverty, unemployment, and size of inner-city population) suggest that crime rates should have been falling during this period, not climbing. How, then, can the problem of rising crime rates be reconceptualized?

According to Cohen and Felson, the presence of a motivated offender is only one of the necessary preconditions to an assault, a sexual assault, a homicide, a break-and-enter, or some other "direct-contact predatory violation." For crimes like these to occur, two other conditions

WHAT DOES IT INCLUDE?

ROUTINE ACTIVITIES THEORY

First, there must be a motivated offender. Second, a suitable target against which the criminal motivation may be directed must be available. Third, there must be an absence of capable guardianship.

BOX 6.2

Repeat Victimization

Studies of crime victims tell us that some people are more likely than others to be victimized; they also tell us that those who have been victimized once are more likely to be victimized again. The extent of repeat victimization is illustrated in the following table, which shows data collected in the 2000 British Crime Survey (BCS). Like other victimization surveys, the BCS attempted to assess crime levels directly by asking respondents about their experiences with crime. Specifically, the 2000 BCS measured the victimization of people living in private households during the calendar year 1999. Of course, this table does not include data relating to nonvictims.

Number of Times Were Victimized, 1999

	Once	Twice	Three times or more
PROPERTY			
Vandalism	68%	16%	16%
Burglary	80	13	7
Vehicle Thefts	76	17	7
Other Household Theft	77	14	9
Theft from the Person	96	3	1
VIOLENCE			
Common Assault	65	17	18
Wounding	74	12	14
Robbery	76	14	10
ALL BCS VIOLENCE	65	17	18
Domestic Violence	43	26	31
Acquaintance	72	14	15
Stranger	79	13	8
Mugging	80	12	8

Source: C. Kershaw, T. Budd, G. Kinshott, J. Mattinson, P. Mayhew, and A. Myhill (2000), *The 2000 British Crime Survey.* London: The Home Office: 68. Used by permission.

must be met. There must also be a "suitable target" against which the criminal motivation can be directed (e.g., a home to break into, a person to assault, goods to steal). Furthermore, there must be an "absence of capable guardianship." In sum, a motivated offender must meet a suitable target in the absence of anything (or anyone) that might prevent the crime from occurring.

Cohen and Felson suggest that variations in crime levels are determined not only by the numbers of people willing to commit crimes but also by the numbers of suitable targets and by the levels of guardianship that are routinely exercised over these targets. Even where the numbers of suitable targets and the levels of guardianship are stable, higher crime rates can be expected if the tempos and rhythms of social life affect the rate at which motivated offenders encounter suitable targets in the absence of capable guardianship. For Cohen and Felson, illegal activities must be understood as behaviours that depend on, and feed off, the population's "**routine activities**." As the structure of routine activities changes, so does the frequency with which crimes occur.

How does all this help explain why crime rates changed as they did after the Second World War? Cohen and Felson contend that changes in patterns of routine activities made it far more likely that offenders would encounter suitable targets in conditions of weak guardianship. This period witnessed a broad shift in the locus of routine activities. More and more women, whose lives had previously revolved around the household, entered or returned to the paid labour force or school. Also, vacations became longer and travel became cheaper, so holidays were more likely to be spent away from home. The frequency with which people dined at restaurants increased; this gave rise to a booming fast-food industry. At the same time, divorce rates increased and people who were single were waiting longer to get married. Both changes pointed to a significant rise in the number of smaller, single-person households. As a result, leisure interests previously pursued at home were now being pursued elsewhere, among nonfamily members.

Not coincidentally, this period also witnessed "a revolution in small durable product design" (Cohen and Felson, 1979: 500). A general increase in the standard of living, combined with technological advances, resulted in a wide range of lightweight, durable consumer goods flooding the consumer market. The demand for tape recorders, television sets, and stereo equipment increased, as it later did for products such as personal computers, CD players, and VCRs (Felson, 1998).

According to Cohen and Felson, all of these changes had a profound impact on the rates of direct-contact predatory crime. By increasing the number of suitable targets and reducing guardianship levels, these changes provided criminals with greater opportunities; as a result, crime rates rose quickly. The shift in routine activities away from the home exposed more people to criminal dangers from which they previously had been insulated. Moreover, more people were leaving their homes unoccupied for longer periods of time, and thus depriving their homes of capable guardianship. At the same time that guardianship was being reduced, homes were being stocked with more highly desirable durable consumer goods that were easy to steal, carry, and sell or use. One need not agonize over the question of criminal

Routine activities theory
A theory that besides the presence of a motivated offender, a suitable target and the absence of capable guardianship are vital to the completion of a crime.

motivation, Cohen and Felson conclude, in order to understand an increase in crime over the period.

ADVANCES IN THE STUDY OF VICTIMIZATION OPPORTUNITY

In the past several years, a large body of research has been published regarding the questions raised by opportunity theories of victimization (Cohen, Kluegel, and Land, 1981; Felson, 1998; Kennedy and Forde, 1990; Rodgers and Roberts, 1995; Rountree and Land, 1996; Skogan and Maxfield, 1981; Tremblay and Tremblay, 1998). As a result, the field has grown in a number of distinct ways.

THEORETICAL REFINEMENTS

Terance Miethe and Robert Meier (1994) have refined and modified the theoretical approach to the study of victimization opportunity. They have proposed a "structural-choice model of victimization." Building on the work of earlier writers (Cohen, Kluegel, and Land, 1981), they maintain that opportunity theories highlight the importance of four factors: the physical proximity of targets to a pool of motivated offenders; the target's exposure to high-risk environments; target attractiveness; and the absence of guardianship. They also contend that current theories of victimization opportunity suggest two propositions. *First*, routine activities or lifestyles foster a structure of criminal opportunity by enhancing the contact between potential offenders and potential victims. *Second*, the subjective value of a person or of property, and the level of guardianship exerted over person or property, determine which targets are chosen for victimization. Thus, their model implies that while patterns of routine activities expose some people or property to greater risks, which specific targets are selected by offenders will depend on the rewards and risks associated with those specific targets. For Miethe and Meier, then, proximity and exposure are "structural" factors because they predispose people to differing levels of risk. In the same vein, target attractiveness and guardianship are "choice" components because they determine which targets are selected, in contexts characterized by particular levels of risk.

Hot spots

High-crime locations.

Some elaborations of opportunity theory focus on how arguments about criminal opportunity are compatible with arguments about the spatial distribution of crime. In Chapter 2 we discussed the research on "**hot spots**" undertaken by Lawrence Sherman and his colleagues (1989). In their analysis of calls for police service in Minneapolis, they found that a relatively small number of urban locations (i.e., addresses and intersections) hosted relatively large amounts of crime. Their explanation of this pattern emphasizes the need to focus on the routine activities of places. In other words, crime rates are high at specific locations because of how those locations are used by the people we find at them. Similarly, most interpretations of social disorganization emphasize how neighbourhood disorganization affects offending; yet it is equally reasonable to assume that social disorganization affects levels of criminal opportunity (Bursik and Grasmick, 1993; Smith, Frazee, and Davison, 2000).

Marcus Felson (1998), one of the architects of routine activities theory, has written recently about the relationship between the character of communities and levels of criminal opportunity. Of special interest to Felson is the urban form he describes as the "metroreef." These "communities" emerge when "metropolises themselves begin to fuse into a single organism, a seemingly endless suburban sprawl at moderate or low metropolitan density" (1998: 87). We might recognize the concentration of population in southern Ontario spreading out from Toronto in all directions as a clear example of such a "metroreef." According to Felson, metroreefs promote crime because of the way they "unpack" everyday activities. Four related aspects of this unpacking process can be identified:

Dispersing by construction As metroreefs develop, they spread homes and public buildings across metropolitan space. The resulting areas are characterized by single-family homes; by large, low buildings on vast lots; and by wide roads and huge parking areas. Environments like this make it very difficult for neighbours to keep an eye on each other's property. Also, police find it harder to patrol these areas effectively.

Proliferating households In the metroreef, young couples and the elderly generally maintain their own households. Boarders are rare, divorce rates are high, and college and university students tend to move away from home. As a result of all this, people in the metroreef are spread out over more households; thus, within each household there are fewer people available to discourage theft. Also, when people are dispersed across more households, fewer activities outside the home take place in family groupings.

Spreading people over many vehicles In the metroreef almost everyone depends on a car for transportation. The huge parking lots that these cars require increase the number of criminal opportunities. Thousands of very expensive cars, and their contents, sitting unsupervised for hours at a time, attract thieves and vandals. People who walk to and from cars in underground parking garages or massive parking lots are vulnerable to a variety of forms of criminal exploitation.

Dispersing activities away from the home   In the metroreef, reliance on cars has reduced the connections people have to their immediate environment, and perhaps the interest they have in it. People are willing to travel farther to work, shop, and socialize. Felson notes as an example that the corner grocery store has been replaced by the mega-supermarket. The former would have attracted local residents, who most likely would have walked there; the latter attracts strangers from a much wider area, who almost certainly drove there.

Felson's analysis points out how the social organization of everyday life in the metroreef makes available a large number of criminal opportunities to those who are inclined—for whatever reason—to take advantage of them.

Some writers (Osgood et al., 1996; Riley, 1987) have argued that offending (like victimization) can itself be understood as a function of routine activities. In other words, the routine activities that people engage in increase or decrease the likelihood that they will find themselves in situations that encourage or allow offending behaviour. Osgood and colleagues argue that for a range of criminal and deviant behaviour, situations conducive to offending are especially prevalent when routine activities often place people in unstructured social activities with peers in the absence of authority figures. The lack of structure leaves time available for deviance. Also, when peers are present various types of crime and deviance are not only easier to accomplish, but also more rewarding. Finally, the absence of an authority figure (such as a parent or a teacher) means that it is less likely that anyone will assume responsibility for the social control of the offending behaviour.

Kennedy and Forde (1999) have attempted to develop what they refer to as "routine conflict theory." This argument seeks to understand the social roots of violence by integrating routine activities theory with arguments about how violent responses to conflict situations are learned. For Kennedy and Forde, it is meaningful to speak of "routine conflict" in two respects. *First*, the conflict situations—often potentially criminally violent ones—in which individuals find themselves, emerge out of the routine interactions in which they engage. These conflicts may involve a fight over money, sex, or drugs, or they may involve trivial disagreements arising from perceived slights. They may lead to threats, or to physical harm, or to a parting of the combatants before real trouble begins. Conflicts may have long histories—which suggests that the combatants have been feuding for years—or they may spark between strangers who have never met before (Kennedy and Forde, 1999: 9). *Second*, how an individual responds to a conflict situation is a function of the "scripts" that individual has learned as part of the socialization process. In other words, when we find ourselves involved in conflict, we rarely understand what is happening as a "completely new situation" involving a "completely novel solution." More typically, we draw on our past experiences with conflict; our actions are informed by our sense of what has worked in the past and therefore is likely to work again. In sum, Kennedy and Forde argue that violent routines are available to people based on what they have learned and on what they expect to happen in particular situations.

This theory maintains that individuals come to situations with a predisposition to behave in particular ways. Moreover, individuals learn "repertoires" for managing their daily lives, much as they learn other aspects of their lifestyles. These repertoires include guidelines regarding how routinely encountered conflict situations should be managed. Kennedy and Forde also note that individuals learn how to act when confronted by the actions of others; they also learn that reactions to perceived threats are tempered by the situations in which they find themselves. Certain environments (e.g., bars, sporting events) may be more likely than others to encourage routine acts of violence.

BROADENING THE VIEW OF RISK

Traditionally, researchers interested in the factors that place people at increased risk of victimization have focused on a relatively narrow range of "lifestyle factors," including alcohol consumption, frequency of nighttime activities outside the home, and a range of demographic indicators such as sex, age, and social class. All of these are thought to be indicative of differences in the kinds of roles people play in society. More recently, some researchers have begun to argue that it is important to extend the range of lifestyle risk factors. Two such variables are of particular interest: offending behaviour and prior victimization experience.

With respect to offending behaviour, several studies have shown that an important, if imperfectly understood, relationship exists between offending and victimization (Jensen and Brownfield, 1986; Sampson and Lauritsen, 1990; Richie, 2000). In short, people who engage in offending behaviour face an increased risk of criminal victimization. There are two very reasonable explanations for this. *First*, as lifestyle models argue, people tend to associate with those who are socially and demographically like themselves. By implication, offenders tend to associate with other offenders. Moreover, offenders often victimize those who are most accessible to them, so it should come as no surprise that those who tell researchers they have offended are also likely to tell them they have been victimized. A *second* explanation emphasizes the character of offending behaviour itself rather than the social demographic characteristics of those who engage in it. Those who engage in prohibited behaviour often make perfect victims because they are unlikely to want the police to be involved in any investigation of their activities. In this sense, offending behaviour can be seen as increasing one's vulnerability to predatory crime (Kennedy and Baron, 1993).

For many people, this link between offending and victimization greatly complicates our understanding of crime. In popular discourse we are encouraged to think of "criminals" and "victims" as two separate categories of people who differ not only behaviourally but also morally. Yet the empirical evidence suggests that the picture is not so straightforward. Victims and offenders share many characteristics in common—both, for instance, are typically young and typically poor. And offending is a risk factor for victimization. And victimization is a risk factor for offending (Agnew, 1992; Fleisher, 1995; Widom, 1995). In other words, for a wide variety of understandable reasons, people who have been criminally exploited by others may be more likely to engage in certain types of criminal behaviour themselves. Clearly, the relationship between offending and victimization is very complex and does not conform neatly to our idealized moral vision of how the world *should* look.

A *second* factor that is generating strong interest among those who study victims is "prior victimization" (Farrell, 1995; Farrell, Phillips, and Pease, 1995; Johnson, Bowers, and Hirschfield, 1997; Hope, 1995). Analyses of victimization data suggest that much victimization is multiple victimization. Stated differently, people who have been victimized once are more likely to be victimized again. There are some crimes—for example, wife assault—for which we are not surprised to learn this. Yet several studies suggest that the phenomenon may be somewhat more widespread than this. An initial act of victimization seems to increase the risk of later victimization, for both property and personal crime.

Ken Pease and Gloria Laycock (1996) use the term "hot dot" to refer to a victim who is repeatedly victimized. In a sense, hot dots are the ultimate hot spots. In their review of the problem of repeat victimization, Pease and Laycock maintain that available research supports the following conclusions:

- An individual's past criminal victimization is a useful predictor of his or her subsequent victimization.

- The greater the number of previous victimizations, the greater the likelihood that the individual will experience victimization in the future.

- High-crime areas differ from low-crime areas at least in part because in high-crime areas a small number of victims are victimized at excessive rates.

- When victimization recurs, it tends to do so soon after the prior occurrence.

- The same offenders seem to be responsible for the bulk of repeated offences against a victim.

- Many factors, from policing styles to the nature of criminal justice information systems, inhibit a more detailed understanding of how repeat victimization contributes to the crime problem.

Two general kinds of explanations can be offered for patterns of repeat victimization. One argument suggests that the social or demographic characteristics that put people at risk for the first victimization may continue to place them at risk after that first victimization. The other maintains that there may be something in the victimization experience itself that increases the risk of further victimization. We might assume that an offender who has burglarized a house once would not want to do so again, yet this may not be the case—a house that has recently been burglarized successfully may be an even more desirable target for a second run. After all, the offender probably has some prior knowledge about when the house is unoccupied and how easy it is to gain access. Also, the burglar can safely assume (given the empty cardboard boxes on the front lawn) that the stolen television and VCR have been replaced by new equipment. There is research evidence to support the conclusion that both prior risk factors and increased vulnerability due to the victimization experience may be important sources of repeat victimization (Wittebrood and Nieuwbeerta, 2000).

SPECIFYING THE OFFENDER'S ROLE

In a very basic way, the ideas generated by opportunity theory have reoriented criminologists' thinking about the causes of crime. Opportunity theories have provided an additional piece to the puzzle as to why and where criminal events occur. A major limitation of these theories is that they have tended to pay little attention to the role of the offender or to the relationship between offender and victim. Rather, it has been assumed that probabilities of offending can be worked out on the basis of sets of conditions relating to opportunities.

BOX 6.3

Offending and Victimization

What is the nature of the relationship between offending and victimization? Stephen Baron (1997) attempted to answer this question by investigating a group that is at high risk for both kinds of behaviour—male homeless street youth. He conducted detailed interviews with 200 street youth, about a variety of issues but especially their involvement in criminal events as offenders and as victims. His findings were illuminating in several respects.

First, almost all of the interviewees had suffered some kind of criminal victimization, and most had been victimized repeatedly.

Second, there seemed to be a strong relationship between offending and chronic victimization. The more violent crimes the offender had committed, the more likely he was to report having been victimized. It is quite likely, Baron reasons, that the "capricious nature" of these crimes left the offender vulnerable to serious physical injury. Also, offenders who behave violently are often themselves at risk of violent retribution at the hands of those they have victimized.

Third, and less expected, Baron found that violent offending can sometimes deter victimization. Those who are themselves not inclined to behave violently may be reluctant to try to steal from someone who is known to have no such inhibitions.

Fourth and finally, youths from abusive families are more likely to be victimized. Perhaps their experiences in abusive homes encouraged them to develop provocative and belligerent interactional styles that made them likely targets for victimization. Baron concluded that it is important to focus future analytical attention on the relationship between offending and victimization—especially as such issues affect those, like homeless youth, who are at high risk of both.

The view of the offender that is generally considered most consistent with opportunity theories of victimization derives from the classical school of criminology (see Chapter 5). In one sense, opportunity theories reflect key assumptions of the social control and deterrence arguments. The suggestion that crimes are less likely to occur when capable guardianship is present is consistent with such arguments. In a related way, opportunity theories are perfectly compatible with rational choice theories of the offender (Clarke and Felson, 1993; Nagin and Paternoster, 1993). It is assumed that offenders make rational decisions about criminal action based on the offending opportunities that the environment presents to them.

Recent attempts to arrive at a neoclassical version of rational choice theory recognize that the rationality of criminal offenders is often compromised. For example, many offenders make decisions about crime commission while under the influence of drugs or alcohol. As well, the fear that a criminal opportunity might slip away may encourage them to make their behavioural choices quickly or in the absence of detailed information (Wright and Decker, 1994). Given contingencies such as this, modern rational choice theorists often speak of a "limited" rather than a "pure" rationality (Cromwell et al., 1991).

CRIME AS INTERACTIONS

An important theoretical question in the study of criminal situations relates to how these events unfold over time. They are set in motion by offenders who are inclined to make use of available criminal opportunities. To explain why they follow their particular courses of action, we must consider the specific behavioural choices that offenders, victims, and others make in the situations in which they find themselves. It is especially important to understand how the choices each participant makes influence the choices made by others. Victims and offenders act and react, and in so doing exert mutual influence. Stated differently, crimes have an interactional character: what any one participant does depends on what others do. Interactional dynamics have not attracted as much attention as issues such as offender motivation; even so, a general appreciation of how criminologists attempt to understand these interactions is necessary.

VICTIM PRECIPITATION

One of the concepts most often employed in the study of crime dynamics is that of **victim precipitation**, according to which the opportunity for crime is created by some action of the victim. In an early and influential study of 588 criminal homicides in Philadelphia, Marvin Wolfgang (1958) reported that about one-quarter of the time, the victim could be said to have precipitated his or her own murder. In these cases, Wolfgang noted, it was the eventual victim who—often under the influence of alcohol—was the first to brandish a weapon or threaten deadly force. The eventual offender, fearing for his or her own safety, either intentionally or unintentionally reacted to the threat in a way that proved fatal for the victim. In a stereotypical case, an altercation between two individuals at a bar escalates to the point where one of the parties produces a gun or a knife or a broken bottle and says to the other party, "I'm going to kill you." The other party responds with haste and force, and suddenly the person who uttered the threat is lying dead on the barroom floor.

Victim precipitation
Occurs when the opportunity for crime is created by some action of the victim.

WHAT DOES IT MEAN?

VICTIM PRECIPITATION

This occurs when the opportunity for crime is created by some action of the victim.

The concept of victim precipitation encourages us to understand the outcome of a crime situation as the joint product of the behaviours of the offender and the victim, rather than simply in terms of the offender's motivation. In the case of the barroom encounter, the killing can be said to have resulted not from the killer's actions but from the killer–killed interaction. It is important to point out that what people *intend* their words or their actions to mean in cases like this is much less important than *how the words are interpreted* by others in the interaction. The person who brandishes a broken beer bottle and threatens death to a disputant may be expressing mere bravado rather than serious intent to harm the other party. To the disputant, whose judgment is clouded by alcohol and who believes the threat to be real, other interpretations of the situation are well out of reach. With respect to cases like this, we have little trouble understanding the explanatory value of the concept of victim precipitation. The homicide would probably not have occurred, we can conclude, if the victim had not initially behaved in an aggressive fashion; thus, the victim was an active contributor to his or her own violent demise.

To what degree can the explanatory logic of victim precipitation be generalized to other types of events? In theoretical terms, this is a tough question. For instance, is it reasonable to argue that crimes such as robbery, theft, and sexual assault can also be victim precipitated? In events like these, does it make sense to argue that victims actively contribute to their own victimization?

Amir (1971) concluded from a study of over 600 rape cases in Philadelphia that about one case in five was victim precipitated. Amir classified rapes as victim precipitated if the victim "actually, or so it was deemed, agreed to sexual relations but retracted before the actual act or did not react strongly enough when the suggestion was made to the offender" (266).

We might be inclined to agree that victims who initially threaten their offenders in some sense precipitate a homicide; we would not agree that victims who initially say yes to sexual relations precipitate rape if they subsequently say no. For one thing, the assumption in the latter case seems to be that the female rather than the male is responsible for the level of male sexual arousal and that if that arousal is not satisfied, the female must bear the violent consequences. Also, it seems to imply that a subsequent decision not to engage in sex, when there has been some initial agreement to do so, is appropriately understood as precipitous of violence. Finally, homicide and sexual assault differ in a fundamental way that is obscured by the haphazard application of the concept of victim precipitation. The types of homicides described by Wolfgang involve events in which victims threaten their offenders with deadly force and are repaid in kind. In the cases of rape described by Amir, the victim was not behaving in a threatening or aggressive fashion, and the violence exhibited by the offender could not have been understood as "payment in kind."

Amir's study illustrates a serious concern that many people have with the concept of victim precipitation: it is difficult to separate the moral dimensions of the concept from its explanatory dimensions. The claim that victims precipitate victimization seems uncomfortably close to the suggestion that victims should be blamed for their victimization. Many criminologists contend that victim blaming should be avoided at all costs (Timmer and Norman, 1984). At the same time, most people can express some degree of empathy for the battered wife who, after years of being subjected to violence, kills her abusive husband. To call a killing of this type "victim precipitated" does not usually elicit a charge of victim blaming.

For some criminologists, the solution is to recognize that crude attempts to sort crimes into precipitated and unprecipitated categories are doomed to failure. Victims and offenders may contribute to the unfolding of a criminal event in a variety of ways, and thus a broader taxonomy of victim and offender roles is necessary (Fattah, 1991; Karmen, 2001). Another solution involves recognizing that it is often inappropriate to speak of victim and offender roles, since doing so minimizes our understanding of how the actual circumstances of events determine who shall bear what label. In other words, there is a need to move beyond the study of victim precipitation to "the full round of interaction," which involves not only the eventual victims and offenders but also other event participants (Luckenbill, 1984).

Situated transaction
Process of interaction involving two or more individuals that lasts as long as they find themselves in one another's presence.

THE SITUATED TRANSACTION

Goffman (1963) defines a **situated transaction** as a process of interaction involving two or more individuals. To understand criminal events as situated transactions, we must focus on what goes on between the participants rather than on what any one of them does individually. According to Goffman (1959), human behaviour is acted out as though part of a thea-

WHAT DOES IT MEAN?

SITUATED TRANSACTION

This refers to a process of interaction involving two or more individuals that lasts as long as they find themselves in one another's presence. If we are to understand criminal events as situated transactions, we need to emphasize the study of what goes on between the participants rather than what any one of them does.

Symbolic interactionism
The role of linguistic interaction in developing a social identity and functioning according to shared norms and values.

trical performance. What's important in the interaction is the impression the actor gives to others. Based on this impression—which generally involves the playing out of a particular role in a specific situation—individuals extract information about others in the interaction. When enough information has been obtained for each individual to define the situation to his or her satisfaction, the roles can be properly acted out (Martin, Mutchnick, and Austin, 1990: 332). With these definitions in hand, individuals are able to sustain and complete a number of transactions throughout their daily lives. But these transactions do not always have positive outcomes.

In his analysis of 70 homicides in California, Luckenbill (1977) utilized an approach that draws on **symbolic interactionism**. Like other researchers, he reported that these murders tend to occur in informal settings and generally involve people who know each other. What distinguishes his approach, however, is his view that homicide is a product of situated transactions rather than of the behaviour of individual participants. For Luckenbill, situated transactions should be viewed as "character contests" in which efforts by the disputants to "save face" result in deadly combat.

BOX 6.4

Stages in the Situated Transaction

David Luckenbill has argued that homicide can be understood as a situated transaction. It is a transaction in that "an offender, victim and possibly an audience engage in an interchange which leaves the victim dead," and it is situated in that the "participants interact in a common physical territory" (1977: 196). Based on an analysis of 70 homicide events in a California county, Luckenbill contended that these incidents typically move through six stages:

- *Stage 1:* The opening move in the transaction is an action undertaken by the (eventual) victim and defined by the (eventual) offender as an offence to "face." For example, the victim says, "Get lost" or "What are you staring at?"
- *Stage 2:* The offender interprets the victim's words or actions as personally offensive.
- *Stage 3:* The offender makes an opening move in salvaging "face" or protecting "honour"—in short, the offender retaliates verbally or physically.
- *Stage 4:* The victim responds in an aggressive manner. His or her actions suggest a working agreement that the situation is suited to violent resolution. By cheering or heckling, onlookers may encourage the movement toward violence. They may also block a convenient exit for one or both parties, or prevent others from breaking up the fight.
- *Stage 5:* There is a physical interchange, typically brief and precise.
- *Stage 6:* The brief battle is over. At this point the offender flees or remains at the scene, either voluntarily or as a result of force applied by bystanders.

This perspective on criminal events is not meant to imply that situated transactions are restricted to one type of crime. The kinds of transactions that result in acquaintance rape differ from those that result in homicide. And even with homicide, some transactions are more "situated" than others (Williams and Flewelling, 1988). For example, it is incorrect to argue that the victims of mass murderers or serial killers are combatants committed to battle. (This is not to deny that such crimes also have situational dynamics.)

Often, transactions are so complex that they blur whatever distinctions we try to make between victims and offenders or between different types of offenders. Frequently, the interaction that the eventual victim and eventual offender are engaged in determines the character of the outcome (Felson and Messner, 1996: Miethe and Drass, 1999). How useful is it for us to say that individuals are of a certain "criminal type" when we know that their behaviour can be affected so strongly by the situations they face and the roles they believe they must play? We do not—as we do in cases of victim precipitation—look to the victim for the causes of the violence, but rather to the victim–offender exchange. With respect to the homicides described by Luckenbill, it should be clear that up until the moment of battle, either party could have pulled out of the exchange or responded differently, and the results would have been quite different. Questions about who should have done what (and when) to prevent the violence are likely to elicit more than one answer. In his study of street youth, Baron confirmed the importance of transactions in determining who is the victim and who is the offender. He reported that the more violent the altercations street youths participated in (as offenders), the greater their risk for violent victimization (see Box 6.4).

THE SOCIAL ORGANIZATION OF CRIME AND DEVIANCE

Joel Best and David Luckenbill (1994) have attempted to develop a comprehensive typology of criminal transactions. These transactions, they argue, differ in a number of ways from one another. Some last only seconds (a mugging); others can last several days or even weeks (blackmail). Some involve people in face-to-face contact; others involve people separated by great distances. Some involve only one or two individuals; others involve a great many more.

Best and Luckenbill identify three main categories of transactions. The first, *individual deviance,* consists of one individual playing a deviant or criminal role—for example, a person involved in illicit drug taking. The second, *the deviant exchange,* involves two people (or more) playing cooperative roles vis-à-vis each other. Drug dealing, the sale of pornography, and prostitution all involve deviant exchanges. The third, *deviant exploitation*, involves parties in conflict. In deviant or criminal exploitation, at least one individual is performing an offender role and at least one is playing the "target." Like the other forms of deviant transaction, deviant exploitation has some characteristic subtypes (see Box 6.5).

BOX 6.5

Criminal Exploitation

In *Organizing Deviance*, Joel Best and David Luckenbill develop a typology that distinguishes between different types of criminal exploitation. Schematically, the differences take the following form:

	Target's Definition of the Situation	
Target's awareness	Exploitation	Exchange
Open	Coercion	Extortion
Closed	Surreptitious exploitation	Fraud

The four types are classified in terms of two dimensions: the target's awareness, and the target's definition of the situation. Thus, we are encouraged to ask two questions. Is the target (or victim) of the offence aware of what is going on while it is going on? And does the target define the transaction as one that involves exploitation or one that involves an exchange?

In coercion, the target surrenders goods or services because the offender uses or threatens violence. Rape, robbery, and murder are obvious examples of coercion. In the case of extortion, the offender threatens to harm someone or something that is being held hostage unless payments are made. Extortion includes the crimes of blackmail and kidnapping. In both cases, the target recognizes the crime for what it is; thus, both can be said to occur under conditions of open awareness. However, extortion—much more so than coercion—takes the form of an exchange or a bargain being struck.

Surreptitious exploitation and fraud occur under conditions of closed awareness. Targets may eventually recognize that they have been victimized; they do not recognize it while the transaction is occurring. With surreptitious exploitation the offender uses stealth to take or damage the property of the target. Break-and-enter and vandalism are clear forms of exploitation, but they typically occur outside of the target's awareness. With fraud the offender uses trickery to make the target believe that a legitimate transaction has occurred. Thus, the target may believe that she received the proper change from a cashier when actually she has been short-changed. Or the target may believe that he has paid an honest contractor to pave his driveway when, in fact, he paid an unscrupulous con artist for a service that was never received. In both cases the transaction looked like an exchange, and in both cases the fraudulent nature of the exchange was outside the target's awareness.

According to Best and Luckenbill, once we recognize that deviant or criminal transactions are organizationally complex, we gain some distinct analytical advantages. *First*, the classification scheme distinguishes between individual deviance, deviant exchange, and deviant exploitation, and this allows us to see similarities among forms of rule breaking that we might not think had very much in common. Usually, we don't think about what murder has in common with fraud, or what skid row drinking has in common with suicide. *Second*, offenders' careers typically involve several kinds of transactions, each of which has its own properties, which can be distinguished using this scheme. Robbing a store to get the money to buy drugs involves one kind of transaction (exploitation), buying the drugs involves another (exchange), and taking the drugs involves still another (individual deviance). An individual's crimes can be understood as organized in terms of their frequency and the offender's degree of engagement in various types of transactions. Of course, different kinds of transactions carry different kinds of risks and present offenders with different sorts of problems requiring solution.

THE SIGNIFICANCE OF INTERACTIONAL ISSUES

The research on victim–offender interactions challenges many of the stereotypes that are inherent in other theoretical approaches. With respect to motivational theories, for instance, we are sometimes led to argue that crimes occur only because criminals are determined to commit them. Theories that focus only on opportunity, if not carefully interpreted, seem to suggest that crimes occur because motivated offenders find the opportunities to translate their inclinations into action.

In contrast, interactional theories suggest that more than motivation and opportunity are needed to understand why and how crime occurs. Crimes are the outcome of social exchanges between people who find themselves in specific circumstances and must make quick decisions about how they should respond to each other's behaviour (Felson and Messner, 1996). A robbery does not occur merely because an offender with an inclination to rob encounters an opportunity conducive to robbery. The potential victim may resist in ways that turn a potential robbery into an attempted murder. The potential victim of an attempted break-and-enter may "overreact" by killing the offender. Victims of property crimes contribute to interactions through the steps they take—or don't take—to protect their property; their actions, or lack thereof, send a message to the potential offender about the risks of trying to steal the property. In sum, victims are not merely passive objects of an offender's predatory desires; nor are they necessarily active contributors to their own victimization. They are, however, key event participants whose actions shape and constrain event outcomes.

Similar comments apply to other participants. For instance, Luckenbill in his study of homicide revealed that the role of bystanders in situated transactions should not be minimized. He found that the presence of bystanders and the actions they took shaped the course of the transaction. In the early stages they sometimes increased the likelihood of mortal battle by encouraging the offender to interpret an offensive remark as requiring a firm response; in the later stages they sometimes supplied a weapon or blocked the exit of the potential victim. Of course, just as bystanders may facilitate the occurrence of a crime, they may also prevent crimes or transform one type of crime into another. A bystander who has the presence of mind to call "911" on witnessing an assault or who is familiar with cardiopulmonary resuscitation (CPR) may prevent an assault from becoming a murder.

SUMMARY

The pressure to behave in a criminal fashion is not sufficient to explain why people commit one type of crime and not another. Researchers who take a routine activities approach explain variations in levels of crime across places and over time based less on variations in the numbers of individuals motivated to commit crime than on variations in the opportunities to commit crime. The concept of opportunities revolves around the notion that some individuals have certain lifestyles or follow certain routines that make them more vulnerable to criminal victimization. This lifestyle exposure, coupled with the presence of motivated offenders and the absence of capable guardians, makes becoming a victim of crime more likely.

Crimes involve choices—by offenders, victims, and others—all of which affect the outcome. Crimes can thus be said to have an interactional character: what any one participant does depends on what others do. An important consideration here is the role played by the victim, who together with the offender and other main players comes to be involved in what is called a situated transaction. In such transactions the characteristics of the individuals involved come to define the direction that the crime will take. In the early stages of interactions it is often difficult to predict who will be the eventual victim and who the offender. It is the actions that occur that clearly define these roles.

Harm and guilt are clearly worked out only after the fact, and often depend on the actions of third parties.

Interactional approaches suggest, then, that crimes are the outcome of social exchanges between people who find themselves in specific circumstances and who must make quick decisions about how they should respond to one another's behaviour. Their responses determine the outcomes. These outcomes are not always predictable, in that they can be affected by many factors in the situation. Interactional approaches help us determine the effectiveness of various strategies used by victims or police in deterring or preventing crime.

QUESTIONS FOR REVIEW AND DISCUSSION

1. Why do you think young males are more likely to live risky lifestyles than any other group?
2. What do you think will be the major change in future lifestyles that will make individuals in society more vulnerable to crime? less vulnerable?
3. Are there steps that can be taken to reduce the likelihood that individuals who confront each other in an interaction will escalate this dispute to violence?
4. The police play an important role as third parties in defining behaviour as criminal or noncriminal. What are the pluses and minuses of police using more discretion in deciding what should be treated criminally and what should be treated as a noncriminal dispute?
5. Are we likely to see a drop in crime as young people who follow risky routines become older and less likely to be involved in these types of behaviour?

INFOTRAC COLLEGE EDITION

Explore InfoTrac College Edition, your online university library, which includes hundreds of popular and scholarly journals in which you can find articles related to the topics in this chapter. Visit InfoTrac through your Web browser (**www.infotrac-college.com**), or through this book's Web site (**www.criminalevent-3e.nelson.com**).

WHAT'S ON THE WEB?

For chapter links and quizzes, check out the accompanying Web site at **www.criminalevent-3e.nelson.com**.

Chapter 7

Crime's Aftermath: The Consequences of Criminal Events

WHAT'S IN CHAPTER SEVEN

In this chapter we review the theories that deal with the aftermath of criminal events. We also examine moral panics—those extreme reactions to crime whereby the public responds intensely to the threat of criminal acts. These reactions strongly affect the actions of claimsmakers, who often set the public agenda for responding to criminal events.

INTRODUCTION

This chapter is concerned with what happens in the aftermath of the criminal event. The issues, theories, and research discussed remind us that for analytical purposes, it makes little sense to say that criminal events end when the thief flees the scene or when the victim of homicide falls to the floor. Just as important is how participants and the rest of us respond to criminal events.

Several of the questions addressed in this chapter relate to the experiences of offenders and victims. How do offenders who are apprehended contend with the criminal status accorded them? What are the effects of crime on victims? How do victims cope with these losses, and why do some manage better than others?

But we must not restrict ourselves to the event participants. Criminal events elicit responses from many individuals and groups in society. As we will see, **fear of crime** is a pervasive problem, especially in large urban areas. Obviously, to some extent the aftermath of criminal events must be seen as an outcome of the event transaction as well as the wider social context in which these events occur. For example, the level of injury experienced by a victim of violence will be related to decisions made by the victim to resist the offender and decisions by the offender to actively overcome that resistance (Kleck and Sayles, 1990; Ziegenhagen and Brosnan, 1985). A "random" murder that is

Fear of crime
A concern or anxiety relating to the possibility of criminal victimization and usually assessed in social research through the measurement of attitudes or reported behaviours.

given sensationalist treatment by the mass media will elicit more public fear than a murder involving drinking partners (Best, 1999; Liska and Baccaglini, 1990). And an offender who is caught selling illegal drugs when society is in a state of panic about drug crimes can expect less sympathy than an offender who is apprehended during a period when the level of concern is lower.

HOW MUCH DOES CRIME COST?

Any attempt to discuss the consequences that crimes have for victims, and victims' efforts to cope with these consequences, is beset by some rather serious research problems. Perhaps the most notable is the "specification problem" (Fattah and Sacco, 1989). In short, it is not always clear what a crime's effects were, and what they were not (Miller, Cohen, and Wiersema, 1996).

Some costs of crime are more obvious than others. With respect to financial loss, it is obvious that the economic cost sustained when someone steals a purse from a victim equals the cost of replacing the purse and its contents. But suppose the victim reacts to the theft by deciding to install deadbolt locks, and to take taxis instead of walking to evening destinations. Suppose as well that she decides that instead of carrying cash she will write cheques for her pur-

---

BOX 7.1

The Cost of Crime

The amount of money spent on justice services (police, courts, and corrections) is considered by many to be one of the more substantial costs of crime to our society. In the Canadian context, what do we know about these costs?

- Three cents of every dollar governments spent in 1996–97 was on policing, courts, and correctional services.
- Spending on six key sectors of the justice system—policing, courts, legal aid, criminal prosecutions, adult corrections, and youth corrections—totalled almost $10 billion in 1996–97. That is roughly $337 for every person in Canada.
- Of the $10 billion that was spent, the largest amount was on policing (59 percent), followed by adult corrections (20 percent). Smaller amounts were spent on courts (9 percent), legal aid (5 percent), youth corrections (5 percent), and criminal prosecutions (3 percent).
- When adjusted for shifts in the population, spending on justice services in 1996–97 was down 2 percent from the previous year.
- In 1996–97 almost 120,000 people were employed full-time by the justice system. Over half of these people worked for police services (62 percent).

Source: Sandra Besserer and Jennifer Tufts (1999), "Justice Spending in Canada," *Juristat* 19(12).

chases in the future. Should the costs of the locks, the taxi fares, and chequing accounts be considered an economic cost of the crime? This issue assumes even more importance when we recognize that financial losses are perhaps the easiest to calculate, given that there is a convenient standard of measurement (Kennedy and Sacco, 1998).

With respect to physical injury, if the victim sustained a broken arm, that injury clearly should be considered a consequence of the crime. But if stress resulting from the crime aggravated a pre-existing health condition, is it correct to say that the incident caused physical harm even though there were no apparent physical injuries? The problems with efforts to assess the costs of crime for victims emerge logically from the types of research methods applied. Typically, information about victimization outcomes—like other information about victims—comes from victim surveys or from specialized samples of crime victims.

Two general strategies can be used to investigate how victims are affected by crime. *First*, survey respondents can be asked directly about the losses they experienced. These questions—like all questions that ask people to report on past events—are subject to errors as a result of faulty memory, dishonesty, and misunderstanding (Skogan, 1986). Usually, these questions focus on the most obvious losses to the victim, such as injury or stolen or damaged goods. Though these questions are useful up to a point, they focus attention only on what happened during or immediately after the event, and reveal little about longer-term impacts. With victimization surveys, respondents are asked about events that occurred in some specified period preceding the survey (typically a year or six months); therefore, our data about problems that emerge later are often minimal.

Respondents can also be asked how they changed or limited their behaviour in response to the victimization. These questions require respondents not only to recall accurately when their behaviour changed but also to understand the causes of their behaviour.

A *second* research strategy involves the researcher rather than the survey respondents making judgments about the effects of the victimization experience. Suppose we are interested in determining whether the victim's involvement in a criminal event increased feelings of anger. Instead of asking victims directly if they are angry about the experience, we might compare victims and nonvictims in terms of the responses they give to more general questions about feelings of anger. If we discover that victims are more angry than nonvictims, we might conclude that the victimization experience is responsible

BOX 7. 2

The Costs of Violence

Mark A. Cohen, Ted R. Miller, and Shelli B. Rossman (1994) have attempted to systematically enumerate the costs of violent victimization.

Cost category	Party that directly pays the cost
Direct property losses	
1. Losses not reimbursed by insurance	Victim
2. Losses reimbursed by insurance	Society
3. Administrative costs: insurance reimbursement	Society
4. Recovery by police	Society
Medical and health care	
1. Charges not reimbursed by insurance	Victim
2. Charges reimbursed by insurance	Society
3. Administrative overhead of insurance coverage	Society
Victim services	
1. Expenses charged to victim	Victim
2. Expenses paid by service agency	Society
3. Temporary labour and training of replacements	Society
Lost workdays	
1. Lost wages for unpaid workers	Victim
2. Lost productivity for paid workdays	Society
Lost school days	
1. Forgone wages due to lack of education	Victim
2. Forgone nonmonetary benefits of education	Victim
3. Forgone social benefits due to lack of education	Society
Lost housework	Victim and family
Pain and suffering/quality of life	Victim
Loss of affection/enjoyment	Victim's family
Death	
1. Value of life	Victim
2. Funeral and burial expenses	Victim's family
3. Loss of affection/enjoyment	Victim's family
4. Psychological injury/treatment	Victim's family
Legal costs associated with tort claims	Victim or victim's family
Long-term consequences of victimization	
1. Future victims	
2. Future social costs	

Cost category	Party that directly pays the cost
Fear of crime	Potential victim
Precaution expenditures/effort	Potential victim
Criminal justice system	Society
1. Police and investigative costs	Society
2. Prosecutors	Society
3. Courts	Society
4. Legal fees	
a. Public defenders	Society
b. Private	Offenders
5. Incarceration costs	Society
6. Nonincarceration sanctions	Society
7. Victim time	Victim
8. Jury and witness time	Jury/witness
Victim services	
1. Victim service organizations	Society
2. Victim compensation programs	Society
3. Victim time	Victim
Other noncriminal programs	
1. Hot lines and public service announcements	Society
2. Community treatment programs	Society
3. Private therapy/counselling	Society/offender
Incarcerated offender costs	
1. Lost wages	Offender/family
2. Lost tax revenue and productivity	Society
3. Value of lost freedom	Offender
4. Psychological cost to family	Family of offender
"Overdeterrence" costs	
1. Innocent individuals accused of offence	Innocent party
2. Restriction of legitimate activity	Society
3. Cost of additional detection avoidance by offenders	Offender
"Justice" costs	
1. Constitutional protections to avoid false accusations	Society
2. Cost of increasing detection rate to avoid differential punishment	Society

for some of the difference. This is standard social scientific practice; however, the results may not be clear, since we probably asked the questions about victimization and about feelings of anger in the same interview. So it is impossible to determine what is the cause and what is the effect. It is reasonable to argue that victimization results in feelings of anger; but it may be just as reasonable to argue that people who have an angry demeanour are more likely to become victims of crime.

The costs of crime for victims are generally considered to fall under four major categories: financial, physical, emotional, and behavioural.

FINANCIAL CONSEQUENCES

As noted, financial costs are among the most obvious costs associated with victimization. As with all types of costs, these can be direct or indirect. Direct costs include the value of the property stolen or damaged as well as any costs associated with medical care. According to the Insurance Information Centre of Canada, the average claim by homeowners and tenants for losses through break-and-enter amounted to $4,364 in 1998–99, and the average claim for commercial businesses amounted to $4,456. In 1998–99 the insurance industry paid out roughly $366 million in property loss claims associated with break-and-enters (Tremblay, 2000). There are also indirect financial costs— for example, those reflecting lost work time, child care costs, or expensive lifestyle changes. Also, direct costs do not include any long-term losses arising from criminal victimization (see Box 7.3, page 200).

PHYSICAL CONSEQUENCES

UCR 2 data gathered from 164 policing agencies in Canada indicate that in 1999 around 40 percent of victims of violence suffered some kind of physical injury. In around 35 percent of cases the injuries were "minor"; in around 4 percent they were "major"; less than 1 percent of cases resulted in death (Statistics Canada, 1999—Shelf Table 4.5).

Victimization data allow us to analyze the physical consequences of crime. Data from the 1999 General Social Survey (GSS) tell us that victims sustain physical injury in a minority of violent incidents. In 1999, victims (male and female) were injured in roughly 18 percent of violent incidents (Besserer and Trainor, 2000).

Victimization studies are quite useful in telling us about the direct injuries incurred from criminal victimization, but tell us relatively little about longer-term effects. Although it is not evident in surveys of this type, the injuries that result from physical encounters can lead to a worsening of existing health problems. Also, when the victim's mobility is restricted he or she may be less able—or even unable—to exercise or to meet nutritional requirements.

EMOTIONAL CONSEQUENCES

Victims can experience a variety of emotional reactions to crime, from mild to extreme. These reactions may include shock, mistrust, sleeplessness, anger, stress, depression, and a diminished capacity to enjoy life events (Mayhew, Maung, and Mirrlees-Black, 1993; Tjaden and Thoennes, 1998a). Victims may also express a sense of guilt—that is, they may blame themselves for what has happened. Table 7.1 gives the frequencies of various emotional effects reported by victims who responded to the 1993 Canadian Violence Against Women Survey (VAWS).

One of the most significant effects that has been associated with victimization is an increase in fear of crime (Johnson, 1996; Keane, 1995; Tjaden and Thoennes, 1998a). Serious crimes—especially crimes of violence—may result in a **vulnerability conversion** (Lejeune and Alex, 1973), as victims develop a sudden understanding that they are more susceptible to the dangers of life than they thought.

Fear is not the only emotional reaction that victimization elicits. Another common one is anger. Victims of crime often feel outraged that their property or person has been violated by an offender. Interestingly, though researchers have spent a great deal of time and energy researching how victimization promotes fear, we know considerably less about the relationship between victimization and anger. Data from the 2000 British Crime Survey (BCS) indicate that to some crimes, anger is a common response. For instance, victims of break-and-enter tended to express shock and fear and to experience difficulty sleeping; more than two-thirds also reported feeling angry (Kershaw et al., 2000).

Janoff-Bulman and Frieze (1983) maintain that serious criminal victimization is stressful in large part because it is unusual and because, unlike more routine stressors, it does not trigger well-developed coping mechanisms. These events make evident people's "psychological baggage" and suggest to them that they need to question not only their assumptions of invulnerability but also other assumptions underlying their day-to-day existence.

Vulnerability conversion
Especially for victims of violence, development of a sudden understanding by victims that they are more susceptible to the dangers of life than they thought.

TABLE 7.1

EMOTIONAL EFFECTS OF INTIMATE VIOLENCE

	Victimization by:		
Emotional effect	Spouses	Dates and boyfriends	Strangers
Anger	30%	31%	32%
More cautious/less trusting	18	32	36
Fear	21	27	31
Lowered self-esteem	18	12	7
Shame/guilt	10	11	9
Problems relating to men	10	16	6
Depression/anxiety	14	6	4
Upset/confusion/frustration	4	4	5
Shock/disbelief/disgust	3	4	5
Increased self-reliance	10	2	3
Other*	13	6	3
No emotional effects	13	9	12

* Includes sleeping problems, hurt, disappointment.

Source: H. Johnson, *Dangerous Domains* (Toronto: Nelson Canada, 1996), p. 203. Used by permission of Statistics Canada.

One such assumption is that "the world is meaningful." Most of us prefer to go through life believing that things happen for a reason—that good things happen to good people and that bad things happen to bad people. It is comforting to think that all things considered, the world makes sense. We can believe it because we also believe that we can exercise a certain amount of control over what happens to us. A serious, random act of crime can challenge this assumption. In the aftermath of such an event, the world seems to make less sense—we have become victims of misfortune even though we may have tried hard to keep ourselves safe.

Criminal victimization can also undermine an individual's positive self-concept. Victims may develop feelings of weakness and helplessness and believe that they could have done more than they did to avoid being victimized. Traditionally, society has reinforced this view by holding victims responsible for what has happened to them.

It is not only violent interpersonal crimes that have emotional consequences. Among property crimes, burglary can invite a strong response (Hough, 1985; Smith and Hill, 1991), in part because it is viewed as a crime with the potential for violence. Typically, victims are away from home when the offence occurs; but they are still forced to contemplate what might have happened had they been at home. Also, because a burglary could threaten violence against other members of the household, each member of the household may feel concern not only for his or her own personal safety but also for the well-being of other family members. Finally, because burglary represents an invasion of privacy and often involves theft of or damage to objects that have sentimental value, the emotional response can be severe (Hough, 1985).

It has often been argued that victims' psychological distress can be magnified by social and criminal justice agencies charged with the responsibility of helping them (Rosenbaum, 1987). In particular, the police have sometimes been accused of failing to provide victims with the emotional support they require and often expect (Carter, 1985; Skogan and Wycoff, 1987). The 1999 GSS found that victims—especially victims of violence—were less likely than nonvictims to have positive attitudes toward the police (Tufts, 2000). Moreover, levels of satisfaction were lower for people who reported a higher number of victimizations. Victims may feel that the police are not doing enough to help them or to recover stolen property. When property is recovered, they may wonder why it is not returned to them more promptly.

To some extent, victims' discontent with the police reflects the routine nature of police work. Some victims of even minor crimes expect a rapid response when they phone the police. Yet dispatchers, overwhelmed by calls for service, may assign minor crimes a very low priority. As a result, victims feel let down by the police. Similarly, victims who know they have been victimized may expect the police officer who arrives on the scene to accept their version of the story at face value and then engage in hot pursuit of the offender. For the police officer, the situation may be more ambiguous, and he or she may find it necessary to ask questions in order to make sense of the event. Also, the officer's experience may suggest that "hot pursuit" is pointless because the offender is unlikely to be found in this way, if at all.

Much of the research on emotional reactions to victimization suggests that they are likely to erode slowly over time (Burt and Katz, 1985; Hough,

1985). There is also some evidence that symptoms sometimes persist, or even re-emerge months after the incident (Sales, Baum, and Shore, 1984). These findings imply that the recovery process may not be as linear as is sometimes believed.

The emotional consequences of crime and victimization are not restricted to victims. It has also been argued that members of offenders' families often experience considerable pain and anguish as they attempt to make sense of the offender's actions (May, 1999). Self-help and counselling groups have been established to help offenders' families cope with the social stigma that derives from being related to an offender. Through their engagement in such groups, members of offenders' families strive to be understood as "the other victims of crime" (Howarth and Rock, 2000).

BEHAVIOURAL CONSEQUENCES

Some of the behaviours that result from victimization are directly related to physical injuries or economic losses. For example, victims may need to take time off work for medical care or to repair and replace property. The 1999 GSS found that a significant number of violent crime victims found it difficult to engage in important life activities as a result of the incident. Around 25 percent of victims of violence found it difficult to carry out their main activity for a variety of reasons, ranging from the need to seek medical attention to the need to consult with insurance agents. Of those who experienced such disruptions, 41 percent reported that it was just for one day; another 40 percent were affected for between two and seven days; 8 percent reported being affected for between eight and fourteen days (Besserer and Trainor, 2000).

Avoidance behaviour

Behaviour by which victims seek to distance themselves from the kinds of people or situations they perceive as dangerous.

Victims exhibit a variety of behavioural reactions to crime; many of these are intended to make them safer. A common response is **avoidance behaviour**—that is, victims seek to distance themselves from the kinds of people or situations they perceive as dangerous (DuBow, McCabe, and Kaplan, 1979). At an extreme this may involve changing residences or neighbourhoods (Dugan, 1999). Victims may also try to fortify their homes by installing new locks or an alarm system, or they may purchase firearms or enrol in a self-defence course. Ironically, victims who engage in these behaviours are often less likely than others to feel safer as a result (Lurigio, 1987).

Victims also seek help from others. As we noted in Chapter 1, a common response (although less common than many think) is to contact the police. It seems that victims are most likely to do this when they see some practical or tangible reason for it. But even before they contact the police, they often contact friends or family members for advice. Sometimes the victim isn't sure the event was a crime, or that it was serious enough to warrant police intervention. Friends and family members can help clarify matters by reminding the victim of standards against which the event can be judged (Greenberg, Ruback, and Westcott, 1984).

This information-seeking behaviour has two important implications. *First*, it helps explain why—according to some research—victims often wait well over an hour after an incident before notifying the police (Greenberg, Ruback, and Westcott, 1984). *Second*, it demonstrates that the victim's decision is not necessarily an individual one; it often reflects the social influence of others to whom the victim has access immediately following the crime (Greenberg, Ruback, and Westcott, 1984).

In the longer term, victims may engage in some type of collective participation (DuBow, McCabe, and Kaplan, 1979). The most obvious form this takes is membership in a community crime prevention group such as **Neighbourhood Watch** (Rosenbaum, 1988). Or they may involve themselves in one of the many generic or more specialized victims' groups that have proliferated in recent decades (Weed, 1995).

Neighbourhood Watch
A community crime prevention program in which residents monitor neighourhood life and exert guardianship over each other's property.

A common reaction is to tell others the story of the crime (Wachs, 1988). The 1999 GSS found that victims of violence are likely to turn to family members, friends, and co-workers to discuss what happened (Besserer and Trainor, 2000). Lejeune and Alex (1973) reported that this is a near-universal tendency among mugging victims. They observed as well that listeners are as interested in hearing the story as the victim is in telling it. Telling the story of one's victimization may have important therapeutic value: when others react in supportive ways or tell similar stories, the victim may find it easier to make sense of the event and to place it in perspective.

The behavioural reactions of victims can be easily overstated, because most people are familiar with someone who has responded to crime in perhaps an extreme manner. But generally speaking, most crime victims do not make major or basic lifestyle changes (Hindelang, Gottfredson, and Garofalo, 1978). Our lifestyles are a product of our family responsibilities and occupational commitments, so they can't be changed easily.

There is a tendency in the criminological literature to think about such changes as **costs of victimization** that limit behaviour; yet victimization can also have benefits. As Skogan (1987) points out, when people change their

Costs of victimization
Losses of a physical, financial, emotional, and social nature that can be attributed to the victimization experience.

BOX 7.3

Assessing the Long-Term Costs of Victimization

Research on the impact of victimization on victims has tended to focus on short-term consequences. With respect to financial costs, for instance, victimization researchers have typically equated the cost of being victimized with whatever "out-of-pocket" expenses can be directly attributed to the incident.

But it is obvious that victimization has longer-term effects. This has been powerfully demonstrated by research undertaken by Ross Macmillan (2000). Through a sophisticated analysis of Canadian and American victimization data, Macmillan estimated income losses over the life cycle that are associated with violent victimization.

His findings included the following:

- The income losses attributable to violent victimization are "age graded." The greatest costs are associated with victimization incidents that occur in adolescence.
- Criminal violence affects earnings in later life by disrupting processes of educational and occupational attainment. In other words, violent victimization seems to affect the commitment to and effort put into education; it also affects academic performance. A major result of decreased educational attainment is a reduction in the status of the occupations the affected individual enters in young adulthood.
- According to data from the 1993 GSS, lifetime loss in income from a violent victimization that occurs in adolescence is a remarkable $237,200. The expected income loss from sexual assault is $241,600, from robbery $262,400, and from assault $212,800.
- The costs of criminal victimization are not borne equally by all in society. The poor and the young have especially high levels of victimization and are most likely to be affected by the costs of victimization. In this way, criminal victimization can be understood as reinforcing the marginalization of the socially and economically disadvantaged.

behaviour in other circumstances in response to negative experiences, we call this "learning." To the degree that such learning makes people less vulnerable without dramatically affecting their quality of life, it may be beneficial.

COPING WITH THE COSTS OF VICTIMIZATION

Victims differ in their ability to cope with the costs of criminal victimization (Resick, 1987; Sales, Baum, and Shore, 1984; Skogan, 1987). Victims who are isolated from supportive others may find it more difficult to manage the stresses associated with crime than those whose families and friends are able to lend emotional or practical assistance. People with more economic resources may find it less difficult to absorb economic losses and to replace stolen or damaged property. Also important are prior psychological functioning and previous history as a victim. Individuals who are already suffering from depression may respond to criminal victimization more negatively; so may those who have already been victimized by crime.

One way that victims try to cope with the costs of victimization is by reevaluating the event (Taylor, Wood, and Lichtman, 1983). In so doing, they redefine the situation to make it less threatening to their self-esteem or their future plans. In short, they heed the various cultural adages that advise us to "look on the bright side." Taylor and colleagues suggest that victims follow a number of evaluative strategies to achieve this. For instance, they may compare themselves with less fortunate others. Provided one chooses the criteria for comparison carefully, one can always find examples of people who have lost more or suffered more. Alternatively, despite suffering or loss, the victim may try to discover ways in which the event was beneficial. That is, the victim may say, "I sure learned my lesson" or "I won't ever get myself into that situation again."

Agnew (1985b) suggests that this process resembles the neutralization process that Matza and Sykes (1961) described in their explanation of why offenders commit crime. However, instead of convincing themselves that a particular criminal act was not really wrong—which is what offenders do—victims try to convince themselves that particular acts of victimization were not really harmful. For instance, they may invoke a "denial of injury" in order to minimize the harm caused. Or they may articulate a "denial of responsibility" to minimize the guilt or shame that accompanies self-blame. These neutralizations, claims Agnew, allow victims to avoid feelings of fear and other negative emotions that sometimes accompany criminal victimization.

OFFENDER OUTCOMES: SOCIAL STIGMA AND LABELLING

In a simple way, a victim's loss is often an offender's gain. Losing cash or property in a theft, or losing a physical encounter, can translate into wins for the offender. Of course, the offender risks apprehension and punishment, but as we noted in previous chapters, these risks are often slight. Proponents of punishment or rehabilitation contend that when offenders are apprehended, the criminal justice system can play an important role in discouraging further

Labelling theory
The theory that frustration created by particular social arrangements, such as identifying a person as a criminal, may motivate criminal behaviour.

offending. A school of thought known as **labelling theory** proposes a markedly different view of how the frustration created by particular social arrangements can motivate criminal behaviour (Becker, 1963; Gibbs, 1966; Kitsuse, 1962; Rubington and Weinberg, 1987). Labelling theorists maintain that the social response to minor and sporadic criminal acts can create conditions that increase the likelihood of more serious patterns of criminality.

Labelling theorists strongly emphasize how the responses of the police and the criminal justice system to people identified as offenders create problems for those who must bear the label of "criminal." Such a label can be understood as a form of stigma that makes it difficult for those on whom it has been imposed to lead normal lives. An individual who has been labelled a criminal, thief, delinquent, or troublemaker often finds it difficult to obtain employment or to maintain friendships with others, who tend to react to the powerful emotional content of the label. People who have been labelled can easily become frustrated by their personal circumstances, or come to perceive as hypocritical the responses of those who condemn their conduct. Increasingly, legitimate associations become less available, and illegitimate associations more so.

WHAT IS IT?

LABELLING

A label is a form of stigma that makes it difficult for those on whom it has been imposed to lead normal lives. An individual who has been labelled a criminal, thief, delinquent, or troublemaker often finds it difficult to obtain employment or to maintain friendships with others, who tend to react to the powerful emotional content of the label. People who have been labelled can easily become frustrated by their personal circumstances, or come to perceive as hypocritical the responses of those who condemn their conduct. Increasingly, legitimate associations become less available, and illegitimate associations more so.

Secondary deviance
The idea that the effect of feedback that consistently provides the message that one is a disreputable person may eventually lead to the acceptance of the definition.

Self-fulfilling prophecy
The theory that people who are perceived as beyond redemption will come to act as if they are.

Labelling theorists contend that societal reactions have a strong impact on how labelled people see themselves. Feedback that consistently sends the message that one is a disreputable person may eventually lead to acceptance of that definition. This can create a criminal self-identity—that is, **secondary deviance** (Lemert, 1951). The problems created by the labelling process increase the likelihood that the labelled person will develop a stable pattern of criminal behaviour. Labelling theory describes a kind of **self-fulfilling prophecy**: people who are treated as if they are beyond redemption will come to act as if they are. The police and other criminal justice agencies are supposed to reduce involvement in crime; labelling theory suggests that they very often have the opposite effect.

Criminologists have criticized the labelling approach for redirecting attention from the individual onto the agencies of social control, and for failing to develop a body of supporting empirical evidence (Gove, 1975; Sagarin, 1975; Wellford, 1975).

SOCIAL OUTCOMES: INDIVIDUAL, ORGANIZATIONAL, AND GOVERNMENTAL RESPONSES

Crimes have implications not only for those who are directly involved but also for others who have only secondhand knowledge of these events. So criminologists also consider how the public, government officials, and various private interests respond to crime.

PUBLIC FEAR OF CRIME

Researchers have been investigating public reactions to crime since the early 1970s. Much of this research has focused on the fear of crime. Surveys indicate that serious crime is statistically rare and that the fear of becoming the victim of a serious crime is much more pervasive. Fear of crime may now be as serious a problem as crime itself. Journalists have taken notice of this, and have covered this issue extensively in recent years.

WHAT IS THE FEAR OF CRIME?

Even though the term **fear of crime** is widely used in the popular press and social scientific literature, there is little consensus as to what it means. Both *fear* and *crime* are complicated terms. *Fear* typically suggests an emotional or physiological reaction. We recognize that we are afraid when our mouths go dry, our hearts begin to pump, and the blood drains from our faces. Criminologists do not employ the term in the same way; after all, they rarely have access to people when they are actually afraid (Mirrlees-Black, Mayhew, and Percy, 1996).

Fear of crime
A concern or anxiety relating to the possibility of criminal victimization and usually assessed in social research through the measurement of attitudes or reported behaviours.

Most research on the fear of crime comes from surveys (often victimization surveys) that ask members of the public about their beliefs or perceptions regarding crime. These surveys usually treat fear as an attitude or a perception rather than as an emotion. Also, criminologists usually treat fear as a personal rather than an altruistic matter, in the sense that they ask people about their worries regarding their own safety or the safety of their property. However, Warr (1991) contends that people often are fearful not for their own safety but for the safety of other family members. For instance, parents may express less fear if asked about their own safety but more fear if asked about the safety of their children.

Skogan (1993) suggests that at least four distinct meanings of fear are reflected in the research literature. The first of these, *concern*, focuses on the extent to which people understand crime to be a serious problem in their communities. Concern is a judgment that people make about the frequency and seriousness of crime in the local environment. Using this definition, it is possible for a person to be concerned about crime without being personally fearful (Furstenberg, 1971).

WHAT IS IT?

FEAR OF CRIME

Fear is usually treated as an attitude or a perception rather than as an emotion. Also, criminologists usually treat fear as a personal rather than an altruistic matter, in the sense that they ask people about their worries regarding their own safety or the safety of their property. However, people often are fearful not for their own safety but for the safety of other family members.

A second definition of fear emphasizes *risk*. Research that uses this definition employs questions asking respondents how likely they think it is that they will become victims of crime at some point in the future. This definition does not include an explicit emotional dimension; however, the assumption is that people who perceive their chances of being a victim of crime to be high will be more afraid.

Fear can also be understood in terms of a *threat*. This definition stresses the potential for harm that people believe crime holds for them. Respondents to surveys are often asked questions along the lines of "How safe do you feel walking alone in your neighbourhood at night? Would you say you feel very safe, reasonably safe, somewhat unsafe, or very unsafe?" Questions like this are asking people how likely they think it is they would be harmed if they were to expose themselves to risk.

Finally, fear can be defined in terms of *behaviour*. Surveys may ask people not how they feel about their safety or how likely they are to be subject to harm, but about what they do (or say they do) in response to crime. For example, respondents may be asked whether they engage in "avoidance behaviour," or about the precautions they take to protect themselves from crime.

In this research it is not only the concept of fear that is problematic but also the concept of crime. Though it is rarely stated explicitly, the kinds of crime to which reference is made are those of a direct, predatory nature. Respondents are usually asked how much they worry about crimes such as robbery or burglary, or how safe they feel on neighbourhood streets. Less often are they asked how much they fear corporate crime or violence in the family (Warr and Stafford, 1983).

PATTERNS IN FEAR

The term *public fear of crime* encourages the view that fear is a problem evenly shared by all members of society (Miethe, 1995). However, as in the case of other social problems, the burden of fear falls more heavily on some than others. Two broad sets of factors have been shown to be related to differences in the fear of crime. One set relates to characteristics of individuals, the other to characteristics of their social environments.

Both sets of factors are important to a comprehensive understanding of fear of crime. The individual-level factors—gender, age, and socioeconomic or minority status—are often interpreted as measures of social and physical vulnerability. They explain why some people—women, the aged, the poor, racial minorities—may feel especially susceptible to criminal victimization or less able to cope with the consequences of victimization. In contrast, the environmental factors describe dangers in the environment itself. When crime rates are higher, when public order is tenuous, and when people learn about local crime by talking to friends and neighbours, they define their environments as less safe.

INDIVIDUAL-LEVEL FACTORS

GENDER

Of all the factors that have been related to fear of crime, the strongest effects are associated with gender (Stanko, 1995). Women are much more likely than men to express anxiety about crime (Johnson, 1996; LaGrange and Ferraro, 1989; Skogan and Maxfield, 1981). For one thing, women are more likely to be smaller and less physically capable than the typical male offender, and to perceive themselves that way (Gordon and Riger, 1989). These physical differences are reinforced by traditional gender-role socialization processes that encourage women to think of themselves as vulnerable to a variety of forms of danger and that discourage them from developing assertive methods for dealing with threatening behaviour (Sacco, 1990).

Another important factor explaining the higher levels of fear among women is the specific fear of rape (Gordon and Riger, 1989; Johnson, 1996). Men are unlikely to express worry about being victimized sexually; yet this crime seems to be at the core of women's fears for their personal safety. Warr (1985) contends that women see rape as both serious in its consequences and frequent in its occurrence. They tend to estimate the risks of rape as relatively high and the consequences as relatively severe, and this has a significant impact on their fear.

Also according to Warr, rape is a "perceptually contemporaneous offence." In other words, it can occur not only as an isolated act but also in connection with other crimes such as robbery and burglary. In other words, these crimes are even more fear-provoking for women because they are associated with sexual danger.

AGE

It is widely believed that fear of crime is especially prevalent among the elderly. Despite their lower victimization rates, older people tend to express greater concern for their personal safety (Baldassare, 1986; Garofalo, 1981b; Skogan and Maxfield, 1981; Yin, 1980). Journalists, policymakers, and many social scientists often contend that their greater fear has a basis in reality (Cook and Skogan, 1990; Fattah and Sacco, 1989).

It can be argued that older people suffer high levels of fear of crime for much the same reasons women do. Both groups tend to be less physically able, and to have fewer resources for coping with the threat of crime and the consequences of victimization (Yin, 1980).

Many researchers have challenged the idea that the elderly are more afraid of crime (Moeller, 1989; St. John and Heald-Moore, 1996; Yin, 1982). LaGrange and Ferraro (1987) contend that researchers who have found that fear increases in old age tend to measure fear by asking questions about feelings of safety while on the street alone at night. They maintain that though older people are more likely to give answers indicating anxiety about their personal safety, this question really has nothing to do with the day-to-day lives of most older people. For a variety of reasons relating to health, finances, and general lifestyle, older people do not typically find themselves walking alone on the street at night. This means that their answers are more hypothetical than descriptive of the everyday realities of the elderly.

Data from the 1999 GSS show that for three different measures of fear, large differences exist between men and women; across age groups the differences are much smaller and less consistent (see Table 7.2).

RACE AND INCOME

Personal safety is a greater problem for low-income individuals and for visible minorities (Miethe, 1995; Skogan and Maxfield, 1981; Will and McGrath, 1995). The differences are not as great as for gender, but they are significant. Two factors have been advanced to explain why. *First,* income and race are

TABLE 7.2

FEAR OF CRIME BY SEX AND AGE, 1999 GSS

	Feel somewhat or very worried when waiting for or using public transportation after dark	Feel somewhat or worried when home alone in the evening or after dark	Feel somewhat or unsafe when walking alone in my area after dark
Gender			
Females	64%	29%	18%
Males	29	12	6
Age			
15–24	44	19	13
25–44	47	22	10
45–64	48	20	11
65+	37	17	10

*Excludes people who do not engage in these activities.

Source: Sandra Besserer and Catherine Trainor (2000), "Criminal Victimization in Canada, 1999," *Juristat* 20 (10): 14. Used by permission of Statistics Canada.

indicators of access to resources. Economic and racial minorities are often less able to take taxis, install alarm systems, and take other measures that might make them feel safer. *Second*, in many cities there are very clear patterns of racial and economic segregation, and many neighbourhoods with large numbers of low-income or minority residents are also neighbourhoods with very high rates of crime. This means that at the level of individuals, measures of race and income are related to fear because they are "proxy" measures for neighbourhood of residence.

ENVIRONMENTAL FACTORS

We are more likely to feel anxious about our personal safety in some settings than others. Warr (1990) has shown that people are more afraid of crime when they are alone, when they are in an unfamiliar setting, and when it is dark. Other research has shown that people are more likely to feel safe in settings that are open to observation, that offer no hiding places for potential offenders, and that would be easy to escape if necessary (Fisher and Nasar, 1995). All of this alerts us to the fact that fear is not just a social psychological characteristic that some people have and other people do not have; it is also a response to the social contexts in which we find ourselves.

THE COMMUNITY SETTING

Generally speaking, fear of crime is a more significant problem in big cities than in small towns (Baumer, 1978; Garofalo, 1981b; Moeller, 1989). The simple explanation for this is that big cities have higher crime rates; urbanites' greater fear is a rational response to the realities of big-city crime.

But this is not necessarily the whole story. The urban sociologist Claude Fischer (1981) suggested that fear is a more significant problem in cities because the "public world of city life" routinely presents residents with situations that increase their feelings of insecurity. As we travel through urban public places, we are likely to encounter people who are strangers not only in the personal sense but also in a cultural sense. Because cities are hotbeds of lifestyle innovation, Fischer argues, we always run the risk of finding ourselves on the street, in an elevator, or on a subway platform with people whose style of dress or public behaviour strikes us as weird or threatening. Though many of the strangers we encounter are not criminals or delinquents, our unfamiliarity with groups whose lifestyles differ dramatically from our own may undermine our sense of security in cities.

Within communities, levels of fear vary from one neighbourhood to another. Some of this is of course due to differences in crime rates (Miethe and Lee, 1984). Those who live in neighbourhoods where the levels of crime are higher are more likely to be concerned about their personal safety and the safety of their property.

Levels of fear in a given neighbourhood are also affected by "social disorder" or **incivility** (LaGrange, Ferraro, and Supancic, 1992; May and Dunaway, 2000; Skogan, 1990b). These terms refer to those low-level breaches of the social order that, while not strictly criminal, often seem to be related to a sense of unease. There are two basic types of incivilities. *Physical incivilities* include conditions such as abandoned buildings, unkempt residences, and strewn trash and litter. *Social incivilities* include public drinking or drug use, panhandlers, and groups of noisy youths. In a study of reactions to disorder in 40 neighbourhoods, Skogan (1990b) found that although disorder tends to be a problem where crime is also a problem, disorder intensifies the levels of fear that are based on the local crime rate.

Why does social disorder promote fear of crime? The usual answer is that it signals that local social controls are breaking down. Typically, incivility is

Incivility
Physical conditions such as abandoned buildings and strewn trash, as well as social conditions such as public drinking or drug use.

BOX 7.4

Community Disorder

According to some researchers, including R. LaGrange and colleagues (1992) and Wesley Skogan (1990b), public concern about disorder is usually gauged by asking respondents to indicate how serious a problem various types of disorder are in their neighbourhoods. Typically, people are asked about disorders such as the following:

- trash and litter lying around
- dogs barking loudly or being a nuisance
- inconsiderate or disruptive behaviour
- graffiti on sidewalks and walls
- vacant houses and unkept lots
- unsupervised youths
- noisy neighbours
- people drunk or high on drugs in public
- abandoned car parts lying around
- kids or adults trespassing in people's yards

seen as an indication that people in the neighbourhood don't care much about themselves or their community. The subtext here is that neighbourhoods that can tolerate incivility can also tolerate more serious threats to person or property (Kelling and Coles, 1996).

THE INFORMATION ENVIRONMENT

Fear of crime is a reaction to both what we experience and what we see and hear. Since fear of crime is more pervasive than crime itself, it makes sense for us to ask what role various information sources play in promoting crime-related anxieties.

WHAT ARE THEY?

INCIVILITIES

Incivilities include physical conditions such as abandoned buildings, unkempt residences, and strewn trash and litter, and social conditions such as public drinking or drug use, panhandlers, and groups of noisy youths.

It seems reasonable to assume that the mass media do much to promote fear of crime (Heath and Gilbert, 1996). After all, crime figures prominently in both news and entertainment media, and Canadians are avid consumers of mass media (see Chapter 1).

Yet despite the apparent logic of this, researchers have had trouble establishing a clear link between people's media diets and their fear of crime (Doob and MacDonald, 1976; Heath and Gilbert, 1996; Sacco, 1995). This is partly because it is hard to research the issue: it is not always easy to determine what people learn from the mass media and what they learn from other sources (Doob, 1982). Most of us not only watch television news and read newspapers but also talk to friends or neighbours about what we hear and read.

Even when we take these limitations into account, the media's effects on fear of crime are not as strong as we might expect. It is too simplistic to argue that people respond in predetermined ways to media messages about crime. People approach the media with their own predispositions, personal histories, and beliefs about media credibility, and all of these affect how they interpret the information they receive (O'Keefe, 1984; Schlesinger et al., 1992).

Although we are heavy consumers of media content, what we learn does not necessarily have much relevance to our judgments about our personal safety. In fact, we seem to base our judgments far more on other sources. It is quite possible that the news about crime that moves through interpersonal channels in the form of gossip and rumour is more likely to induce fear than news that comes to us in broadcast or print form (Bursik and Grasmick, 1993; Skogan and Maxfield, 1981). For example, when we learn about crime by talking to our neighbours, we are learning about victims of whom we may have some personal knowledge. In these situations we cannot dismiss what we hear by telling ourselves that the victims are nameless and faceless and that they live somewhere else.

In comparison, the average crime story that we read about in the newspaper is stripped of much of its emotional content and is likely to involve victims who are much more anonymous. Moreover, the typical media crime story provides us with so little information about victims, offenders, or the circumstances of the crime that we learn relatively little that will help us assess the risks in our neighbourhoods, our workplaces, or anywhere else our daily routines take us (Gordon and Riger, 1989). Most crime news is "non-local" in character and thus not relevant to the judgments we need to make about the threats we face in local environments. Consistent with this view is the finding reported by some researchers that news coverage is likely to affect fear when the media give prominent treatment to random violent crimes that occur locally (Heath and Gilbert, 1996; Liska and Baccaglini, 1990).

COMMUNITY REACTIONS

What implications do individuals' reactions to crime have for their communities? Theorists have provided two general answers to this question. The first, derived from the pioneering French sociologist Emile Durkheim, suggests that public reactions to crime can make important contributions to the cohesion and stability of social life:

Crime brings together upright consciences and concentrates them. We have only to notice what happens, particularly in a small town, when some moral scandal has just been committed. [People] stop each other on the street, they visit each other, they seek to come together to talk of the event and to wax indignant in common (Durkheim, 1933: 102).

According to this perspective, crime shocks our sentiments and reaffirms our commitment to the common values the crime violated. Our communal opposition to crime unites us: we speak out against crime, we are more vigilant in exercising informal social control, we join concerned citizens' groups, we support the toughening of laws intended to control crime. The overall effect is to strengthen social integration, and to strengthen social control in such a way that crime rates decline or at least stabilize.

In sharp contrast, others have suggested that because crime generates fear, it is more likely to drive people apart (Conklin, 1975; Di Iulio, 1989; Goodstein and Shotland, 1982). John Conklin argues that when people are less afraid of crime, they are more likely to trust others and to think positively about their communities, and less likely to restrict their activities and reduce their social interactions with other community members. In contrast, when levels of fear are high, people are more likely to stay home at night and less likely to get to know or to be interested in their neighbours. Some may even be tempted to flee the community for a safer haven. Overall, then, crime does not build communities up as the Durkheimian model contends; rather, it undermines communities by weakening interpersonal ties.

This view implies that public reactions to crime weaken informal social controls. When the streets are empty and people stop caring what happens to their neighbours, potential offenders may feel freer to take advantage of criminal opportunities.

There is research to support both perspectives. But generally speaking, the argument that crime drives people apart seems to have more empirical validity (Skogan, 1981, 1990b). Note that the two arguments are not necessarily inconsistent with each other.

Liska and Warner (1991) apply the routine activities theory of Cohen and Felson (1979) to suggest why elements of both arguments are useful. They contend that the Durkheimian view is correct in claiming that public reactions to crime reassert social controls in ways that stabilize crime rates or push them down. However, their view of the process by which this happens is closer to the position taken by Conklin than to the one advanced by Durkheim.

BOX 7.5

Can Crime Cause Crime?

Some researchers have argued that public reactions to rising crime rates can amplify subsequent increases in crime rates. The central mechanism in this process is the breakdown of informal social control at the community level. Lynne Goodstein and Lance Shotland (1982) described the process by which crime rates spiral upward as follows:

> The cycle begins with actual increases in the crime rate or with the occurrence of one or several particularly noteworthy crimes. Such crimes might include an unsolved murder or a series of sexual assaults for which an offender has not been apprehended.

> In the next stage, information about these crimes and the threats that they pose to other members of the community is disseminated widely. People learn via the mass media or rumour networks that crimes are increasing and/or that even they might be at risk.

> As the information circulates, people begin to fear for their safety. This fear causes them to withdraw from community life. They stay home at night rather than go out and report that their enjoyment of the community has declined.

> As people withdraw from the community, the delicate web of social relations begins to break down, as do the various informal social controls that regulate conduct. Thus, as the streets become less populated, they are subject to less control because citizen surveillance of them is reduced.

> As the levels of community control decline, the levels of crime may be expected to rise; and as the levels of crime continue to rise, the cycle begins to repeat itself.

Goodstein and Shotland's argument is consistent with the theoretical view that crime is made more likely by the absence of controls that would check it. As the authors note, empirical evidence supports each of the individual linkages just described. What is less clear is the validity of the overall model, which has not been rigorously tested.

Routine activities theory emphasizes the role that opportunities play in the commission of crimes (see Chapter 6). Social patterns that separate people from their property and from their family members increase the opportunities for crime. Liska and Warner agree that public reactions to predatory crimes (such as robbery) keep people at home and away from strangers. Though this reduces their sense of community, it also allows them to exert greater guardianship over their persons and property. As this happens, opportunities for crime are decreased and greater control of crime is achieved.

More recently, Bellair (2000) has argued that the relationship between crime and informal social control is extremely complex. Robbery and stranger assault can reduce informal surveillance of the street; but at the same time, informal surveillance of the street can reduce the prevalence of robbery and stranger assault. In other words, the effects flow in both directions. Bellair also reports that though some crimes, such as robbery, may reduce the informal control that residents exert over the street, other crimes, such as break-and-enter, may increase these controls.

CLAIMSMAKING

Fear can strengthen the public's concerns about crime. People's reactions to crime can be determined by the actions of special interest groups. Some writers refer to the processes by which laws are passed and legal reforms are initiated as **claimsmaking** (Best, 1995; Loseke, 2000; Spector and Kitsuse, 1977). In the claimsmaking process, a group offers assertions about the existence of some problem that requires a policy solution. It then attempts to gain public support for its claims and to attract the attention of public officials and the mass media. Becker (1963) describes the claimsmaker as a "moral entrepreneur" who is best exemplified by the crusading reformer. According to Becker there is "some evil which profoundly disturbs" these reformers, who believe that "nothing can be right in the world until rules are made to correct it" (147–8).

Claimsmaking
The making of assertions about the existence of some problem that requires a policy solution.

In the early stages, claims may reflect a narrow set of relatively private interests (Pfuhl, 1986; Ross and Staines, 1972). Claimsmakers may see themselves as representing those who have been victimized by some condition, or who feel directly threatened by it (Weeks et al., 1986). But claims can also be issued by agencies seeking to expand their mandates, or by professional groups seeking to enhance their status. Researchers have suggested that the pressure for the passage of computer crime laws is largely the result of the crusading efforts of computer crime "experts," who by publicizing the issue gain recognition for themselves and their work (Hollinger and Lanza-Kaduce, 1988).

Best (1990) asserts that with respect to legislative and other policymaking bodies, claimsmakers can be either insiders or outsiders. Insiders include political lobbyists, representa-

WHAT DOES IT MEAN?

CLAIMSMAKER

The claimsmaker is a "moral entrepreneur," best exemplified by the crusading reformer who believes that rules must be formulated to combat the evil in the world.

tives of powerful professional organizations, and members of government, all of whom have relatively direct access to those who make public policy. In contrast, outsiders have no direct access and must rely more heavily on taking their message directly to the public. In so doing, outsiders hope to enlist members in their cause. How a given claimsmaking process unfolds depends on several factors, two of which require particular attention.

The *first* involves the amount of opposition that claimsmakers encounter in their attempts to convince the public and policymakers that a particular remedy is necessary. Some kinds of claimsmaking are more adversarial than others. Issues that do not have an adversarial quality are sometimes referred to as **valence issues**. Child abuse, crimes against the elderly, and computer crime are valence issues, in the sense that most people would readily agree that they are problems requiring public intervention. In contrast, efforts by claimsmakers to organize public support for interventions directed against abortion or pornography are often met by resistance or by counterdefinitions of what the problem really is (Ross and Staines, 1972).

A *second* factor affecting claimsmaking is the wider social context in which the process unfolds. Prevailing social values and beliefs can facilitate or hinder claimsmaking. Based on an analysis of many case studies of criminalization, Hagan (1980) argued that successful claimsmakers have usually appealed effectively to dominant cultural values. For example, the social problem of crime against the elderly emerged in the 1970s because a "ripe issue climate" existed in which rising crime, the needs of crime victims, and the needs of the elderly were already seen as important problems.

Criminalization is clearly a form of claimsmaking, yet the passage of a law is not always enough to satisfy claimsmakers. Much contemporary claimsmaking about crime is directed toward changing how behaviour that has already been criminalized is treated by the criminal justice system. The recognition in recent years that crimes against women, victims' rights, impaired driving, crimes against the elderly, stalking, and hate crime are issues requiring more vigorous enforcement or innovative approaches attests to the validity of this observation (Best, 1999).

In general, when we understand responses to crime as the product of claimsmaking, conflict, and power (rather than of social consensus), this alerts us to the biases of these responses. This in turn casts doubt on the value of approaches that characterize the law as a neutral arbiter that can be understood without reference to the societies that produced it.

Valence issues

Issues that do not have an adversarial quality.

EXTREME REACTIONS: THE MORAL PANIC

Public reactions to crime can generally be characterized as subtle and routine (Hindelang, Gottfredson, and Garofalo, 1978). Typically, crime dominates neither our personal nor our public agendas. Sometimes, however, the media, the government, and members of the public respond to crime in a much more intense fashion. The sociologist Stanley Cohen (1972) used the term **moral panic** to describe such episodes. Goode and Ben-Yehuda (1994) explain:

> During the moral panic, the behaviour of some members of a society is thought to be so problematic to others, the evil they do, or are thought to do is felt to be so wounding to the substance and fabric of the body social that serious steps must be taken to control the behaviour, punish the perpetrators and repair the damage. The threat this evil presumably poses is felt to represent a crisis for that society: something must be done about it and something must be done now; if steps are not taken immediately, or soon, we will suffer even graver consequences. The sentiment generated or stirred up by this threat can be referred to as a kind of fever; it can be characterized by heightened emotion, fear, dread, anxiety, hostility and a strong feeling of righteousness (31).

Moral panic
The behaviour of some members of society is seen as so problematic, evil, or harmful to the society that it becomes a social imperative to control the behaviour, punish the offenders, and repair the damage (e.g., the Great European Witch Hunts).

According to Goode and Ben-Yehuda, moral panics have several distinguishing characteristics:

- A heightened concern over some behaviour or the group that is thought to be responsible for it.
- An increase in hostility toward the individuals in question.
- A substantial or widespread consensus regarding the seriousness and the nature of the problem.
- A public reaction that seems out of proportion to the size of the problem.
- A volatile character such that panics emerge and subside rather suddenly.

In recent years we have witnessed several episodes that could be described in these terms. The social response to illegal drugs (Reinarman and Levine, 1989), serial killers (Jenkins, 1994), child abduction (Best, 1988), and random violence (Best, 1999) provide illustrations of this concept.

One clear example of moral panic that has attracted the attention of several researchers is the satanic crime scare that emerged as a visible public issue in the 1980s (Richardson, Best, and Bromley, 1991; Victor, 1993). Late in the decade it was argued on several fronts that North America was in the midst of a serious crime wave resulting from the conspiratorial actions of thousands of satanic cult members. The allegations included claims about graveyard desecrations, the molestation of children in day care centres, the satanic involvement of serial killers such as the Son of Sam, the use of fantasy role-playing games to recruit teen satanists, the covert actions of business leaders active in satanic worship, and police and government cover-ups of evidence that could expose the conspiracy (Richardson et al., 1991; Jenkins, 1992; Jenkins and Meier-Katkin, 1992; Victor, 1993).

WHAT IS IT?

MORAL PANIC

"During the moral panic, the behaviour of some members of a society is thought to be so problematic to others, the evil they do, or are thought to do is felt to be so wounding to the substance and fabric of the body social that serious steps must be taken to control the behaviour, punish the perpetrators and repair the damage" (Goode and Ben-Yehuda, 1994).

The claims were promoted in several ways by several groups. The bizarre and sensationalist nature of the claims made them an attractive topic for afternoon talk shows and other "tabloid television" programs as well as for "legitimate" news organizations. A watershed event in this respect was the 1988 broadcast of an American TV special on satanic crime, hosted by Geraldo Rivera. The media fascination with these allegations was reinforced by a developing therapeutic community that claimed to have uncovered clinical evidence of the effects of satanic abuse and that promised effective treatment. Also, many police departments developed units to fight occult crime, and the policing of satanic activity became a new law enforcement specialization (Hicks, 1991).

Careful analyses of these claims showed that they lacked substance (Bromley, 1991). Supporting "evidence" was at best ambiguous and at worst nonexistent. Moreover, the claims often defied logic and strained credibility. Still, the overriding belief that satanists often posed as "respectable" members of society allowed those caught up in the panic to discount critics—because, of course, they could be satanic conspirators as well.

According to Jenkins and Meier-Katkin (1992), the satanic crime issue was rooted in the political concerns of the fundamentalist religious right. The issue was framed and promoted in a way that reflected the concerns of Christian fundamentalists at a time when this movement was undergoing rapid expansion.

According to Goode and Ben-Yehuda (1994), three theories can be used to explain the development of moral panics. The first, the **grassroots model**, views these panics as originating in the mood of the public. The concerns

Grassroots model
Views moral panics as originating in the mood of the public.

expressed by the mass media and by politicians are a reaction to public sentiment, not the cause of it.

A second theory, the **elite-engineered model**, argues that moral panics are
deliberate attempts by economic or political elites to promote public concern
about some issue that does not involve their interests. Moral panics are a
means of manipulating consciousness; elites resort to them to divert attention
from real social problems, the solutions to which might undermine their
interests.

The third perspective, and the most common, is **interest-group theory**.
Unlike the elite-engineered model, this perspective does not see the power or
resources that create moral panics as narrowly concentrated in the hands of a
small group. Instead, power is understood as more diffuse and more plural-
istic. The implication is that moral panics are set in motion by the actions of
politicians, crusading journalists, or professional associations.

Goode and Ben-Yehuda contend that the elite-engineered model does not
seem to explain most moral panics; the other two perspectives are of greater
value, especially in combination. The grassroots model allows us to see which
fears and concerns are available as the raw materials for moral panics; the
interest-group model allows us to understand how these raw materials are
intensified and mobilized.

SUMMARY

Victimization has financial, physical, emotional, and behavioural costs, and
the ability to adjust depends on a number of factors. Victims who are alone
may find it more difficult to manage the stresses associated with crime than
those whose families and friends are able to lend emotional or practical assistance. People with more economic resources may find it less difficult to absorb
economic losses and to replace stolen or damaged property. Also important
are prior psychological functioning and previous history as victims.
Individuals who are already suffering from depression may respond to criminal victimization more negatively; so may those who have already been victimized by crime.

Criminality also has consequences for the offender. Labelling theorists
emphasize how the responses of the police and the criminal justice system
create problems for those who must bear the label of "criminal." This label is
a form of stigma that makes it difficult for those people to lead normal lives.
An individual who is labelled a criminal, thief, delinquent, or troublemaker

Elite-engineered model
Argues that moral panics represent the deliberate attempt on
the part of the economic or political elite to promote public concern about some issue that does
not involve the public's interests.

Interest-group theory
Moral panics can be set in
motion by the actions of small
groups, such as politicians, crusading journalists, or professional associations.

often finds it difficult to obtain employment or to maintain friendships with others. People who have been labelled often feel frustrated by their personal circumstances, and view as hypocritical the response of those who condemn their conduct. Increasingly, legitimate associations become less available and illegitimate ones more so. Feedback that consistently sends the message that one is disreputable may eventually cause one to accept that definition. The overall effect of labelling, then, may be to create a criminal self-identity, or secondary deviance. In sum, the labelling process increases the likelihood that the labelled person will develop a stable pattern of criminal behaviour.

Fear of crime can increase in the aftermath of crime. *Fear* can be approached from at least four distinct angles: "concern," a judgment that people make about the frequency and seriousness of crime in the local environment; "risk," how likely people think it is that they will be victims of crime; "threat," the potential for harm that people believe crime holds for them; and "behaviour," which focuses on what people do (or say they do) in response to crime.

Public discussion of crime is often fuelled by special-interest groups pushing for stronger interventions by the police and the criminal justice system. These "claimsmakers" seek to get certain issues and problems on the forefront of the public agenda. Moral panic represents an extreme response: an intense reaction to crime problems and strident calls for action, even when the crimes being committed are few in number and not widely threatening to the public.

QUESTIONS FOR REVIEW AND DISCUSSION

1. Are there ways we can properly compensate crime victims for their losses? Should the offenders be involved in this process?

2. Can we use the label of "offender" in a positive way to help us rehabilitate offenders back into the community, or is it the case that once people offend they cannot be expected to behave normally again?

3. Is the fear of crime a realistic assessment of the risk of crime or a reflection of an overreaction to crime?

4. Do you agree that people should not change their behaviour in response to their fear of crime? Does not changing behaviour raise their chances of being victims, or does it keep the chances of victimization the same?

5. Can you identify different moral panics that have occurred and explain what the reactions to these panics have been?

INFOTRACT COLLEGE EDITION

Explore InfoTrac College Edition, your online university library, which includes hundreds of popular and scholarly journals in which you can find articles related to the topics in this chapter. Visit InfoTrac through your Web browser (**www.infotrac-college.com**), or through this book's Web site (**www.criminalevent-3e.nelson.com**).

WHAT'S ON THE WEB?

For chapter links and quizzes, check out the accompanying Web site at **www.criminalevent-3e.nelson.com**.

Part 3

Domains of Crime

Chapter 8
Crime and the Family and Household

In this chapter we focus on crime in the family and in the household. Our interest in criminal events in this domain centres on two substantive issues. The first is family violence: How do we make sense of the ways in which family members victimize each other? The second is crime against the household: many types of property crime can be understood as crimes in which the household unit is the victim.

INTRODUCTION

In Part Two we presented the theoretical perspectives that criminologists have used to explain criminal behaviour and the evolution of criminal events. Part Three focuses on how criminal events cluster in particular social domains. Chapters 9 and 10 are concerned with the leisure and work domains. In this chapter we analyze the domain of the family and the household.

In these chapters we discuss crime events in an integrated fashion, reviewing what we know from current research about offenders, victims, the circumstances in which these events occur, and so on. As we proceed we will alert you to the relevant theories that best explain the aspect of the event we are examining. Some theories, especially those that focus on motivation, are more useful when analyzing the precursors of crime events. Generally speaking, transactions are best understood from opportunity perspectives; the aftermath can be analyzed using insights drawn from theories about reactions to crime.

Throughout these chapters we encourage you to refer to the theories we have reviewed when thinking about the research findings being discussed. These theories constitute a road map for guiding us through the details of research findings; they help us identify commonalities in social behaviour, and they provide an understanding of the complexities of social interaction. We begin with a description of the family and household domain.

THE FAMILY AND THE HOUSEHOLD

In the literature of social science, the concept of family has several different meanings. A narrow definition views the family as "husband and wife, with or without never-married children of any age, living at home, or a lone parent with or without one or more never-married children at home" (Devereaux, 1990: 33). Broader definitions suggest that the concept of family includes any adult–child grouping (e.g., with lesbian or gay parents), and all intimate cohabitating or consciously committed support groups, including childless couples, communes, and networks of friends (Luxton, 1988).

In general, we understand the **family** as any relatively enduring pattern of social relationships through which domestic life is organized (Miller, 1990). Customarily, the family is seen as a distinct kind of intimate group in that its relationships are based on kinship. However, our definition of a family is as much a matter of culture as it is of **social organization**. For instance, our cultural view of the family as a unit of procreation leads many people to define a family in which the father is absent as a "broken" home (Wells and Rankin, 1986).

The **household** is generally understood as the social and physical setting within which family life is organized. Many surveys—such as those used in the census—lead us to equate families with households, but in so doing they may distort the empirical realities of family relations. Family relations often extend beyond the particular household. For instance, husbands and wives who are separated usually maintain separate households, although—perhaps because of dependent children—family relations may be sustained.

From a wealth of demographic data it is clear that family relations have changed a great deal in recent years (Almey, 2000; Le Bourdais, Neill, and Turcotte, 2000; Milan, 2000) For example:

- In the past few decades Canadians have seen a decrease in marriages, an increase in common law marriages, and a rise in the break-up of all types of unions.
- The instability of many common law arrangements and the rising rate of the dissolution of all types of unions suggest that more people will spend more time living alone or in the context of a larger number of short-term relationships.

Family and household domain
Enduring pattern of social relationships through which domestic life is organized.

Social organization
Coherence and continuity in the social environment, and rational co-operation among individuals and social institutions.

- In 1932 less than 0.5 percent of lone-parent families were the result of births to women without a partner. By 1996 the figure had risen to 22 percent.

- In 1994–95 nearly 9 percent of Canadian children under age 12 were living in a stepfamily.

- In 1997 there were 44 births for every 1,000 women in Canada aged 15 to 49—less than one-half the figure in 1959, when there were 116 births per 1,000 women in this age group.

- Canadian families now have fewer children living at home than they did in the past. This reflects both a decline in birth rates and an increase in the number of "empty nesters" and in the proportion of couples who have never had children.

- Couples are living longer and living better after their children leave than ever before.

Obviously, the Canadian family is changing. We are witnessing a move away from the conventional single-family unit toward variations that include single parents, multiple singles, and lone individuals. As a result of these varying structures, social relations within families are different from what we would have expected in the past. Also, more and more households are now occupied by the elderly, with the result that this group's dependence on their children is increasing.

FAMILY VIOLENCE

Our culture's tendency to idealize the family as the most intimate and nurturing of social groups long discouraged research into the extent to which violence is a part of family life (Miller, 1990). Only very gradually, in large part through the efforts of claimsmakers, has it come to be recognized that **family violence** is a social problem. In the 1960s the problem of child abuse emerged as a policy and research issue (Best, 1990; Nelson, 1984; Pfohl, 1977). In the 1970s wife abuse moved onto the agendas of researchers and criminal justice professionals (Loseke, 1989; Tierney, 1982). In the 1980s elder abuse came to be recognized as a form of family violence requiring attention (Leroux and Petrunik, 1990). To a far lesser degree, criminologists have also researched and theorized about other forms of family violence, including sibling violence (Pagelow, 1989) and adolescent violence toward parents (Agnew and Huguley, 1989).

Family violence
Child abuse, wife assault, elder abuse, and other forms of physical coercion that are contextualized by domestic living arrangements.

PRECURSORS

Any discussion of the preconditions of family violence must begin with a close look at the social organization of families, which contain within them the seeds out of which violent episodes grow.

CHARACTERISTICS OF FAMILIES

Interpersonal conflict theory has been used to shed light on how families run into the kinds of problems that lead to interpersonal violence. The following draws on insights provided by Gelles and Straus (1988).

First, family life provides the social setting for omnipresent conflict. Family members spend a great deal of time with one another and interact across a wide variety of dimensions. They also make a great number of decisions, from how to spend money and who will spend it, to where vacations will be spent and how they will be paid for, to who will prepare dinner and what dinner will be. The frequency of interactions like this, coupled with their intensity (often high), sets the stage for conflict. Also, because the family is a heterogeneous social grouping—that is, it includes within it males and females and people of different ages—it also provides the context for the playing out of gender or generational conflicts that have societal origins. Because family members usually know one another well, they are well aware of one another's weaknesses and vulnerabilities. This intimate knowledge makes it easier for conflicts to escalate into violent exchanges.

Second, family life is private life. What happens between family members often takes place behind closed doors. The private character of family life reflects a consensus view that families are different from other social groupings. The privacy of the family has structured how the police and the courts have responded to intrafamily violence. Neighbours, friends, and co-workers may not know about violence that occurs between family members, and even if they do know about it, they may regard it as none of their business. Moreover, the view that violence in the home is a family matter may be shared by the victims of violence. All of these factors reinforce the low visibility of violent conflict in the home and suggest the extent to which it is immune from many of the informal social controls that regulate violent behaviour among nonintimates. Those who take a feminist perspective argue that concerns for the privacy of the home simply shield the abuser from the sanctions of the criminal justice system. These concerns, they continue, reflect a bias toward maintaining power relationships in families that favour men, while ignoring the injustices perpetrated against women.

Third, cultural attitudes toward family violence are highly ambivalent. In the family, unlike in the workplace or other more formal settings, physical violence continues to be tolerated. This is most evident with respect to the spanking of children (Davis, 1994). Most parents believe that in certain circumstances it is perfectly appropriate for one family member to use physical force against another family member. This is not to suggest that spanking is necessarily abusive (although it well may be), but rather that rules about violence in the home differ from rules about violence in other social domains. Nor does the tolerance of physical violence extend to dependent children alone. In the recent past, violent behaviour by husbands against wives was tolerated in much the same way that parental violence toward children is tolerated now. Most people still continue to regard violence among siblings as normal and natural and—despite obvious physical consequences—not really a form of violence at all.

Fourth, the family is a hierarchical institution. In other words, some family members have more power than others (Sagrestano, Heavey, and Christensen, 1999). Obviously, parents are more powerful than children. As power control theory would predict, in traditional patriarchal family structures, which are characterized by the presence of an adult male authority figure, the husband is assumed to have the right to make decisions that are binding on other family members (Hagan, Gillis, and Simpson, 1985). Such authority relations, which are recognized by law, create a situation that allows those with more power to behave with relative impunity toward those who have less power. Also, the widespread support for existing authority relations allows those with power to believe they have a right to expect compliance from those who are less powerful. Violence can thus be understood as one effective means of gaining compliance.

INEQUALITY IN FAMILY RELATIONS

Consensus views of the family have been challenged by those who see that inequalities in family relations render some people more vulnerable than others to intrafamily violence. Our tendency to categorize the major forms of family violence as "wife assault," "child abuse," and "elder abuse" reflects this fact. The consequences of this "hierarchy of family violence" rest most heavily on the shoulders of women, who historically have been economically dependent on men. Not surprisingly, as both children and adults, females face a greater risk than males of violence from family members. Victimization surveys typically show that the overwhelming majority of victims of partner violence are women (Johnson, 1996; Tjaden and Thoennes, 1998a). These differences are most pronounced when more serious forms of violence are considered. Data from the Canadian General Social Survey (GSS) indicate that women are twice as likely as men to report being beaten by a partner, five times more likely to report being choked, and almost twice as likely to report being threatened with a gun or knife. Women are also more likely than men to report repeat victimizations and to report having experienced injury (Bunge, 2000a).

According to Locke (2000a), spousal homicides account for around 15 percent of all solved homicides. The average annual rate of homicide victimization in Canada between 1979 and 1988 was 10 wives for every 3 husbands per million couples. In other words, over that period more than three times as many wives (1,486) as husbands (433) were killed by spouses.

Some studies have found that within families, women may be as violent as men. This has led some observers to suggest that we need to focus more attention on the "battered husband" (Steinmetz, 1977–78). However, these studies do not indicate the context, motives, or consequences associated with the violent acts (DeKeseredy and Hinch, 1991; Johnson, 2000). By most measures of victimization—who initiates the violence, who uses violence offensively rather than defensively, and extent of injury—there is little question that women are more often and more seriously victimized (Johnson and Bunge, 2001). This is illustrated by the data in Figure 8.1.

Figure 8.1

Percentage of male and female victims reporting consequences and outcomes of spousal violence, Canadian GSS data, 1999

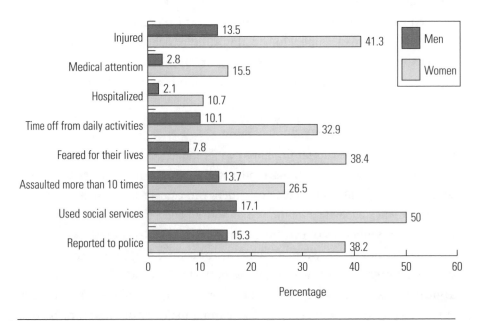

Source: H. Johnson and V.P. Bunge (2001). "Prevalence and Consequences of Spousal Assault in Canada." *Canadian Journal of Criminology* (January): p. 37. Used by permission of Statistics Canada.

Patterns of violence against children also reflect patterns of inequality and dependency. Family assaults of children—that is, assaults by either parents or siblings—are alarmingly common. According to UCR data, children are most likely to be victimized by acquaintances (52 percent of cases); however, they are also more likely to victimized by family members (24 percent) than by strangers (19 percent) (Locke, 2000b). Within families, parents are the most likely perpetrators of violence against children. In 1999, 66 percent of the victims of physical assault and 42 percent of the victims of sexual assault were victimized by parents (Locke, 2000b). Regardless of the type of abuse or the age of the child, children who are victims of parental abuse are most likely to be victimized by their fathers.

As with assault, most young homicide victims were killed by a parent—typically the father (Locke, 2000a). In 1998 there were 82 homicide victims in Canada under age 18; 72 percent of these were killed by a family member.

Another form of abuse that reflects hierarchy and dependency relationships is elder abuse, the victims of which may be infirm and reliant on a spouse or on an adult-child caregiver for the basic necessities of life (Pillemer and Finkelhor, 1988; Quinn and Tomita, 1986). Our understanding of elder abuse as a social problem is much less developed than for some other forms of family violence, in part because researchers have been interested in such crimes for a much shorter time.

In the 1999 GSS, elderly respondents reported very little physical or sexual violence. Around 1 percent reported such victimization at the hands of a spouse, an adult child, or a caregiver (Bunge, 2000b). However, around 7 percent reported some form of emotional or financial abuse, most often committed by a spouse. Available UCR data also suggest that rates of violent elder abuse are quite low. In 1999, 802 such cases were identified in a sample of data collected from 164 policing agencies. These victims were most likely to be victimized by adult children or spouses (Bunge, 2000b).

ISOLATION AND ECONOMIC STRESS

Conflict, privacy, ambivalent attitudes about violence, and inequality are not the only contributors to violence in the family. When families are isolated from the wider community of kin, friends, and neighbours, the negative effects of privacy can increase (Straus, 1990). In such circumstances, those who behave violently may become increasingly insensitive to prevailing community standards of appropriate conduct. Furthermore, they and their

---

BOX 8.1

Risk Factors for Wife Assault

Victimization surveys are an important source of information about the kinds of factors that put some people at higher risk of particular types of crime. The British Crime Survey (BCS)—like all victimization studies—shows that wife assault does not occur randomly and that various factors put some women at greater risk. These factors include:

- *Previous victimization.* Being victimized previously by wife assault increases the risk of subsequent victimization.
- *Separation.* Women who are separated from their partners are at much higher risk of domestic violence than women in other social statuses.
- *Gender inequality.* Egalitarian relationships place women at lower risk than relationships characterized by greater gender inequality.
- *Poverty.* Women in economically precarious households are at greater risk than women in more stable economic environments.
- *Youth.* As women become older, their risk of violent victimization in the home declines.

Source: S. Walby and A. Myhill, *Reducing Domestic Violence...What Works?* London: Home Office Research. Used by permission.

---

victims may lose or find less accessible the social supports that could be crucial in ending or preventing violence.

Economic stress can also contribute to violent conduct. The Violence Against Women Survey (VAWS) and several other studies have shown that low income is related to wife assault (Johnson, 2000). As strain theories would predict, a husband or father who is out of work may use violence to compensate for feelings of inadequacy that the perceived failure to play the breadwinner role may promote (Frieze and Browne, 1989). This interpretation is consistent with the widely reported finding that rates of family violence are generally higher among lower-income groups (Straus and Smith, 1990). Strain may also arise from noneconomic sources such as illness or the death of a loved one. In the case of child abuse or elder abuse, strain may originate in the demands of the caregiving experience itself (Fattah and Sacco, 1989).

TRANSACTIONS

In general terms, the location and timing of violent events reflect the importance of the precursors discussed earlier. Most violent events involving family members take place in the home. Typically, spousal homicides occur in private residences—most often in the home of the victim (Bunge, 2000a). The reason is fairly obvious: the home is where family members are most likely to confront one another in privacy.

Intrafamily violence is most likely to erupt in the evening or late at night. Arguments that begin in the early evening may turn violent if they are unresolved as the night wears on (Gelles and Straus, 1988). Also, the late-night and early-morning hours bring with them a reduction in the options available for resolving the matter without violence. It is too late to call a family member or to leave the house to visit a friend. Stressful events that fuel tensions or challenge parental or patriarchal authority increase the likelihood of a violent episode involving children. Despite the attention paid to the physical mistreatment of very young children, it seems that much family violence is directed at teenage children, whose various forms of adolescent rebellion may be viewed as requiring strict physical discipline (Pagelow, 1989).

Sometimes the factors that make a violent event more likely come into sharp relief. Gelles and Straus (1988) note that violent events occur with greater frequency during the Christmas and Easter holidays. At these times the sources of economic and noneconomic stress can be especially pronounced. Family members spend more time than usual together and may entertain unrealistically positive expectations about how others will behave. Also, family celebrations may involve drinking alcohol, and this in itself can make violence more likely.

PATTERNS OF FAMILY VIOLENCE

Perhaps the most distinctive characteristic of family violence is its repetitive and cyclical character. Many other forms of victimization result from chance encounters between victim and offender; in contrast, the intimate relationships in which family members are involved increase the probability that violent events will reoccur or escalate. Minor acts of violence may be self-reinforcing when those who engage in them come to see violence as an effective means of achieving compliance, and when the use of violence carries few sanctions (Johnson, 1996). Most victims try to resist the physical violence, but their resistance is more likely to be passive (reasoning with the offender, trying to get help) than active (Harlow, 1991). Silverman and Kennedy (1993) note that most spousal homicides are not the result of a sudden "blowup," but rather represent the culmination of serial violence, which is fuelled by drugs and alcohol, a lack of problem-solving skills, and the effects of long-standing quarrels and antagonisms. Many cases of family violence escalate into more serious forms of victimization. At a minimum, the physical violence that does occur is probably part of a much larger pattern involving a variety of forms of emotional and psychological mistreatment.

Increasingly, researchers are contending that we must focus on the various contexts in which different types of family violence occur. For example, with respect to partner violence, Johnson and Ferraro (2000) argue that several distinct subtypes can be identified. "Common couple violence" is not part of a general pattern and arises mainly in the context of a specific argument in which one of the partners responds violently to the other. In contrast, "intimate terrorism" involves violence as just one tactic in a general pattern of control. "Violent resistance" refers to the use of violence as a form of self-defence. Finally, "mutual violent control" suggests a pattern in which both husband and wife are controlling and violent in a situation that "could be viewed as two intimate terrorists battling for control" (Johnson and Ferraro, 2000: 950).

THE AFTERMATH

Family violence can have severe physical consequences and even result in death (Johnson and Ferraro, 2000). Some evidence suggests that violence in the home is more likely to result in injury than other types of violence (Harlow, 1991). This finding can be explained by the repetitive character of family violence and by the relatively limited ability of victims to escape violent encounters.

SHORT- AND LONG-TERM CONSEQUENCES OF FAMILY VIOLENCE

Violence has emotional and psychological as well as physical effects. Victims of violence in the home, like other victims of violence, experience many forms of fear, trauma, and stress (Bunge, 2000a; Kershaw et al., 2000). Indeed, violence in the home may be more likely than other forms of violence to produce these consequences since it usually occurs in environments that are assumed to be "safe" (Burgess, Holmstrom, and McCausland, 1977). Being victimized by an intimate can produce greater stress, since victims have to cope with the fact that the violence was at the hands of someone they trusted (Sales, Baum, and Shore, 1984).

Despite the seriousness of their injuries, victims may decline to seek medical aid so as to avoid having to explain to others the sources of the injury. The stigma of being a victim keeps many from seeking help. And those who do seek help may encounter emergency room personnel who are less than sympathetic. According to Kurz (1987), some ER staff describe abused wives as "AOBs" (alcohol on breath) and as troublesome people who deserve the predicament in which they find themselves.

For similar reasons, victims of family violence may decline to report the incident to the police (Klaus and Rand, 1984). For many female victims of spousal abuse, calling the police is a last resort, even when the violence is severe. Victimization surveys suggest that the victim's fear that the offender will seek revenge figures largely in the decision not to report. The victim may also fear that an arrest could lead to a loss of financial support.

In the past, police were reluctant to intervene in family situations, and when they did intervene they were often reluctant to remove the offender (most often the husband) from the situation. More and more, however, the police are enforcing the law as it applies to family violence (Fleury et al., 1998). Williams and Hawkins (1986) contend that applying sanctions to offenders may deter future offending. As we noted in our review of deterrence theories in Chapter 5, there is a strong stigma associated with arrest (Dutton et al., 1992).

There is also a strong sentiment among victim groups that more must be done to help victims of family violence. The number of safe houses is considered inadequate to meet the needs of women who feel at risk. At a more basic level, some claim, it is unfair that women have to flee their homes for safety's sake.

Providing resources such as shelters is helpful in managing the more serious forms of violence, but most of the time the day-to-day problems that people encounter do not come to the attention of the authorities. Many of these problems are, however, known to neighbours, friends, and others. We are becoming increasingly aware of situations of serial violence, eventually resulting in homicide, in which outsiders knew of the conflict for a long time but were either reluctant to intervene or were not taken seriously by authorities when they did attempt to intervene.

One important issue being considered by researchers interested in the aftermath of family violence is how violent behaviour by one family member promotes violent behaviour by others. The courts are growing more willing to accept the psychological consequences of violence as a defence for killing; in other words, they beginning to accept that we cannot always rely on the notion of rational behaviour when establishing why people act as they do. Arguments that an act was performed in the "heat of passion" have always been recognized when one partner kills another in a jealous rage. Yet the idea that violence begets violence is only now being taken seriously in the courts.

FAMILY VIOLENCE AND DELINQUENCY

The use of physical violence against children may increase the risk that they will themselves behave in violent or nonviolent criminal ways (Widom, 1995).

Physical punishment may induce conformity in children in the short run; in the longer term it may create the very problems it is intended to prevent (Straus, 1991).

How does physical violence against children increase the risk of delinquency? *First*, according to social control theorists, the bonds between juveniles and their parents (and other conformist models) provide a certain amount of insulation against involvement in delinquency. A high degree of parental attachment means that the parent is better able to teach the positive social skills that will facilitate an individual's success at school and in the workplace (Currie, 1985; Patterson and Dishion, 1985). Obviously, parental abuse may weaken this bond and lessen the degree of juvenile sensitivity to parental expectations of appropriate behaviour (Rankin and Wells, 1990).

Second, when a parent is abusive, the child or adolescent may seek to avoid contact. According to control theorists, delinquency is prevented when parents are able to monitor and supervise the behaviour of their children. So if children seek to avoid contact with an abusive parent, delinquency may well increase (Gottfredson and Hirschi, 1990; Thornberry, 1987).

Third, violent delinquency may be a form of acting out on the child's part (Agnew, 1985a). Children may run away from home or engage in other "escape crimes." Their resulting homelessness, combined with a lack of labour market skills, may increase the likelihood that they will make use of available delinquent or criminal opportunities to support themselves (McCarthy and Hagan, 1991). Also, they may behave violently toward classmates or other acquaintances as a way of expressing their frustration with the abusive home situation.

Fourth, growing up in a violent home may provide children with lessons in the use of violence as a means of achieving goals and controlling others (Hanson et al., 1997; Sprott and Doob, 2000). A child who witnesses spousal violence may come to see it as a legitimate means of resolving conflict (Fagan and Wexler, 1987; McCord, 1991). According to Hotaling, Straus, and Lincoln (1990), homes in which child assault or spousal assault occurs have higher rates of sibling violence and higher rates of violence by the dependent children against children outside of the home.

CRIMES AGAINST THE HOUSEHOLD

Crimes against households are very common in Canada. Table 8.1 shows the rates of the various forms of household victimization investigated in the 1999

BOX 8.2

Portrait of the Batterer

What are the characteristics of men who violently victimize their female partners? To answer this question, R. Karl Hanson and colleagues (1997) collected a range of information from almost 1,000 male residents of Edmonton. Using self-report data, the researchers compared men who did and men who did not behave violently toward their partners. The researchers summarized the profile of the batterer that emerged from the data as follows:

> The portrait of the abusive man suggested by this research is one of a lifestyle characterized by violence, anger and subjective distress. He is likely to have been raised in a violent home in which his parents hit him as well as each other. His own aggressive, disobedient behavior during his youth developed into Antisocial Personality Disorder as an adult. He has a long history of impulsive behavior including motor vehicle infractions, substance abuse and impulsive violence. He feels deeply dissatisfied with himself and his intimate relationships. His feelings of subjective distress are dominated by anger and hostility. He is worried about other men being interested in his partner, and, importantly, feels justified in using force to keep her in line (Hanson et al., 1997: 204).

GSS. The overall rate of reported household victimization is 218 incidents per 1,000 households.

According to UCR data, in 1999 roughly 1.3 million property crimes were reported to the police. Rates for this category, which includes but is not restricted to crimes against households, have been decreasing since 1991. A reduction in break-and-enters (which make up one-quarter of all property crimes reported to police) contributed to this decline (Tremblay, 2000).

PRECURSORS

The routine activities theory of predatory crime (see Chapter 6) explains such crimes in terms of how offenders encounter opportunities for offending. Modern lifestyles send people outside the home for long periods of time to work and pursue leisure activities; as a result, many households are left unoccupied and unguarded, which enhances their appeal as targets for crime.

Not all households are equally likely to be victimized. The patterns of household victimization as revealed by victimization surveys and UCR data suggest that opportunities for property crimes are structured. In general, rates of household crime are higher in urban than in nonurban areas (Cohen and Cantor, 1981; Maguire and Bennett, 1982). For example, according to the 1999

TABLE 8.1

HOUSEHOLD VICTIMIZATION RATES PER 1,000 HOUSEHOLDS, BY TYPE OF INCIDENT, URBAN/RURAL LOCATION, AND HOUSEHOLD INCOME, CANADA, 1999

Type of incident

	Break-and-enter/ attempt	Motor vehicle theft / attempt	Theft, household and property/ attempt	Vandalism	Total house-hold
Canada	48	41	62	56	218
Urban	52	44	66	70	232
Rural	32	30	49	53	164
Income groups					
<$15,000	53	27	57	46	183
15,000–29,999	52	36	67	65	220
30,000–39,999	50	43	79	73	245
40,000–59,999	50	51	73	72	247
60,000+	58	50	75	86	279

Source: S. Besserer and C. Trainor (2000), "Criminal Victimization in Canada, 1999," *Juristat 20*(10): p. 22.

GSS the rates of household theft were 66 and 49 incidents per 1,000 house-holds for urban and rural areas respectively (Besserer and Trainor, 2000). These differences may arise from the fact that formal and informal social controls are often less effective in urban centres. Alternatively, larger cities may provide a fertile breeding ground for criminal subcultures that provide an intricate network for distributing stolen goods.

Not all urban neighbourhoods face the same risk of household crime. Residents of socially disadvantaged areas may face greater risks than those who reside in more affluent areas (Evans, 1989; Maguire and Bennett, 1982). Low-income areas have many characteristics that may increase the prevalence of household crime. Lower income may result in fewer precautions being taken to protect the household (i.e., security costs money). Low-income areas also contain a disproportionate number of single-parent households; this leaves children with generally lower levels of adult supervision (Maxfield, 1987; Smith and Jarjoura, 1989). Mixed land use in these areas may mean the presence of bars and stores that bring a large number of strangers through the neighbourhood. Under such conditions, it may be more difficult to know who does and who does not belong in the area (Lynch and Cantor, 1992). Finally, residential instability and social heterogeneity are greater in poor areas, and this may undermine the development of collective community sentiments and thereby diminish effective informal social control at the local level (Bursik and Grasmick, 1993). In other words, as people become less tied to one another, they have less reason to worry about what others think and to conform to others' expectations.

The fact that poor *areas* have higher rates of household victimization than more affluent ones does not necessarily mean that poorer *households* have higher rates of victimization than their more affluent counterparts (Maguire and Bennett, 1982). In fact, several studies have shown that the risk of many forms of household victimization does not have a clear-cut relationship with household income. This is consistent with the patterns in Table 8.1. Households with incomes less than $15,000 reported break-and-enter rates of 53 incidents per 1,000 households. Households with incomes of $60,000 were burglarized at a very similar rate—50 incidents per 1,000. This may be because offenders choose the more affluent targets in less affluent areas, or the wealthier homes located near such areas (Waller and Okihiro, 1978; Cohen and Cantor, 1981; Cohen, Kluegel, and Land, 1981).

Victimization research also suggests that some types of housing are more susceptible than others to various forms of household crime (Massey, Krohn, and Bonati, 1989). Most susceptible are dwellings that offer the thief or the burglar easy access or that provide cover during the commission of the crime. Thus, the risk of break-and-enter is higher when a housing structure offers multiple points of entry, when doors or windows are covered by trees or shrubs, when the house is on a corner or near a major route that allows easy escape, and when neighbours' houses do not directly overlook the target (Bennett and Wright, 1984; Evans, 1989). The 1999 GSS found that household victimization was highest for semidetached and row houses and for duplexes (Besserer and Trainor, 2000).

Studies in which burglars themselves served as informants have provided information regarding what types of household settings are likely to be "high risk" for this type of victimization (Wright, Logie, and Decker, 1995). For example, Reppetto (1974) interviewed 100 convicted burglars, who identified several characteristics that made a household a more attractive target: ease of access, appearance of affluence, inconspicuous setting, isolated neighbourhood, absence of police patrols, and lack of surveillance by neighbours.

Many studies have found that burglaries are quite likely to occur when houses are empty—often during daylight hours (Evans, 1989; Mirrlees-Black, Mayhew, and Percy, 1996). The rhythms and tempos of family life affect the risk of household crime in other ways. A good deal of traffic in and out of the home is an expected characteristic of large families. Doors are more likely to be left open or unlocked, and property may not always be put away, which makes such homes an attractive target for thieves (Smith and Jarjoura, 1989). Also, the summer months bring warm temperatures, open windows, and houses left empty by vacationers; all of these factors may increase the opportunities for household crime (Sacco and Johnson, 1990).

TRANSACTIONS

We often think about opportunities for crime as an objective feature of the social environment (i.e., an open door invites theft), but the situation is more complicated than this. Criminal opportunities also have a subjective quality. For criminal events to occur, a potential offender must define the open door as an opportunity for theft. One person may see the large shrubs blocking a residential window as nothing more than interesting landscaping; another may see this shrubbery as providing cover during a robbery attempt.

What are the characteristics of the property offender? Like many other types of predatory offenders, these individuals tend disproportionately to be young males, many of whom come from socially disadvantaged backgrounds (Maguire and Bennett, 1982; Waller and Okihiro, 1978). Data from the 1999 UCR indicate that most break-and-enter offenders are adult males; 62 percent of them were over age 18, and among both adults and youth, over 90 percent were males (Tremblay, 2000).

PROFESSIONAL VERSUS AMATEUR THIEVES

It is useful to distinguish between two broad types of property offenders (Evans, 1989). On the one hand, there is the professional offender, who is sometimes characterized as the "good burglar" (Shover, 1973, 1983) and as the "elite of the criminal world" (Cromwell, Olson, and Avary, 1991). These individuals have a considerable degree of technical competence and are connected

BOX 8.3

Trends in Break-and-Enter

In Canada, rates of break-and-enter (and many other crimes) have been falling since 1991. Because break-and-enters are such a large proportion of property crimes, these substantial decreases have affected both the rate of property crime and the overall crime rate. In 1999 the UCR information systems recorded 318,448 break-and-enters. That was roughly one in every four property crimes.

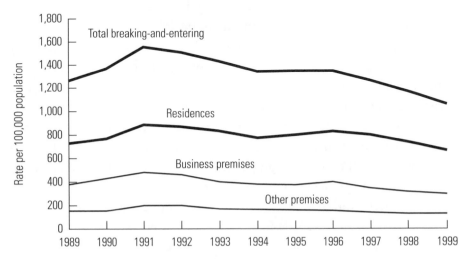

Figure 8.2

Breaking-and-entering incidents, by type, Canada, 1989–99

Source: S. Tremblay, "Crime Statistics in Canada, 1999," *Juristat* 20(5): p. 9. Used by permission of Statistics Canada.

to a network of other thieves and tipsters as well as to fences to whom they sell stolen property. Professional thieves think of themselves as "specialists" and understand their offending in occupational terms; they speak of pulling a "job" or "working" a particular area (Maguire and Bennett, 1982). Most of their crimes are carefully planned and involve rational assessments of specific risks and benefits.

The professional offender usually figures prominently in media portrayals of household crime and in police rhetoric about the typical offender. However, several researchers argue that popular images of the cool, calculating, highly specialized, and rational property offender may be exaggerated. According to Cromwell, Olson, and Avary (1991), much of what we know about these offenders comes from interviews with offenders or ex-offenders,

Rational reconstruction
Occurs when individuals recall their crimes and suggest there was more planning than actually took place.

Occasional offenders
Commit crimes when opportunities or situational inducements present themselves.

Recidivism
Repetition or recurrence of delinquent or criminal behaviour or behaviour disorder, especially following punishment or rehabilitation.

who may be engaging in **rational reconstruction.** In other words, in recalling their crimes, they may tend to suggest that far more planning took place than was actually the case. Professionals are sometimes said to seek opportunities for crime. But according to Cromwell and colleagues, these offenders do not so much seek opportunities as develop a special sensitivity to the opportunities they happen to encounter.

Hough (1985) suggests that notwithstanding the activities of some unspecified number of professional household thieves, these individuals are probably responsible for only a minority of the crimes revealed in victimization surveys. This speculation is supported by the fact that surveys generally uncover a large number of crimes that point to amateurish offenders with little technical knowledge or experience (Felson, 1998). Many household crimes are committed by unsophisticated offenders, most of whom are probably juveniles. These **occasional offenders** commit crimes when opportunities or situations present themselves (Evans, 1989). Irrespective of the level of professionalism of the offender, property crimes such as break-and-enter are motivated by instrumental needs (Bennett and Wright, 1984). These crimes do not reflect expressive needs such as anger or revenge; rather, they are prompted by the offender's desire to obtain the property of the victim.

Engagement in household theft, as well as movement out of this type of crime with advancing age, can be understood in terms of control theory. Household theft easily resists detection (Maguire and Bennett, 1982). Offenders learn from their own and others' experiences that their chances of getting caught committing a particular crime are very slim (Bennett and Wright, 1984). But they also recognize that if they become known to the police as thieves and fail to vary their methods of crime commission, their chances of getting caught will increase over time; this reduces the attractiveness of this form of crime (Cromwell, Olson, and Avary, 1991). The professional thief can be said to have a lengthy criminal career; in contrast, many juvenile offenders commit crimes only rarely, and do so with even less frequency as they get older (Shover, 1983). The number of repeat offenders, as measured by the **recidivism** rate for burglary, is higher for break-and-enter than for many other crimes, but many juvenile offenders do not repeat the crime at all (Maguire and Bennett, 1982).

As events, crimes against households can be relatively uncomplicated. Quite often, an opportunistic thief passes a house and notices some item of value lying unguarded on the front lawn or in the driveway (Lynch and

Cantor, 1992). Seeing no one around, the thief grabs the item and continues on his or her way. Similarly, under cover of darkness in the early hours of the morning, the thief may happen on an unlocked car and steal either its contents or the car itself.

Break-and-enter varies in terms of how much planning it requires. In many break-and-enters a young offender targets a house not far from his or her own residence (Brantingham and Brantingham, 1984; Cohen and Cantor, 1981; Hough, 1985). The proximity of the target reflects two distinct considerations: the offender's relatively limited mobility (e.g., too young to drive), and his or her direct knowledge of the contents and routine activities of the household (i.e., they have been in it before, in the course of routine activities). In cases like this, entry may be "child's play" (Maguire and Bennett, 1982). The offender tests the door and, if it is open, enters the house. Data from the 1998 BCS and other surveys indicate that most of the time some degree of force was used to gain entry (Budd, 1999). The thief moves through the house quickly, more interested in getting in and out with something of value than with the wanton destruction of property (Maguire and Bennett, 1982; Waller and Okihiro, 1978). The items stolen often include money, alcohol, and light electronic goods such as portable TV sets and VCRs.

The more professional burglar often selects a target more carefully. This selection process may have several stages: the offender decides which neighbourhood will be victimized, and which block in the neighbourhood, and which house on the block (Taylor and Gottfredson, 1986). The offender may cultivate relationships with "tipsters" who can provide information about vacant homes and potentially large "scores" (Shover, 1973). Some tipsters may be "fences" attempting to boost their inventory; others may be thieves who for some reason cannot undertake the crime themselves. Also, in the course of their regular travels through the neighbourhood, thieves may watch out for homes that look empty or that promise easy entry. Waiting at a traffic light may provide potential burglars with the opportunity to view potential targets without attracting attention (Cromwell, Olson, and Avary, 1991).

RISK, EASE OF ENTRY, AND REWARD

Irrespective of the level of professionalism, burglars who are intent on break-and-enter must consider three questions: Can they get away with the crime (risk)? Can they commit the crime without great difficulty (ease)? Can they get anything out of it (reward) (Bennett, 1989)? Of these three factors, the first (degree of risk) is probably the most important. Homes that are difficult to surveille from other homes present the offender with fewer risks. The mere presence of passersby may not influence the decision to offend, since thieves are concerned not about being seen, but rather about being seen *and* reported (Cromwell, Olson, and Avary, 1991).

Probably the most important aspect of risk is whether the home is occupied or not. The presence of a car in the driveway or signs of movement or activity in the house may encourage the potential offender to look elsewhere (Bennett, 1989). Some offenders engage in sophisticated **occupancy probes** to establish whether the household is vacant.

An occupied home is to be avoided not only because of the risk of detection but also because of a concern on the part of the offender that if someone is home, the crime of break-and-enter could escalate into a more serious offence. Some researchers (Kennedy and Silverman, 1990; Maxfield, 1990) have observed that although a rare occurrence, there is a higher-than-expected number of homicides involving elderly victims in their homes. This may be because the elderly occupy households that seem uninhabited during the day. The burglar, surprised by an unexpected encounter, may strike out against the elderly person, with fatal consequences. All of this suggests that offenders may not be quite as adept at assessing occupancy as is sometimes thought (Hough, 1985).

The second factor (ease of entry) concerns how hard it would be to enter the residence. Usually this factor cannot be assessed until the offence is under way (Bennett and Wright, 1984). Often it is a simple matter to break a door or a window; even the presence of special locks and security hardware may not serve as a strong deterrent (Lynch and Cantor, 1992; Maguire and Bennett, 1982). Many professional burglars report that they can, if they have to, deal effectively with alarms or watchdogs; but they also report that the large number of households that are unprotected by such measures makes attempted burglary of protected homes unnecessary (Maguire and Bennett, 1982).

The final factor (the potential reward) is probably the least important consideration. Offenders who engage in break-and-enter may be unable to determine before committing the crime whether anything of value is to be gained (Lynch and Cantor, 1992; Miethe and Meier, 1994). As noted earlier, information from a tipster may decrease uncertainty, and higher-status households may hold the promise of greater rewards. However, usually the thief can

Occupancy probes
Imaginative methods that the offender uses to determine whether anyone is home.

BOX 8.4

Occupancy Probes

In their interviews with burglars, Cromwell, Olson, and Avary (1991) discovered that these offenders use several imaginative methods to determine whether anyone is home.

1. If working as part of a team, the most "presentable" burglar knocks on the door or rings the doorbell. If someone answers, the burglar asks for directions or for a nonexistent person.
2. The burglar rings the doorbell and, if someone answers, claims that his or her car broke down and that he or she needs to use the phone. If the resident refuses, the burglar leaves without attracting suspicion. If the resident consents, the burglar can check out the merchandise in the home as well as whatever security measures exist.
3. The burglar telephones the residence to be broken into from a nearby phone and then returns to the residence. If he or she can hear the telephone ringing, it is unlikely that anyone is at home.
4. The burglar targets a house next to a residence that has a "for sale" sign on the front lawn. Posing as a buyer, the burglar can then examine the target household from the vantage of the sale property.

One informant in the Cromwell et al. study would dress in a tracksuit, jog to the front door of the target household, remove a piece of mail from the potential victim's mailbox, and ring the doorbell. If anyone answered, he would say that he found the letter and was returning it. The tracksuit suggested a reason why a stranger might be ringing a doorbell in the neighbourhood; the apparently neighbourly gesture suggested that he was a good citizen and therefore above suspicion.

be fairly certain that something of value will be collected in the course of the crime (Cromwell, Olsen, and Avary, 1991).

THE AFTERMATH

Property crime results in substantial economic loss. In 1998 the average claim for residences and businesses for losses sustained in break-and-enters was over $4,000. The items most often stolen were TV sets, stereos, and other pieces of AV equipment. In 1998, theft of motor vehicles and motor vehicle parts cost consumers $600 million (Tremblay, 2000). Some of the net loss for property crimes can be mitigated by either recovery or insurance. Members of lower-income groups are less likely to have insurance, and so generally experience the greatest net loss for household crimes.

All of this provides only a partial picture of the impact of household crime. Illegal entries that escalate into assaults, robberies, sexual assaults, or homicides have very direct and immediate physical consequences (Warr, 1988). Because incidents of this type are relatively rare, and because household crimes generally involve rather small net losses, these crimes are sometimes assumed to have little psychological impact on victims. That is not the case, especially with respect to break-and-enter (Budd, 1999). Many victims—especially women—may be badly shaken by the event (Maguire and Bennett, 1982). Victims may experience feelings of vulnerability, concern that the offender will return, and fear of being alone—even in situations that are not directly related to household crime. They may also experience long-term sleeping disorders or require tranquillizers for an extended period.

Many crimes against households are not reported to the police. Data from the 1999 GSS indicate that about 44 percent of all household crimes were reported (62 percent of attempted or successful break-and-enters, 60 percent of thefts of motor vehicles or motor vehicle parts, 32 percent of thefts of household property, and 34 percent of acts of vandalism) (Besserer and Trainor, 2000). With property crime as with personal crimes, when victims fail to report, it is because they define the incidents as not worth reporting or because they do not believe there is much the police can do. Victimization data suggest that property crimes are more likely to be reported than personal crimes in part because insurance policies require that they be reported before insurance money can be collected. The 1999 GSS found that the likelihood of reporting household crime was related to the total loss associated with the incident. Thus, unreported household crimes—at least in the legal context—are generally less serious than those that come to the attention of the police.

Victims who report household crime do so in the hope that the police will be able to apprehend the offender and recover the stolen property. At a minimum, victims expect the police to undertake an investigation and treat them with some sympathy (Maguire and Bennett, 1982). In the aftermath of household crime, victims may seek the help of a friend, neighbour, or landlord in addition to or instead of that of the police. When losses are substantial, victims may seek compensation through private insurance.

Reported household crimes carry with them a small likelihood of arrest. In 1999 only about 13 percent of break-and-enters were cleared, and of the total number of these offences, only about 8 percent were cleared by charge (Shelf Table 4.19). These crimes have low clearance rates because by the time they are reported to the police, the perpetrator is long gone. Also, there is no immediate suspect, as there typically is for crimes against persons (Maguire and Bennett, 1982).

In the aftermath of the crime, offenders are probably less concerned with arrest than with the uses to which they can put the stolen merchandise. Cash or alcohol can be used for "partying." Although the offender may keep and use some stolen merchandise, there is a limit to how much loot one person can use this way. Also, retaining too many stolen goods can increase the risk of arrest.

Much of what is stolen may be converted into cash through sale. A substantial market exists for stolen goods (Cromwell and McElrath, 1994)—especially for lightweight electronic goods—but typically, offenders recoup a relatively small amount from each item. Some stolen goods are sold directly to private buyers for their own use. These people may see this exchange not as a criminal activity but as "good business." Their reasoning may be, "It was already stolen, and if I don't buy it someone else will" (Cromwell, Olson, and Avary, 1991). Merchandise can also be sold to "fences," who purchase the items for resale. Some fences are businesspeople who do not have a criminal record; others are ex-thieves (Maguire and Bennett, 1982).

One popular public response to the increase in property crime has been to attempt to make homes less vulnerable to attack. "**Target hardening**" activities include installing deadbolt locks and bars on windows, purchasing alarms and watchdogs, and developing programs (such as Neighbourhood Watch) that increase the surveillance of property.

Target hardening
Increasing protection of premises to deter a criminal through fear of detection or because the target has been made inaccessible.

SUMMARY

Violent events within families can be attributed in part to the value our society places on family privacy. Feminist researchers see family violence as reflecting the power differentials within families—in other words, men use violence against women and children as a form of control over their actions (Simpson, 1989: 611).

To understand family violence we must consider the stresses placed on families, the reluctance of victims to report the violence, how parents manage conflict and anger (and why they manage these the way they do), the breakdown of social control mechanisms that restrain interpersonal violence, and the paucity of deterrence strategies. The uncovering in recent years of the extent of family violence, coupled with changes in societal values, has done much to redefine violent events within families as criminal events. Changes in the law and in how the police enforce it are reinforcing this new definition.

Property crime is a booming business. The target of most of this crime is the household, which is filled with portable appliances that can easily be transported and resold. Much property crime is opportunistic in nature, and involves the presence of a thief at a place where and time when property is unguarded and easy to steal. A lot of the property crime committed by youthful offenders falls into this category. The more complicated crime of break-and-enter, which often requires considerable planning and technical expertise, tends to be committed by professional burglars, who not only take the time to plan the event but also ensure that the merchandise can be disposed of after the fact. Sometimes, owing to a miscalculation by the offender, residents may be unexpectedly encountered during the household burglary. The consequences—especially for elderly victims—can be fatal.

Many property crimes are not reported to the police. People who do not report may feel that there is little the police can do to solve the crime or that the crime is not serious enough to warrant reporting. Increasingly, homeowners are engaging in target-hardening activities intended to discourage both opportunistic and professional burglars.

There is growing interest in confronting crimes that occur in or are directed toward the household. Intrafamily violence is attracting a great deal of public attention, and demands have been growing that more action (in the form of education and changes in the law) be taken to reduce the likelihood that this kind of violence will occur. Attempts have been made to give victims of family violence greater protection under the law and to provide them with safe havens, as well as to treat offenders (see Chapter 11). As our review of family violence has shown, it is important to consider different theoretical approaches to the problem. New perspectives that draw attention to such things as power differentials in families are providing us with explanations of family violence and with possible ways to respond to it.

There are many different views regarding why people commit property crimes. Obviously, not everyone who is given the opportunity to steal does so. Depending on your perception of human behaviour, you might assume that people will steal if they know they won't get caught (social control), if they see others doing the same thing (cultural influence), or if they feel pressured by social circumstances (strain). All of these explanations rely on the idea that the offender has the opportunity (and some skills) to commit the crime and little fear of apprehension. Probably, the most effective means of combatting property crime is to limit the opportunities for it.

QUESTIONS FOR REVIEW AND DISCUSSION

1. Why has there been so much resistance to the claim that family violence is a serious problem?

2. How can we use strain theory to explain wife assault?

3. Many people argue that sibling violence is normal and that this kind of violence is very different from the kinds of violence we label "wife assault" and "child abuse." Do you agree? Explain.

4. Recently, many notorious court cases have revolved around family violence issues (perhaps the O.J. Simpson case is the best example). Is the high level of media attention devoted to these cases a good thing or a bad thing?

5. Marcus Felson has argued that in the past few decades, the decrease in levels of household occupancy and the proliferation of "lightweight durable consumer goods" has resulted in a "deskilling of crime." How valid is this proposition with respect to crimes against the household?

6. With respect to your own residence, how might a potential thief or burglar make decisions about "risk," "ease," and "reward"?

INFOTRAC COLLEGE EDITION

Explore InfoTrac College Edition, your online university library, which includes hundreds of popular and scholarly journals in which you can find articles related to the topics in this chapter. Visit InfoTrac through your Web browser (**www.infotrac-college.com**), or through this book's Web site (**www.criminalevent-3e.nelson.com**).

WHAT'S ON THE WEB?

For chapter links and quizzes, check out the accompanying Web site at **www.criminalevent-3e.nelson.com**.

Chapter 9

Crime and Leisure

WHAT'S IN CHAPTER NINE

In this chapter we examine the nature of crime that takes place when people pursue recreation and leisure activities. We consider the view that leisure acts as a corrupter of youth and makes social control difficult. The contexts in which leisure-based criminal events take place include the street and bars, dating relationships, and vacation travel.

INTRODUCTION

In this chapter we discuss a second social domain that is significant to the study of criminal events—the leisure domain. The relationship between leisure and crime has several interesting dimensions. People who are "at leisure" seem to be especially at risk for many different types of criminal victimization. Furthermore, many types of offending—especially juvenile offending—are themselves forms of leisure. Our language reflects this fact when, for instance, we describe illegal drug use as "recreational drug use," and when we describe stealing a car for fun as "joyriding." The leisure preferences of young people are often seen as a cause of crime. This is evident in periodic scares in our society about the criminogenic effects of violent television, popular music, fantasy role-playing games, and video games.

We will also see that certain leisure settings, such as bars and sports complexes, are often scenes of crime and victimization. The street is also a likely location for crime victimization, as we begin to adopt lifestyles that take us away from our homes and into public areas in search of leisure pursuits. We begin our review of the relationship between leisure and criminal activities with a discussion of the concept of leisure.

WHAT IS LEISURE?

Leisure
Free time (after work, familial, and other obligations are met) that can be used for play or recreation.

Leisure can be defined in a variety of ways (Wilson, 1980). We often use the term in an objective way to describe the "spare time" or "free time" that is left over after paid work and other obligations (such as child care) have been taken care of (Iso-Ahola, 1980). However, leisure has a subjective as well as objective character. In other words, leisure is not just free time, but free time that is used in a particular way—usually for play or recreation. Leisure activity can be regarded as intrinsically satisfying in that it provides its own rewards (Roberts, 1983). Also, we usually assume that leisure activities are freely chosen and that leisure interaction occurs among peers. In contrast, family- or work-related activities tend to be less voluntary and are characterized by authority relations enforced by law or custom.

Like other scarce resources, leisure time is unequally distributed (Jones, 1994). Teenagers and the elderly tend to have more leisure time than young parents and the middle-aged. And because household tasks and child care responsibilities reduce free time, men generally have more leisure time than women. People also differ with respect to their leisure preferences and the resources they have to pursue them. Those in higher-income groups are more likely to frequent restaurants; young people are more likely to go to bars, movies, or video arcades (Provenzo, 1991). The elderly are less likely to go out in the evening for leisure of any kind (Golant, 1984). Elderly people who do engage in leisure outside the home tend to visit friends or family.

The amount of leisure time that people have available to them and the uses to which they put it are important elements of what we refer to as *lifestyle* (see Chapter 6). Moreover, the leisure content of people's lifestyles has important implications for the kinds of criminal events in which they are involved, as offenders or as victims. Opportunity theories are especially attentive to the linkage between lifestyle and crime.

PRECURSORS

What does leisure have to do with the timing, location, and relative involvement of particular types of people in particular types of criminal events? There are two answers to this question. The first stresses how specific types of leisure activities motivate offenders toward, or free them from constraints against, offending. The second suggests that leisure activities and settings facilitate encounters between offenders and potential victims. These perspectives are not contradictory, but they do differ in their fundamental emphases. The former is offender-centred; the latter is opportunity-centred.

LEISURE AS A CORRUPTER

Arguments about the corrupting influences of leisure have typically been made with respect to youthful offenders. Throughout this century, every major form of youth leisure preference has been characterized by interest groups as a corrupter of young people. Feature films, rock 'n' roll, rap and heavy metal music, video games, comic books, Saturday morning cartoons, and television commercials have all, at one time or another, been accused of weakening youthful inhibitions, providing negative role models, destroying childhoods, and disrupting the bonds between adolescents and adult authority figures (Best, 1990; Gray, 1989; Maguire, Sandage, and Weatherby, 2000; Tanner, 2001).

Literally hundreds of studies have investigated the potentially negative effects of television violence. This issue has been the focus of attention from the public as well as Royal Commissions in Canada and presidential panels in the United States (Tate, 1998). The argument that television violence has some causal relationship with real-life violence seems to be supported by much anecdotal evidence (in the form of so-called copycat crimes, for example) and by common sense. We know that television is a powerful persuader; otherwise, advertisers would not spend so much money buying commercial time

---

BOX 9.1

Patterns of Television Viewing

One major form of leisure that has been the source of much controversy is television viewing. According to Statistics Canada:

- Estimates of television viewing reached a two-decade low in the fall of 1999; viewers in almost every province spent less time in front of their TV set.
- Canadians watched television for an average of 21.6 hours per week—almost one hour less than in 1998, and well below the peak of 23.5 hours reached in 1988.
- Viewing declined in all provinces except Newfoundland and British Columbia, which posted small increases. Demographically, all age and sex groups watched less.
- Viewers spent two-thirds of their viewing time watching foreign productions— largely American-produced programs. The most popular categories were drama and comedy, followed by news and public affairs.

Source: *The Daily*, Statistics Canada, January 25, 2001. Used by permission of Statistics Canada.

to convince consumers to purchase their products. We also know that television is a violent medium and that young people—who are most likely to behave violently—have high levels of exposure to such content.

However, despite anecdotal evidence and commonsense notions, it is not at all clear what effects television violence has on viewers, or how strong those effects are. The effects of television violence on criminal motivation are probably limited by several factors. *First*, according to UCR data, violent crimes account for only a small proportion of total crime. So unless we want to argue that television violence affects nonviolent crime in some as yet undetermined fashion, the amount of crime that could be causally linked to violent content is limited, even if the effects on violence are substantial. In fact, some researchers *have* suggested that the real effects of television may be on property rather than violent crimes (Hennigen et al., 1982). The basis for this argument is that the emphasis in the media on consumerism raises people's expectations regarding the amounts of material goods to which they think they are entitled (Surette, 1992). However, the link between television and property crime has not received sufficient research attention to warrant firm conclusions.

Second, given that criminal motivation is a complex issue, any effects produced by media exposure must be understood in the context of many other factors that encourage or restrain offending. The amount of variation attributable to media exposure is likely to be smaller than many observers would argue. Some researchers claim that 5 to 10 percent of violent and nonviolent behaviour is attributable to exposure to media violence (Surette, 1992). Whether this means that television violence is a relatively important or unimportant factor in real-life violence remains unresolved.

Third, many research experiments have shown that exposure to violent content in laboratory settings triggers violent arousal, but the same effects are not necessarily produced by media exposure in the real world (Howitt, 1998). In lab experiments, subjects may be encouraged to behave violently (or at least not discouraged from doing so); in contrast, violent behaviour in most social contexts is discouraged. Also, how violence is measured in the lab (e.g., the willingness of children to play with violent toys, or of subjects to administer a harmless electrical shock to another person) may not have much to do with the willingness of people to beat, assault, rob, or kill others. Studies that try to link television violence to aggressive behaviour in real-life settings have often been less successful than those that try to find these effects in the laboratory.

All of this suggests that the relationship between television violence and criminal violence is more complicated, and perhaps less substantial, than we

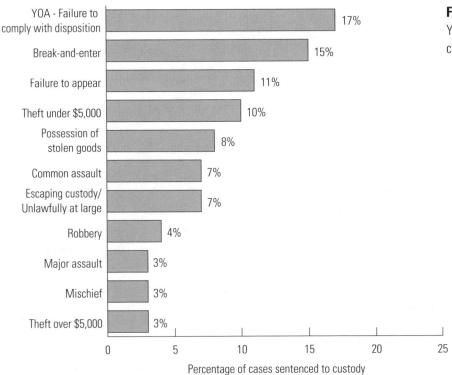

Figure 9.1

Youth court cases by offence category, Canada, 1996–97

Source: Stevenson, K., J. Tufts, D. Hendrick, and M. Kowalski (1998). *A Profile of Youth Justice in Canada.* Ottawa: Statistics Canada. Used by permission of Statistics Canada.

sometimes think. Much of the research supports the view that television violence may influence the behaviour of a pool of at-risk individuals who may be especially susceptible to its effects. In other words, television violence may be most likely to affect the behaviour of individuals already predisposed to behave aggressively. Unfortunately, we lack detailed knowledge of the size of this at-risk pool or of the factors that put these people at risk. Media violence may not cause interpersonal aggression in any direct way, but it may reinforce pre-existing tendencies or shape them in particular ways. In the case of copycat crimes, for instance, media violence may not motivate someone to commit a crime, but it may affect *how* that person commits a crime.

The effects of television (or movie) violence may often be short-term. Anyone who has ever left a movie theatre feeling excited or energized may intuitively understand the nature of this temporary arousal. We know that such effects tend to dissipate rather quickly as we return to the family, work, or school responsibilities that structure our lives. Thus, whether people behave violently after this arousal may have as much to do with the situations and circumstances in which they find themselves as with their level of arousal. That being said, it is important to note that we know relatively less about the long-term effects of high levels of media violence on cultural beliefs and social practices.

Sociologist David Phillips (1983) illustrated how some of the effects might work. In a number of studies, he showed that media portrayals of homicide or suicide may exert temporary effects on the rates of such behaviour. In the case of homicide, for instance, Phillips studied what happened to homicide rates after highly publicized prizefights. These media events are especially interesting because they involve violence that is both widely publicized and generally condoned. Having carefully assessed homicide trends, Phillips was able to show that in the few days immediately following a highly publicized fight, homicide rates increased by about 12 percent; also, that these effects could not be attributed to seasonal, monthly, or other temporal patterns.

Critics contend that the findings of studies like these are not convincing. Howitt (1998) points out that homicides do not occur randomly over time but vary according to the day of the week and month of the year. Similarly, prizefights are not random events; in fact, the date of a title bout is very carefully selected to maximize the investment of the promoters. Given the nonrandomness of both the cause (the bouts) and the effect (the homicides), it is possible that the statistical relationship between the two suggests a spurious outcome rather than a real causal process.

Of broader significance to Canadians is Howitt's conclusion:

Although American research dominates research in the field as in many others, it is a fairly gross assumption to imply that what is true of America must be true of the rest of the world. Media systems worldwide vary markedly from American norms and the programming varies from country to country, despite the homogenizing effect of satellite television. Since crime rates vary markedly from country to country, one might assume that these "cultural" baselines of crime may enhance or buffer media effects (Howitt, 1998: 71).

The rancorous public debate over television violence has strong similarities to the debate over video games. The content of these games is typically violent, and because they are interactive, they may be more likely than television viewing to produce delinquency. Though we have not yet amassed a significant body of research on the subject of the criminogenic influences of video games, so far concerns about the effects of these games on serious criminal offending seem to be overstated (Provenzo, 1991).

Regarding adults (as opposed to juveniles), public alarm about the effects of pornography on sex crimes reflects concerns similar to those voiced by critics of television violence. Again, people who try to draw direct causal links between violent pornography (e.g., "slasher" movies that combine sexual scenes with violent ones) and sex crimes are ignoring the complexity of the issue. A large body of experimental literature suggests that exposure to this kind of pornography promotes negative attitudes toward women, a greater acceptance of rape myths (e.g., that rape victims are to blame for what

BOX 9.2

Pornography and the Law

Pornography as a form of cultural expression has always been controversial. Child pornography is more likely than any other kind to excite public indignation and raise worries about possible criminogenic effects.

In January 2001 the Supreme Court of Canada upheld a law criminalizing the possession of child pornography. The court recognized this law as an appropriate and constitutional means for preventing the exploitation of children; however, it also identified two areas where freedom of thought must be protected. *First*, there is a need to protect people who write or draw sexually explicit depictions of children for their own enjoyment. *Second*, there is a need to protect those who create visual depictions of themselves engaged in sexual activity—assuming that the sexual activity is itself legal.

According to the SCC decision:

> The costs of prohibiting such materials to the right of free expression outweighs any tenuous benefits it might confer in preventing harm to children … To ban the possession of our own private musings falls perilously close to criminalizing the mere articulation of thought.

These distinctions may make legal sense. But critics pointed out the complexities of the problem. For example, the court had not clarified whether someone who views child pornography on the Internet is guilty of possession, even if that individual does not print out or download the material. If the police came into the room and pornographic images are on the screen, is the individual breaking the law?

Clearly, in this area and also in many others, new technologies are complicating the role of law.

Source: K. Makin, 2001, "Top Court Rules 9–0: Child Porn Law Stays," *The Globe and Mail*, January 27.

happens to them), and a decreased sensitivity toward female victims of violence (Malamuth, 1983; Malamuth, and Donnerstein, 1984). Yet, as in the case of television violence, the effects of violent pornography on perpetrators of sex crimes may be most evident in men who are already predisposed to behave violently toward women.

LEISURE AND FREEDOM FROM SOCIAL CONTROL

In the case of juveniles, it is sometimes argued that patterns of leisure activity increase the likelihood that crimes will occur by freeing youth from the social controls that might otherwise check or restrain delinquent conduct. This position builds on the arguments suggested in the theories presented in Chapter 5.

Typically, juvenile leisure is pursued out of the sight of parents and teachers and in the presence of peers (Agnew and Peterson, 1989; Osgood et al., 1996). The modern video arcade, like the pool hall of an earlier era, is off-limits to adults. "Hanging out" at the video arcade or mall or on the street corner may provide the behavioural freedom that makes group delinquency possible. A study by Riley (1987) of juvenile crime in England and Wales found that offenders and nonoffenders engaged in different types of leisure activities. Nonoffenders generally spent more time with parents and around the home; offenders were more likely to spend their time in peer activities away from home. Also, offenders were more often out in the evening, were expected home later, and were more likely to spend their money on youth-oriented amusements. These leisure activities removed some of the obstacles to delinquency by lessening the chances of apprehension and by providing exposure to behavioural contexts that facilitated delinquent action.

In contrast, leisure activities organized by adults and leisure time spent with parents can be expected to decrease the likelihood of delinquency by strengthening social bonds and thereby rendering delinquency less attractive (Agnew, 1985a; Messner and Blau, 1987). One study found that "hanging out" and social activities such as dating and partying were associated with higher levels of delinquent involvement, whereas organized leisure was associated with lower levels of delinquent involvement (Agnew and Peterson, 1989). However, the researchers also reported that it is not enough for youths to be engaged in "positive" leisure for a decrease in delinquency to occur—they must also enjoy the activity. In other words, coercive leisure cannot be expected to bring about a decrease in offending behaviour.

When it comes to the development or freeing of delinquent motivation, leisure may affect males more than females (Riley, 1987). In part, as power-control theory has argued, this is because female adolescents have tradition-ally been subject to higher levels of control, which restrict their leisure options (Hagan, Gillis, and Simpson, 1985; Singer and Levine, 1988). These gender differences may be rooted in patterns of family socialization. Risk-taking behaviour is encouraged in male children; female children are generally sub-jected to significantly greater parental control (see Chapter 5). Gender differ-ences in delinquent leisure may reflect these patterned gender differences in risk-taking and control.

However, Tanner (2001) notes that the behaviour of boys also has a sig-nificant effect on the routine leisure activities of female adolescents. Girls are often missing from deviant youth cultures because males exclude them. Male delinquents do not always relish female participation except as ancillaries or as objects of sexual goals. As Tanner points out, there is really no reason to think that delinquent males are any less sexist than nondelinquent males.

LEISURE ACTIVITIES AND OPPORTUNITIES

Leisure activities are important occasions for criminal events of various types, as evidenced by the times when and places where crimes occur. A large number of personal victimizations occur in the evenings and on weekends, when most people are "at rest," when they have dropped their more serious work roles, and when the formal social controls of the school and the work-place are not operative (Luckenbill, 1977; Melbin, 1987). Also, personal vic-timizations occur disproportionately in leisure settings—that is, in informal contexts that host a wide range of activities such as drinking, gambling, dancing, and playing games. In a study of high school youth in Tucson, Arizona, Jensen and Brownfield (1986) found partying, cruising, and visiting bars—in general, the social pursuit of fun—to be significantly related to vic-timization risk.

Bars are good examples of **permissive environs.** Bars are the site of many criminal events, and so are the blocks where they are located (Roncek and Maier, 1991; Roncek and Pravatiner, 1989). There are many reasons. Bars do most of their business in the evening, when people are released from many of the social controls that structure their working days. Bars also deal in cash and liquor, which are easily stolen and easily used by the offender. Furthermore, bars tend to place no real restrictions on who can enter, and they are especially popular among young people. Finally, alcohol consumption increases the probability of interpersonal conflicts; it also impairs judgments regarding the scale of these conflicts (Engs and Hanson, 1994).

Permissive environs
Social settings, such as bars and parties, where individuals feel free of many of the constraints that operate in other settings, such as the school and the work-place.

Generally, activities that bring people out of their homes in the evening increase the likelihood of personal and household crime (Kennedy and Forde, 1990). Messner and Blau (1987) found that the volume of leisure activity *in* the home (indexed by levels of reported television viewing) is related to lower rates of victimization, while the volume of leisure activity *outside* the home (indexed by the number of sports and theatrical facilities) is related to higher rates of victimization.

A similar and consistent pattern has been revealed by victimization surveys. Violent and household victimizations increase as evening activities outside the home increase. This relationship is independent of marital status, employment status, and age (Kennedy and Sacco, 1998; Gottfredson, 1984). Going out on weekends increases these risks more than going out during the week. Engaging in leisure pursuits increases risk more than going to work or to school (Lasley and Rosenbaum, 1988; Sacco, Johnson, and Arnold, 1993).

Risky lifestyle

A regular pattern of activities that exposes individuals to higher levels of risk of criminal victimization.

Leisure can be part of a **risky lifestyle** that has dangerous consequences (Kennedy and Forde, 1999). Clearly, some types of leisure are riskier than others. Young single males are more likely than others to go to bars where— as we have seen—the risks are higher. In contrast, elderly people are less likely to leave their homes for leisure in the evening; when they do they are less likely to come into contact with potential offenders.

Several studies suggest that forms of leisure that are themselves criminal may pose especially high victimization risks (Gottfredson, 1984; Jensen and Brownfield, 1986; Lauritsen, Sampson, and Laub, 1991; Sampson and Lauritsen, 1990). In part this is because offenders make good victims: they are unlikely to call the police, and if they do they will likely have difficulty establishing their credibility.

TRANSACTIONS

The content of criminal events varies across leisure settings and activities. Criminologists have paid particular attention to the street, bars, dating, and tourism.

THE STREET

For many youths, the street is itself a leisure setting (Kennedy and Sacco, 1998). For others, it is the route they take from one setting to another or from these settings to their homes (Felson, 1998). Criminal events in the street seem to support the argument of opportunity theorists that people are victims of routines that leave them vulnerable to offenders. Actually, research indicates that despite the horror stories from inner-city areas suggesting that people of all ages are vulnerable to crime, young males are more likely than any other group to be involved in "risky" routines on the street (Stevenson et al., 1998). Their behaviour tends to be more public than that of most other groups, and they frequent the street to a greater degree than others.

YOUNG MALES

As stated previously, the groups most vulnerable to assaults in public places are young, unmarried males who frequent bars, go to movies, go out to work, and spend time out of the house walking or driving around (Felson, 1998). This lifestyle exposes them to risk. Victimization data support the conclusion that much violent crime involving youths takes place in public places. For example, Canadian UCR data indicate that in 1997, 35 percent of violent victimizations of youthful victims took place in public areas, and another 17 percent in commercial settings or public institutions. Many of these incidents occurred in parking lots or on public streets (Stevenson et al., 1998). Violent crime is often spontaneous; that being said, its targets tend to be people who are in places that are conducive to violent conflict. This observation does not account for the motivation behind violent crime, but it does explain the high levels of victimization among particular groups based on their exposure to certain settings and activities. Kennedy and Forde (1990) report a similar pattern for robberies: young, unmarried males who frequent bars and who are out walking or driving around are more likely to be victims of this crime.

The behaviour of young males who just hang around on the street is often seen as criminogenic. According to Skogan and Maxfield (1981), urban residents are most afraid of run-down urban areas where teenagers are hanging around on street corners. Even if the loitering is harmless and the individuals who are engaging in it never become involved in crime, the street is seen as a dangerous place.

When these youths are loosely attached to one another, those whom they encounter in street situations are likely to be acquaintances, and the chances of violence are likely to be low. When individuals are more closely affiliated, as in a gang, the chances of violence increase, although—as Kennedy and Baron (1993) report—violence may not be a routine outcome of activity by gangs on the street. Much of the crime engaged in by gangs actually occurs as a result of contact with other gangs. Minor theft and robbery certainly occur, but not to the extent the public believes. Also, the view that gangs pursue violence for violence's sake, as would be predicted by the subculture-of-violence theory, is not substantiated by the research.

Individuals on the street who are potential offenders can also be victims. Young men in risky areas can easily become targets of assaults and robberies. When alcohol or drugs are involved, spontaneous conflicts may arise between individuals who are complete strangers to each other. Motivation in the violence that occurs among young males, whether in gangs or not, may simply be based on tests of character (Luckenbill, 1977).

Any women who are present in street environments are less likely to become involved in conflicts directly; however, they may act as third parties in escalating or defusing the conflict. Women alone tend to avoid areas they perceive as risky (especially the street) and situations that could lead to violence or loss of property. Of course, women can be targets of theft just as easily as men—purse snatching is all too common. That being said, street crime seems to be predominantly the domain of young men, both as offenders and as victims.

According to Hocker and Wilmot (1985: 38), the precursors of assaults and robberies may depend on conflict styles, which vary with individual personality and with the social situations individuals confront. These researchers assume that people develop patterned responses to conflict. Response styles are based on past experience and on learning (i.e., on observing others' behaviour and trying out different responses).

Third parties play an important role in conflict escalation and de-escalation. Young boys often jokingly exhort their friends to physically restrain them when they are confronting a foe. The opponent is advised, "You're lucky he's holding me back, or you'd be sorry!" This type of posturing, which is facilitated by third parties, can work to dissipate conflict, but it can also have the opposite effect. The joking may become serious, and third parties may promote the conflict instead of acting to reduce it. However, even when one participant lands a blow that in legal terms could be considered criminal assault, it is probably not viewed as such by the parties involved. There is likely too much confusion as to the identities of the instigator and the victim (Van Brunschot, 2000). Only when serious physical harm is inflicted do these situations lead to the involvement of a formal third party (i.e., the police).

Kennedy and Baron (1993) found that members of punk gangs were prepared to absorb a great deal of verbal abuse; they became involved in a fight only when they felt a need to protect themselves, not when they felt that backing down would make them look foolish. This finding does not suggest that the members of punk gangs were unprepared for violence; nor does it suggest that they would just walk away if attacked; rather, it suggests that the crime in which they engaged was more likely to be a spontaneous outburst of violence than a conscious, planned event (Gottfredson and Hirschi, 1990).

VANDALISM

People's attitudes toward city streets are affected not only by the presence of gangs but also by graffiti and other signs of vandalism and decay (see Chapter 7). When people see these signs, and the patterns of movement around them, their fears are often awakened. Though **vandalism** is not a criminal event in the conventional sense (i.e., an event in which at least two parties are involved in a criminal action), we can still approach it in event terms. Vandalism differs from other criminal events in that there is a time delay between the offence and the victimization.

Vandalism
The deliberate damaging or destruction of public or private property.

Criminologists have paid more attention to the consequences of vandalism than to its causes. Some criminologists (Skogan, 1990b; Kelling and Coles, 1996; Wilson and Kelling, 1982) identify vandalism as a major contributor to the public's declining sense of security in a given neighbourhood. Wilson and Kelling contend that disorder and crime are inextricably linked in a kind of developmental sequence. Wilson (1983: 78) notes that social psychologists and police officers tend to agree that if a building window is broken and left unrepaired, the remaining windows will soon be damaged. Vandalism occurs more often in areas where surveillance is low. By generating "untended" behaviour, vandalism leads to a breakdown of community controls and to the degeneration of the neighbourhood into one that may become criminogenic. The fear that accompanies this degradation may discourage people from routinely using the streets, and from providing informal surveillance as a means of constraining disorderly behaviour. As vandalism increases and the neighbourhood continues to decline, residents may move to safer, more congenial environments.

Though abandoned buildings seem to be the most frequent targets of vandalism, we are witnessing the growth of public vandalism, which involves tagging (writing graffiti on) walls, public vehicles, and whatever else is available. Graffiti-filled trains and stations have long been the scourge of public transit in New York and have created the impression that the system is dangerous, even though there are fewer incidents of crime on that city's subway than on the streets above it (Felson, 1998). New York City's transportation department has taken extreme steps to ban all graffiti on its subway trains. Similar strategies have been used in other cities.

Most tagging takes place at night, when there is little possibility of detection. However, graffiti writers are becoming bolder and are sometimes recognized for their skill at leaving their mark in daylight hours. This bravado may be the natural response of taggers who have come to see themselves as artists; to most people, however, graffiti is simply vandalism.

What motivates most vandalism? Thrill-seeking and the fact that it doesn't seem to harm anyone are probably significant causative factors. Notwithstanding the efforts made to curtail it in many cities, vandalism is almost impossible to detect and deter.

BARS

People go to bars (taverns, lounges, and so on) to relax, meet friends, listen to music, and drink. Most bars escape the frenzied aggressiveness that may lead to crime; some attract it (Kennedy and Sacco, 1998). In these locations, where alcohol and drugs mix with loud music and bravado, violence often erupts. Bar owners are growing more and more concerned about this violence but often don't know how to reduce it. They hire bouncers to remove the most raucous clients, but sometimes these bouncers incite more violence. When one asks college or university criminology students where they would go to find a fight on any given night, they can easily list two or three notorious bars in town where violence regularly occurs. Apparently these places attract a clientele that tends to be more aggressive than average—a conclusion that supports the subculture-of-violence perspective.

Most of the criminal events that occur in bars are minor assaults, especially between young males. This is consistent with the finding that many victimization incidents occur when people are drinking. The 1999 General Social Survey (GSS) found that in half of violent crime incidents the victim stated that the incident was related to the use of alcohol or drugs by the accused, or the victim, or both (Besserer and Trainor, 2000). These events may also involve vandalism (breaking windows, chairs, and tables). Events involving interpersonal conflict may conclude without violence, with the protagonists either walking away or being pulled away from each other. When there is escalation, violence may erupt. All of this suggests that such events are spontaneous; however, the idea that certain bars attract this type of problem implies that some individuals go to those bars in search of trouble. Luckenbill's (1977) charac-

BOX 9.3

Risk Factors for Courtship Violence

With respect to courtship violence, who is at risk of offending and victimization? The Centers for Disease Control in Atlanta, Georgia, have drawn on a large body of empirical research to provide the following profiles:

Characteristics of Victims
- Women aged 12 to 18 who are victims of violence are more likely than older women to report that their offenders were acquaintances, friends, or intimate partners.
- The likelihood of becoming a victim of dating violence is associated with having female peers who have been sexually victimized, lower church attendance, greater number of past dating partners, acceptance of dating violence, and personally having experienced a previous sexual assault.

Characteristics of Perpetrators
- Studies have found the following to be associated with sexual assault perpetration: the male having sexually aggressive peers; heavy alcohol or drug use; the man's acceptance of dating violence; the male's assumption of key roles in dating such as initiating the date, being the driver, and paying dating expenses; miscommunication about sex; previous sexual intimacy with the victim; interpersonal violence; traditional sex roles; adversarial attitudes about relationships; and rape myths.
- Men who have a family history of observing or experiencing abuse are more likely to inflict abuse, violence, and sexual aggression.
- As the consumption of alcohol by either the victim or the perpetrator increases, the rate of serious injuries associated with dating violence also increases.

Source: Centers for Disease Control and Prevention: www.cdc.gov

terization of the "character contest" seems to apply to such situations (see Chapter 6). The jostling and shoving that precede a fight may be combined with insults and threats. When the fight breaks out, those around the combatants may add fuel to it by offering encouragement or by joining in.

DATING VIOLENCE

According to popular thinking, adolescent dating is a context for innocent exploration, whereas violence is a feature of conflict-ridden and constricting marital relationships (Sugarman and Hotaling, 1989). But in recent years, dating violence has been recognized as existing in some unknown proportion of dating relationships. To a large degree, difficulties in estimating the size of the problem reflect inconsistencies in how abusive behaviour is measured.

Most of the contemporary discussion about dating violence has focused on the subject of date rape (Karmen, 2001; Gabor, 1994). Because these rapes occur in a social context where consensual sex is a possibility, until recently the tendency has been to view date rape as something other than "real rape" (Bechhofer and Parrot, 1991). This has led to a victim-blaming strategy, as well as to a widespread willingness to dismiss the injury or trauma experienced by victims. A more realistic appraisal links date rape to culturally supported dating rituals that reflect patriarchal assumptions about male power and privilege (DeKeseredy and Kelly, 1993). Research suggests that male sexual aggression is more likely when males exert greater control over the dating process—that is, when they control the initiation of dating, assume responsibility for expenses and transportation, and choose the dating activity (Harney and Muehlenhard, 1991).

Male control may translate into sexual aggression in two distinct ways. *First*, many men interpret a woman's willingness to allow the male to make decisions about where they will go on a date, what they will do, and who will pay for it, as a sign of interest in sexual activity (Johnson, Palileo, and Gray, 1992). These men may be reasoning that if women don't object to coming back to their room or accompanying them to a secluded spot, they must be interested in sex, even if they say otherwise. Also, because dating is a leisure activity in late adolescence or early adulthood, it often involves the use of alcohol (or other drugs). This means that courtship sexual violence often occurs in contexts that involve alcohol consumption (Meadows, 1998). A woman's heavy consumption of alcohol may be interpreted by the male as a sign of sexual interest (Benson, Charlton, and Goodhart, 1992; Vogel and Himlein, 1995).

Second, to the extent that the male controls the circumstances of dating, he controls the opportunities for offending. For instance, when he controls transportation he can effectively impede the female's ability to escape a situation in which sexual assault is likely. A woman who is in an isolated spot with a sexually aggressive male may be reluctant to leave the car because she has been warned that even greater dangers confront women who are not protected by male companions. Not surprisingly, date rapes typically occur in the home of the offender, inside an automobile, or in some other isolated location (Harney and Muehlenhard, 1991). The Violence Against Women Survey (VAWS) found that 20 percent of date-related sexual assaults took place in the home of the male, and another 25 percent in a car; a further 24 percent occurred in the victim's home, 21 percent in another public place, and 10 percent in someone else's home (Johnson, 1996). The consequences of male control—misinterpretation of sexual interest and the creation of opportunity—often work in concert. For example, "parking" combines privacy, which provides the opportunity for sexual aggression, with the likelihood that the male will overestimate the female's willingness to engage in sexual relations (Muehlenhard and Linton, 1987).

In courtship violence, like marital violence, violence is supported by the patriarchal belief that the use of force by men against women is legitimate (DeKeseredy and Kelly, 1993; Lloyd, Koval, and Cale, 1989). Women who are assaulted by boyfriends frequently cite jealousy or attempts to terminate the relationship as the precipitating factors. Ironically, such dating violence may be viewed as a sign of love by either or both parties.

"Stalking," as defined by academics and criminal justice practitioners, suggests a related problem (Lowney and Best, 1995). Typically, stalking involves various forms of criminal harassment in which an offender follows, telephones, or otherwise physically and emotionally intimidates a victim. The available data clearly indicate that in the overwhelming majority of cases of stalking, the offender is male and the victim is female. In terms of their relationships, the largest proportion of victims are harassed by ex-partners (ex- spouses or boyfriends) (Tjaden and Thoennes, 1998b). This pattern is illustrated by the UCR data on criminal harassment shown in Figure 9.2. As Figure 9.2 also demonstrates, when males are harassed, their offenders are more likely to be casual acquaintances than former partners (Kong, 1996).

TOURISM

It is impossible to ignore the growing importance of tourism in our society. Large amounts of money are spent on tourist attractions, and people are allocating more and more of their disposable income to travel. Despite the growing awareness that tourists are not immune to crime, hotels and travel agencies have been slow to warn tourists about potentially dangerous areas. Tourists tend to be easy targets for pickpockets and robbers. Nor is it just the property that tourists take with them that is at risk. One scam involves thieves reading the identification tags of departing travellers and then burglarizing their now unoccupied homes!

Victimization of travellers is hardly a recent phenomenon. In the Middle Ages, castles were built in the south of France to protect pilgrims travelling through areas inhabited by thieves and robbers. And although modern

FIGURE 9.2

Female victims harassed by ex-husbands, male victims harassed by casual acquaintances, 1994 and 1995

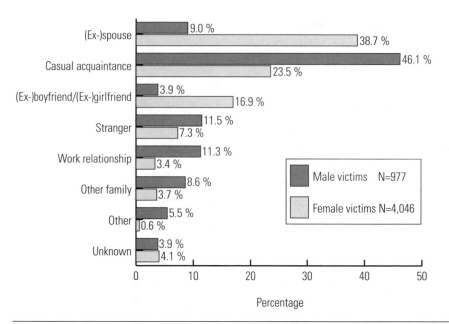

Source: Kong, R. (1996). "Criminal Harassment." *Juristat* 16(12): p. 4. Used by permission of Statistics Canada.

tourism has left the impression that tourists are not likely to be victims, they *are*, and they need to take precautions to protect themselves. Tourists are becoming increasingly aware of their vulnerability; as a result, many are staying away from once-popular tourist destinations.

Major outbreaks of violence against tourists receive widespread media attention; often this attention comes with advice to tourists about how they can protect themselves. Attacks on foreign tourists in parts of East Africa and Egypt have led to a worldwide alert to avoid these areas. Canadians have recently received highly publicized warnings about travel in Florida—a popular destination for families and the elderly. Also, travel agencies and tour groups now steer clients away from areas they consider dangerous. The governments of many countries issue warnings to their nationals to avoid certain areas—in particular, areas characterized by political instability or violence against tourists. In circumstances like this, travellers may become a target of local anger and frustration. Some countries are responding to crime against tourists by developing programs to enhance security in resort areas and to educate travellers about the hazards they may encounter in certain areas. Tourist-directed crime seems to be best explained by opportunity theorists, who view tourists as vulnerable targets in areas where surveillance may be low and precautions more difficult to take.

A tourist is more likely to be a victim of theft or robbery than of personal attack. Most commonly, luggage is stolen or pockets are picked. As thieves develop sophisticated techniques for picking or jimmying locks, they are preying more and more on cars as well. In one scam the thief drives along a beach road that is not too crowded and checks out the parked cars. If there are signs of an attractive target (e.g., a foreign licence plate or a rental car), and if the owner is nowhere to be seen (and thus presumably down at the beach), the thief parks behind the car, approaches it, and breaks through its lock (with special tools, this can be accomplished easily). Then the thief quickly searches the car and exits with whatever loot he has found. Slashing a tire prevents the victim from attempting pursuit.

Tourists may also run into problems simply because they do not understand the local language or customs. In one case, a 16-year-old Japanese exchange student was shot and killed in a Louisiana neighbourhood because he did not understand the warning "Freeze!" The youth had been looking for a Halloween party and did not stop when he was accosted by Rodney Peairs, who later said that he felt his life was being threatened by the costumed youth. Peairs was acquitted under a Louisiana law that allows citizens to use deadly weapons to protect themselves. In response to the student's tragic death, the Japanese government is publishing a guide of helpful phrases for U.S.-bound tourists. The guide will include about 30 phrases that few Japanese learn in their language classes, among them, "Get lost," "Watch out," and "I mean it" (Sanger, 1993: A9). Not only the translations but also the different cultural meanings of the 30 phrases will be imparted to teach visitors that the person issuing the warning is serious.

Victimization data can help us understand how tourism and other forms of travel affect our chances of becoming crime victims. Using survey data, Wellford (1997) estimated the victimization rates of domestic travellers in the United States. His findings were not what we might expect. He found that for all types of crime, victimization rates for domestic travellers were substantially lower than those for the general population. Also, gender differences with respect to victimization were the same for travellers as for the general population.

How do we reconcile these results with our assumptions about the dangers of travel? Wellford suggests that routine activities theory offers one way of understanding the results. Perhaps crime rates are lower for travellers in large part because they tend to take more concrete steps to control target suitability and guardianship. For example, tourists are generally more likely to go out in groups and to spend their time in well-travelled "tourist areas." This interpretation is consistent with the observation that those notorious cases of tourist victimization that we read or hear about typically seem to involve people who wandered off the beaten path into high-crime areas or who took the "wrong" exit ramp off the highway. Clearly, the topic of tourism and victimization deserves more focused attention.

THE AFTERMATH

Victimizations that occur in leisure settings often go unreported. For example, the tourist-victim may not speak the local language or know how to find the police. If the loss or the injury is not great, the tourist-victim may decide that reporting the incident to the police is not worth it. Victimizations may also go unreported when the leisure activity is itself regarded as a form of disreputable behaviour. Victims who have been drinking or who encounter offenders in a known "deviant context" (i.e., in a bar with a notorious reputation) may be reluctant to bring the incident to the attention of the police. Given the generally negative attitude toward many forms of youthful leisure activities, it is not surprising when crimes in these settings go undiscovered or unrecorded by police.

Victims respond in various ways to crimes committed against them in leisure settings. One common response is to avoid encounters or circumstances of the type during which the victimization occurred. Leisure activity is by definition discretionary activity, so it is easier to avoid than home- or work-related activities. Thus, the victim of courtship violence may refrain from dating, and the jogger who has been mugged may stop jogging and take up "mall walking," perceiving it to be safer than running on city streets or park paths.

A participant in a street fight or barroom brawl may prefer to seek revenge rather than report the crime to police. Of course, the status of these individuals as "victims" may itself be questionable, as they themselves may have struck the first blow or picked the fight. Also, many criminal events involving young males are of little interest to police, who are being encouraged more and more to manage their workloads by assigning a higher priority to the victimization of women and children than to that of young males.

The long-term consequences of leisure-related victimizations are not yet evident. The effects may be short-lived (except when it comes to sexual assaults). The punks that Baron (1989) talked with simply shrugged off their own victimization, regarding it as a routine hazard of life on the street. The degree to which individuals are deterred from becoming involved in leisure-related crimes may have more to do with the risk of being hurt than with the risk of being arrested. This is not to suggest that the police do not deter; their presence on the street and in bars plays an important role in keeping potentially dangerous behaviour under control. The evidence seems to indicate that the behaviour of young males on the street and in other settings can change from passive to violent fairly easily, especially given the fact that victims and offenders are often hard to distinguish and that public guardians (police and citizens) are not always available to stop a brewing conflict from becoming serious.

The need for guardianship has long driven the policy whereby police attempt to maintain a high profile on the street. This high profile has been achieved through the use of random patrol (i.e., cars cruising neighbourhoods looking for problems). However, patrol tactics seem to have little influence on the amount of neighbourhood crime (see Chapter 3). As a result, police departments are now experimenting with neighbourhood mini-stations and increasing foot patrols and neighbourhood consultations—tactics they believe can prevent and deter crime more effectively than a highly visible police presence in the form of random patrol. The most effective guardians against crime are not the police, but rather other people who frequent leisure settings and who call the police when needed.

There have been attempts to control crime by influencing how leisure is used. Especially conspicuous have been efforts to develop **positive leisure** alternatives for young people who are actually or potentially delinquent (Agnew and Peterson, 1989). This approach reflects the maxim, made explicit in social control theory, that "idle hands are the devil's workshop." Youths get themselves into trouble—through various forms of "hanging out"—because they lack positive options. The reasoning behind the positive-leisure approach is that summer camps, organized clubs, and other so-called forms of healthy recreation will expose youths to an environment that discourages involvement in crime and delinquency.

A similar approach focuses on the need to control "negative" and "corrupting" forms of youth leisure. This approach reflects the view that if they are left to make their own leisure choices, youths will almost always make the wrong ones. The past several decades have witnessed many crusades intended to impose legal and social restrictions on the ability of young people to make their own choices. These campaigns were directed against feature films in the

Positive leisure
Forms of leisure activity that link adolescents to conformist others and that are thought to insulate against delinquency.

1930s; comic books and rock 'n' roll in the 1950s; "drug-influenced" protest music in the 1960s; and rap and heavy metal music, fantasy role-playing games (e.g., Dungeons and Dragons), and video games in the late twentieth and early twenty-first centuries. Television violence has been subject to recurrent crusades every five or ten years since the 1960s (Best, 1990; Gray, 1989). However, there is an ironic character to crusades like these. According to Tanner (1992: 228) they reflect a perennial tendency on the part of adults to rediscover, to stigmatize, and to attempt to control the culture and behaviour of the generations that follow them. The Elvis Presley and Beatles fans and the hippies and student radicals of earlier eras now express bewilderment and concern about the corruptive nature of the cultural worlds in which they believe their own children to be immersed. Contemporary charges that modern heavy metal music inspires teen suicide and sexual promiscuity, or that it promotes mysticism and devil worship, tell us more about how anxieties about youth are reproduced across generations than about the uniquely deviant characteristics of contemporary youth.

SUMMARY

When people are "at leisure," they are also at risk of involvement in criminal events, as offenders or as victims. The links between leisure activity and criminal activity are highly complex. It has been argued that some forms of leisure can cause crime—for example, that the content of youth-oriented media may provide the motives for crime. It has also been suggested that peer activities may provide freedom from the social controls that might be expected to inhibit offending.

Much leisure activity takes place in public spaces. Street crime involves people who are passing through an area from one place to another or who are simply "hanging out." In these contexts, crime itself can be a form of leisure, as seems to be the case with vandalism and graffiti writing. In leisure settings such as streets and bars, it is often difficult to distinguish offender from victim when a conflict escalates into assault or some other form of violence. This form of opportunity crime tends to be based on the risky lifestyles of the individuals involved, and is more likely to be deterred by retribution than by reporting the crime to the police.

In date rape, the routine activity of courtship takes on a criminal character when aggressive behaviour translates into sexual assault against an unwilling participant. Much of this behaviour goes unreported. Tourism crime targets people who are at leisure in unfamiliar places; their lack of understanding of which areas are safe or unsafe may put them at risk. It is often difficult for tourists who have been victimized to find someone to whom to report the crime. They may decide they simply don't want the hassle of getting involved with the police in a foreign country. Increasingly, travel agencies and governments are briefing tourists on how to travel safely and advising them of areas to avoid altogether. A tourist's most effective deterrent against crime is to not travel in unsafe areas at all; this removes the opportunity for crime.

Some leisure pursuits place people at particular risk of victimization. The risky lifestyles in which people engage may make the search for a "good time" result in a "bad time." It must be emphasized that in the leisure domain, as in other domains, the processes we are describing are not deterministic. In other words, exposure to criminogenic influences or to threats of victimization does not necessarily result in a criminal event; these things only make a criminal event more probable by bringing together opportunities for crime with motivations to offend.

QUESTIONS FOR REVIEW AND DISCUSSION

1. Why are bars the site of so much crime? Can you name some bars in your area that are associated with high rates of crime?

2. Is dating violence a serious problem on your campus? What measures (if any) have been taken by school officials to deal with the problem?

3. How do you account for the recurrent tendency on the part of adults to view the cultural trappings of adolescents as troublesome?

4. In what ways can vandalism be understood as a juvenile form of leisure activity?

5. How do patterns of leisure activity change over the life cycle? What implications do these changes have for victimization risk?

6. Why are many of the crimes committed against tourists never reported to the police?

INFOTRAC COLLEGE EDITION

Explore InfoTrac College Edition, your online university library, which includes hundreds of popular and scholarly journals in which you can find articles related to the topics in this chapter. Visit InfoTrac through your Web browser (**www.infotrac-college.com**), or through this book's Web site (**www.criminalevent-3e.nelson.com**).

WHAT'S ON THE WEB?

For chapter links and quizzes, check out the accompanying Web site at **www.criminalevent-3e.nelson.com**.

Chapter 10

Crime and Work

WHAT'S IN CHAPTER TEN

In this chapter we discuss the three forms of the relationship between work and crime. First we examine how different types of work can expose individuals to varying forms and levels of victimization risk. Second we examine how people who are employed in legitimate work activities take advantage of their positions to commit crimes. Third we look at crime that takes on the character of work in the context of an ongoing illegal enterprise.

INTRODUCTION

In this chapter we consider crime in the social domain of the workplace. This social domain was largely neglected by criminologists until recently (Gill, 1994). Our discussion is organized around two broad topics.

The *first* is the relationship between participation in the legitimate labour force and the occurrence of criminal events. Two major issues concern us here. In what ways are patterns of victimization associated with patterns of employment? That is, how do our jobs affect the victimization risks we face? And in what ways does seemingly honest work make available opportunities for criminal behaviour, involving either employers (or employees) or members of the public?

The *second* major theme of this chapter is crime as an occupational activity. Here we examine "enterprise crime," which involves exploiting opportunities for the development of criminal business.

CRIME, EMPLOYMENT, AND UNEMPLOYMENT

The Canadian labour force has undergone several important changes in the past few decades. Female labour force participation has increased greatly in recent years, especially among married women. The types of jobs available have also changed in the past two decades. Employment in the manufacturing sector has fallen since 1979, but the availability of jobs in the service sector has increased. However, compared with goods-producing jobs, service jobs tend to pay less and to more often involve part-time work. Unemployment remains especially prevalent among young people and members of minority groups, who as we already know are at high risk for involvement in criminal events as both victims and offenders. Although Canadians between age 15 and 24 comprise only 8 percent of the total working-age population, they account for 30 percent of all unemployed Canadians (Stevenson et al., 1998).

The nature of work itself has also undergone important changes. Many of these changes are attributable to technological innovations, especially in computer technology. These changes, which are intended to make the workplace more efficient—and from the employer's viewpoint, more profitable—have affected the pacing and timing of jobs. Many employees have computer hookups in their homes that allow them to reduce the amount of time required at their formal places of work. Fax machines quicken the pace at which information can be transmitted, and cellular telephones have begun to blur, for many, the distinction between private time and work time.

EMPLOYMENT AND VICTIMIZATION

How do patterns of employment and experiences in the labour force relate to patterns of involvement in criminal events? One approach to this question is to ask whether employed and unemployed individuals face different victimization risks. This question is not as straightforward as it first seems. For one thing, who exactly are we comparing employed people to? When we define "unemployed" broadly, to include not only those who are unemployed but also those who are retired, institutionalized, or sick, or who define their main activity as "homemaker," the victimization risks associated with being employed are generally higher for most types of crime. This is because those who constitute this other broad reference group are likely to be people whose social and demographic characteristics are usually associated with lower victimization rates. But when we compare those who are employed with those who are looking for work and unable to find it, the disadvantages associated with employment diminish in many surveys. In other words, unemployment is associated with higher victimization risk (Miethe and Meier, 1994).

UNEMPLOYMENT AND OFFENDING

The relationship between unemployment and offending is studied much more often than the relationship between unemployment and victimization. Most of the theories of offending we reviewed in Chapters 4 and 5 would lead us to expect that the risks of offending are greater for unemployed people. Theories that emphasize the role of **social inequality** in the generation of crime quite naturally suggest that not having a job may encourage the development of criminal motivations. Moreover, this view is perfectly consistent with common sense.

Social inequality
Results when one social group is underprivileged compared with another.

For many reasons we would expect measures of unemployment to be related, in empirical studies, to measures of criminal offending (Fagan and Freeman, 1999):

- Some property crimes may be committed out of a sense of need or desire for things that people want but cannot buy. People who lack a stable income may experience greater temptations to take what is not theirs.
- Occupational status arguably is an important mechanism for integrating people into conventional society; that is, jobs provide a "stake in conformity" (Toby, 1974). Not having a job may weaken the hold that conformist institutions have over people.
- Being unemployed may result in the adoption of behaviours, such as drug use, that are themselves associated with criminal offending (Hartnagel and Krahn, 1989).
- Unemployment may be related to family instability and thus to the ability of parents to monitor the criminal behaviour of dependent children (Sampson, 1987).
- Since rates of unemployment are high among young people, who seem to be most "crime prone," we might expect the criminogenic effects of unemployment to be especially strongly related to offending among this segment of the population.

Despite these theoretical and commonsense connections between unemployment and offending, several criminologists question the validity of this relationship (Chiricos, 1987; Freeman, 1983; Gottfredson and Hirschi, 1990). Many researchers argue that unemployment is causally related to crime but are unsure of the size and significance of the effect. Others dispute whether being unemployed has any independent causal influence on the propensity to behave criminally.

Sorting out the relationship between unemployment and offending is no simple task. *First*, just as efforts to measure crime are fraught with difficulties, so is it difficult to measure unemployment in any valid way (Gramling, Forsyth, and Fewell, 1988). Unemployment is usually measured in terms of the number of people who are not employed but who are actively looking for work. Measures like this exclude those who have "dropped out" of the labour pool. This bias in our measures of unemployment may end up including those who are most highly motivated to gain entry to the "conventional world" and excluding those who are least motivated. The overall effect may be to weaken the measured relationship between crime and unemployment.

Second, some researchers have argued that not only unemployment per se but also the quality of labour force experiences is related to criminal offending (Hartnagel and Krahn, 1989). Precarious, low-paying jobs that offer few of the advantages generally associated with employment are counted as "employment" in labour force surveys, even though such jobs may not provide a strong cushion against the various criminogenic influences to which the jobholder may be exposed. *Third*, many researchers try to study the relationship between unemployment and crime at the aggregate level (e.g., by asking whether the national unemployment rate is related to the national crime rate) (Chiricos, 1987). This may be too broad for the investigation of this issue, in that it may obscure relationships that exist at the community and neighbourhood levels.

Despite the popular view of the relationship between unemployment and crime, studies support alternative interpretations. For instance, some researchers have suggested that delinquent involvement is greater among employed teenagers than among unemployed ones (Tanner, 2001). The former group, it is argued, may be less susceptible to parental controls and more susceptible to delinquent peer influences. Other researchers have suggested that crime causes unemployment, not the other way around (Fagan and Freeman, 1999). Perhaps people who are criminally inclined are less interested in conforming to the routines demanded by legitimate labour force participation (Wilson, 1983). Still others maintain that the relationship between crime and unemployment is "spurious" in the sense that no real relationship exists between them; the appearance of a relationship is created by the fact that being unemployed and behaving criminally are both related to a "common cause" such as a low degree of self-control (Gottfredson and Hirschi, 1990).

In sum, it may be impossible to generalize about the relationship between unemployment and crime. The nature of the relationship may depend on the type of crime, the social characteristics of the labour force group, and the social policies in place to assist those who are not employed (Allan and Steffensmeier, 1989; Currie, 1985). Cantor and Land (1985) have argued, moreover, that the rate of unemployment may have more than one type of effect on the overall rate of crime. Consistent with arguments made earlier in this chapter, they suggest that unemployment may encourage the development of criminal motivation among some people. This implies that unemployment is positively related to the crime rate—that is, the crime rate increases as the unemployment rate increases. However, Cantor and Land also suggest that the unemployment rate may have a negative effect on the crime rate. This effect is related not to criminal motivation but to criminal opportunity. According to Cantor and Land, the unemployed are much less likely to engage in routine activities that take them away from the home for predictable and extended periods. In other words, unemployment may be related to increases in the level of guardianship exercised over persons and property. Also, because the unemployment rate can be understood, at least in part, as a general indicator of the overall well-being of the economy, we can assume that when the unemployment rate is high, there will be fewer goods in circulation for thieves to steal.

We have reviewed the relationship between employment (and unemployment) and the likelihood of committing crime. Next we examine how particular forms of labour force participation make crime possible. Two issues concern us here. What is the relationship between the jobs people have and the victimization risks they face? And how do the jobs people have provide them with opportunities to behave criminally?

VICTIMIZATION AND WORK

Public awareness of workplace stress has been increasing in recent years. Work-related stressors include job demands and hours of work, the threat of layoff, poor interpersonal relations, the risk of accident or injury, harassment, discrimination, and even fear for one's life.

INDIVIDUAL AND OCCUPATIONAL CHARACTERISTICS

Although it is not generally recognized, the threat of criminal victimization may be an important source of job stress for many people. Victimization surveys tell us that the chances of being a victim of crime are not randomly distributed across occupational groups. This is not surprising, given that occupations differ with respect to the work they require of people and with respect to where, when, and under what conditions that work is done. As we will see, the characteristics of some jobs increase risk, and the characteristics of other jobs decrease risk. These differences are often obscured when the victimization experiences of the employed are compared with those of the unemployed.

Yet even when we compare the victimization risks associated with different occupations, it can be difficult to determine whether it is the job itself or the characteristics of the people who hold that job that affects the risk of victimization. For instance, if we were to discover that part-time employees of fast-food restaurants face especially high risks of victimization, we would not necessarily be justified in concluding that there is something about cooking or serving hamburgers that makes one more vulnerable to criminal danger (although there may be!). Fast-food employees tend to be teenagers, and in view of the relationship between age and victimization, the higher risks may involve age-related rather than work-related factors. In fact, we might not even be surprised to discover that though these employees report higher rates of crime, the experiences they tell us about typically occur outside of work rather than on the job. In sum, a cursory review of victimization risks and occupations can easily mislead us.

Information about how victimization risks vary across occupations is hard to come by. This is because the statistical rarity of victimization incidents often prevents survey researchers from computing separate victimization rates for a detailed inventory of occupations. Some research indicates that risks are higher for members of the military (Harlow, 1991), probation officers (Lindner and Bonn, 1996), police officers, welfare workers, those who work in bars (Mayhew, Elliott, and Dowds, 1989), and other occupations that involve regular and frequent contact with high-risk populations.

A large-scale study of occupational differences in victimization risk was undertaken by Block, Felson, and Block (1984), who calculated the victimization rates for 426 occupations using data on 108,000 crime incidents reported to U.S. National Crime Survey (NCS) interviewers between 1973 and 1981. For the five offences these researchers examined—robbery, assault, burglary, larceny, and automobile theft—victimization risk was inversely related to "occupational status," which they defined as the average income for each occupation. In other words, as the average income of an occupation increased, the risks of being victimized decreased. The study also showed wide variations in levels of victimization risk. For instance, for all offences, recreation workers (e.g., at amusement parks) and hospitality workers (e.g., busboy, dishwasher, server) were among the top five for risk of victimization. Sheriffs and police officers had the highest assault rates; taxi drivers and newspaper vendors were among the most often robbed. The lowest rates of victimization were found among certain farm workers, and among telephone and electrical workers, opticians, stenographers, and radio operators.

The authors readily acknowledged that data of this sort are difficult to interpret:

> On the one hand, better jobs tend to provide more good things in life, presumably including safety and security from crime. More income and credit allow people to purchase security devices, safer locations to live in, better parking spots and the like. Better jobs may also help people avoid public transit and unfavourable hours for trips to work and elsewhere. Better credit allows avoidance of cash. In general, more resources, including money, credit and control over time, should help people to obtain security from crime.

> On the other hand, better jobs may bring with them more luxury goods to attract offenders. Higher strata individuals may also go out more at night, enjoying sport and cultural events or visiting restaurants or other night spots. Good jobs are often found within a metropolis rather than in rural areas with lower risk. One suspects that modern offenders have little trouble finding the higher occupational strata in order to victimize them, security efforts notwithstanding (Block, Felson, and Block, 1984: 442).

So analyses of the victimization rates of different occupational groups are interesting and informative, but they do not necessarily tell us very much about crimes that occur in the workplace. This requires a more focused investigation of the crimes that happen while people are at work.

A more recent analysis of NCS data from 1992 to 1996 provides a helpful discussion of the relationship between work and victimization risk (Warchol, 1998). The analysis revealed that the most common violent crime experienced by victims working or "on duty" at the time of their victimization was simple assault. Also, as Table 10.1 shows, the rate per 1,000 workers of violent workplace victimization varies quite dramatically across occupations. These data

Part 3: Domains of Crime

TABLE 10.1

OCCUPATIONS OF VICTIMS OF NONFATAL WORKPLACE VIOLENCE, 1992–96

Occupation	Number of victims per 1,000 workers
Medical	
Physicians	15.7
Nurses	24.8
Technicians	21.4
Others	10.7
Mental health	
Professional	79.5
Custodial	63.3
Other	64.0
Teaching	
Preschool	3.6
Elementary	16.0
Junior high	57.4
High school	28.9
College/university	2.5
Technical/industrial	4.4
Special education	40.7
Other	10.1
Law enforcement	
Police	306.0
Private security	117.3
Corrections officer	217.8
Other	61.5
Retail sales	
Convenience/liquor store	68.4
Gas station	79.1
Bar	91.3
Other	17.5
Transportation	
Taxi driver	183.8
Bus driver	45.0
Other	10.0

Source: G. Warchol (1998), Bureau of Justice Statistics Special Report, *National Crime Survey: Workplace Violence*, Washington D.C.: U.S. Department of Justice. Used by permission.

suggest that for the occupational categories listed, the highest rates of violent workplace victimization are experienced by those involved in law enforcement, and the lowest rates are experienced by teachers.

PRECURSORS

In very general terms, workplace settings have characteristics that both encourage and inhibit victimization. On the one hand, full-time employees spend many hours "at risk" of whatever threats the workplace presents. On the other hand, workplace settings tend to be much more highly structured than, for instance, leisure settings and thus more subject to a variety of social controls that discourage victimization. Some degree of order and control is usually deemed necessary if the organizational goals of the workplace are to be achieved efficiently.

How much crime happens in the workplace? As stated, answers to this question are not easy to derive from most kinds of existing data sets, which are usually intended to answer more general types of questions. Data from a 20-year analysis of NCS data provide some clarification (Zawitz et al., 1993). This analysis revealed that with respect to violent crime, about 14 percent of incidents occurred while the victim was working or "on duty." In contrast, 16 percent of incidents occurred while the victim was participating in an activity at home (i.e., rather than sleeping), and 29 percent occurred while the victim was engaged in a leisure activity away from home. In the case of burglary, 21 percent occurred while the victim was at work, compared to 15 percent while the victim was sleeping and 25 percent while the victim was pursuing a leisure activity away from home. For crimes of theft, the two most common activities for victims at the time the crime was committed were leisure away from home (21 percent) and working (19 percent). However, these data underestimate the relative proportion of **workplace crime** in that they represent proportions of the total number of incidents—that is, incidents involving those who are *and* those who are not members of the paid labour force.

Data from the 1988 British Crime Survey (BCS) allow us to separate out the proportion of workplace crimes reported by employed respondents (Mayhew, Elliott, and Dowds, 1989). These findings reveal that 71 percent of thefts, 22 percent of assaults, 11 percent of robberies, and 13 percent of vehicle thefts occurred while respondents were at work. In all cases, the vast majority of crimes occurred while the victim was inside the workplace rather than in

Workplace crime
Criminal events that emerge out of relations formed by labour force participation in the context of legitimate or illegitimate economies.

some other work-related location, such as out-of-doors at work or on the street near the workplace.

One type of worksite for which detailed information about victimization risk is readily available is schools. In recent years much attention has been paid to schools as settings that pose serious criminal dangers to both students and teachers (Kaufman, Chandler, and Rand, 1998; May and Dunaway, 2000; Rountree, 2000; Sheley and Wright, 1998).

According to Canadian UCR data for 1997, 9 percent of all criminal incidents involving youth were committed on school property. Violent offences accounted for 38 percent of all incidents at schools (Stevenson et al., 1998). To some degree, the high proportion of violent incidents reported to have occurred at schools reflects the influence of zero-tolerance policies toward violence. In earlier periods, many of these incidents would have been handled informally by teachers or principals. The existence of these policies makes it more likely that the police will become involved (and that incidents will end up in police data systems). The absence of long-term victimization data makes it difficult to formulate alternative estimates of school violence.

How do workplace characteristics relate to variations in the levels of workplace danger? Data from victimization surveys have been used to describe the types of workplace conditions that seem to facilitate employee victimization (Collins, Cox, and Langan, 1987; Lynch, 1987). These studies suggest that the risks of becoming a crime victim on the job are greater in the following circumstances:

- When the job involves face-to-face contact with a large number of people on a routine basis. That is, if the workplace restricts access to authorized persons, the risks of crime are lower.
- When the job involves handling money.
- When the job involves overnight travel or travel between worksites.
- When the job involves the delivery of passengers or goods.

The importance of these factors becomes apparent when we assess them in reference to routine activities theory and associated concepts such as exposure and guardianship. People who work in settings that leave them unprotected and at the same time exposed to a large number of people (some of whom may be "motivated offenders") are more likely to be victimized in the workplace.

Victimization studies also indicate that it not the characteristics of the victims (such as sex and age) but rather the nature of the work that affects an individual's likelihood of becoming a crime victim in the workplace. The structure of school populations would lead us to expect more crime than we observe in that setting.

Schools, after all, concentrate on a daily basis the age groups at greatest risk of offending and victimization. Toby (1995) contends that the risks associated with school populations are compounded by the requirement of compulsory attendance. Disruptive or troublesome students who do not wish to attend school are required to do so. For this reason, he suggests, junior high schools have more serious rates of victimization than senior high schools.

Also, until recently schools have been relatively open settings, easily accessible to potential offenders who do not attend them. These "intruders" may include not only the stereotypical predator but also the angry parent or the student who is upset at having been expelled. Although schools are capable of exercising some degree of guardianship against victimization, a school of above-average size that allows students considerable freedom of movement may provide many settings that facilitate criminal activity. In school buildings, more victimizations typically take place in less supervised areas, such as hallways and rest rooms, than in more controlled places such as classrooms and libraries (Garofalo, Siegel, and Laub, 1987).

The routine activities associated with some work locations tend to make them less vulnerable to crime. Desroches (1995) notes that department stores and supermarkets are known to carry large amounts of cash yet are generally not perceived as desirable targets by robbers. Supermarkets are likely to have security equipment, and there are often many people in the store at any given time. The high shelves in most grocery stores do not allow the potential thief an unobstructed view of the setting, and because there are usually two exits, it is difficult to control movement in and out of the store. Furthermore, the separation of the cash registers by relatively wide aisles makes the collection of the stolen money a time-consuming activity. In short, targets like this offer too many risks for too little money.

TRANSACTIONS

Much of the violent victimization that occurs in the workplace results from conflicts between employees and customers or clients. A bartender tells an inebriated customer he is "cut off," a teacher tries to enforce classroom discipline, a sales clerk refuses to permit a return of merchandise, a police officer tries to intervene in an argument, and so on.

The situational context of much workplace victimization is revealed in a study by Salinger and colleagues (1993) of assaults of flight attendants. This study found that flight attendants have rates of assault as much as 10 times higher than the average. Most assaults involved a conflict between passenger and attendant over some mandatory flight regulation relating, for example, to baggage arrangements or food or drink service. The researchers found that first-class passengers, who are only 10 percent of the travelling public, accounted for 20 percent of assaults—a finding that may be explained by the higher expectations of service, passengers' perception of their status relative to that of the attendant, and the consumption of alcohol. The study also found that assaults are most likely to occur during takeoffs or landings, which are the most distressing times for passengers who are afraid of flying. Also, at takeoff the authority role of the attendant may not yet be clearly understood.

Violent school crimes, except perhaps those involving intruders, are probably more likely than other workplace crimes to include as participants offenders and victims who are known to each other (Whitaker and Bastian, 1991). According to Garofalo, Siegel, and Laub (1987), many of these events result from

> frictions from peers arising from normal daily activities. School grounds and trips to and from school provide ample opportunities for interactions that can escalate into relatively minor victimizations. "Weapons" often consist of available items grabbed on the spur of the moment. Items stolen from victims often seem to be the targets of malicious, even mischievous motivations (333).

THE AFTERMATH

Victimizations in the workplace do not seem to differ much from other types of victimizations in terms of levels of property loss and injury (Whitaker and Bastian, 1991). Data from the 1997 Canadian UCR suggest that few physical injuries resulted from incidents in schools (Stevenson et al., 1998); fewer than 5 percent of victims reported serious physical injuries. This probably reflects the fact that violent incidents that occur in schools are unlikely to involve the use of a weapon.

As with other social domains, much of the crime that occurs in the workplace is not reported to the police (Warchol, 1998). As noted earlier, school crime is an exception since mandatory reporting rules often apply. At least two

BOX 10.1

School Massacres

In the late 1990s and early 2000s several high-profile incidents in Canada and the United States led to a widespread concern about the threat of mass murder in schools. Though these incidents are statistically rare, the horrific violence associated with them has had profound consequences for how politicians, security experts, and parents think about school safety.

Criminologists John Alan Fox and Jack Levin note that for the public, "lethal violence inside the school struck a nerve" (2001: 94). To some degree, these incidents were made all the more shocking by their contexts. Because they did not occur in minority communities in urban centres, where drugs and street violence are seen as pervasive, they shocked the consciousness of those who tended to believe they were safe from violence.

Fox and Levin observe that the search for explanations of these incidents quickly settled on the family. Popular wisdom suggests that bad kids come from bad homes. Though parenting is an important factor, these researchers also direct our attention to the social dynamics of schools. With respect to perhaps the most notorious incident of school violence—the mass murder at Columbine High School in April 1999—the schoolyard snipers were seen by others as "geeks" or "nerds." Largely excluded from student cliques and from the mainstream of school life, they banded together with fellow outcasts in what they called the "Trench Coat Mafia." The image of themselves they attempted to construct emphasized power, invincibility, and incivility. Fox and Levin conclude:

> Birds of a feather may kill together. Harris, the leader, would likely have enjoyed the respect and admiration from Klebold, who in turn would have felt uplifted by the praise he received from his revered buddy. In their relationship, the two boys got from one another what was otherwise missing from their lives—they felt special, they gained a sense of belonging, they were united against the world. As Harris remarked, as he and his friend made last-minute preparations to commit mass murder: "This is just a two-man war against everything else" (Fox and Levin, 2001: 94).

characteristics of the work domain may discourage reporting. *First*, many work environments have alternative means for dealing with crime. The handling of an incident often proceeds no further than bringing it to the attention of a supervisor or private security officer (Warchol, 1998). Businesses, restaurants, and even schools may choose to avoid the publicity associated with the visit of a police patrol car by dealing with less serious incidents themselves.

Second, employees who are victimized as a result of their dealings with the public may be persuaded by their employers that these incidents only occur

BOX 10.2

Feeling Safe at Work

Crime in the workplace has become a public issue, and many people are feeling less secure at work than they used to be. But we know relatively little about the character of workplace fear of crime. Esther Madriz (1996) used data from the American NCS to investigate the factors that affect fear at work. She found that people are more likely to judge the workplace as unsafe when

- they live in bigger cities
- they have contact with potential offenders
- they handle money in their jobs
- they work in places that employ fewer security measures
- they work evenings
- they use public transportation
- they have been victims of crime in the past

Madriz notes that many of these factors are related not only to fear of crime but also to the actual risks of victimization.

when they are not doing their work properly. In other words, they may come to believe that "cooling off" belligerent customers or clients is one of their job responsibilities. Even in severe cases, the victim may fear being blamed for having started the incident by behaving rudely toward the customer (Salinger et al., 1993).

Jobs can become hazardous when they expose employees to clients and situations that provide opportunities for crime. One step that can be taken to deter these crimes is to provide employees with the resources they need to deal with client-related problems. Also, employers must be ready to react strongly to crimes that occur on their premises; this will ensure that their employees can do their jobs with a greater sense of security.

CRIME AND LEGITIMATE WORK

Many people—including many criminologists—tend to think about criminal offending and legitimate work as mutually exclusive. But as Fagan and Freeman (1999) note, the relationship between crime and legitimate work is hardly that simple. Many individuals are simultaneously involved in legitimate labour *and* the world of crime. Crime, after all, need not take all that much time and energy; and legitimate jobs do not necessarily remove criminal motivation, especially if they pay badly. Even more importantly, legitimate jobs often provide workers with criminal opportunities to which they would otherwise not have access. In this section we explore some of the ways that work makes offending possible.

WHAT IS OCCUPATIONAL CRIME?

The scope of work-related crime is potentially as broad as the types of jobs that exist in an economic system (Croall, 1987). An employee with unsupervised access to his employer's inventory may find that his job provides a unique opportunity for theft. A physician or a lawyer may charge for services she hasn't performed (Arnold and Hagan, 1992). Stores may use illegal sales practices to defraud the public. Large corporations may engage in the sale and manufacture of dangerous products, pollute the environment, and maintain unsafe working conditions. Work-related crime ranges from pilfering by a disgruntled employee to the gargantuan thefts associated with the savings and loans scandal in the United States (Sherrill, 1997).

Modern interest in the concept of work-related crime is usually traced back to the writings of the famous American criminologist Edwin Sutherland (see Chapter 4). Sutherland (1940) used the term **white-collar crime** to refer to crimes committed in the context of work by people of high status and respectability. He saw a need to correct the imbalance in criminological thinking that associated crime almost exclusively with the actions of the poor and the powerless. Through a study of major American corporations, he sought to prove that individuals who are fully and gainfully employed, and whose jobs accord them considerable power and economic security, are often responsible for serious breaches of the law.

Since Sutherland's time the concept of white-collar crime has undergone adjustments that reflect changes in the meaning of white-collar work. For Sutherland the term *white-collar crime* denoted the criminal conspiracies of major corporations. Today many forms of work—for example, sales and computer programming—do not involve manual labour, yet even so cannot be considered positions in some sort of economic or corporate elite. This is why criminologists have introduced such terms as *professional crime, elite deviance, corporate crime, organizational crime, respectable crime,* and *business crime.* Our interest in social domains as the context of criminal events requires us to pay close attention not only to the crimes of powerful jobholders but also to the crimes of those whose jobs denote lower-ranked positions. Encompassing

White-collar crime
A crime committed by a person of respectability and high status in the course of his or her occupation.

Occupational crime
Violation of legal norms governing lawful occupational endeavours.

both types of crime is the term **occupational crime,** which Akers (1985: 228) defines as the "violation of legal norms governing lawful occupational endeavours."

There are different varieties of occupational crime. Some kinds are intended to provide only the jobholder with direct benefits. The person who pilfers from an employer does so for personal benefit; the same with the bank teller who embezzles or the systems analyst who steals computer time. In these situations the agency or organization is the victim and the employee is the offender.

But other times the organization is not the victim but rather a weapon being used against those outside of the organization or at the bottom of the organizational hierarchy. In these situations, the crime may profit the jobholder *indirectly*, in that direct benefits accrue to the organization itself. In these circumstances the victims may be other business organizations (e.g., a corporation hires industrial saboteurs to steal competitors' secrets), or clients or customers (e.g., a corporation engages in deceptive advertising or sells untested pharmaceutical or food products), or low-level organizational members (e.g., employers maintain unsafe working conditions or violate laws relating to labour relations). Furthermore, in some situations the victim is society at large. Political bribery, tax fraud, and polluting the environment fall into this category, in the sense that society in general suffers for these crimes.

Occupational crimes also vary by setting. Some types involve an offender acting alone or with a handful of offenders. Medical fraud and dishonest household repair schemes typically involve the actions of a single offender, who is dealing directly with victims and whose activities are not dependent on institutional support from co-workers. At the other extreme, **corporate crime** can involve "large vertical slices" of complex organizations (Snider, 1993: 321). In these situations it can be difficult to say who did and who did not behave criminally, since each individual's actions contribute in small ways to the criminal event.

We now examine the social organization of work routines in order to understand how and why occupational crimes occur.

Corporate crime
Acts committed by businesses in the interests of generating profit and avoiding losses and prosecution.

PRECURSORS

The relationship between work routines and criminal offending can be understood with reference to the concepts of opportunity and motivation (Coleman, 1987, 1991). In other words, the social organization of work may

BOX 10.3

Occupational Delinquency

Although most adolescents spend some part of their youth in the labour force, criminologists have spent very little time investigating their work-related delinquency. John Paul Wright and Francis T. Cullen (2000) attempted to investigate this issue using survey data collected from over 300 employed juveniles enrolled in eight high schools. The research revealed the following:

- Two-thirds of the students reported committing at least one work-related delinquent act in the previous year. The most common acts included calling in sick (when the individual was not), giving away goods or services for nothing and without permission, and drinking alcohol or using drugs while on the job.
- The overall quality of the workplace had no effect on the likelihood of engaging in delinquency.
- The likelihood of delinquency was related to the presence of delinquent peers in the workplace.
- Youth who were delinquent outside the workplace were more likely to be delinquent on the job.
- Individuals with delinquent propensities are selected (by themselves or by others) into work environments in which delinquency is more likely.

give people the means with which to violate the law, and their feelings about their work or employers may supply them with reasons for doing so.

In terms of opportunity, some work routines give employers or employees access to people and things to victimize. Doctors have access to patients, lawyers have access to clients, corporations have access to markets, and bank tellers have access to "other people's money" (Calavita and Pontell, 1991). While this access does not necessarily result in criminal action, it does make such action possible.

According to Coleman (1987, 1991), at least four factors influence the evaluation of opportunities to commit white-collar crime. The *first* factor is the perception of how large a gain can be expected from using the opportunity. The *second* is the perception of potential risks associated with the opportunity. The exploration of criminal opportunities is more likely when effective control is lacking. For example, many professional groups claim to be self-regulating, and discourage the efforts of government agencies to investigate them except in the most extreme cases. Also, many crimes that are associated with large corporations are so complex that they are policed only with great difficulty. Some observers have argued that the power of professional groups and large corporations discourages effective enforcement by state agencies (Hagan, 1992). The *third* factor is the degree of compatibility between the use of the opportunity and the potential offender's beliefs, attitudes, and ethical view of the situation. *Fourth* and finally, the evaluation of the opportunity is based on the potential offender's perception of the benefits of one opportunity relative to other opportunities to which that person has access.

The motivations for occupational crime are a matter of considerable debate. Some observers claim that these motivations reside in the nature of work itself or in the wider socioeconomic setting of the workplace. Insofar as capitalism promotes a "culture of competition" that encourages the pursuit of economic profit, the profit motive can be said to be the criminal motive (Calavita and Pontell, 1991). But the ways in which particular businesses and industries are organized can also serve as important motivating factors. Industries that experience severe competition, that are engaged in the sale or distribution of potentially dangerous—and therefore highly regulated—goods, or that operate in an uncertain economic environment may feel pressure to operate unlawfully in order to achieve organizational goals (Keane, 2000; Snider, 1993).

In very large corporations or businesses, pressures to behave criminally may be accentuated by the pressure placed on underlings to achieve organizational goals. In what Simon and Eitzen (1993) describe as "corporate Frankensteins," senior management may establish goals or quotas that everyone knows cannot be achieved within the limits imposed by current regulations. At the same time, management may be able to insulate itself from any covert criminal actions that result from these corporate objectives (Hagan, 1992). Those who make decisions about criminal wrongdoing may be actively or passively discouraged from reporting their activities to senior management (Coleman, 1987). If the acts are discovered by enforcement agencies or the public, management can then disavow any knowledge of wrongdoing. If the acts are not discovered, management can claim credit for the high profit yields (Snider, 1993).

The role of market forces in criminal events is illustrated clearly by the case of the Ford Pinto. This car was placed on the market in 1970, largely in response to fears of competition from Japanese car manufacturers. Lee Iacocca, who was president of Ford at the time, told his engineers they had to produce a car that weighed less than 2,000 pounds and that cost less than $2,000. The Pinto met these specifications, but it also contained serious design flaws. Most critical was the placement of the gas tank, which increased the likelihood that the car would explode in a rear-end collision. It was later discovered that the corporate officers had known about this design flaw and about the actions that could be taken to correct it. But instead of acting on this knowledge, they calculated the cost of these modifications and compared them with the costs likely to be incurred in lawsuits resulting from injuries to or deaths of Pinto drivers. The costs of the improvements were estimated to be greater than the costs associated with death and injury, so Ford decided not to repair the defect.

Some criminologists have emphasized the significant role played by "definitions of the situation"—definitions that favour criminal offending (Keane, 2000). Coleman (1987) proposes the following six such definitions:

1. Defining acts of theft as "borrowing."
2. Denying that white-collar crimes result in any real harm.
3. Claiming that the laws prohibiting the behaviour are unfair or unjust.
4. Claiming that certain types of criminal behaviour are necessary if organizational goals are to be achieved.
5. Claiming that the behaviour is normal and "everybody does it."
6. Claiming that employee theft is not really stealing since the money was owed (e.g., uncharged overtime).

Thus, acts that might be seen as criminal by others are often seen as excusable behaviours by the embezzler who defines theft as "borrowing" and by the corporate executive who defines the violation of fair labour laws as "just good business."

Much of the debate about the motivations to commit occupational crime has centred on questions about the distinctiveness of occupational offenders. Many criminologists have long contended that white-collar offenders differ from street criminals in important ways. Many white-collar offenders are neither poor nor powerless. Their crimes are not impulsive, irrational, or the product of inadequate planning. Thus, many of the factors that are usually associated with crime and criminals have little to do with the behaviour of white-collar offenders, especially those at the top of corporate hierarchies. It follows that the causes of these types of crime must lie elsewhere.

In contrast, the architects of the "general theory of crime," Gottfredson and Hirschi (1990), argue that the similarities between street criminals and occupational criminals are more important than the differences. For Gottfredson and Hirschi, the key explanatory mechanism for both groups is "self-control." Special theories are no more necessary to explain the criminal in a legitimate business than they are to explain the criminal in the university, the military, or the church. People who have low self-control are likely to engage in a variety of types of crime and deviance, as the opportunities to do so present themselves.

Gottfredson and Hirschi argue that because occupations that present significant criminal opportunities tend to be occupations that require a considerable degree of self-control, the rates of occupational crime are lower than is popularly believed. Moreover, they suggest that when differences in opportunity are taken into account, demographic correlates of street and occupational crime are similar. They conclude that there is no need to presume special motivational circumstances in the case of the occupational offender, such as "the culture of competition" and other types of factors described here. Instead, they assert that "the distinction between crime in the street and crime in the suite is an *offence* rather than an *offender* distinction [and] that offenders in both cases are likely to share similar characteristics" (Gottfredson and Hirschi, 1990: 200).

Benson and Moore (1992) used data on the sentencing patterns for a large number of white-collar crimes (bank embezzlement, bribery, income tax evasion, false claims, and mail fraud) and common crimes (narcotics offences, postal forgery, and bank robbery) to test some of the implications of Gottfredson and Hirschi's theory. Specifically, they attempted to determine whether white-collar offenders were as "criminally versatile" as common offenders, and whether they were as prone to as wide a range of deviant activities. They found that a minority of white-collar offenders behaved as the theory predicted; most did not.

According to Benson and Moore, low self-control is not the only path to occupational crime. Offenders with high self-control may employ it to pursue ego gratification in an aggressive and calculating manner. The culture of competition rewards these individuals by giving them positions of trust and opportunities for committing serious (and often undetected) crimes. In between those with high self-control and those with low self-control are individuals who may or may not take advantage of occupational opportunities depending on their personal situations. For these individuals, fear of economic or occupational failure can create a circumstance in which a once adequate level of self-control is now inadequate; when this happens the individual's ability to resist occupational opportunities for crime can be weakened.

TRANSACTIONS

It is difficult to determine how much crime is committed in the course of legitimate work. There are many reasons, the main one being that this kind of crime is often almost impossible to detect. Corporate crimes that victimize consumers, clients, or members of the public are very often "invisible" (Coleman, 1987). For example, people who are ill do not necessarily know that their illness is the result of inadequately tested drugs. Workers who are injured by hazardous working conditions may be inclined to blame themselves rather than their employers for their injuries (Croall, 1987). Our terminology encourages this tendency: we routinely call such occurrences "accidents" rather than "assaults."

Unlike more garden-variety forms of offending, occupational crimes are largely hidden from public view. The employee who has access to opportunities for offending often escapes public scrutiny. The offender who uses a computer to embezzle can often do so in such a way that the crime goes undetected by the employer, co-workers, and enforcement agencies. Corporate conspiracies are even less visible. Evidence about corporate decisions regarding offending is not accessible to those outside the corporation. Moreover, because a corporate crime may involve actions by members at all levels of the organization, many of those participating in the event may not even be aware of the true character of their actions.

As with other categories of crime, occupational crimes do not come to the attention of policing or regulatory agencies as a result of vigorous enforcement practices. At the same time, victims may be poorly positioned to know about (so that they can respond to) the occupational crimes that victimize them. The regulatory agencies that are supposed to police and scrutinize corporate behaviour face many obstacles. According to Snider (1992), these obstacles include the following:

- The massive economic and political power of corporations, which favours nonenforcement.
- Lack of staff and funds.
- Frequent lack of support from the governments that appoint them.
- The high cost of investigating complaints.
- Support only from weak consumer or labour groups.
- Minimal accountability to the public or the media.

A consequence of these obstacles is that many occupational crimes that are discovered are not reported. A business that learns its employees have been embezzling funds may not wish the matter to be widely known because it could reduce public trust in the company. In other words, the long-range negative consequences of reporting may be seen to outweigh any immediate benefits.

Police data on occupational offences are of only limited use. These offences are underreported, and often (e.g., in the case of fraud) it can't be determined whether they occurred in the context of work. This is partly because occupational crime is a conceptual rather than a legal category. Victimization surveys can supplement official record-keeping systems, but these too are limited, given the absence so often of a "direct victim" and the inability of the victim to recognize occupational and corporate offending.

THE AFTERMATH

Our best estimates suggest that the crimes committed by people in the course of legitimate occupational activities result in considerable levels of financial and physical harm and loss of life (Simon, 1996). Snider (1993) contends that "corporate crime is a major killer, causing more deaths in a month than all the mass murderers combined do in a decade." According to one estimate, Canadians are 10 times more likely to die as a result of unsafe or unhealthy workplace conditions as they are to be murdered (Reasons, Ross, and Paterson, 1981). It is estimated that the economic costs of corporate crime also exceed the costs of "street" crimes such as burglary and larceny. In the United States, one particularly notorious case of corporate offending, the savings and loans scandal, will end up costing American taxpayers as much as $500 billion (Gabor, 1994).

Controlling crimes that occur in the context of legitimate work roles is no easy task. It is sometimes assumed that the public is less concerned about occupational crimes than about more direct forms of predatory crime; however, this does not seem to be the case (Hans and Ermann, 1989). Even so, the fact remains that the low level of visibility associated with occupational crimes makes effective deterrence difficult (Coleman, 1987). Some studies suggest that threats of legal sanction have less impact on corporate crime than does the market environment in which companies operate (Keane, 2000; Simpson and Koper, 1992).

ENTERPRISE VERSUS ORGANIZED CRIME

Sometimes crime can be thought of as an occupation or business. We can define **enterprise crimes** as the "sale of illegal goods and services to customers who know that the goods or services are illegal" (Haller, 1990: 207). What constitutes an illegal good or service ultimately depends on what the law disallows. The sale of illegal drugs or pornography, the operation of illegal gambling houses, loan sharking, and "contract killing" are all examples of enterprise crime.

Enterprise crime
Sale of illegal goods and services to customers who know that the goods and services are illegal.

Enterprise crime is usually referred to by criminologists and others as "organized crime." This concept conjures up a number of familiar images gleaned from movies like *The Godfather,* television shows like *The Sopranos,* and newspaper coverage of "mob trials" (e.g., the trial of John Gotti). However, for reasons that will become clear, the concept of organized crime obscures rather than enhances our understanding of the types of events in which we are interested.

WHAT IS ORGANIZED CRIME?

The study of enterprise crime has been compromised by what some writers have referred to as the "official myth of organized crime" (Kappeler, Blumberg, and Potter, 2000). Typically, the term *organized crime* has been used to refer to long-term, highly organized criminal syndicates that are involved in a number of criminal businesses. These syndicates are said to be organized along ethnic lines, and to have well-established patterns of recruitment and

---

BOX 10.4

Types of Organized Crime Groups

In her recent analysis of organized crime in Canada, sociologist Margaret Beare (1996) contends that organized crime groups can be distinguished with respect to their degree of dependence on organized crime activity. She suggests that this typology is useful for helping us distinguish groups at any one point in time, and that it also describes the various forms that any one group might take at different points in time. In Canada, more and more attention is being paid to the activities of outlaw motorcycle gangs and Chinese and Vietnamese groups. Similarly, American observers are expressing concern about the increasing involvement of Cuban, African-American, Jamaican, Russian, and Aboriginal groups in organized crime activities (Finckenauer and Waring, 1998; Beare, 1996).

La Cosa Nostra
Literally "our thing." This term is understood as the formal designation of the Italian-American crime syndicate which dominated enterprise crime during the twentieth century.

authority, and to function in much the same way as legitimate business corporations (Cressey, 1969). According to this view, organized crime functions largely as an "alien parasitic conspiracy" (Smith, 1975).

The most widely discussed group of organized criminals in the criminological and popular literature on the subject is the Mafia, also known as **La Cosa Nostra.** This particular form of criminal conspiracy is said to have dominated organized crime in North America for most of the twentieth century, although its significance is generally thought to have declined in recent years (Jacobs, 1999; Reuter, 1995).

How useful is it to think of organized crime as the exclusive domain of alien ethnic conspirators? Critics contend that the tendency to equate organized crime with particular types of criminal organizations discourages our understanding of the many and various other parties involved in organized crime. In other words, there is more to organized crime than organized criminals: there are also victims, customers, regulators, suppliers, customers, competitors, and innocent bystanders. The criminal association is only one part of a much larger web of social relationships.

Even more basically, the concept of organized crime is confusing and misleading (Friedrichs, 1996). Logically, we might suggest that it refers to any type of activity involving two or more offenders acting in coordinated fashion. From this perspective, two juveniles who break into a house would be engaging in organized crime. But the term is almost never used this way. Instead, it is used to refer to large-scale criminal efforts that are diverse in nature and that seem to have little in common beyond the fact that we associate them with particular stereotypical notions of who organized criminals are. Adding to the confusion, the term *organized crime* is sometimes used to refer to a particular type of activity (as in the statement, "Gambling is a form of organized crime"), and other times to particular groups of criminals (as in the statement, "We must prosecute members of organized crime"). This usage results in circular reasoning. For example, if we say, "Organized crime is involved in the drug trade," we have not really said anything, because the drug trade by definition is an organized crime and any group involved in this activity must necessarily be involved in organized crime. Recently, Margaret Beare (1996) has argued that the most useful way to think of organized crime is to view it as a "process" rather than as a structure or a group. In other words, organized crime is not a type of crime, but rather a way of committing crimes.

TABLE 10.2

THE COMMITMENT OF LEGITIMATE AND ILLEGITIMATE GROUPS TO CRIME

Existence of group is independent of, and therefore separate from, OC activity ⟶		⟶ Existence of group is dependent on, and therefore explained by, OC activity	
Characteristics	**Characteristics**	**Characteristics**	**Characteristics**
Criminal activity is secondary to the ongoing purpose of the existing group structure.	Structure is in place for political/ideological or task-oriented reason. OC may be used to provide the funds to reach the goals.	The sense of tradition/ethnic cohesion is provided within the continuation of a historical structure that may have been created originally around a political ideology.	Groups are created strictly for the purpose of efficiently carrying out OC crimes. If OC was no longer a group activity, the group would have no reason to exist.
Existing structure or circumstantial advantages may facilitate the OC activity, but OC is not the reason the group exists.	OC activity is accepted as a necessary part of the operation of these groups. However, without the OC activity, the groups would change but continue to exist.	The group's main reason now for existing is to carry out OC.	This category tends to include the newer OC groups that are still in a state of flux.
Group is seen to be legitimate in spite of OC activity. Group activities are much broader.			
Examples	**Examples**	**Examples**	**Examples**
Aboriginal groups that engage in OC criminal activity.	Terrorist groups involved in OC to generate funds.	Asian triads/Mafia.	Russian, Jamaican, and Nigerian OC groups.
	Outlaw motorcycle gangs.		Colombian cartels.

Source: M.E. Beare, *Criminal Conspiracies* (Scarborough: Nelson Canada, 1996). Used by permission.

One way to circumvent some of these definitional difficulties is to shift our attention away from alien, parasitic conspiracies and "organized crime" and toward the study of enterprise crime.

PRECURSORS

As already noted, enterprise crime involves selling and distributing illegal goods and services. What kinds of social conditions make enterprise crime likely? The *first* condition, of course, is the existence of laws prohibiting the goods and services in question. In other words, enterprise crime is made possible when the law creates market opportunities. Prohibition, which was in force in the United States between 1920 and 1933, directly created an opportunity for financial gain that was soon exploited by criminal entrepreneurs (Packer, 1969; Schelling, 1967). Similarly, attempts to use the law to control the availability of illicit drugs—such as marijuana and cocaine—or to use high rates of taxation to control the availability of legal drugs such as tobacco, make enterprise crime possible. The gap between what people want and what the law allows them to legitimately have suggests an important way in which our society creates the conditions for enterprise crime. This point is obscured when we think of such crime as merely the product of an alien, parasitic conspiracy.

A *second* factor is systematic corruption. To the extent that enterprise criminals have access to police or political officials who are interested in cooperating with them, the agencies of legal control may be neutralized. Bribery and corruption offer some enterprise criminals protection from the law and make other enterprise criminals the objects of much more aggressive enforcement. Just as in the more legitimate sectors of the economy, the establishment of cozy relationships between those who do the policing and those who are supposed to be policed may help the latter strengthen their control of the market. Where bribery and corruption don't exist, criminal enterprise markets are more unstable.

A *third* factor is the existence of partnerships. These arrangements play the same role in illegal businesses as they do in legal ones: they allow entrepreneurs to share risks—especially the risk of business failure—and they allow people with different types of resources to pool those resources. This means that individuals who have capital, political influence, or managerial skills can combine their talents in ways that increase the potential for profit.

This emphasis on partnerships suggests that instead of being hierarchically or bureaucratically organized, enterprise crime is much more likely to involve informal styles of association (Ianni and Reuss-Ianni, 1972; Haller, 1992). Partnerships may arise when they are deemed necessary or desirable for business purposes, and they may be dissolved when they have served their purpose or when they cease to be profitable. Moreover, Haller (1990) notes, within these partnerships not everyone need be thought of as equal. Some entrepreneurs may exercise much more power than others because they have the political or economic resources that enable them to participate in several enterprises simultaneously.

Haller (1990; 1992) suggests that like the Chamber of Commerce or the Rotary Club, La Cosa Nostra should be viewed not as an organization that operates illegal (or legal) businesses, but rather as an association that businesspeople join partly to further their business careers.

Finally, Haller notes, many economic factors shape illegal enterprises, and these factors both enhance and reduce cooperation. Enterprises that involve importing drugs such as cocaine and heroin may require a high degree of cooperation among many groups in both the exporting and the receiving country. Drug networks also exist at local levels. Also, large drug deals require a large initial investment. Factors like these encourage monopolies, since few groups have the contacts or the economic resources to bring off large transactions. The market for marijuana is structured quite differently. This illicit commodity does not have to be imported and can be distributed on a small scale by independent entrepreneurs, who are catering to the needs of a small, local clientele. Markets of this type are much more resistant to monopolization.

TRANSACTIONS

If we think about enterprise crime as a type of business, the questions to which we seek answers are not unlike the ones we might ask regarding more legitimate businesses. What is the nature of the market? How are goods and services produced and distributed? What are the sources of capital that underwrite the costs of doing business? How do the various groups involved in these businesses cope with changing markets? What types of people are attracted to this particular line of work, and why?

Criminologists are especially interested in the fact that the business is illegal (Haller, 1990). As economist Thomas Schelling (1967) notes, when a

---

BOX 10.5

Criminal Business Organizations in Vancouver

Robert M. Gordon (2000) investigated various criminal organizations around Vancouver. Specifically, he collected information about 128 known gang members. Of the forms of criminal organization—street gangs, wanna-be groups, and criminal business organizations—it is the last that relates most directly to the study of what has traditionally been called organized crime.

Gordon found that criminal business organizations are carefully structured and highly sophisticated. Most of their members are adults engaging in crime mainly for economic reasons. Unlike street gangs, these groups try to maintain a low public profile. Gordon focused on 24 members of six criminal organizations. His research revealed the following:

- Members tended to be older, better educated males. They were less likely to be economically disadvantaged (in large part because their illegal enterprises were so successful).
- Typically, these enterprises engaged primarily (but not exclusively) in the supply of illegal goods and services (such as illegal drugs). Other business activities included robbery and extortion.
- The lucrative character of the business associations made it difficult for some members to leave. Most had minimal work skills and could not expect to command comparable incomes in the legitimate economy.
- Members were more likely to have immigrated to Canada than, for example, street gang members; they were also more likely to be members of a visible ethnic group. Sixteen of the 24 were of Vietnamese or Chinese ethnic origin.
- Data gathered from the offenders themselves—and from their probation officers—indicated that membership in these organizations may have provided members with a cultural bond and helped them cope with what they experienced as a sense of ethnic marginality.

---

business is made illegal, entry into the marketplace is restricted to those who are willing and able to behave criminally. In other words, illegal business is perhaps most attractive to those who have no strong reservations about acting in ways that are prohibited by law.

As we pointed out earlier, much has been made of the ethnic character of organized crime. Apart from La Cosa Nostra, commonly cited groups include the Chinese Triads, the Jamaican Posse, and associations loosely referred to in the popular press as the Colombian, Irish, and Vietnamese "mafias." This emphasis on ethnicity has often reinforced the popular view that criminal enterprise is an "alien" problem.

Over four decades ago, Daniel Bell (1953) rejected this view, arguing that organized crime serves as a "queer ladder of social mobility" in societies that emphasize material success but fail to provide all racial and economic groups with equal opportunities for achieving it. Like Robert Merton (1938), Bell maintained that groups that find the legitimate channels of upward mobility blocked may turn to illegal alternatives. A key implication of this argument is that enterprise crime, seen as a form of economic activity, is most attractive to those who are at or near the bottom of the social hierarchy.

O'Kane (1992), like Bell, has argued that involvement in enterprise crime is characterized by ethnic succession rather than by any enduring criminal conspiracy. Particular ethnic groups may dominate organized crime until legitimate channels of upward mobility become generally accessible. At that point the influence of a particular group may decline, as other groups move in to fill the void created by the outward movement. Thus, the Italian presence in organized crime, which peaked just before Prohibition, was preceded by an Irish and Jewish presence and succeeded by a Cuban and African-American presence. The emergence in Canada of Vietnamese, Chinese, and Aboriginal gangs suggests a similar process of ethnic succession.

This is not to say that the domination of enterprise crime by any particular group is irrelevant to how markets are structured or exploited (Light, 1977). Members of ethnic groups may be able to draw on their cultural capital in ways that enable them to be especially effective in particular types of enterprise crime. They may also share particular cultural traditions that facilitate criminal organization. According to Ianni (1971), the significance of the family as a central organizing theme in Italian culture has contributed to the creation of remarkably durable criminal enterprises structured along kinship lines.

A second important implication that flows from the illegal nature of criminal enterprises relates to the role of regulation. Obviously, when a market is declared illegal, it cannot be controlled by government agencies responsible for mediating disputes or resolving conflicts (Reuter, 1984b). Criminal entrepreneurs cannot seek recourse for the harm done against them by going to the police or initiating lawsuits. One mobster cannot sue another because a promised shipment of heroin was not delivered or because a promise to influence the vote of a labour union was not kept. This is why violence, or the threat of violence, looms so large in the business affairs of criminal entrepreneurs. Violence is one of the few means by which contracts can be enforced and compliance with agreements can be assured (Black, 1983).

The criminal events that are central to enterprise crime are complicated, but much popular thinking on the subject glosses over these complexities. We are used to thinking about enterprise crime as nothing more than the acts of vicious gangsters whose ways of thinking and acting are foreign to the societies in which we find them. This makes for good pulp fiction, but it is not very illuminating. Organized crime events are shaped by the societal context and are in no fundamental way alien to it. The gap between popular demand and efforts to legally control supply makes illegal markets possible in the first place. By declaring these markets off-limits to legal regulation, society creates circumstances in which the potential for violence is considerable. Society is stratified, and it imposes restrictions on upward mobility. As a result, some of those who are adversely affected come to see enterprise crime as a viable means of achieving socially accepted goals.

THE AFTERMATH

In 1998 the Solicitor General commissioned a study of the impact of organized crime on Canadian society (Solicitor General Canada, 1998). Here are some of the report's findings:

- The Canadian illegal drug market is between $7 and $10 billion dollars per year.
- Economic crimes such as securities and telemarketing fraud cost Canadians $5 billion per year.
- Between $5 and $17 billion is laundered in Canada each year.
- As many as 16,000 people are smuggled into Canada each year.
- Counterfeit products (i.e., their production and sale) cost Canadians as much as $1 billion each year.
- The illegal smuggling of tobacco, alcohol, and jewellery costs the government as much as $1.5 billion a year in taxes.

Public reactions to enterprise crime often fail to take account of the wider context. As we have argued, this is necessary if we are to understand this type of crime. When we read about a gangland killing in an urban ethnic restaurant or a police seizure of drug assets off the B.C. coast, we rarely consider the social character of these crimes. We are encouraged to think about organized crime as a force at war with "decent society"—as something that preys on citizens and threatens to corrupt our public officials and undermine our basic social institutions. Rarely are we encouraged to think about criminal enterprise as a logical product of social conditions. As McIntosh (1975) argued, criminal entrepreneurs are part of a larger configuration that includes not only the criminal but also victims, police, politicians, customers, and others. The activities of the criminal entrepreneur cannot be understood by focusing on the entrepreneur alone. As these larger configurations change, so do the types of events in which criminal entrepreneurs are likely to be involved. In the absence of this more complex and detailed understanding, enterprise crime will be seen as alien and parasitic.

How is enterprise crime to be controlled? The idea that enterprise crime is an alien, parasitic conspiracy rather than a social product supports the position that this type of crime is a law enforcement problem. From this perspective, enterprise crime is best controlled by aggressively prosecuting criminal entrepreneurs. But when we conceptualize the problem in terms of criminal enterprise rather than in terms of organized crime, we recognize that this "gangbuster mentality" has serious limitations. If enterprise crime really does function like other economic markets, the removal of criminal entrepreneurs through arrest and imprisonment cannot significantly affect market operations, since these actions will have no effect on the demand for illegal goods. We recognize this fact quite explicitly when it comes to legal markets. When an entrepreneur who sells legal goods—for instance, shoes—is removed from the market as a result of death, illness, or retirement, shoes remain available (Van den Haag, 1975). This is because the demand for shoes will prompt others to enter the market to fill the void. It can be argued that an aggressive policy of prosecution may actually increase the prices for illegal goods and services, and the profits to be made from them, by increasing the risks of involvement in these businesses.

SUMMARY

The roles we play in the workplace structure the kinds of involvement we are likely to have in various types of criminal events. Some jobs increase employees' risks of criminal victimization; others provide them with opportunities to victimize others, be they subordinates, co-workers, clients, customers, or society at large. Also, various types of enterprise crime constitute a form of work.

Criminology has long focused on how exclusion from the world of legitimate work motivates criminality. Though this remains an important (if unresolved) issue, it is equally important to understand how the organization of work fosters or hinders criminality. Theories that emphasize the role of social inequality in the generation of crime quite naturally suggest that not having a job may encourage the development of criminal motivations. Victimization risks differ between those who are employed and those who are not. More importantly, particular forms of labour force participation make crime possible. Relevant here are two factors: the relationship between the jobs people have and the victimization risks they face, and the ways that jobs provide people with opportunities to behave criminally.

Victimization risk at work is inversely correlated to occupational status, measured by income; those in lower-income occupations are more vulnerable. However, occupation alone is not enough to establish victimization risk. The workplace setting can strongly influence opportunities for crime. Risk may be heightened by the fact that money is available to be stolen. Sometimes the nature of the job can have a provoking effect on customers, who may vent their anger and frustration at the employee. Crimes that occur in these circumstances are not easy to deter and are underreported. In the aftermath of violent encounters, employees may accept the blame or assume that the employer will blame them for handling the situation poorly. Often these incidents are handled informally to avoid the complexities associated with police involvement.

Work-related crime ranges all the way from pilfering by a disgruntled employee to the gargantuan thefts associated with the S&L scandal in the United States. Sutherland (1940) used the term *white-collar crime* to refer to crimes committed by people of respectability and high status in the course of their occupation. He saw a need to correct the imbalance in criminological thinking that associated crime almost exclusively with the actions of the poor and the powerless.

Occupational crimes can be distinguished in two important ways. *First*, they differ with respect to the nature of the offender–victim relationship. Some kinds of crimes are intended to provide direct benefits only for the jobholder, as in the case of the employee who steals. In these instances the agency or organization is the victim and the employee is the offender. Other times the organization itself may be used to attack those outside of the business or at the bottom of the organizational hierarchy. With respect to these criminal events the crime may profit the jobholder indirectly, in that more direct benefits accrue to the organization itself. Finally, more general patterns of victimization result from crimes that inflict harm on very broad segments of society. These crimes include political bribery, tax fraud, and industrial pollution.

Second, occupational crimes differ according to the nature of the organizational settings in which they occur. Some types of occupational crime involve either a lone offender or a small number of offenders (e.g., medical frauds and dishonest household repair services). At the other extreme, corporate crime can sometimes involve "large vertical slices" of complex organizations. In these situations it may be difficult to say who did and did not behave criminally, since each individual's actions constitute only a small portion of the criminal event.

Gottfredson and Hirschi (1990) contend that the mechanism of self-control is as applicable to understanding the behaviour of occupational criminals as it is to understanding the behaviour of street criminals. In their view, what distinguishes occupational crime from street crime is not the offender but rather the offence. People who have low self-control are likely to engage in a variety of types of crime and deviance as opportunities present themselves. Despite the significant financial and physical harm caused by occupational crimes, their low visibility makes them difficult to detect and deter.

We can also view crime as operating in a marketplace in which illicit substances and services are sold to customers who know they are illegal. Instead of viewing these activities in terms of ethnically based organized crime, we instead use the term *enterprise crime*. Enterprise crime occurs as a result of laws that prohibit certain goods and services. In other words, enterprise crime is made possible when the law creates market opportunities. Enterprise crime needs the presence of systematic corruption, partnership arrangements between illegal and legal businesses, and favourable market conditions such as a monopoly on the illegal goods.

When we conceptualize the problem of "organized crime" in terms of criminal enterprise rather than in terms of organized crime, it becomes apparent that law enforcement responses to crime have serious limitations. If enterprise crime functions like other economic markets, removing criminal entrepreneurs through arrest and imprisonment cannot significantly affect market operation or reduce the demand for illegal goods.

QUESTIONS FOR REVIEW AND DISCUSSION

1. What criminological factors would help to explain why taxi drivers tend to experience high rates of robbery?

2. What measures could be taken to reduce the problems of crime and victimization in high schools? Would these solutions interfere with the basic mission of schools to provide education?

3. Do you agree that corporate crime is a more serious problem than street crime? How do corporations discourage us from adopting this view?

4. In reference to a job you currently hold (or perhaps a previous summer job), what opportunities for crime did your employment make available to you?

5. How do television and movie portrayals of organized crime distort public understanding of the problem? Can you think of some specific examples?

6. "Despite their differences, most offender-based theories lead us to expect a higher rate of crime among people who are unemployed than among people who are employed." Discuss this statement.

INFOTRAC COLLEGE EDITION

Explore InfoTrac College Edition, your online university library, which includes hundreds of popular and scholarly journals in which you can find articles related to the topics in this chapter. Visit InfoTrac through your Web browser (**www.infotrac-college.com**), or through this book's Web site (**www.criminalevent-3e.nelson.com**).

WHAT'S ON THE WEB?

For chapter links and quizzes, check out the accompanying Web site at **www.criminalevent-3e.nelson.com**.

Part 4

Responses to Crime

Chapter 11

Summary and Review of Public Policy Responses to Crime

WHAT'S IN CHAPTER ELEVEN

In this chapter we begin by reviewing the criminal event perspective. We then examine the potential public policy responses implied by this perspective, focusing on public safety and crime prevention issues. We conclude by discussing recent initiatives in community policing.

INTRODUCTION

The objectives of this chapter are *first*, to summarize what we have learned in previous chapters about the nature, causes, and consequences of criminal events, and *second*, to sketch some of the major policy responses available to us. These objectives are interrelated, in that what we can do about criminal events should follow logically from a detailed understanding of their causes and content.

SUMMARY OF FINDINGS ON THE CRIMINAL EVENT

We began in Chapter 1 by discussing some important concepts guiding the study of criminal events. Most notably, we emphasized that there are no simple answers to the questions, What is crime? and How is crime to be studied? It is too glib to say that crime is simply behaviour that violates the law. Such a definition obscures our view of the complex social realities that demand our attention. We emphasized a need to recognize that there is more to crime than the behaviour of a lawbreaker. As social events, crimes involve not only offenders but also other participants, including victims, the police, witnesses, and bystanders, all of whom act and react within particular social and physical circumstances. We discussed as well how the mass media and day-to-day conversations influence public views of crime. Unfortunately, media images of crime tend to exaggerate the frequency of serious violent crime and to emphasize the sensationalist character of both crime and its solutions.

In Chapter 2 we introduced the criminal event framework. Most fundamentally, we observed that criminal events are social events in the sense that they involve interaction between human beings. The dynamics of this interaction shape the content of the event and thus the consequences for those involved. We discussed the roles played by the principal protagonists in criminal events: offenders, victims, bystanders, and the police. In examining the social and demographic characteristics of victims and offenders, we noted that for many categories of crime, offenders and victims have much in common (a finding contrary to what media reporting usually leads us to believe). Both victims and offenders tend to be young, socially disadvantaged, and—for many categories of crime—males. There are of course important exceptions to this pattern. For obvious reasons, corporate crimes are not typically perpetrated by disadvantaged young males, and many forms of violence (such as rape and domestic assault) uniquely victimize women. We also pointed out that criminal events do not occur with equal frequency in all types of communities or within communities, or at all types of locations.

In Chapter 3 we saw that the data on crime are derived mainly from two types of investigative strategies: observations and reports. Some researchers attempt to gather information about crime through their observations of crime in naturalistic settings and/or in experimental and quasi-experimental settings. But most contemporary research focuses on reports of crime from police, victims, and offenders. Though there is much debate about the innate superiority of one type of report over another, we suggested that each type must be approached in terms of its own particular strengths and weaknesses. Different types of reports provide us with different perspectives on and data about criminal events. Their variable nature does not make them unusable; however, we should be critical and judicious when employing their data.

Chapters 4 to 7 described the major theoretical orientations that have dominated criminology in recent decades. We defined criminological theories as generalized explanations of criminal phenomena. We look to theories to make sense of our observations of the empirical world. Conversely, we look to the empirical world for confirmation or refutation of our theoretical views.

Theoretical interest in crime has generally meant theoretical interest in offenders. For this reason we devoted two chapters to describing alternative conceptualizations of the offender. Chapter 4 focused on theories that derive from "positivist" views of the offender: Chapter 5 presented explanations based on "classical" thought. The distinction between positivist and classical views has to do with the degree to which human will is thought to dominate social action. Broadly stated, positivist theories seek to understand why offenders do what they do, whereas classical theories emphasize the significance of rational choice in influencing the behaviour of the criminal offender.

Chapter 4 discussed many of the causal theories that have been offered to explain criminal behaviour. Some of these theories emphasize biological, constitutional, or genetic causes of criminal conduct, but most emphasize social factors. We examined two main types of social explanations. The *first* considers how socially induced frustration can contribute to the development of criminal motivations. Robert Merton argued that the gap between people's aspirations and what is actually available to them can lead to a form of frustration, which in turn leads to criminal conduct.

The *second* social explanation of criminal motivation stresses the role of culture. Subcultural theories suggest that people learn motivations to behave criminally the same way they learn motivations to do anything else. The emphasis here is on the immediate environment that offenders operate in and on how these environments foster the learning of cultural lessons supporting criminal conduct. The most important early proponent of this view was Edwin Sutherland, whose theory of differential association emphasized that crime should be viewed as a learned behaviour. The subcultural theorists who have followed Sutherland encourage us to think about the relationship between criminal behaviour and exposure to criminal cultures. Theorists such as David Matza and Gresham Sykes contend that we need to appreciate how lessons that might motivate offending can be learned from mainstream culture.

In Chapter 5 we focused on offenders' decision-making processes rather than on their motivations. According to theorists of the classical school there is little to be gained from searching for unique factors that motivate offending behaviour. They suggest instead that such behaviour is better understood in relation to the formal and informal social controls that might be expected to restrain offending behaviour. When these controls are ineffective or when individuals are insensitive to them, potential offenders are primed to become actual offenders. In these circumstances, people are free to act in ways that, criminal though they may be, reflect rational self-interest. Social controls that discourage individuals from engaging in the criminal pursuit of self-interest include their social bonds to conformist others, their relationships with their communities, and the sanctions promised by the legal system.

The theoretical explanations discussed in Chapter 6 differ fundamentally from those presented in previous chapters. Specifically, they do not focus on the behaviour of offenders, but rather on the opportunities to which offenders have access, and on the situations in which they find themselves. According to these theories, an individual who is ready, willing, and able to break the law will not necessarily do so. Other elements must come into play, and depending on how these elements come together, the offender may end up committing one type of crime rather than another.

Opportunity theories suggest that the ways in which people "distribute their lives" over time and across space either increase or decrease the number of criminal opportunities to which offenders have access. Lifestyle exposure theory contends that individuals who pursue lifestyles that bring them into contact with likely offenders or that put them in dangerous places face higher victimization risks. Similarly, routine activities theory suggests that crimes result when motivated offenders, suitable targets, and an absence of capable guardianship converge in time and space. Other theories reviewed in Chapter 6 focus on how the interactions between offenders and their victims influence criminal outcomes. Relatively simple theories that speak of "victim precipitation" have been replaced in recent years by theories about crime as a situated transaction that is the product not only of an offender's will or motivation but also of social interaction.

In Chapter 7 we discussed theories and research relating to the aftermath of criminal events. We examined the variety of ways—obvious and not so obvious—that involvement in these events may affect victims and offenders. For instance, labelling theorists maintain that society's reaction to minor or petty acts of nonconformity may result in stigmatization, which frustrates the labelled person and thereby contributes indirectly to more serious violations of the law. We also discussed how the effects of crime extend beyond the immediate victim. For example, the fear of crime can have important implications for the well-being of individuals and their communities. In extreme cases the public response in the aftermath of criminal events may amount to a panic.

Our theoretical elaboration of criminal events led us to conclude that it is worth investigating these events in the context of particular social domains. Social domains can be defined as the major spheres of life in which we spend most of our time and energy. Three of these domains—the family and the household, recreation and leisure, and the workplace—provided the organizing themes for the substantive analysis of criminal events presented in Chapters 8 to 10. We argued that a comprehensive examination of criminal events in these domains requires us to focus on three important components: precursors, the transaction, and the aftermath. This approach helps us understand *first*, how social arrangements affect the distribution and timing of criminal events, *second*, why some groups in society are more likely than others to be involved in criminal events, whether as offenders or victims, *third*, why particular types of criminal events have the content they have, and *fourth*, how victims and others are affected by these events.

Our discussion of criminal events in specific social domains in Chapters 8 to 10 enabled us to apply the theoretical and research lessons that emerged from earlier chapters. In Chapter 8 we took up the issue of criminal events in the home. Two general categories of events were discussed. The *first* was interpersonal violence in the context of familial relationships. This sort of violence emerges from and reflects the social organization of family life. The very factors that lead us to idealize family life—intimacy and privacy—increase the risks of danger to more vulnerable family members. The data clearly indicate that women and children suffer most from violence in the home.

The *second* major type of criminal event in the family and household domain is property crime. Break-and-enter and the theft of household goods are very common crimes and result in substantial financial loss. We suggested that much of this crime is opportunistic in nature and involves rational offenders who encounter opportunities for theft. Our discussion of family life and family organization revealed how routine activities create such opportunities.

In Chapter 9 we took up several issues relating to criminal events in the leisure domain. We saw that especially in the case of juveniles, leisure is often understood as a "cause" of crime. It has been argued that many leisure pursuits that youths engage in promote criminal conduct directly or indirectly. This argument has been made most passionately with respect to television violence, but it also encompasses most other leisure activities pursued by young people. We also saw how leisure pursuits may free youths from social controls and at the same time provide them with opportunities for offending. Finally, we investigated how particular leisure contexts—the street, bars and taverns, dating, and tourism—provide settings for criminal events.

A final social domain, the workplace, was discussed in Chapter 10. The nature and degree of people's involvement in the work domain has important implications for the kinds of criminal events they engage in. Two major issues emerged from our discussion of the work domain. The *first* was the relationship between involvement in the legitimate world of work and involvement in criminal events. Particular kinds of work expose employees to particular kinds of victimization and offending risks. Jobs that involve handling money, travel between remote worksites, or regular exposure to high-risk populations increase the risks people face at work. Highly publicized homicides in the workplace have brought this issue into sharp relief. The jobs people have may also provide them with unique opportunities to break the law. For instance, corporate criminals have access to highly profitable offending opportunities and very often remain insulated from controls that are supposed to deter their behaviour.

The *second* major issue discussed in Chapter 10 was crime as a form of work. Like legitimate business enterprises, criminal enterprises are sensitive to market conditions, endeavour to forge stable partnership arrangements, and attempt to manage their relationships with state agencies that try to control their activities.

In the course of this book we have emphasized an appreciation for the variety and the complexity of criminal events. Though these events occur in diverse social domains and involve different categories of actors, this does not mean they are not amenable to criminological analysis. Throughout our analysis of criminal events, the same fundamental questions kept recurring: Why do offenders and victims come together when they do, as they do, and where they do? Why does the event evolve as it does? What are the consequences of the event for its participants? Instead of seeking highly specific answers to these questions, we have attempted to link specific concerns to theoretical ones. We have also been attentive to the pictures of criminal events that are revealed to us by the main criminological data sources. We conclude here with a brief consideration of how understanding these events in criminological terms helps us make sense of public attempts to deal with the problem of crime.

RESPONDING TO CRIME

Criminal events occur because offenders encounter opportunities to violate the law. Controlling the occurrence of these events could involve discouraging potential offenders. Depending on our theoretical model, we could remove the factors that we believe motivate offending, or we could make crime seem less rewarding to those who regard it as a rational course of action. With respect to the latter strategy, we have commented repeatedly on the role of legal deterrence.

Instead of trying to prevent criminal events by controlling offenders, we could try to empower victims so that they are more resistant to victimization. One way to achieve this would be to develop policies that allow potential victims greater access to law, or that teach them measures they can take to make themselves less vulnerable to crime. Similarly, we could try to reduce the number of criminal opportunities available to offenders by manipulating the physical environments and social situations in which crimes occur.

THE GET-TOUGH APPROACH

These preliminary observations suggest several fronts along which any battle against crime could be conducted. Too often our thinking about crime is less imaginative than it could be. Fed by sensationalist media reporting and political rhetoric, we tend to think of "getting tough" as the most appropriate response to crime: hire more police, hand down longer sentences, and build more prisons.

Some observers have argued that get-tough responses to the problem of crime are inherently limited (Donzinger, 1996; Standing Committee on Justice and the Solicitor General, 1993). As they see it, the problem is twofold. *First,* there is little convincing evidence that we are controlling crime effectively when we simply invest more resources in the criminal justice system (Graham, 1990). *Second,* when we view the criminal justice system as the principal social mechanism for responding to crime, we approach the problem in a reactive rather than a proactive manner and thus never really address the underlying factors associated with crime and criminality.

As with other social problems, it is perhaps more sensible to think about strategies of prevention. **Crime prevention** has been defined as "the anticipation, recognition and appraisal of a crime risk and the initiation of some action to reduce or remove it" (National Crime Prevention Institute, 1986: 2). Clearly, the criminal justice system is itself part of an overall crime prevention strategy, for two reasons: the threat of legal penalty is meant to deter potential offenders; and prison terms, in their capacity to either punish or rehabilitate, are intended to prevent reoffending.

Crime prevention
The anticipation, recognition, and appraisal of a crime risk and the initiation of some action to reduce or remove it.

BOX 11.1

Are Boot Camps a Viable Solution to Juvenile Crime?

One solution to the crime problem that is popular with conservative policymakers is the boot camp. These military-style correctional facilities reflect the widespread view that misbehaviour among juveniles emerges out of a basic lack of discipline. The quick fix that boot camps promise is especially popular among politicians who wish to demonstrate that they are "cracking down" on delinquents. Tabloid talk show hosts like Maury Povich and Sally Jesse Raphael find it easy to exploit for ratings purposes the pain and suffering caused by both crime and boot camp solutions. It is often assumed that boot camps produce the desired outcomes; the available research suggests otherwise. Specifically, recent studies indicate the following:

- Boot camps do not have a significant impact on recidivism.
- Compared to prisons, they are not more cost-effective and are sometimes less cost-effective.
- Boot camps result in needless incarceration, because judges who support them may use them simply because they are available, when offenders might otherwise have been put on probation.

Source: A.W. Saleno (1994), "Boot Camps: A Critique and Proposed Alternative," *Journal of Offender Rehabilitation* 20: 147–58. J. Shamsie, S. Nicholl, and K.C. Madsen (1999), *Antisocial and Violent Youth.* Toronto: Lugus.

Get-tough approaches to crime tend to involve options that are associated specifically with the criminal justice system. As used by criminologists, the term *crime prevention* is more broadly based, referring to strategies or tactics that might involve the police (or other criminal justice functionaries), but are rooted in the physical and social character of the local community (Lab, 1992; van Dijk and de Waard, 1991). From this perspective, crime prevention involves a range of strategies, including installing lights on city streets, initiating citizen police patrols, developing Neighbourhood Watch programs, mounting public information campaigns, locking doors, carrying weapons or alarms, and introducing programs aimed at reducing unemployment or poverty.

Advocates of the get-tough approach often claim that they are merely responding to a public demand that something be done about crime swiftly and decisively. But the relationship between public opinion and the get-tough agendas of conservative governments is perhaps more complicated than it is often made out to be. There is indeed support for some get-tough policies, but there is also public support for alternatives to harsh punishment (Cullen et al., 1998; Tufts, 2000). In particular, the public seems willing to support programs of early intervention directed to helping young children avoid a life of crime and less coercive sanctions for youthful and first-time offenders.

PUBLIC HEALTH AND PUBLIC SAFETY

Public policy in the area of health care suggests interesting parallels to the issue of crime prevention (Anderson, Grandison, and Dyson, 1996). One way society can deal with medical problems is to wait until people get sick and then make health care services available to them. Similarly, we can wait until people commit crimes and then take action by using criminal justice resources to catch and then confine or treat them. The use of the word *rehabilitation* in reference to prison programs suggests a quite literal application of the medical model to our thinking about crime and punishment.

> ### WHAT DOES IT MEAN?
>
> ### CRIME PREVENTION
> Crime prevention refers to strategies or tactics that, though they may involve the police (or other criminal justice functionaries), are rooted in the physical and social character of the local community.

In the field of public health, most policy planners recognize the value of applying limited resources in a preventive rather than a reactive manner. If we can prevent illness, we won't need to treat it after the fact. This is why people are advised to get regular medical checkups, exercise, and watch their diets. We could view the problem of crime in a similar way. It is more sensible to take action *before* crimes occur than after harm has been done. Public health–style approaches to violence emphasize four basic elements (Anderson, Grandison, and Dyson, 1996; Durant, 1999; Potter and Saltzman, 2000):

1. Identifying patterns and epidemics of violence.
2. Conducting epidemiological research on the causes of violence.
3. Designing and evaluating prevention interventions.
4. Implementing prevention programs.

Borrowing from the language of public health, we can think of crime prevention as having primary, secondary, and tertiary dimensions (Brantingham and Faust, 1976; Lab, 1992; van Dijk and de Waard, 1991). *Primary* prevention includes programs aimed at either the entire community or the population at risk. Good examples of primary prevention are crime prevention programs that teach risk-reducing skills to large audiences (Davis and Smith, 1994; Sacco and Silverman, 1982). Pamphlets, brochures, and posters providing information on family violence are examples of (mass media) primary prevention. *Secondary* prevention refers to programs aimed at those segments of the population that are at especially high risk (or, in public health language, that show early symptoms of the problem). Examples of secondary prevention include targeting high-crime areas for special treatment (such as neighbourhood redevelopment or Neighbourhood Watch programs) and installing security equipment in schools that have experienced problems with intruders. *Tertiary* prevention refers to strategies that are intended to prevent the recurrence of crime. Examples of tertiary prevention include victim–offender mediation, training courses for drunk drivers, treatment programs for wife assaulters, and various forms of diversion and community service.

Despite the valuable insights the public health model provides, its application to crime prevention is problematic (Graham, 1990). *First*, the model is so wide-ranging that it is unclear where we should draw the boundaries between what is and what is not a crime prevention practice. *Second*, the distinctions between primary, secondary, and tertiary prevention are often less clear in practice than in theory. *Third*, attempts to classify crime prevention practices in this way assume that our understanding of what causes crime—and therefore, how it can be prevented—is more scientifically precise than it really is. Harries (1990) further cautions that public health as an institution has at present neither the resources nor the personnel to make a lasting impression on the problem of crime incidence.

In the rest of this section and in the two sections that follow we examine three major approaches to crime prevention that extend well beyond traditional get-tough approaches. Each picks up an important theme in the study of criminal events; in combination they form the basis for what many would argue is a comprehensive approach to crime prevention. **Opportunity reduction** focuses on how social and environmental factors could be brought to bear on the reduction of crime opportunities. **Social development approaches** look to create social conditions that discourage long-term serious offending, and that empower potential victims while at the same time contributing to the rebuilding of communities. **Community-based policing**—or problem-oriented policing—considers how the policing role could be expanded beyond the narrow reactive role that brings the police into criminal events only when the events are either already under way or finished.

CRIME PREVENTION THROUGH OPPORTUNITY REDUCTION

As we have seen, the event conceptualization of crime emphasizes the importance of opportunity in determining where and when crimes occur. Only when people who are ready, willing, and able to offend encounter conditions

Opportunity reduction
Focuses on how social and environmental factors can be brought to bear on the reduction of crime opportunities.

Social development approach
An approach to crime prevention which attempts to create social conditions that discourage long-term serious offending and that empower potential victims, while at the same time contributing to the rebuilding of communities.

Community-based policing
Expansion of the policing role beyond the traditional narrow reactive role.

BOX 11.2

Guns and the Law

Recent changes in Canadian gun laws have been highly controversial. Though public opinion polls have shown widespread support for tighter controls over firearms, gun owners are strongly concerned that their personal liberties will be compromised. Whatever their shortcomings, the intent of these laws is to control the death and injury produced by the misuse of firearms. The emphasis on preventing death and suffering and on the need to reduce the consequences of crime is consistent with a public health approach. What exactly do the new laws involve? Below are the main legal requirements of the *Firearms Control Act*:

- The key feature of the act is a registry of people and firearms. All firearms owners must have applied for a licence by December 31, 2000, must register all firearms by December 31, 2002, and must remember to safely store all firearms.
- The *Firearms Control Act* and regulations apply to all persons (including visitors) and to all businesses that possess firearms.
- Before a licence is issued, safety checks are to be done on all applicants.
- Applicants who wish to acquire firearms must pass the Canadian Firearms Safety Course.
- To register a firearm, the applicant must first have a licence.
- All firearms must be stored unloaded and locked.
- Visitors bringing firearms into Canada must declare their firearms in writing.
- Previously registered restricted firearms—such as handguns—must be registered again.
- Handguns with a short barrel (105 mm or less) or those that discharge 25- or 32- calibre ammunition are prohibited.

Source: Ministry of Justice Web site cfc-ccaf.gc/general_public/highlights

favourable to offending are criminal events likely to develop. So from a policy standpoint, actions that control the appearance or accessibility of opportunities to engage in crime may help prevent much crime. The important implication of this approach is that we can manage the risks of crime without changing the character of offenders. Because the emphasis in opportunity reduction is on modifying the situations in which crimes occur, crime prevention through opportunity reduction is sometimes referred to as **situational crime prevention** (Clarke, 1993).

Situational prevention is based on two important assumptions. *First*, crimes are prevented most effectively when we are attentive to their particular characteristics (Brantingham and Brantingham, 1990; Gottfredson and Hirschi, 1995). So the first step in opportunity reduction is careful crime

Situational crime prevention
Efforts to prevent crime that focus on the suppression of criminal opportunities (rather than, for instance, the reform of offenders).

analysis: Who commits these crimes? When are they committed? Where do they most often occur? What do offenders hope to achieve by committing them? How might certain characteristics of the physical environment contribute to them? Are there natural forces of guardianship that could be activated in the situations in which crimes typically occur? The answers to questions like these help crime prevention planners tailor specific solutions to specific crime problems.

Second, offenders' decisions are based on their assessment of the various costs and benefits associated with a particular course of action (Cornish and Clarke, 1986). How easily can a crime be committed? Is anyone who might take action to prevent the crime standing guard? Are there less risky ways of obtaining the rewards that the commission of the crime promises? Offenders seek answers to these questions and then behave in ways that reflect their best interests. If the opportunities conducive to crime can be made less attractive or less plentiful, many types of crimes—especially those that are largely opportunistic in nature—may occur much less often. According to Clarke

---

BOX 11.3

Safety Precautions Taken by Canadians

Surveys suggest that many people routinely take measures to protect themselves from crime. Respondents to the 1999 Canadian General Social Survey (GSS) were asked a variety of questions about the precautions they took. One set of questions asked respondents what they had done in the 12-month period preceding the survey:

- 27 percent of Canadians had changed their activities or avoided certain places.
- 21 percent had installed security hardware.
- 3 percent had taken a self-defence course.
- 2 percent had changed their phone number.
- 1 percent had changed their residence.
- Far fewer than 1 percent indicated that they had purchased a gun.

Respondents were also asked about their routine behaviours:

- 57 percent locked doors for safety when alone in a car.
- 44 percent checked the backseat for intruders when returning to their car alone.
- 42 percent planned travel routes with safety in mind.
- 13 percent carried something to defend themselves or to alert others.
- 10 percent stayed home at night because they were afraid to go out alone.

Overall, the survey suggested slightly lower levels of such behaviour than were revealed by the previous GSS in 1993.

Source: S. Besserer and C. Trainor (2000), "Criminal Victimization in Canada," *Juristat* 20(10). Used by permission of Statistics Canada.

(1992), situational prevention involves increasing the risks and decreasing the rewards associated with crime. As offending situations become riskier, more difficult, and less rewarding, rational offenders will be discouraged from offending.

One obvious way that people make crimes more difficult to carry out is through target hardening. This refers to measures that decrease the vulnerability of personal or household property. Entry into a house with locked doors and windows is more difficult than entry into a house without them. Various forms of access control, such as locked gates and entry phones, also increase the degree of effort needed to commit certain crimes.

The risks involved in the commission of crime can be increased by measures that make it more likely—or at least make it *seem* more likely—that the

---

BOX 11.4

Situational Prevention and Gang Violence

As crime prevention specialists have become more skilled at implementing principles of situational prevention, it has become clear that the approach has broad applicability. Common uses of the approach suggest that it is best suited for controlling minor nuisance crimes such as trespassing and vandalism. However, it has also been used to control much more serious offences.

The Los Angeles Police Department employed situational prevention principles in an attempt to reduce levels of assault and homicide. This program, known as Operation Cul de Sac (OCDS), involved efforts to control and reroute traffic so as to "design out" crime by reducing the opportunities to commit it.

Traffic barriers were placed in neighbourhoods where gangs and gang violence had become especially serious problems. Police data indicated that most drive-by shootings and violent gang encounters occurred in clusters on the periphery of neighbourhoods linked to major thoroughfares. To control the problem, the police closed all of the major roads leading to and from these identified "hot spots" by placing cement barriers at the ends of the streets that led to these roads. This redesign in effect created cul-de-sacs.

This approach assumes that though gang violence may have deep-seated structural causes, it also has significant opportunity dimensions. So instead of focusing on the "root causes" of gang violence, it focuses on "proximate causes."

An evaluation of the program showed that the number of homicides and assaults in the OCDS area fell significantly after two years, and rose again after it ended. (In a comparison area, it remained constant.) Importantly, the evaluation also showed that crime was not displaced to other areas.

Source: J. Lasley (1998), "'Designing Out' Gang Homicides and Street Assaults," *National Institute of Justice: Research in Brief*, Washington D.C.: U.S. Department of Justice. Used by permission.

offender will be discovered and apprehended. A high level of surveillance by security guards, citizen patrols, and security cameras clearly is intended to serve this purpose. Perhaps less obvious is the role played by other types of crime prevention measures, such as locks. As Felson (1992: 32) notes:

> The strategic role of a lock is not to prevent entry! Rather, its strategic role is to force the offender to make a lot of noise, in hope that others will hear that noise. Ideally, the potential offender will take a look at the lock, note the noise it will force him to make, fear the consequences of that noise, and decide against committing the crime.

Prevention involves more than establishing defensible space. According to Merry (1981), a neighbourhood may be architecturally designed to discourage crime but still not be adequately defended, because it has little or no social cohesion. Krupat and Kubzansky (1987: 61) note:

> Even when buildings are low and the entrances and public spaces focus around a small set of families, people will not react to crime when they believe that they are on someone else's turf, when they do not consider the police effective or when they fear retribution.

Among the most popular measures intended to activate natural surveillance at the local level are Block Watch and Neighbourhood Watch programs sponsored by the local police. The intent of these programs is to encourage neighbourhood residents to "share information about local crime problems, exchange crime prevention tips, and make plans for engaging in surveillance ('watching') of the neighbourhood and crime-reporting activities" (Rosenbaum, 1987: 104). Surveillance programs increase interaction among neighbours and at the same time remove opportunities for crime.

The U.S. Bureau of Justice Statistics reported in 1986 that about one family in five lives in a neighbourhood with a surveillance program and that in those areas, 38 percent of residents participate (Garofalo and McLeod, 1988). In Canada, evidence suggests that though awareness of these programs has been high, actual levels of participation have been somewhat lower (Solicitor General, 1984).

Finally, crime can be made less attractive by reducing the rewards associated with it. For example, requiring bus riders to have exact change decreases the amount of money that must be handled by any particular bus driver; this makes robbing drivers a less attractive proposition. Similarly, markings that identify individual ownership of property may discourage the conspicuous use of stolen merchandise and seriously hurt the chances for resale.

The most sophisticated forms of situational prevention employ knowledge about all elements of the criminal event. Paul and Patricia Brantingham (2001), the foremost authorities on this approach, identify several such elements:

1. *The offender.* All crimes require an offender. Traditional approaches to crime prevention focus on changing the offender's motivation; in contrast, situational approaches direct our attention to the routine activities of offenders and to their patterns of decision making.

2. *Target.* All predatory crimes have targets or victims. Situational approaches are sensitive to the role played by victim precipitation and carelessness.

3. *Site.* Every criminal event has a site—a discrete location in space and time—at which the criminal action by the offender against the target takes place. These sites can be analyzed to reveal patterns that will help prevention planners understand the spatial (and temporal) regularities in crime occurrence (Rossmo, 2000).

4. *Situations.* Crimes require specific behavioural settings and situations. Just because a potential offender and victim find themselves in each other's presence does not mean that a crime will happen. It is also essential that the offender define the situation as appropriate. This could involve, for instance, the absence of official protectors—guardians or property managers such as landlords or security guards.

5. *Mechanics of the crime.* The criminal event model of crime prevention also directs our attention to the sequence of actions the offender must take to accomplish the crime once the offender, target, site, and situation have combined to create a criminal opportunity. Most criminal action sequences are short and technically simple, but they are sometimes quite complex. Knowledge of the mechanics of this process makes possible the development of strategies intended to disrupt this sequence.

The Brantinghams contend that situational prevention strategies must not only account for each of these factors but also be informed by an awareness of their various combinations. The many ways in which each combines and intersects with the others suggest to careful planners a wide range of prevention opportunities.

Unquestionably, opportunity reduction has been effective in a variety of specific settings and with respect to a variety of offences (Clarke, 1993, 1994). But this approach has its critics. Some suggest that removing opportunity is more likely to displace crime than to prevent it (Gabor, 1990b). In other words, if we make it difficult for a motivated offender to offend in one situation, he or she may simply find another situation more conducive to offending. If one store takes precautions to prevent theft, can we really be sure the would-be thief will not simply seek out targets where these precautions have not been taken? The evidence suggests that displacement may be a problem with some types of crime and some types of offenders. That being said, many forms of opportunity reduction do in fact prevent crimes—they don't simply displace them (Brantingham and Brantingham, 1990).

More specific forms of opportunity reduction invite more specific criticisms. Various target-hardening methods, such as installing locks on doors and bars on windows, may be faulted for encouraging a "fortress mentality" that enhances fear of crime in society (Graham, 1990). Some critics see the use of electronic surveillance as part of a gradual shift toward a "surveillance society" (Lyon, 1994). Critics of Neighbourhood Watch programs claim that despite the highly favourable publicity they receive and the high regard in which they are held by police and politicians, there is little evidence that they accomplish what they are supposed to accomplish. According to Rosenbaum (1987):

> There is some evidence to suggest (a) if given the opportunity to participate, residents in the majority of high-crime neighbourhoods would not participate, and (b) when citizens do participate, the social interaction that occurs at meetings may lead to increases (rather than decreases) in fear of crime, racial prejudice and other crime-related perceptions or feelings. More important, there is little evidence that these block/neighbourhood meetings cause local residents to engage in neighbourhood surveillance, social interaction, and bystander intervention—behaviours that are posited as the central mechanism for strengthening informal social controls and reducing opportunities for crime (127).

Perhaps the most common and general criticism of opportunity reduction approaches is that by placing so much emphasis on reducing opportunities for crime, they ignore the underlying causes of crime (Waller and Weiler,

1984). It has been argued that because these strategies do not address the root causes of crime, they achieve short-term benefits at best. If we wish to consider these root causes, we must turn to another important approach: crime prevention through social development.

CRIME PREVENTION THROUGH SOCIAL DEVELOPMENT

Crime prevention through social development focuses not on the criminal act but rather on the serious, repeat offender (Gabor, 1990a). As we saw in previous chapters, research suggests that a relatively small number of offenders are responsible for a disproportionately large number of crimes. These offenders begin their criminal careers early in life and end them (if at all) late in life. Over the course of their offending careers, they commit a wide variety of predatory offences. The research also indicates that these individuals tend to come from disadvantaged backgrounds, that they abuse alcohol and other drugs, and that they have experienced serious family problems as well as school- and employment-related problems.

Any number of social problems, from family victimization to poverty and racism, provide fertile breeding grounds for crime. Advocates of the social development approach see community building as a comprehensive strategy that reduces crime by discouraging potential offenders and strengthening potential victims. Crime prevention through social development aims to correct the criminogenic social conditions that are assumed to be the root causes of crime (National Crime Prevention Centre, 2000). This approach focuses on long-range prevention; it seeks to eliminate the underclass, from which serious repeat offenders typically emerge (Standing Committee on Justice and the Solicitor General, 1993).

Advocates of this approach contend that investing early in children, schools, and families pays long-term financial dividends (Cohen, 1998). Though the prevention of crime is not reducible to money issues, it does have financial dimensions. It is less costly to prevent a child from going down a criminal path than it is to deal with an adult offender (Parks, 2000). These savings can be of several types:

- savings in welfare assistance
- savings in special education
- savings to the criminal justice system
- savings to crime victims
- increased tax revenue from higher earnings

BOX 11.5

Some Social Development Principles

As the body of research relating to crime prevention through social development accumulates, it is becoming clear that there are some important principles that should guide such interventions.

1. *Intervene early.* The risks of becoming delinquent almost certainly develop early in childhood. For youths at greatest risk, waiting until adolescence may be too late.

2. *Intervene in multiple settings.* Interventions that simultaneously occur in schools, in the home, in the peer group, and in the neighbourhood are preferable to interventions in only one setting. For one thing, children are more responsive to lessons that are reinforced across settings.

3. *Move beyond the individual child.* The larger context should be taken into account. Children do not function in a vacuum; family, peer, and classroom contexts are integrally related to a child's functioning.

4. *Motivate children, teachers, and parents.* Despite their good intentions, programs often fail because parents and teachers do not reinforce desired behaviours by exhibiting them.

5. *Set and enforce appropriate limits.* It is essential that programs be prepared to sanction negative behaviour as well as reward positive behaviour.

6. *Use modelling as a positive influence.* It is essential that children have adequate access to prosocial behaviours that can be modelled.

7. *Involve the community.* The level of violence in schools and in homes is related to the character and viability of the broader community. So it is important that prevention efforts take the community into account.

8. *Provide adequate alternatives.* Effective programming is about providing positive alternatives to aggression and violence.

Source: R. Prinz (2000), "Research-Based Prevention of School Violence and Youth Antisocial Behavior: A Developmental and Education Perspective," in *Preventing School Violence: Plenary Papers of the 1999 Conference on Criminal Justice Research and Evaluation—Enhancing Policy and Practice Through Research*, Vol. 2. Washington D.C.: U.S. Department of Justice. Used by permission.

Some data to illustrate this have been provided by the National Crime Prevention Centre (N.D.). Basing its results on a fictional but typical case, this study found that the costs of a delinquent career generated by a repeat offender before the age of 18 were roughly $511,500.

The notion that crime can be prevented by eliminating the social ills that breed crime (especially teenage crime) is not new. There is a long history of social reformism that argues we can best fight crime by fighting poverty, racism, unemployment, and other forms of social disadvantage (Graham,

1990; Rosenbaum, 1988). The social development approach differs from these older approaches in its more systematic efforts to identify and attack the root causes of crime.

Because predatory crime is part of the "tangle of pathologies" (Wilson, 1987) that characterizes the lives of the socially disadvantaged, our policy approaches to crime prevention must extend beyond the criminal justice system into the areas of family, education, housing, and health policy (Canadian Criminal Justice Association, 1989; Graham, 1990).

Advocates of the social development approach do not see crime prevention as the exclusive domain of any one social or governmental agency. Rather, they strongly emphasize the need to establish partnerships and crime prevention councils at the federal and municipal levels (Kellam, 2000). These councils would bring together groups with a stake in a broad range of social welfare issues: voluntary agencies, the police, those with responsibility for health, family, employment, and housing policy, and so on. The idea behind all this is that once ownership of the crime problem is shared, more comprehensive solutions will be developed.

The social development approach has been more popular in some European countries than in North America, but it is clearly gaining momentum in Canada and the United States (Donzinger, 1996; Waller, 1989). Some advocates of opportunity reduction maintain that social development strategies fail to recognize that crime is not a homogeneous event, and that different crimes require different intervention strategies (Brantingham, 1989).

Other critics question whether we in this society have the political will to launch social development programs, and whether—in this time of fiscal restraint—we are ready to make the financial commitments that such comprehensive programs would require. It has also been questioned whether the links between crime and factors such as family upbringing, employment, and school experience are as obvious and as straightforward as proponents of social development programs make them out to be. The social development approach draws our attention to a long and unwieldy list of causative factors, and as we have seen, there is honest debate among criminologists about the relative importance of these factors (Graham, 1990). There is a tendency to group together all "positive" interventions as likely to reduce crime; the empirical record suggests that not all of them do. For example, preschool and weekly home visits by teachers, and parent training about risk factors for delinquency, may reduce youthful engagement in crime, whereas subsidized work programs for at-risk youth may not (Sherman et al., 1998). All of these social development initiatives may have some merit and therefore be worthy of public support, but it does not follow that they are all equally likely to reduce crime.

For the purposes of presentation we have drawn a distinction between opportunity reduction and social development, but there is not really an inherent conflict between these two approaches. In the same way that we have borrowed from different theories to explain criminal events, we can borrow from these different perspectives to create an integrated approach to crime prevention. Many policymakers have advocated that these strategies be combined with community policing to form an integrated approach to crime prevention (Canadian Criminal Justice Association, 1989; Standing Committee on Justice and the Solicitor General, 1993).

COMMUNITY-BASED POLICING

Gottfredson and Hirschi (1995) argue that the natural limits of law enforcement are set by the spontaneous nature of crime: the offender sees that he or she can get something for nothing and seizes the opportunity. No increases in law enforcement, they suggest, can truly deter this type of behaviour. Research in Canada (Koenig, 1991) and elsewhere (Bayley, 1985; Jackson, 1989) has provided strong evidence that there is no relationship between the level of crime in a society and the number of police available to control this crime (Felson, 1998; Koenig, 1991). Gottfredson and Hirschi (1990: 270) maintain that in the overwhelming majority of robberies, burglaries, assaults, homicides, thefts, and drug deals, "the offender does not know or care about the probability of being observed by the police." The primary role of the police, they suggest, is to respond to criminal activity and to maintain social control; there is no evidence that increasing police tactical resources reduces crime rates.

Unfortunately, police resources have become scarcer, and what the police do primarily is respond to complaints (not crime), maintain visibility in neighbourhoods, and control traffic. In a study of police activity, Lawson (1982) found that the police spend only 10 to 15 percent of their time engaged in actual law enforcement. Bayley (1994) reports that patrol officers, who are responsible for most contacts with the general population, rarely make an arrest. In the United States there is less than one arrest per officer per fifteen working days. According to Ericson and Shearing (1986), Canadian police officers make on average one criminal arrest per month, and encounter a recordable criminal offence only once a week. The police spend the rest of their time on order maintenance.

The pressures of order maintenance and restricted resources have forced police agencies to rethink their law enforcement strategies (Rosenbaum, 1998). The police role has expanded partly because the police are the only 24-hour social agency that is easy to reach and that will make house calls. As we discussed earlier, the 911 line leaves police overwhelmed with calls that require them to serve not a law enforcement function, but rather a regulatory or order maintenance function (Kennedy and Veitch, 1997). As Bayley (1994) points out, most of the time the police do not use the criminal law to restore calm and order:

> The police "sort out" situations by listening patiently to endless stories about fancied slights, old grievances, new insults, mismatched expectations, indifference, infidelity, dishonesty, and abuse. They hear about all the petty, mundane, tedious, hapless, sordid details of individual lives. None of it is earthshaking, or worthy of a line in a newspaper—not the stuff that government policy can address, not even especially spicy: just the begrimed reality of the lives of people who have no one else to take their problems to (20).

The police are being urged to become more actively involved in crime prevention. This is partly a response to the increased levels of unease that people are feeling in urban areas. Given the assumption of routine activities theory that crime is made possible by the availability of offenders and victims and *also* by the absence of visible guardians (such as the police), it is hard to believe that the police have *no* deterrent effect on crime. But for many reasons, hiring more police does not necessarily reduce crime. In earlier chapters we examined the role of the police in defining criminal events. The criteria that the police use to determine whether to make an arrest are shaped by a number of factors: the nature of the police organization and its strategies of policing, differing interpretations of criminal events, differing assessments of the characteristics and motivations of participants in those events, variations in the interpretations of the law and the cooperation of the public, and so on. We will soon consider how each of these factors influences the new problem-oriented strategies—referred to as community-based policing—that are

BOX 11.6

Crime Concentration and Police Problem Solving

How should police do "problem-oriented policing"? One answer to this question suggests that the police need to collect better crime data and need to think imaginatively about how to use that data. A good example of problem-solving logic is provided by John Eck (2001). Eck contends that traditionally, police managers have not been attentive enough to how crimes are clustered. We know, Eck says, that 10 percent of the places with the most crime account for about 60 percent of crime, that 10 percent of offenders are involved in about 50 percent of the offences, and that 10 percent of victimized people are involved in about 40 percent of victimizations. The implications of this are profound. It is possible that a community has a high crime rate because a small number of offenders are committing a lot of crime (career criminals), or because a small number of victims are repeatedly being victimized (hot dots), or because a small number of places are hosting a large number of events (hot spots). Eck nicknames these problems "ravenous wolves," "sitting ducks," and "dens of inequity" respectively. Clearly, these represent quite different types of crime problems. Merely knowing that the crime rate is high or that it has increased doesn't tell us whether we have a wolf problem, a duck problem, or a den problem, or some combination. For instance, if a housing project has a high rate of break-and-enter, we need to know whether this rate reflects a small number of offenders victimizing a lot of residences; or a small number of victims being repeatedly victimized; or a certain group of residences getting victimized repeatedly no matter who lives there. Perhaps it is even more complicated: perhaps the problem is 80 percent wolf, 10 percent duck, and 10 percent den, or some other such combination. These differences matter because wolf, duck, and den problems require different types of police interventions.

Wolves. The primary response to a pure wolf problem is, of course, to remove the wolves through incapacitation or rehabilitation. This is the traditional approach of the criminal justice system. Because many offenders use tools, another wolf solution is to make those tools less effective. For instance, metal detectors in schools can be used to systematically disarm potential wolves.

Ducks. Duck problems require different solutions than do wolf problems. Since victims and offenders must persistently come together at the same place for a crime problem to occur, one approach to preventing repeat victimization is to keep victims away from offenders, or places where offenders tend to gather. Also, potential victims can be encouraged to improve their use of tools—to install locks, increase lighting, and do other things to help them detect and avoid offenders. Police crime prevention programs can be important sources of relevant information and hardware.

Dens. Den problems require still other types of tactics. Dens can be made less accessible to victims or offenders, or they can be removed permanently. For example, the open hours of ATM machines can be limited. The typical den solution involves changing the physical environment. Again, the police can be expected to play an active consultative and facilitative role with respect to implementing crime prevention through environmental design.

Eck's analysis shows that a careful and judicious analysis of crime data by policing agencies can point out a range of options that are not obvious in the context of traditional models of policing.

intended to help the police deal with crime. But first we consider the changes that have taken place over the years in how the police function.

In the nineteenth century the mandate of the police was order maintenance (Wilson, 1983). The order maintenance or compliance role of the police was coterminous with "community relations." The police were to protect the community from disorderly behaviour and to control conflict where they found it (Monkkonen, 1983). This role required them to act as "watchmen," keeping track of comings and goings in the community and looking out for behaviour that might constitute a threat to public order. The compliance role is associated with the "proactive" policing we discussed in earlier chapters. As Klockars (1985: 106–7) has stated, the police are not law enforcement agencies, but rather regulatory institutions; their job is not to enforce laws but to regulate relationships between people.

The main objective of compliance law enforcement is to secure conformity with the law through means that induce that conformity (Reiss, 1984). Compliance systems return to the original mandate of the police, whereby one seeks to create law-abidingness through preventive or remedial actions. With these systems the main focus of policing shifts from detecting and penalizing violators to providing incentives to individuals to comply with the law. Compliance-based policing recognizes the need to include the public in controlling social disorder, beyond merely reporting crime to the police. The public is encouraged to include the police as intermediaries in situations of community conflict (Normandeau and Leighton, 1993).

The public has been demanding more social order since at least the 1850s (Monkkonen, 1983). In comparison with crime control, order control as practised by the police has had a long and successful record. As Monkkonen notes, Victorian morality has triumphed on most of North America's city streets. We expect, and get, quiet and predictable behaviour from almost everyone. Vice is no longer highly visible. Yet the dramatic rise in crime rates, and the apparent ineffectiveness of the police in dealing with crime and its consequences, has again raised concerns about social order. Monkkonen attributes increases in crime rates to a number of factors, including urbanization and demographic change. Early in the twentieth century, changes like these narrowed the focus of police agencies to crime control alone; problems of general order maintenance were left to other agencies.

The main objective of crime control or deterrence law enforcement is to detect violations of the law, identify the offenders responsible for those violations, and penalize the perpetrators. The goal is to diminish the likelihood of future offences both by the offender (specific deterrence) and by others who may contemplate the same criminal act (general deterrence) (Reiss, 1984: 91). Until recently, contemporary policing had as its stated objective the apprehension of offenders through arrest; this led to "reactive" policing, which still dominates the work of police agencies (Reiss, 1984: 84).

Police are now beginning to realize that crime control requires broadening their mandate to once again include order maintenance or compliance law enforcement (Greene, 1998). But this notion is being resisted by police agencies, which still regard law enforcement as their principal mandate. The internal workings of police organizations are such that peacekeeping and order maintenance functions are perceived as residual matters (Bayley, 1994: 34). Real policing, some argue, involves making arrests. As Kelling (1999) notes, many people—including many police—view community policing as "soft" policing "comparable to community relations, or worse yet, social work" (Kelling, 1999: 10). However, Kelling notes, the styles of police work that are associated with crime fighting are inherently more conservative than community policing, which is inherently proactive. Traditional policing requires police to respond to citizen requests for assistance; in contrast, community policing requires officers to scan for problems, diagnose and try to limit the damage, and restore victim–offender and community relations. According to Kelling, the equation of community policing with soft policing is troublesome because it supports the view that "real" crime problems require "real" solutions, and thus fails to appreciate how community policing styles can be effective even when crime problems are serious.

The philosophy of community-based policing challenges this view. The problem is that many compliance-based actions are still without legitimation in police organizations. Also, little training is provided for compliance-based operations. As Mastrofski (1983: 34) notes, the crime-fighting and the non-crime public service functions coexist uneasily in the police profession. The former dominates training curricula, career incentives, and organization evaluations; the latter dominates the workload.

Notwithstanding all this, community-based policing has replaced professional crime control policing as the dominant ideological and organizational model of progressive policing in Canada (Murphy, 1993). Bayley (1988: 226) identifies four main features of community-based policing: community-based crime prevention; proactive service as opposed to emergency response; public participation in the planning and supervision of police operations; and the shifting of command responsibility to lower-level ranks. Accompanying these organizational and procedural changes is an emphasis on identifying and solving problems, which are defined in terms of breaches of both law and social order. Furthermore, the solutions to these problems do not reside merely in the rules and regulations of the police service; they also acknowledge the concerns and desires of the community in which the problems occur.

According to Goldstein (1990), community-based policing requires at least five major adjustments in current thinking.

- *First*, police officers must be encouraged to search for alternatives to law enforcement. This encouragement must be reflected in a consistent, agency-wide commitment to improving the quality of police service.

- *Second*, the police must not restrict their attention to actions that have the potential to reduce crime. Sometimes crime is only the final consequence of unresolved, noncrime-related problems.

- *Third*, consistent with the view that policing encompasses all of a community's problems, those that do not fit strict law enforcement criteria must also be addressed.

- *Fourth*, some effort must be made to understand the nature of the problems encountered in a given area before any alternatives are set out. Too often, alternatives are prescribed that simply do not work because they are not suited to the area being policed. Like other large organizations, police services have difficulty resisting internal pressures to follow established but rigid objectives and procedures.

- *Fifth*, police must be open to the idea of allowing other agencies to fulfil the job in conjunction with or in place of the police. According to Goldstein (1990: 104), this strategy "is intended to dissuade the police from applying a generic response to a generic problem, or to applying a single response haphazardly to a wide range of different types of problems."

Bayley (1988: 226) suggests that if it is done correctly, community-based policing will constitute the most fundamental change in policing since the rise in police professionalism early in this century. Therefore, it is important that community policing initiatives be rigorously evaluated (Kennedy, 1991; Chicago Community Policing Evaluation Consortium, 2000) so that we can understand how and why they actually work. In the absence of good evaluation data, there is the risk that the police may simply end up doing the same thing as before, but labelling it as something else, or doing something differently, but not as well as before.

At the heart of the community-based policing concept is neighbourhood team policing, which involves the long-term assignment of officers to a particular area. (For a discussion of the experience in Halifax with this strategy, see Clairmont, 1990.) This strategy allows officers to make a commitment to an area and to assume a broader level of authority in providing policing that is more sensitive to community needs. Neighbourhood team programs have not been embraced by many police managers, who see the decentralization associated with this approach as limiting their control over their officers (Scheingold, 1984: 134). Also, the aggressive patrol tactics used in crime control may diminish police rapport with the public, and thereby undermine the effectiveness of community-based policing (Scheingold, 1984: 135). Finally, their fear of being seen as indecisive may cause many officers to play the role of enforcer rather than that of peacemaker (Palenski, 1984: 35).

Police must look to community members to support them in their efforts to bring about order in the community. This support can take the form of self-help, as discussed earlier, or it can involve a kind of coproduction, whereby the police use community members as supporters of police activity (Krahn and Kennedy, 1985). Coproduction can range from passive responses, such as locking doors, to more active responses, such as participating in crime prevention programs and acting as informants (Skolnick, 1966). As Black (1980) points out, since the typical criminal act occurs at an unpredictable time and place, the police must rely on citizens—most often the victims of a crime—to involve them.

Resources for community-based policing (outside of community support) have been hard to come by. Police budgets are still based on number of calls for service and on crime rates. Community-based policing, directed as it is at problem solving and at making referrals to outside programs, may create an impression of reduced activity; in turn this may suggest that budgets can be cut. The use of alternative programs also brings the police into conflict with other agencies; this makes it more difficult for them to define their role in the community and to obtain the resources they need to meet their objectives (Kennedy and Veitch, 1997). Despite these problems, the solutions that have been offered for handling demands from the public—including initiatives like building community police stations—have been quite successful. Walker and Walker (1993) document Victoria's positive experiences with mini-stations, which have worked in that city to reduce strain on centralized police functions and have increased the police department's ability to solve problems at the community level.

It is very difficult for some police agencies to remain apolitical when they are fighting for budget allocations and arguing for certain policing strategies. The lobbying by communities and by volunteers in community-based policing programs may make the police seem more politically active than local politicians want them to be, and make their requests for more funds even more tenuous. Police chiefs are confronted with a plethora of community constraints, which they must overcome before they can show they are fulfilling the objectives of compliance-based policing. Improving police–community relations is a crucial first step (Sacco, 1998; Shaffer, 1980). The members of the community must get to know the police as concerned and sympathetic individuals, as well as controlling and disciplining law officers. Without communication and cooperation between the police and the public, effective and fair policing is impossible.

SUMMARY

One response to crime is to see it as a public health problem that is best addressed by removing some of the major instruments that bring about injury (e.g., guns). A second view advocates that social institutions and resources be mobilized as a means for empowering victims to defend themselves against criminal attack. Because public health institutions already face tough challenges in dealing with diseases and injuries unrelated to crime, our heavy reliance on the police to confront the crime problem is unlikely to change, at least in the near future.

We can look at prevention from the perspective of either opportunity reduction or social development. Prevention can involve a number of things, from target hardening to increased surveillance. It can also set as a priority the targeting of violence, and offer ways for averting violence. Situational prevention is based on two important assumptions: that crime is most effectively prevented when we attend to the particular characteristics of the type of crime in question; and that we are usually dealing with a rational offender who considers risks, benefits, and ease of accomplishment before committing a crime. It follows from this that raising the costs associated with crimes (which are largely opportunistic in nature) may reduce the frequency with which they occur. Neighbourhood Watch and Block Watch programs assume that crime can be prevented by increasing surveillance and, by extension, the risk of detection and apprehension as it is perceived by the potential offender.

In contrast to the other prevention strategies, social development approaches focus on the serious, repeat offender. A relatively small number of offenders may be responsible for a disproportionately large number of crimes. These individuals tend to have in common many social and demographic characteristics. The aim of crime prevention through social development is to correct the criminogenic social conditions that are assumed to be important causes of crime. The focus of social development is on long-range outcomes that enhance social security and reduce crime incidence.

Community-based policing is a new approach that combines opportunity reduction with social development. The police are shifting their attention away from crime fighting (i.e., deterrence-based policing) toward compliance policing, which is more directly integrated with the community. The main objective of compliance law enforcement is to secure conformity with the law through systems that encourage community participation in defining and solving problems. The former emphasis on detecting and punishing violators has given way to an emphasis on providing incentives to individuals as a means of encouraging them to comply with the law.

Compliance-based policing recognizes the need to include the public in controlling social disorder, beyond merely reporting crime to the police. Bringing together a number of services within the community, as well as community members, can help form a multipronged attack on crime, involving re-education, mediation, opportunity removal, **resource mobilization**, the targeting of the roots of crime, and problem solving. Our success in controlling crime and diminishing the incidence of criminal events depends on our ability to understand where crime comes from, and also on our commitment to expend resources in broadening our responses to it.

Resource mobilization
Addressing crime issues in terms of whether the law helps people against victimization.

QUESTIONS FOR REVIEW AND DISCUSSION

1. Why is there a popular tendency to think about "more police and more prisons" as the *obvious* solution to the crime problem?

2. What similarities are there in the ways in which Canadian society approaches the problem of crime and the problem of disease?

3. With reference to the community where you live, to what extent are local crime problems wolf, duck, or den problems?

4. How do policies of situational prevention emerge logically from theoretical ideas that emphasize "rational offenders" and "social control"?

5. What does it mean to say that "there is much more to community-based policing than law enforcement"?

6. According to critics, what are some of the more important limitations of traditional responses that assign the central responsibility for crime control to the criminal justice system?

INFOTRAC COLLEGE EDITION

Explore InfoTrac College Edition, your online university library, which includes hundreds of popular and scholarly journals in which you can find articles related to the topics in this chapter. Visit InfoTrac through your Web browser (**www.infotrac-college.com**), or through this book's Web site (**www.criminalevent-3e.nelson.com**).

WHAT'S ON THE WEB?

For chapter links and quizzes, check out the accompanying Web site at **www.criminalevent-3e.nelson.com**.

GLOSSARY

Actus reus
The mere physical criminal act. (Chapter 1)

Adoption studies
The behavioural comparison of near-birth adoptees to their genetic and their adoptive parents. (Chapter 4)

Aftermath
Events that occur after the committed crime. (Chapter 2)

Age-specific
The crime risk for a certain age group. (Chapter 3)

Anomie theory
Theory that says anomie occurs when cultural norms and goals break down. (Chapter 4)

Atavism
The theory that offenders are less likely to conform to the demands of contemporary social life because they are related to a more primitive evolutionary condition. (Chapter 1)

Attachment
The degree to which children are sensitive to the expectations of parents or teachers. (Chapter 5)

Attachment costs
The costs associated with the loss of weakened ties that may make an arrest a fearsome prospect. (Chapter 5)

Avoidance behaviour
Behaviour by which victims seek to distance themselves from the kinds of people or situations they perceive as dangerous. (Chapter 7)

Battered woman syndrome
The sense of helplessness felt by women who come to believe that they can neither leave an abusive relationship nor effectively act to reduce the violence. (Chapter 1)

Belief
The degree to which youths believe that the conformist values of parents and teachers are worthy of respect. (Chapter 5)

Body type

In order to determine the relationship between physique and criminality, Sheldon categorized ("somatotyped") three basic types of body build—endomorphic, ectomorphic, and mesomorphic—that are associated with a particular type of temperament. (Chapter 4)

Bond, theory of the

Theory that strong social bonds insulate youths against the delinquent environment. (Chapter 5)

Bystanders

Criminal event participants whose presence may affect the course of action even though they are not centrally involved in the event as offenders or victims. (Chapter 2)

Canadian General Social Survey (GSS)

A large Canadian national survey that periodically has as a focus criminal victimization, crime prevention behaviour, and perceptions of crime. (Chapter 2)

Celerity

With reference to deterrence, the swiftness (perceived or objectively measurable) with which an offender is apprehended or punished. (Chapter 5)

Certainty

With reference to deterrence, the likelihood (perceived or objectively measurable) that an offender will be apprehended or punished. (Chapter 5)

Claimsmaking

The making of assertions about the existence of some problem that requires a policy solution. (Chapter 7)

Classical school

A school that views the offender as a "rational person" who would be deterred only by the threat of sanction. (Chapter 1)

Clearance status

A judgment made by the police based on identification of at least one of the offenders involved in an offence. (Chapter 3)

Commitment

The size of the investment of time and energy that a youth has made to a conventional activity, such as getting good grades. (Chapter 5)

Commitment costs

The possibility that arrest may jeopardize people's investments in some legitimate activity. (Chapter 5)

Community-based policing

Expansion of the policing role beyond the traditional narrow reactive role. (Chapter 11)

Conflict pattern

A pattern that occurs in socially disorganized neighbourhoods, where youth often experience the disparity between legitimate goals and legitimate opportunities, and this leads to aggressive behaviour. (Chapter 4)

Conflict theory

Theory that argues that in a complex society, social groups may pursue different interests, and the achievement of success depends on how powerful they are. Responses to crime are interpreted as part of a larger struggle among groups that attempt to use law, or legal control, in pursuit of their own interests. (Chapter 1)

Control theory

A group of theories which proceed from the assumption that criminal behaviour emerges in the absence of controls (internal or external) that might check or contain it. (Chapter 5)

Consensus theory

Theory proposing that laws and punishment be enforced in order to maintain the collective interests shared by members of society. (Chapter 1)

Constitutional structure

Predispositions toward crime are claimed to be expressed by biological factors, such as phenotypes or body types, and psychological propensities. (Chapter 4)

Containment theory

Theory, based on control theory, that youth are insulated from delinquency by inner and outer containments that constrain nonconformist behaviour. (Chapter 5)

Corporate crime

Acts committed by businesses in the interests of generating profit and avoiding losses and prosecution. (Chapter 10)

Costs of victimization

Losses of a physical, financial, emotional, and social nature that can be attributed to the victimization experience. (Chapter 7)

Crime

A behaviour that breaks the criminal law and is liable to public prosecution and punishment. (Chapter 1)

Crime funnel

A "volume-reducing system," meaning that there is a high level of attrition as cases travel through various stages of the criminal justice system. (Chapter 3)

Crime gene

The sociobiological perspective that certain genes may be linked to criminality. (Chapter 4)

Crime myths

Distorted and misleading information that nevertheless is accepted as fact. (Chapter 1)

Crime prevention

The anticipation, recognition, and appraisal of a crime risk and the initiation of some action to reduce or remove it. (Chapter 11)

Crime rate

Measures that calculate the amount of crime relative to the occurrence of some count of events, conditions, or people. (Chapter 3)

Criminal career

A way of thinking about the sequential stages of criminal involvement over the offender's life course. (Chapter 5)

Criminal event

Comprises its precursors, including the locational and situational factors that bring people together in time and space; the event itself, including how the interactions among participants define the outcomes of their actions; and the aftermath of the event, including the reporting to the police, their response, the harm done, the redress required, and the long-term consequences of the event in terms of public reactions and the changing of laws. (Chapter 2)

Criminal pattern

A rational delinquency oriented toward the pursuit of monetary objectives, exemplified by organized theft and the sale of illicit goods or services. (Chapter 4)

Criminological theories

Generalized explanations of why, how, and with what consequences crimes occur. (Chapter 4)

Crude crime rate

Crime rate measures which employ as a denominator the total population in some jurisdiction and thus which take no account of the demographic structure of the population. (Chapter 3)

Cultural goals

Legitimate objectives held by all or by diversely located members of society. (Chapter 4)

Culture of competition

A cultural atmosphere in which crime is promoted by competition that defines wealth and success as central goals of human activity. (Chapter 4)

Defensible space
The physical design of a place that may deter or attract an offender. (Chapter 2)

Deterrence
Theory of prevention in which the threat of punishment or retribution is expected to forestall some act from occurring. (Chapter 5)

Diet
The concept that the behaviour of certain individuals can be affected by their diet. (Chapter 4)

Differential adjudication hypothesis
The theory that delinquents with learning disabilities who are arrested and charged are more likely to be convicted of crimes due to their inability to cope with the process of criminal justice adjudication. (Chapter 4)

Differential arrest hypothesis
The theory that learning disabled children are more likely to be apprehended by the police since they are less likely to conceal their activities. (Chapter 4)

Differential association
The theory that criminal behaviour is learned in the process of interaction with intimate groups. (Chapter 4)

Differential disposition hypothesis
The theory that learning disabled delinquents have a higher chance of receiving harsher sentences than do other delinquents. (Chapter 4)

Direct observation
A technique in which an investigator attempts to develop a theory through exploration, or confirm hypotheses through direct participation in and observation of the community or other social grouping being studied. (Chapter 3)

Duress defence
Some unlawful constraint of influence used to force an individual to commit an act that he or she otherwise would not have committed. (Chapter 1)

Ecological position
Incorporates geographic and economic relationships within a community in the analyses of crime rates. (Chapter 3)

Elite-engineered model
Argues that moral panics represent the deliberate attempt on the part of the economic or political elite to promote public concern about some issue that does not involve the public's interests. (Chapter 7)

Enterprise crime

Sale of illegal goods and services to customers who know that the goods and services are illegal. (Chapter 10)

Ethnographic research

Studies in which the researcher attempts to directly observe and interact with the people being studied in a naturally occurring context. (Chapter 3)

Excuse

Denial of responsibility for an acknowledged wrongful act. (Chapter 2)

Experimental observation

An experimental method, often conducted in laboratories, in which the experimenter creates the conditions necessary for observation rather than searching for naturally occurring situations. (Chapter 3)

Family and household domain

Enduring pattern of social relationships through which domestic life is organized. (Chapter 8)

Family violence

Child abuse, wife assault, elder abuse, and other forms of physical coercion that are contextualized by domestic living arrangements. (Chapter 8)

Fear of crime

A concern or anxiety relating to the possibility of criminal victimization and usually assessed in social research through the measurement of attitudes or reported behaviours. (Chapter 7)

Feminist

A theoretical orientation that critically assesses power relationships in society particularly as those relationships relate to gender inequality. (Chapter 1)

Focal concerns

Concerns around which life in the lower class is organized: trouble, toughness, smartness, excitement, fate, and autonomy. (Chapter 4)

Folk hero syndrome

A residual belief that the criminal should be admired for expressing some degree of resistance to convention. (Chapter 5)

Formal social control

Conventional methods of technology and physical coercion, such as the police force, used to maintain social order. (Chapter 5)

General deterrence

The ways in which individuals, on seeing offenders receiving punishment, will be deterred from breaking the law themselves. (Chapter 5)

General pedigree studies
A nonexperimental approach to the study of intergenerational transmission of genetically predisposed behaviour between related individuals. (Chapter 4)

General strain theory
A focus on negative relationships between people that promote anger, fear, and frustration, which may lead to delinquency. (Chapter 4)

General theory of crime
The theory that criminal activity appeals to people who are impulsive, short-sighted, physical, risk-taking, nonverbal, and, most importantly, have low self-control. (Chapter 5)

Genetics
In criminology, a field of study that attempts to determine how certain presocial factors such as family ties and blood relations influence criminal outcomes (often in conjunction with environmental factors). (Chapter 4)

Grassroots model
Views moral panics as originating in the mood of the public. (Chapter 7)

Hedonism, principle of
The principle that the seeking of pleasure and avoidance of pain are the ultimate aims and motivating forces of human action. (Chapter 1)

Hot spots
High-crime locations. (Chapter 6)

Illegitimate means
Two aspects of the delinquent opportunity structure: opportunity to learn and to play the delinquent role. (Chapter 4)

Improvised news
Similar to rumour; expresses anxieties and uncertainties about some aspect of social life. (Chapter 1)

Incivility
Physical conditions such as abandoned buildings and strewn trash, as well as social conditions such as public drinking or drug use. (Chapter 7)

Informal social control
Casual methods of coercion employed by community members to maintain conformity. (Chapter 5)

Inner containments
The products of effective socialization and the successful internalization of rules regarding acceptable behaviour. (Chapter 5)

Interactional theory of delinquency

The theory that ties to conventional others, which, if weak, increase the likelihood of delinquent behaviour, can be strengthened over time in response to changing circumstances. (Chapter 5)

Interest-group theory

Moral panics can be set in motion by the actions of small groups, such as politicians, crusading journalists, or professional associations. (Chapter 7)

Involvement

Participation in the world of conformity so that little time is left for delinquency. (Chapter 5)

IQ

A measure of intelligence derived from standardized testing procedures that compare individuals' mental and chronological ages. (Chapter 4)

Justification

Accepting responsibility for the act while denying the immorality of the act. (Chapter 2)

Juvenile

In Canada, anyone under age 12 cannot be responsible for their own actions in the criminal sense. Children age 12 to 17 are held culpable for their actions but are held separate from adults when their criminal responsibilities are assessed. (Chapter 1)

Karyotype studies

These claim that an individual's chromosomes—that is, their size, shape, and number—are a causal factor in criminality. (Chapter 4)

Labelling theory

The theory that frustration created by particular social arrangements, such as identifying a person as a criminal, may motivate criminal behaviour. (Chapter 7)

La Cosa Nostra

Literally "our thing." This term is understood as the formal designation of the Italian-American crime syndicate which dominated enterprise crime during the twentieth century. (Chapter 10)

Learning disabilities

Difficulties faced by children and youths with dyslexia, dysgraphia, aphasia, perceptual and motor deficits, poor sensory integration, or minimal brain dysfunction. (Chapter 4)

Legitimate means

Widely accepted routes of achieving cultural goals through institutions. (Chapter 4)

Leisure

Free time (after work, familial, and other obligations are met) that can be used for play or recreation. (Chapter 9)

Life course perspective

Adult criminality is strongly influenced by patterns of childhood behaviour, and changes in people's lives affect the likelihood of involvement in crime. (Chapter 5)

Lifestyle exposure theory

Focuses on patterned ways in which people with certain demographic characteristics distribute their time and energies across a range of activities, and their relation with the risk of victimization by motivated offenders. (Chapter 6)

Mala in se

Crimes that are perceived historically and cross-culturally as wrong. (Chapter 1)

Mala prohibita

Crimes that are condemned through prohibition. (Chapter 1)

Mandatory charge rule

Legal or procedural regulation that requires the police, in domestic violence cases, to make an arrest when they have physical evidence suggesting that an assault has taken place. (Chapter 2)

Mens rea

The wilful quality of a criminal act. (Chapter 1)

Middle-class measuring rod

The middle-class ethic, which people use to compare and determine their status, that prescribes an obligation to strive, by dint of rational, ascetic, self-disciplined, and independent activity, to achieve worldly success. (Chapter 4)

Moral panic

The behaviour of some members of society is seen as so problematic, evil, or harmful to the society that it becomes a social imperative to control the behaviour, punish the offenders, and repair the damage (e.g., the Great European Witch Hunts). (Chapter 7)

Neighbourhood Watch

A community crime prevention program in which residents monitor neighourhood life and exert guardianship over each other's property. (Chapter 7)

Neuropsychological theory

The theory that people with identical IQ scores can have very different patterns of mental strengths and weaknesses (e.g., verbal skill, spatial perception) that can influence behaviour. (Chapter 4)

Neutralization theory
The view that delinquents often use linguistic constructions (i.e., excuses or rationalizations) to reduce the guilt resulting from their delinquent behaviour. (Chapter 4)

Norms
Rules that govern social activities and define social roles, role relations, and standards of appropriate conduct. (Chapter 1)

Occasional offenders
Commit crimes when opportunities or situational inducements present themselves. (Chapter 8)

Occupancy probes
Imaginative methods that the offender uses to determine whether anyone is home. (Chapter 8)

Occupational crime
Violation of legal norms governing lawful occupational endeavours. (Chapter 10)

Offender reports
Data gathered from a sample of known offenders, such as prison inmates. (Chapter 3)

Opportunity reduction
Focuses on how social and environmental factors can be brought to bear on the reduction of crime opportunities. (Chapter 11)

Outer containments
Aspects of the individual's social environment (e.g., primary groups) that help ensure that delinquent behaviour does not occur. (Chapter 5)

Peacemaking
A process that involves reducing punishment/imprisonment and promoting programs that encourage treatment, rehabilitation, alternatives to incarceration, mediation, and enhanced social justice. (Chapter 1)

Permissive environs
Social settings, such as bars and parties, where individuals feel free of many of the constraints that operate in other settings, such as the school and the workplace. (Chapter 9)

Positive leisure
Forms of leisure activity that link adolescents to conformist others and that are thought to insulate against delinquency. (Chapter 9)

Positivist school

The philosophical position, developed by Auguste Comte, that scientific knowledge can come only from direct observation, experimentation, and provision of quantitative data (e.g., finding the cause of crime within the criminal). (Chapter 1)

Power control theory

The theory that due to differential control (i.e., girls are subject to greater control than boys) within the patriarchal family, males have a higher propensity to engage in risk-taking and delinquent behaviour. (Chapter 5)

Precursors

Situational factors that bring people together in time and space. (Chapter 2)

Proactive policing

Police involvement in incidents as a result of their own investigative or patrol activities, which bring to their attention events that may be designated as crimes. (Chapter 2)

Psychopathology

Study of abnormal behaviour. (Chapter 4)

Psychopathy

A sociopathic disorder characterized by lack of moral development and the inability to show loyalty to others. (Chapter 4)

Punishment

Confinement, restriction of activities, infliction of pain, and other measures taken for retribution, to enforce compliance, or to bring about behavioural changes. (Chapter 5)

Rational choice theories

These focus on the offenders' actions and decisions as they are based on perceived benefits rather than on precipitating or psychological factors. (Chapter 5)

Rational reconstruction

Occurs when individuals recall their crimes and suggest there was more planning than actually took place. (Chapter 8)

Reactive policing

The police become involved in criminal events when asked to do so by a member of the public. (Chapter 2)

Recidivism

Repetition or recurrence of delinquent or criminal behaviour or behaviour disorder, especially following punishment or rehabilitation. (Chapter 8)

Resource mobilization

Addressing crime issues in terms of whether the law helps people against victimization. (Chapter 11)

Retreatist pattern

Pattern exhibited by people who are unable to succeed through either legitimate or illegitimate means (double-failures), and who resort to delinquency organized around the consumption of drugs. (Chapter 4)

Risky lifestyle

A regular pattern of activities that exposes individuals to higher levels of risk of criminal victimization. (Chapter 9)

Routine activities theory

A theory that besides the presence of a motivated offender, a suitable target and the absence of capable guardianship are vital to the completion of a crime. (Chapter 6)

School failure hypothesis

The idea that self-perpetuating academic failure resulting from learning disabilities causes frustration and aggressive behaviour. (Chapter 4)

Secondary deviance

The idea that the effect of feedback that consistently provides the message that one is a disreputable person may eventually lead to the acceptance of the definition. (Chapter 7)

Self-defence

Actions taken to protect oneself or one's property, involving reasonable force, in the face of a threat. (Chapter 1)

Self-fulfilling prophecy

The theory that people who are perceived as beyond redemption will come to act as if they are. (Chapter 7)

Self-report studies

Respondents' reports about their involvement as offenders. (Chapter 3)

Severity

With reference to deterrence, the perceived or actual seriousness of the penalty for a legal infraction. (Chapter 5)

Situated transaction

Process of interaction involving two or more individuals that lasts as long as they find themselves in one another's presence. (Chapter 6)

Situational crime prevention
Efforts to prevent crime that focus on the suppression of criminal opportunities (rather than, for instance, the reform of offenders). (Chapter 11)

Situational deterrence
The ways in which the offender's fear of apprehension are related to the specific circumstances of the criminal event. (Chapter 5)

Social bond
In social control theory, the strength and quality of the relationships that link potential offenders to conformist others and that serve to insulate them from criminal influences. (Chapter 5)

Social control
The regulatory institutions of society—especially the law enforcement and judicial systems—and how they operate, encompassing rule enforcement at all levels. (Chapter 1)

Social development approach
An approach to crime prevention which attempts to create social conditions that discourage long-term serious offending and that empower potential victims, while at the same time contributing to the rebuilding of communities. (Chapter 11)

Social disorganization
Long-term, widespread deterioration of social order and control in a population. (Chapter 5)

Social domains
Major spheres of life in which we spend most of our time and energy. (Chapter 2)

Social inequality
Results when one social group is underprivileged compared with another. (Chapter 10)

Social organization
Coherence and continuity in the social environment, and rational co-operation among individuals and social institutions. (Chapter 8)

Sociopathy
Antisocial personality disorder involving a marked lack of ethical or moral development. (Chapter 4)

Specific/special deterrence
The ways in which individuals are deterred from offending or re-offending by receiving punishment. (Chapter 5)

Stigma of arrest
The belief that apprehension by the police may harm one's reputation. (Chapter 5)

Strain theory

The theory that the constant emphasis on success in society and its possible attainment consistently contradicts the actual opportunity facing people—especially at the bottom of society, where the greatest amount of crime occurs. (Chapter 4)

Subculture

A group of people in a dominant culture with different values, evident in their expression of deviant behaviour. (Chapter 4)

Subculture of violence

A subculture in which disproportionate rates of criminal violence are the product of a group's commitment to subcultural values and norms that condone violence as acceptable means of resolving interpersonal conflict. (Chapter 4)

Subterranean values

Values that are held by many in society, although they may conflict with other cherished values. (Chapter 4)

Susceptibility hypothesis

The theory that learning disabled students have unique characteristics, such as impulsiveness and irritability, and thus are more likely to become delinquent. (Chapter 4)

Symbolic interactionism

The role of linguistic interaction in developing a social identity and functioning according to shared norms and values. (Chapter 6)

Target hardening

Increasing protection of premises to deter a criminal through fear of detection or because the target has been made inaccessible. (Chapter 8)

Telescoping

Reporting a crime as occurring during the reference period when it actually occurred at an earlier time. (Chapter 3)

Trace elements

Mineral content in the subject's body determines episodic violence or antisocial behaviour. (Chapter 4)

Trajectories

In the life course perspective, these describe the directions in which lives seem to be moving. (Chapter 5)

Transactions

The interactions between individuals that have led to the outcome of a crime. (Chapter 2)

Transitions

In the life course perspective, specific events that may or may not alter trajectories. (Chapter 5)

Twin studies

A nonexperimental study designed to research and compare criminal predispositions between dizygotic and monozygotic twins. (Chapter 4)

Twinkie defence

When a defendant experiences diminished mental capacity and is therefore not guilty of criminal behaviour due to an overconsumption of junk food. (Chapter 4)

Underclass

A class of society that almost exclusively inhabits segregated, disadvantaged neighbourhoods. (Chapter 1)

Uniform crime reporting system (UCR)

The UCR is a survey collated by Statistics Canada based on crime reports from police departments nationwide. The information is available to the government, criminologists, politicians, and the mass media. (Chapter 3)

Urban legend

Captivating and plausible fictional oral narratives that are widely regarded as true stories. (Chapter 1)

Valence issues

Issues that do not have an adversarial quality. (Chapter 7)

Vandalism

The deliberate damaging or destruction of public or private property. (Chapter 9)

Victim precipitation

Occurs when the opportunity for crime is created by some action of the victim. (Chapter 6)

Victim reports/surveys

Large-scale studies that ask individuals about their experience with crime. (Chapter 3)

Victimless crimes

Criminal events in which a victim does not exist in any direct and immediate way. Examples: gambling or abusing drugs by personal choice. (Chapter 2)

Vulnerability conversion

Especially for victims of violence, development of a sudden understanding by victims that they are more susceptible to the dangers of life than they thought. (Chapter 7)

White-collar crime
A crime committed by a person of respectability and high status in the course of his or her occupation. (Chapter 10)

Workplace crime
Criminal events that emerge out of relations formed by labour force participation in the context of legitimate or illegitimate economies. (Chapter 10)

REFERENCES

Agnew, R. 1985a. "A Revised Strain Theory of Delinquency." *Social Forces* 64(1): 151–67.

——— 1985b. "Neutralizing the Impact of Crime." *Criminal Justice and Behavior* 12: 221–39.

——— 1990. "The Origins of Delinquent Events: An Examination of Offender Accounts." *Journal of Research in Crime and Delinquency* 27(3): 267–94.

——— 1992. "Foundation for a General Strain Theory of Crime and Delinquency." *Criminology* 30: 47–87.

——— 1993. "Why Do They Do It? An Examination of the Intervening Mechanisms between 'Social Control' Variables and Delinquency." *Journal of Research in Crime and Delinquency* 30(3): 245–66.

Agnew, R., and S. Huguley. 1989. "Adolescent Violence toward Parents." *Journal of Marriage and the Family* 51: 699–711.

Agnew, R., and A.R. Peters. 1986. "The Techniques of Neutralization: An Analysis of Predisposing and Situational Factors." *Criminal Justice and Behavior* 13: 81–97.

Agnew, R., and D.M. Peterson. 1989. "Leisure and Delinquency." *Social Problems* 36(4): 332–50.

Agnew, R., and H.R. White. 1992. "An Empirical Test of General Strain Theory." *Criminology* 30: 475–99.

Akers, R.L. 1985. *Deviant Behavior: A Social Learning Approach.* Belmont: Wadsworth.

——— 1994. *Criminological Theories.* Los Angeles: Roxbury Publishing.

Alarid, L.F., V.S. Burton, Jr., and F.T. Cullen. 2000. "Gender and Crime among Felony Offenders: Assessing the Generality of Social Control and Differential Association Theories." *Journal of Research in Crime and Delinquency.* 37(2): 171–99.

Allan, E.A., and D.J. Steffensmeier. 1989. "Youth, Underemployment and Property Crime: Differential Effects of Job Availability and Job Quality on Juvenile and Young Adult Arrest Rates." *American Sociological Review* 54: 107–23.

Almey, M. 2000. "Family Status." *Women in Canada 2000.* Ottawa: Minister of Industry.

Amir, M. 1971. *Patterns of Forcible Rape.* Chicago: University of Chicago Press.

Anderson, J.F., T. Grandison, and L. Dyson. 1996. "Victims of Random Violence and the Public Health Implication: A Health Care or Criminal Justice Issue." *Journal of Criminal Justice* 24(5): 379–91.

Anttila, I. 1974. "Victimology: A New Territory in Criminology." *Scandinavian Studies in Criminology* 5: 7–10.

Arneklev, B.J., H.G. Grasmick, and R.J. Bursik, Jr. 1999. "Evaluating the Dimensionality and Invariance of 'Low Self-Control.'" *Journal of Quantitative Criminology* 15(3): 307–31.

Arnold, B.L., and J. Hagan. 1992. "Careers of Misconduct: Prosecuted Professional Deviance among Lawyers." *American Sociological Review* 57(6): 771–80.

Ayers, C.D., J.H. Herbert, J.D. Hawkins, P.L. Peterson, R.F. Cataleno, and R.A. Abbott. 1999. "Assessing Correlates of Onset, Escalation, Deescalation, and Desistance of Delinquent Behavior." *Journal of Quantitative Criminology* 15(3): 277–306.

Baldassare, M. 1986. "The Elderly and Fear of Crime." *Sociology and Social Research* 70: 218–21.

Balkin, S. 1979. "Victimization Rates, Safety and Fear of Crime." *Social Problems* 26(3): 343–58.

Baron, S. 1989. "The Canadian West Coast Punk Subculture: A Field Study." *Canadian Journal of Sociology* 14(3): 289–316.

Baron, S.W. 1997. "Risky Lifestyles and the Link between Offending and Victimization." *Studies on Crime and Crime Prevention* 6(1): 53–71.

Baron, S.W., and T.F Hartnagel. 1996. "'Lock em up': Attitudes towards Punishing Juvenile Offenders. " *Canadian Journal of Criminology* 38: 191–212.

Bartusch, D.R., D.R. Lynam, T.E. Moffitt, and P.A. Silva. 1997. "Is Age Important? Testing a General versus a Developmental Theory of Antisocial Behavior." *Criminology* 35(1): 13–47.

Baumer, T.L. 1978. "Research on Fear of Crime in the United States." *Victimology* 3: 254–64.

Baunach, P.J. 1990. "State Prisons and Inmates: The Census and Survey." In D.L. Mackenzie, P.J. Baunach, and R.R. Robert (eds.), *Measuring Crime: Large-Scale, Long-Range Efforts*. Albany: State University of New York.

Bayley, D.H. 1985. *Patterns of Policing: A Comparative International Analysis.* New Brunswick: Rutgers University Press.

——— 1988. "Community Policing: A Report from the Devil's Advocate." In J.R. Greene and D. Mastrofski (eds.), *Community Policing: Rhetoric or Reality.* New York: Praeger.

———— 1994. *Police for the Future.* New York: Oxford University Press.

Beare, M.E. 1996. *Criminal Conspiracies.* Scarborough: Nelson Canada.

Bechhofer, L., and A. Parrot. 1991. "What Is Acquaintance Rape?" In A. Parrot and L. Bechhofer (eds.), *Acquaintance Rape: The Hidden Crime.* New York: John Wiley.

Becker, H.S. 1963. *Outsiders: Studies in the Sociology of Deviance.* New York: Free Press.

Beckett, K., and T. Sasson. 2000. *The Politics of Injustice.* Thousand Oaks: Pine Forge Press.

Bell, D. 1953. "Crime as an American Way of Life." *The Antioch Review* 13 (June): 131–54.

Bell, D.J. 1987. "The Victim–Offender Relationship: A Determinant Factor in Police Domestic Dispute Dispositions." *Marriage and Family Review* 12(1/2): 87–102.

Bellair, P.E. 2000. "Informal Surveillance and Street Crime: A Complex Relationship." *Criminology* 38(1): 137–70.

Bennett, T. 1989. "Burglars' Choice of Targets." In D.J. Evans and D.T. Herbert (eds.), *The Geography of Crime.* London: Routledge.

Bennett, T., and R. Wright. 1984. *Burglars on Burglary.* Brookfield: Gower.

Benson, D., C. Charlton, and F. Goodhart. 1992. "Acquaintance Rape on Campus: A Literature Review." *College Health* 40 (January): 157–65.

Benson, M.L. 1985. "Denying the Guilty Mind: Accounting for Involvement in a White-Collar Crime." *Criminology* 23(4): 583–607.

Benson, M.L., and E. Moore. 1992. "Are White Collar and Common Offenders the Same? An Empirical and Theoretical Critique of a Recently Proposed General Theory of Crime." *Journal of Research in Crime and Delinquency* 29(3): 251–72.

Bernard, T.J. 1981. "The Distinction between Conflict and Radical Criminology." *Journal of Criminal Law and Criminology* 72(1): 362–79.

Besserer, S. 1998. "Criminal Victimization: An International Perspective." *Juristat* 18(6).

Besserer, S., and C. Trainor. 2000. "Criminal Victimization in Canada, 1999." *Juristat* 20(10).

Best, J. 1988. "Missing Children: Misleading Statistics." *The Public Interest* 92 (Summer): 84–92.

———— 1990. *Threatened Children.* Chicago: University of Chicago Press.

———— 1995. *Images of Issues.* New York: Aldine de Gruyter.

———— 1999. *Random Violence: How We Talk about New Crimes and New Victims.* Berkeley: University of California Press.

———— 2001. *Damned Lies and Statistics: Untangling Numbers from the Media, Politicians and Activists.* Berkeley: University of California Press.

Best, J., and D.F. Luckenbill. 1994. *Organizing Deviance.* 2nd ed. Englewood Cliffs: Prentice Hall.

Biderman, A.D., and J.P. Lynch. 1991. *Understanding Crime Incidence Statistics.* New York: Springer-Verlag.

Birkbeck, C., and G. LaFree. 1993. "The Situational Analysis of Crime and Deviance." *Annual Review of Sociology* 19: 113–37.

Black, D. 1970. "Production of Crime Rates." *American Sociological Review* 35: 733–47.

———— 1971. "The Social Organization of Arrest." *Stanford Law Review* 23: 1087–111.

———— 1976. *The Behavior of Law.* New York: Academic Press.

———— 1980. *The Manners and Customs of the Police.* New York: Academic Press.

———— 1983. "Crime as Social Control." *American Sociological Review* 48 (February): 34–45.

Blau, J.R., and P.M. Blau. 1982. "The Cost of Inequality: Metropolitan Structure and Violent Crime." *American Sociological Review* 4 (February): 114–29.

Block, C.R., and R.L. Block. 1984. "Crime Definition, Crime Measurement, and Victim Surveys." *Journal of Social Issues* 40(1): 137–60.

Block, R. 1974. "Why Notify the Police? The Victim's Decision to Notify the Police of an Assault." *Criminology* 11(4): 555–69.

Block, R., M. Felson, and C.R. Block. 1984. "Crime Victimization Rates for Incumbents of 246 Occupations." *Sociology and Social Research* 69(3): 442–51.

Blumstein, A., J. Cohen, and D.P. Farrington. 1988a. "Criminal Career Research: Its Value for Criminology." *Criminology* 26(1): 1–36.

———— 1988b. "Longitudinal and Criminal Career Research: Further Clarifications." *Criminology* 26(1): 57–74.

Blumstein, A., J. Cohen, and R. Rosenfeld. 1992. "The UCR–NCS Relationship Revisited: A Reply to Menard." *Criminology* 30(1): 115–24.

Bockman, L.S. 1991. "Interest, Ideology and Claims-Making Activity." *Sociological Inquiry* 61(4): 452–70.

Bograd, M. 1988. "How Battered Women and Abusive Men Account for Domestic Violence: Excuses, Justifications or Explanations." In

G.T. Hotaling, D. Finkelhor, J.T. Kirkpatrick, and M.A. Straus (eds.), *Coping with Family Violence*. Newbury Park: Sage.

Bohm, R.M. 1997. *A Primer on Crime and Delinquency*. Belmont: Wadsworth.

Boritch, H. 1992. "Gender and Criminal Court Outcomes: An Historical Analysis." *Criminology* 30(3): 293–325.

———— 1997. *Fallen Women: Female Crime and Criminal Justice in Canada*. Scarborough: Nelson Canada.

Bottomley, A.K., and K. Pease. 1986. *Crime and Punishment—Interpreting the Data*. Philadelphia: Open University Press.

Box, S. 1981. *Deviance, Reality, and Society*. London: Holt, Rinehart & Winston.

Boyd, N. 2000. "Canadian Criminal Law." In R.A. Silverman, J.J. Teevan, and V.F. Sacco (eds.), *Crime in Canadian Society*, 6th ed., pp. 20–31. Toronto: Harcourt Brace.

Braithwaite, J. 1989. *Crime, Shame and Reintegration*. Cambridge: Cambridge University Press.

Brantingham, P.J., and P.L. Brantingham. 1984. *Patterns in Crime*. New York: Macmillan.

Brantingham, P.J., and F.L. Faust. 1976. "A Conceptual Model of Crime Prevention." *Crime and Delinquency* 22: 284–96.

Brantingham, P.J., S. Mu, and A. Verma. 1995. "Patterns in Canadian Crime." In M.A. Jackson and C.T. Griffiths (eds.), *Canadian Criminology*, pp. 187–245. Toronto: Harcourt Brace.

Brantingham, P.L. 1989. "Crime Prevention: The North American Experience." In D.J. Evans and D.T. Herbert (eds.), *The Geography of Crime*. London: Routledge.

Brantingham, P.L., and P.J. Brantingham. 1990. "Situational Crime Prevention in Practice." *Canadian Journal of Criminology* 32(1): 17–40.

———— 1993. "Situational Crime Prevention in Practice." In R.V. Clarke and M. Felson (eds.), *Routine Activity and Rational Choice*. New Brunswick: Transaction.

———— 2001. "The Implications of the Criminal Event Model for Crime Prevention." In R.F. Meier, L.W. Kennedy, and V.F. Sacco (eds.), *The Process and Structure of Crime*. Vol. 9, Advances in Criminological Theory. Piscataway: Transaction Press.

Brennan, P.A., S.A. Mednick, and J. Volavka. 1995. "Biomedical Factors in Crime." In J.Q. Wilson and J. Petersilia (eds.), *Crime*. Pp. 65–90. San Francisco: Institute for Contemporary Studies Press. Used by permission.

Brezina, T. 1996. "Adapting to Strain: An Examination of Delinquent Coping Responses." *Criminology* 34(1): 39–60.

——— 2000. "Delinquent Problem Solving." *Journal of Research in Crime and Delinquency* 37(1): 3–30.

Brillon, Y. 1985. "Public Opinion about the Penal System: A Cynical View of Criminal Justice." In D. Gibson and J.K. Baldwin (eds.), *Law in a Cynical Society? Opinion and Law in the 1980s.* Calgary: Carswell.

Bromley, D.G. 1991. "Satanism: The New Cult Scare." In J.T. Richardson, J. Best, and D.G. Bromley (eds.), *The Satanism Scare.* New York: Aldine de Gruyter.

Brunvand, J.H. 1981. *The Vanishing Hitchhiker: American Urban Legends and Their Meaning.* New York: Norton.

——— 1984. *The Choking Doberman and Other "New" Urban Legends.* New York: Norton.

——— 1986. *The Mexican Pet.* New York: Norton.

——— 1989. *Curses! Broiled Again!* New York: Norton.

Budd, T. 1999. *Burglary of Domestic Dwellings: Findings from the British Crime Survey.* London: Home Office Statistical Bulletin.

Bunge, V.P. 2000a. "Spousal Violence." *Family Violence in Canada: A Statistical Profile 2000.* Ottawa: Statistics Canada.

——— 2000b. "Abuse of Older Adults by Family Members." *Family Violence in Canada: A Statistical Profile 2000.* Ottawa: Statistics Canada.

Burgess, A.W., L.L. Holmstrom, and M.P. McCausland. 1977. "Child Sexual Assault by a Family Member: Decisions Following Disclosure." *Victimology: An International Journal* 2(2): 236–50.

Bursik R.J. 1999. "The Informal Control of Crime through Neighborhood Networks." *Sociological Focus* 32(1): 85–97.

Bursik Jr., R.J., and H.G. Grasmick. 1993. *Neighborhoods and Crime: The Dimensions of Effective Community Control.* New York: Lexington Books.

Burt, M.R., and B.L. Katz. 1985. "Rape, Robbery and Burglary: Responses to Actual and Feared Criminal Victimization with Special Focus on Women and the Elderly." *Victimology* 10: 325–58.

Burton Jr., V.S., F.T. Cullen, T.D. Evans, L.F. Alarid, and R.G. Dunaway. 1998. "Gender, Self-Control." *Journal of Research in Crime and Delinquency* 35(2): 123–47.

Calavita, K., and H.N. Pontell. 1991. "'Other People's Money' Revisited: Collective Embezzlement in the Savings and Loan Insurance Industries." *Social Problems* 38(1): 94–112.

Calhoun, T.C., and G. Weaver. 1996. "Rational Decision-Making among Male Street Prostitutes." *Deviant Behavior* 17: 209–27.

Canada. 1982. *The Criminal Law in Canadian Society*. Ottawa: Government of Canada.

Canadian Centre for Justice Statistics. 1990. *The Development of Data Quality Assessment Procedures for the Uniform Crime Reporting Survey: A Case Study of Calgary–Edmonton*. Ottawa: Statistics Canada.

——— 1993. *Incident-Based Uniform Crime Reporting Survey*. Ottawa: Statistics Canada.

——— 2000. *The Justice Factfinder, 1998*. Ottawa: Statistics Canada.

Canadian Criminal Justice Associaton. 1989. "Safer Communities: A Social Strategy for Crime Prevention in Canada." *Canadian Journal of Criminology* 31(4): 359–363.

Cantor, D., and K.C. Land. 1985. "Unemployment and Crime Rates in the Post-World War II United States: A Theoretical and Empirical Analysis." *American Sociological Review* 50 (June): 317–32.

Carter, D.L. 1985. "Hispanic Perceptions of Police Performance: An Empirical Assessment." *Journal of Criminal Justice* 13: 487–500.

Cernkovitch, S.A., P.C. Giordano, and J.L. Ruddolph, 2000. "Race, Crime, and the American Dream." *Journal of Research in Crime and Delinquency*. 37(2): 131–70.

Chaiken, J., and M. Chaiken. 1982. *Varieties of Criminal Behavior*. Rand Report r-2814-NIJ. Santa Monica: Rand Corporation.

Chambliss, W. 1975. "On the Paucity of Original Research on Organized Crime: A Footnote to Galliher and Cain." *The American Sociologist* 10: 36–9.

Chambliss, W.J. 1986. "On Lawmaking." In S. Brickey and E. Comack (eds.), *The Social Basis of Law*. Toronto: Garamond Press.

Chermak, S. 1998. "Predicting Crime Story Salience: The Effects of Crime, Victim, and Defendant Characteristics." *Journal of Criminal Justice* 26(1): 61–70.

Chibnall, S. 1977. *Law-and-Order News*. London: Tavistock.

Chicago Community Policing Evaluation Consortium. 2000. *Community Policing in Chicago, Year Seven: An Interim Report*. Chicago: Illinois Criminal Justice Information Authority.

Chilton, R. 1991. "Images of Crime: Crime Statistics and Their Impact." In J.F. Sheley (ed.), *Criminology: A Contemporary Handbook*: 45–65. Belmont: Wadsworth.

Chiricos, T., K. Pagett, and M. Gertz. 2000. "Fear, TV News, and the Reality of Crime." *Criminology* 38(3): 755–85.

Chiricos, T.G. 1987. "Rates of Crime and Unemployment: An Analysis of Aggregate Research Evidence." *Social Problems* 34(2): 187–242.

Clairmont, D. 1990. *To the Forefront: Community-Based Zone Policing in Halifax.* Ottawa: Canadian Police College.

Clark, R.D. 1988. "Celerity and Specific Deterrence: A Look at the Evidence." *Canadian Journal of Criminology* 30(2): 109–20.

Clarke, R.V. 1992. "Introduction." In R.V. Clarke (ed.), *Situational Crime Prevention.* Albany: Harrow & Heston.

——— 1993. *Crime Prevention Studies*, Vol. 1. Monsey: Criminal Justice Press.

——— 1994. *Crime Prevention Studies*, Vol. 2. Monsey: Criminal Justice Press.

Clarke, R.V., P. Ekblom, M. Hough, and P. Mayhew. 1985. "Elderly Victims of Crime and Exposure to Risk." *Journal of Criminal Justice* 23: 1–9.

Clarke, R.V., and M. Felson. 1993. "Introduction: Criminology, Routine Activity, and Rational Choice." In R.V. Clarke and M. Felson (eds.), *Routine Activity and Rational Choice.* New Brunswick: Transaction Publishers.

Clermont, Y. 1996. "Robbery." In L.W. Kennedy and V.F. Sacco (eds.), *Crime Counts: A Criminal Event Analysis.* Toronto: Nelson.

Cloward, R.A. 1959. "Illegitimate Means, Anomie, and Deviant Behavior." The Bobbs-Merrill Reprint Series in the Social Sciences. Reprinted by permission of *American Sociological Review* 24 (April): 164–76.

Cloward, R.A., and L.E. Ohlin. 1960. *Delinquency and Opportunity.* New York: Free Press.

Cohen, A.K. 1955. *Delinquent Boys: The Culture of the Gang.* New York: Free Press.

Cohen, L.E., and D. Cantor. 1981. "Residential Burglary in the United States: Lifestyle and Demographic Factors Associated with the Probability of Victimization." *Journal of Research in Crime and Delinquency* 18(1): 113–27.

Cohen, L.E., and M. Felson. 1979. "Social Change and Crime Rate Trends: A Routine Activity Approach." *American Sociological Review* 44 (August): 588–608.

Cohen, L.E., J.R. Kluegel, and K.C. Land. 1981. "Social Inequality and Predatory Criminal Victimization: An Exposition and Test of a Formal Theory." *American Sociological Review* 46 (October): 505–24.

Cohen, M.A. 1998. "The Monetary Value of Saving a High-Risk Youth." *Journal of Quantitative Criminology* 14(1): 5–33.

Cohen, M.A., T.R. Miller, and S.B. Rossman. 1994. "The Costs and Consequences of Violent Behavior in the United States." in J. Roth and A. Reiss (eds.). *Understanding and Preventing Violence*, Vol. 4. Washington, DC: National Academy Press, 67–166.

Cohen, S. 1972. *Folk Devils and Moral Panics.* London: MacGibbon & Kee.

Coleman, C., and C. Norris. 2000. *Introducing Criminology.* Portland: Willan Publishing.

Coleman, J.W. 1987. "Toward an Integrated Theory of White-Collar Crime." *American Journal of Sociology* 93(2): 406–39.

———— 1991. "Respectable Crime." In J.F. Sheley (ed.), *Criminology: A Contemporary Handbook.* Belmont: Wadsworth.

Collins, J.J., B.G. Cox, and P.A. Langan. 1987. "Job Activities and Personal Crime Victimization: Implications for Theory." *Social Science Research* 16: 345–60.

Conklin, J.E. 1975. *The Impact of Crime.* New York: Macmillan.

Cook, F.L., and W.G. Skogan. 1990. "Agenda Setting and the Rise and Fall of Policy Issues: The Case of Criminal Victimization of the Elderly." *Environment and Planning C: Government and Policy* 8: 395–415.

Cook, P.J. 1977. "Punishment and Crime: A Critique of Current Findings Concerning the Preventive Effects of Punishment." *Law and Contemporary Problems* 41(1): 164–204.

Cornish, D.B., and R.V. Clarke (eds.). 1986. *The Reasoning Criminal.* New York: Springer-Verlag.

Cornwall, A., and H.N. Bawden. 1992. "Reading Disabilities and Aggression: A Critical Review." *Journal of Learning Disabilities* 25(5): 281–8.

Corrado, R.R., and A. Markwart. 1996. "The Evolution of Juvenile Justice in Canada." In R.A. Silverman, J.J. Teevan, and V.F. Sacco (eds.), *Crime in Canadian Society*, 5th ed. Toronto: Harcourt Brace.

Costello, B.J. 2000. "Techniques of Neutralization and Self-Esteem: A Critical Test of Social Control and Neutralization Theory." *Deviant Behavior* 21: 307–29.

Cressey, D.R. 1969. *Theft of the Nation.* New York: Harper & Row.

Croall, H. 1987. "Who Is the White-Collar Criminal?" *British Journal of Criminology* 29(2): 157–74.

Cromwell, P., and K. McElrath. 1994. "Buying Stolen Property: An Opportunity Perspective." *Journal of Research in Crime and Delinquency* 31(3): 295–310.

Cromwell, P.F., J.N. Olson, and D.W. Avary. 1991. *Breaking and Entering: An Ethnographic Analysis of Burglary.* Newbury Park: Sage.

Cullen, F.T., and R. Agnew. 1999. *Criminological Theory: Past to Present.* Los Angeles: Roxbury.

Cullen, F.T., J.P. Wright, S. Brown, M.M. Moon, M.B. Blankenship, and B.K. Applegate. 1998. "Public Support for Early Intervention Programs: Implications for a Progressive Policy Agenda." *Crime & Delinquency* 44(2): 187–204.

Culliver, C., and R. Sigler. 1991. "The Relationship between Learning Disabilities and Juvenile Delinquency." *International Journal of Adolescence and Youth* 3(1–2): 117–28.

Curran, D.J., and C.M. Renzetti. 2001. *Theories of Crime.* 2nd ed. Boston: Allyn and Bacon.

Currie, E. 1985. *Confronting Crime: An American Challenge.* New York: Pantheon.

Cusson, M. 1993. "Situational Deterrence: Fear During the Criminal Event." In R.V. Clarke (ed.), *Crime Prevention Studies,* Vol. 1. Monsey: Criminal Justice Press.

Daly, K., and L. Maher. 1998. *Criminology at the Crossroads.* New York: Oxford University Press.

Daly, M., and M. Wilson. 1988. *Homicide.* Chicago: Aldine de Gruyter.

Davis, C.R., and B. Smith. 1994. "Teaching Victims Crime Prevention Skills: Can Individuals Lower Their Costs of Crime?" *Criminal Justice Review* 19(1): 56–68.

Davis, P.W. 1991. "Stranger Intervention into Child Punishment in Public Places." *Social Problems* 38(2): 227–46.

——— 1994. "The Changing Meaning of Spanking." In J. Best (ed.), *Troubling Children,* pp. 133–53. New York: Aldine de Gruyter.

Dechenes, E.P. 1990. "Longitudinal Research Designs." In K.L. Kempf (ed.), *Measurement Issues in Criminology,* pp. 152–66. New York: Springer-Verlag.

DeKeseredy, W.S., and R. Hinch. 1991. *Woman Abuse: Sociological Perspectives.* Ottawa: Thomson Educational Publishing.

DeKeseredy, W., and K. Kelly. 1993. "The Incidence and Prevalence of Woman Abuse in Canadian University and College Dating Relationships." *Canadian Journal of Sociology* 18(2): 137–59.

Desroches, F.J. 1991. "Tearoom Trade: A Law Enforcement Problem." *Canadian Journal of Criminology* 33(1): 1–21.

——— 1995. *Force and Fear: Robbery in Canada.* Toronto: Nelson Canada.

Devereaux, M.S. 1990. "Decline in the Number of Children." *Canadian Social Trends* 18 (Autumn): 32–4.

DiIulio, J.J. 1989. "The Impact of Inner-City Crime." *Public Interest* 96: 28–46.

Donzinger, S.R. 1996. *The Real War on Crime: The Report of the National Criminal Justice Commission.* New York: HarperPerennial.

Doob, A.N. 1982. "The Role of Mass Media in Creating Exaggerated Levels of Fear of Being the Victim of a Violent Crime." In P. Stringer (ed.), *Confronting Social Issues: Applications of Social Psychology.* Toronto: Academic Press.

Doob, A.N., and G.E. MacDonald. 1976. "Television Viewing and Fear of Victimization: Is the Relationship Causal?" *Journal of Personality and Social Psychology* 37: 170–9.

Dorfman, A. 1984. "The Criminal Mind." *Science Digest* 92(10): 44–7, 98.

DuBow, F., E. McCabe, and G. Kaplan. 1979. *Reactions to Crime: A Critical Review of the Literature.* Washington: U.S. Department of Justice.

Dugan, L. 1999. "The Effect of Criminal Victimization on a Household's Moving Decision." *Criminology* 37(4): 903–30.

Durant, T.J. 1999. "Violence as a Public Health Problem: Toward an Integrated Paradigm." *Sociological Spectrum* 19: 267–80.

Durkheim, E. 1933. *The Division of Labor in Society.* Trans. G. Simpson. Glencoe: Free Press.

———— 1964. *The Rules of Sociological Method.* New York: Free Press. (Orig. pub. in 1938.)

Dutton, D., S. Hart, L.W. Kennedy, and K. Williams. 1992. "Arrest and the Reduction of Repeat Wife Assault." In E. Buzawa and C. Buzawa (eds.), *Domestic Violence: The Changing Criminal Justice Response.* Westport: Greenwood Press.

Dutton, D.G. 1987. "The Criminal Justice Response to Wife Assault." *Law and Human Behavior* 11(3): 189–206.

Eck, J.E. 2001. "Problem-Oriented Policing and Crime Event Concentration." In R.F. Meier, L.W. Kennedy, and V.F. Sacco (eds.), *The Process and Structure of Crime.* Vol. 9, Advances in Criminological Theory. Piscataway: Transaction Press.

Ellis, L. 1982. "Genetics and Criminal Behavior." *Criminology* 20(1): 43–66.

Engs, R.C., and D.J. Hanson. 1994. "Boozing and Brawling on Campus: A National Study of Violent Problems Associated with Drinking over the Past Decade." *Journal of Criminal Justice* 22(2): 171–80.

Ericson, R.V. 1982. *Reproducing Order: A Study of Police Patrol Work.* Toronto: University of Toronto Press.

———— 1991. "Mass Media, Crime, Law, and Justice: An Institutional Approach."
   The British Journal of Criminology 31(3): 219–49.

Ericson, R., and C. Shearing. 1986. "The Scientification of Police Work." In
   G. Boehme and N. Stehr (eds.), *The Knowledge Society*, pp. 129–59.
   Dordrecht: D. Reidel.

Ericson, R.V., P.M. Baranek, and J.B.L. Chan. 1987. *Visualizing Deviance.*
   Toronto: University of Toronto Press.

Evans, D.J. 1989. "Geographical Analyses of Residential Burglary." In D.J. Evans
   and D.T. Herbert (eds.), *The Geography of Crime.* London: Routledge.

Fagan, J., and S. Wexler. 1987. "Family Origins of Violent Delinquents."
   Criminology 25: 643–69.

Fagan, J., and R.B. Freeman. 1999. "Crime and Work." *Crime and Justice: A
   Review of Research* 25: 113–78.

Farrell, G. 1995. "Preventing Repeat Victimization." In M. Tonry, and
   D.P. Farrington (eds.), *Building a Safer Society. Crime and Justice*, Vol. 19.
   Chicago: University of Chicago Press.

Farrell, G., C. Phillips, and K. Pease. 1995. "Like Taking Candy: Why Does
   Repeat Victimization Occur?" *British Journal of Criminology* 35(3): 384–99.

Farrington, D.P. 1989. "Implications of Longitudinal Studies for Social
   Prevention." *Canadian Journal of Criminology* 31(4): 453–63.

Farrington, D.P., S. Bowen, A. Buckle, T. Burns-Howell, and J. Burrows. 1993.
   "An Experiment on the Prevention of Shoplifting." In R.V. Clarke (ed.),
   Crime Prevention Studies. Monsey: Criminal Justice Press.

Fattah, E.A. 1976. "The Use of Victim as an Agent of Self-Legitimation: Toward a
   Dynamic Explanation for Criminal Behavior." *Victimology* 1(1): 162–9.

———— 1991. *Understanding Criminal Victimization.* Scarborough: Prentice-
   Hall.

———— 1993. "The Rational Choice/Opportunity Perspectives as a Vehicle for
   Integrating Criminological and Victimological Theories." In R.V. Clarke and
   M. Felson (eds.), *Routine Activity and Rational Choice.* New Brunswick:
   Transaction.

Fattah, E.A., and V.F. Sacco. 1989. *Crime and Victimization of the Elderly.*
   New York: Springer-Verlag.

Fekete, J. 1994. *Moral Panic: Biopolitics Rising.* Montreal: Robert Davies
   Publishing.

Felson, M. 1987. "Routine Activities and Crime Prevention in the Developing
   Metropolis." *Criminology* 25(4): 911–31.

——— 1992. "Routine Activities and Crime Prevention." *Studies in Crime and Crime Prevention Annual Review* 1(1): 30–4.

——— 1998. *Crime and Everyday Life*, 2nd ed. Newbury Park: Pine Forge Press.

Felson, R.B., W.F. Baccaglini, and S.A. Ribner. 1985. "Accounting for Criminal Violence: A Comparison of Official and Offender Versions of the Crime." *Sociology and Social Research* 70(1): 93-101.

Felson, R.B., A.E. Liska, S.J. South, and T.L. McNulty. 1994. "The Subculture of Violence and Delinquency: Individual vs. School Context Effects." *Social Forces* 73(1): 155–73.

Felson, R.B., and S. Messner. 1996. "To Kill or Not to Kill: Lethal Outcomes in Injurious Attacks." *Criminology* 34(4): 519–45.

Ferraro, K.J. 1989. "Policing Woman Battering." *Social Problems* 36(1): 61–74.

Ferraro, K.J., and J.M. Johnson. 1983. "How Women Experience Battering: The Process of Victimization." *Social Problems* 30: 325–35.

Finckenauer, J.O., and E.K. Waring. 1998. *Russian Mafia in America: Immigration, Culture, and Crime.* Boston: Northeastern University Press.

Fischer, C.S. 1975. "The Effect of Urban Life on Traditional Values." *Social Forces* 53: 420–32.

——— 1981. "The Public and Private Worlds of City Life." *American Sociological Review* 46 (June): 306–16.

——— 1995. "The Subcultural Theory of Urbanism: A Twentieth-Year Assessment." *American Journal of Sociology* 101(3): 543–77.

Fisher, B., and J.L. Nasar. 1995. "Fear Spots in Relation to Microlevel Physical Cues: Exploring the Overlooked." *Journal of Research in Crime and Delinquency* 32(2): 214–39.

Fishman, M. 1978. "Crime Waves as Ideology." *Social Problems* 25(5): 531–43.

Fishman, M. 1981. "Police News: Constructing an Image of Crime." *Urban Life* 9(4): 371–94.

Fishman, M., and G. Cavender. 1998. *Entertaining Crime: Television Reality Programs.* New York: Aldine de Gruyter.

Fleisher, M.S. 1995. *Beggars and Thieves: Lives of Urban Street Criminals.* Madison: University of Wisconsin Press.

Fleury, R.E., C.M. Sullivan, D.I. Bybee, and W.S. Davidson. 1998. "What Happened Depends on Whom You Ask: A Comparison of Police Records and Victim Reports Regarding Arrests for Women Battering." *Journal of Criminal Justice* 26(1): 53–9.

Flowers, R.B. 1989. *Demographics and Criminality: The Characteristics of Crime in America.* New York: Greenwood Press.

Fox, J.A., and J. Levin. 2001. *The Will to Kill: Making Sense of Senseless Murder.* Boston: Allyn and Bacon.

Freeman, R.B. 1983. "Crime and Unemployment." In J.Q. Wilson (ed.), *Crime and Public Policy.* San Francisco: ICS Press.

Friedrichs, D.O. 1996. *Trusted Criminals.* Belmont: Wadsworth.

Frieze, I.H., and A. Browne. 1989. "Violence in Marriage." In L. Ohlin and M. Tonry (eds.), *Family Violence.* Chicago: University of Chicago Press.

Frinell, D.E., E. Dahlstrom III, and D.A. Johnson. 1980. "A Public Education Program Designed to Increase the Accuracy and Incidence of Citizens' Reports of Suspicious and Criminal Activities." *Journal of Police Science and Administration* 8(2): 160–5.

Furstenberg, F. 1971. "Public Reactions to Crime in the Streets." *The American Scholar* 40: 601–10.

Gabor, T. 1990a. "Crime Prevention: The Agenda." *Canadian Journal of Criminology* 32(1): 1–7.

———— 1990b. "Crime Displacement and Situational Prevention: Toward the Development of Some Principles." *Canadian Journal of Criminology* 32(1): 41–73.

———— 1994. *Everybody Does It: Crime by the Public.* Toronto: University of Toronto Press.

Gabor, T., and A. Normandeau. 1989. "Armed Robbery: Highlights of a Canadian Study." *Canadian Police College Journal* 13(4): 273–282. Used by permission.

Gans, H. 1962. *The Urban Villagers.* New York: Free Press.

Garofalo, J. 1981a. "Crime and the Mass Media: A Selective Review of Research." *Journal of Research in Crime and Delinquency* (July): 319–50.

———— 1981b. "The Fear of Crime: Causes and Consequences." *The Journal of Criminal Law and Criminology* 72: 839–57.

Garofalo, J., and M. McLeod. 1988. *Improving the Use and Effectiveness of Neighborhood Watch Programs.* Washington: U.S. Department of Justice.

Garofalo, J., L. Siegel, and J. Laub. 1987. "School-Related Victimizations among Adolescents: An Analysis of National Crime Survey (NCS) Narratives." *Journal of Quantitative Criminology* 3(4): 321–38.

Garofalo, R. 1914. *Criminology.* Boston: Little, Brown.

Gartner, R. 2000. "The Centre for Criminology at the University of Toronto." *The Criminologist* 25(4): 1, 3–4.

Gartner, R., and A. Doob. 1994. "Trends in Criminal Victimization: 1988–1993." *Juristat* 14(13). Statistics Canada.

Gartner, R., and R. Macmillan. 2000. "Victim–Offender Relationship and Reporting Crimes of Violence against Women." In R.A. Silverman, J.T. Teevan, and V.F. Sacco (eds.), *Crime in Canadian Society*. 6th ed. Toronto: Harcourt Brace.

Gartner, G., and B. McCarthy 1996. "The Social Distribution of Femicide in Urban Canada: 1921–1988." In R.A. Silverman, J.J. Teevan, and V.F. Sacco (eds.), *Crime in Canadian Society*, 5th ed., pp. 177–85. Toronto: Harcourt Brace.

Gaskell, G.D., D.B. Wright, and C.A. O'Muircheartaigh. 2000. "Telescoping of Landmark Events: Implications for Survey Research." *Public Opinion Quarterly* 64: 77–89.

Gelles, R.J., and M.A. Straus. 1988. *Intimate Violence.* New York: Simon & Schuster.

Gibbons, D.C. 1988. "Some Critical Observations on Criminal Types and Criminal Careers." *Criminal Justice and Behavior* 15: 8–23.

Gibbs, J.P 1966. "Conceptions of Deviant Behavior: The Old and the New." *Pacific Sociological Review* 9: 9–14.

Gibbs, J.P., and M.L. Erikson. 1976. "Crime Rates of American Cities in an Ecological Context." *American Journal of Sociology* 82(3): 605–20.

Gilbert, N. 1997. "Advocacy Research and Social Policy." *Crime and Justice: A Review of Research*, Pp. 101–48. Chicago: University of Chicago Press.

Gill, Martin. 1994. *Crime at Work: Studies in Security & Crime Prevention.* Leicester: Perpetuity Press.

Gillespie, C. 1989. *Justifiable Homicide: Battered Women, Self Defense, and the Law.* Columbus: Ohio State University Press.

Gillespie, D.L., and A. Leffler. 1987. "The Politics of Research Methodology in Claims-Making Activities: Social Science and Sexual Harassment." *Social Problems* 34(5): 490–501.

Gilsinan, J.F. 1989. "They is Clowning Tough: 911 and the Social Construction of Reality." *Criminology* 27(2): 329-344.

——— 1990. *Criminology and Public Policy: An Introduction.* Englewood Cliffs: Prentice-Hall.

Goff, C., and N. Nason-Clark. 1989. "The Seriousness of Crime in Fredericton, New Brunswick: Perceptions Toward White-Collar Crime." *Canadian Journal of Criminology* 31(1): 19–34.

Goffman, E. 1959. *The Presentation of Self in Everyday Life.* Garden City: Doubleday.

——— 1963. *Stigma: Notes on the Management of Spoiled Identity.* Englewood Cliffs: Prentice-Hall.

Golant, S.M. 1984. "Factors Influencing the Nighttime Activity of Old Persons in Their Community." *Journal of Gerontology* 39: 485–91.

Gold, M. 1970. *Delinquent Behavior in an American City.* Belmont: Brooks/Cole.

Goldstein, H. 1990. *Problem-Oriented Policing.* Philadelphia: Temple University Press.

Gondolf, E.W., and J.R. McFerron. 1989. "Handling Battering Men and Police Action in Wife Abuse Cases." *Criminal Justice and Behavior* 16: 429–39.

Goode, E., and N. Ben-Yehuda. 1994. *Moral Panics: The Social Construction of Deviance.* Oxford: Blackwell.

Goodstein, L., and R.L. Shotland. 1982. "The Crime Causes Crime Model: A Critical Review of the Relationship between Fear of Crime, Bystander Surveillance, and Changes in the Crime Rate." *Victimology* 5(2–4): 133–51.

Gordon, R.M. 2000. "Criminal Business Organizations, Street Gangs and 'Wanna-Be' Groups: A Vancouver Perspective." *Canadian Journal of Criminology* 42(1): 39–60. Used by permission.

Gordon, M.T., and L. Heath. 1981. "The News Business, Crime and Fear." In D.A. Lewis (ed.), *Reactions to Crime.* Beverly Hills: Sage.

Gordon, M.T., and S. Riger. 1989. *The Female Fear.* New York: Free Press.

Gordon, R.M., and J. Nelson. 2000. "Crime, Ethnicity, and Immigration." In R.A. Silverman, J.J. Teevan, and V.F. Sacco (eds.), *Crime in Canadian Society,* 6th ed., pp. 263–74. Toronto: Harcourt Brace.

Gorelick, S.M. 1989. "'Join Our War': The Construction of Ideology in a Newspaper Crimefighting Campaign." *Crime and Delinquency* 35(3): 421–36.

Gottfredson, M.R. 1984. "Victims of Crime: The Dimensions of Risk." A Home Office Research and Planning Unit Report. London: HMSO Books.

Gottfredson, M.R., and D. Gottfredson. 1988. *Decisionmaking in Criminal Justice,* 2nd ed. New York: Plenum.

Gottfredson, M.R., and T. Hirschi. 1986. "The True Value of Lambda Would Appear to Be Zero: An Essay on Career Criminals, Criminal Careers, Selective Incapacitation, Cohort Studies, and Related Topics." *Criminology* 24(2): 213–34.

——— 1988. "Science, Public Policy and the Career Paradigm." *Criminology* 26: 37–55.

———— 1990. *A General Theory of Crime.* Stanford: Stanford University Press.

———— 1995. "National Crime Prevention Policies." *Society* 32(2): 30–6.

Gould, L.C. 1989. "Crime, Criminality, and Criminal Events." Paper presented at the Annual Meetings of the American Society of Criminology, Reno, Nevada.

Gove, W.R. 1975. *The Labelling of Deviance: Evaluating a Perspective.* New York: Sage.

Gove, W.R., M. Hughes, and M. Geerken. 1985. "Are Uniform Crime Reports a Valid Indicator of the Index Crimes? An Affirmative Answer with Minor Modifications." *Criminology* 23(3): 451–501.

Graham, J. 1990. *Crime Prevention Strategies in Europe and North America.* Helsinki: Helsinki Institute for Crime Prevention and Control.

Grainger, B. 1996. "Data and Methodology in the Area of Criminal Justice." In L.W. Kennedy and V.F. Sacco (eds.), *Crime Counts.* Toronto: Nelson Canada.

Gramling, R., C. Forsyth, and J. Fewell. 1988. "Crime and Economic Activity: A Research Note." *Sociological Spectrum* 8: 187–95.

Grattet, R., V. Jenness, and T.R. Curry. 1998. "The Homogenization and Differentiation of Hate Crime Law in the United States, 1978 to 1995: Innovation and Diffusion in the Criminalization of Bigotry." *American Sociological Review* 63: 286–307.

Gray, H. 1989. "Popular Music as a Social Problem: A Social History of the Claims against Popular Music." In J. Best (ed.), *Images of Issues.* New York: Aldine de Gruyter.

Greenberg, D.F. 1992. "Comparing Criminal Career Models." *Criminology* 30(1): 141–7.

Greenberg, M.S., R.B. Ruback, and D.R. Westcott. 1984. "Social Influence and Crime-Victim Decision Making." *Journal of Social Issues* 40(1): 51–76.

Greene, J. 1998. "Evaluating Planned Change Strategies in Modern Law Enforcement: Implementing Community-Based Policing." In J-P. Brodeur (ed.), *How to Recognize Good Policing: Problems and Issues.* Thousand Oaks: Sage.

Gusfield, J. 1963. *Symbolic Crusade: Status Politics and the American Temperance Movement.* Urbana: University of Illinois Press.

———— J. 1989. "Constructing the Ownership of Social Problems: Fun and Profit in the Welfare State." *Social Problems* 36(5): 431–41.

Hagan, J. 1980. "The Legislation of Crime and Delinquency: A Review of Theory, Method and Research." *Law and Society Review* 14(3): 603–28.

———— 1985. *Modern Criminology.* New York: McGraw-Hill.

———— 1989. *Structural Criminology.* New Brunswick: Rutgers University Press.

———— 1992. "White Collar and Corporate Crime." In R. Linden (ed.), *Criminology: A Canadian Perspective.* Toronto: Harcourt Brace Jovanovich.

Hagan, J., A.R. Gillis, and J.H. Simpson. 1979. "The Sexual Stratification of Social Control: A Gender-Based Perspective on Crime and Delinquency." *British Journal of Sociology* 30(1): 25–38.

———— 1985. "The Class Structure of Gender and Delinquency: Toward a Power-Control Theory of Common Delinquent Behavior." *American Journal of Sociology* 90(6): 1151–78.

Hagan, J., G. Hefler, G. Classen, K. Boehnke, H. Merkens. 1998. "Subterranean Sources of Subcultural Delinquency Beyond the American Dream." *Criminology* 36(2): 309–42.

Hagan, J., J. Simpson, and A.R. Gillis. 1987. "Class in the Household: Deprivation, Liberation and a Power-Control Theory of Gender and Delinquency." *American Journal of Sociology* 92(4): 788–816.

———— 1988. "Feminist Scholarship, Relational and Instrumental Control, and a Power-Control Theory of Gender and Delinquency." *The British Journal of Sociology* 39(3): 301–36.

Haller, M.H. 1990. "Illegal Enterprise: A Theoretical and Historical Interpretation." *Criminology* 28(2): 207–35.

———— 1992. "Bureaucracy and the Mafia: An Alternative View." *Journal of Contemporary Criminal Justice* 8: 1–10.

Hamlin, J.E. 1988. "The Misplaced Role of Rational Choice in Neutralization Theory." *Criminology* 26: 425–38.

Hanmer, J., and S. Saunders. 1984. *Well-Founded Fear: A Community Study of Violence to Women.* London: Hutchinson, in association with The Explorations in Feminism Collective, an affiliation of the Women's Research and Resources Centre.

Hans, V.P. 1990. "Law and the Media: An Overview and Introduction." *Law and Human Behavior* 14(5): 399–407.

Hans, V.P., and D. Ermann. 1989. "Responses to Corporate versus Individual Wrongdoing." *Law and Human Behavior* 13(2): 151–66.

Hanson, R.K., O. Cadsky, A. Harris, and C. Lalonde. 1997. "Correlates of Battering Among 997 Men: Family History, Adjustment, and Attitudinal Differences." *Violence and Victims* 12(3): 191–208.

Harlow, C.W. 1991. *Female Victims of Violent Crime.* Washington: U.S. Department of Justice.

Harney, P.A., and C.L. Muehlenhard. 1991. "Factors that Increase the Likelihood of Victimization." In A. Parrot and L. Bechhofer (eds.), *Acquaintance Rape: The Hidden Crime.* New York: John Wiley.

Harries, K.D. 1990. *Serious Violence.* Springfield: Charles C. Thomas.

Harris, M.K. 1991. "Moving into the New Millennium: Toward a Feminist Vision of Peace." In H.E. Pepinsky and R. Quinney (eds.), *Criminology as Peacemaking.* Bloomington: Indiana University Press.

Hartman, D.P., D.M. Gelfand, B. Page, and P. Walder. 1972. "Rates of Bystander Observation and Reporting of Contrived Shoplifting Incidents." *Criminology* (November): 247–67.

Hartnagel, T.F. 1997. "Crime Among the Provinces: The Effect of Geographic Mobility." *Canadian Journal of Criminology* 39(4): 387–402.

———— 2000. "Correlates of Criminal Behaviour." In R. Linden (ed.), *Criminology: A Canadian Perspective.* 4th ed. Toronto: Harcourt Brace.

Hartnagel, T.F., and H. Krahn. 1989. "High School Dropouts, Labor Market Success, and Criminal Behavior." *Youth and Society* 20(4): 416–44.

Heath, L., and K. Gilbert. 1996. "Mass Media and Fear of Crime." *American Behavioral Scientist* 39(4): 379–86.

Hennigen, K.M., L. Heath, J.D. Wharton, M.L. Del Resario, T.D. Cook, and B.J. Calder. 1982. "Impact of the Introduction of Television on Crime in the United States: Empirical Findings and Theoretical Implications." *Journal of Personality and Social Psychology* 42(3): 461–77.

Henry, S., and R. Eaton (eds.). 1999. *Degrees of Deviance: Student Accounts of Their Deviant* Behaviour, 2nd ed. Salem: Sheffield.

Henshel, R.L., and R.A. Silverman. 1975. *Perception in Criminology.* Toronto: Methuen.

Herrnstein, R.J. 1995. "Criminogenic Traits." In J.Q. Wilson and J. Petersilia (eds.), *Crime*, pp. 39–64. San Francisco: Institute for Contemporary Studies Press.

Hickey, E. 1991. *Serial Murderers and Their Victims.* Belmont: Wadsworth.

Hicks, R.D. 1991. *In Pursuit of Satan.* Buffalo: Prometheus Books.

Hindelang, M.J., M.R. Gottfredson, and J. Garofalo. 1978. *Victims of Personal Crime: An Empirical Foundation for a Theory of Personal Victimization.* Cambridge: Ballinger.

Hirschi, T. 1969. *Causes of Delinquency.* Berkeley: University of California Press.

Hirschi, T., and M.J. Hindelang. 1977. "Intelligence and Delinquency: A Revisionist View." *American Sociological Review* 42: 571–87.

Hocker, J.L., and W.W. Wilmot. 1985. *Interpersonal Conflict,* 2nd ed. Dubuque: William C. Brown.

Hodgins, S. 2000. "Biological Factors in Criminal Behavior." In R. Linden, *Criminology: A Canadian Perspective.* 4th ed. Toronto: Harcourt Brace.

Hollinger, R.C., and L. Lanza-Kaduce. 1988. "The Process of Criminalization: The Case of Computer Crime Laws." *Criminology* 26(1): 101–13.

Hope, T. 1995. "The Flux of Victimization." *British Journal of Criminology* 35(3): 327–342.

Hotaling, G.T., and D. Finkelhor. 1990. "Estimating the Number of Stranger-Abduction Homicides of Children: A Review of Available Evidence." *Journal of Criminal Justice* 18: 385–99.

Hotaling, G.T., and M.A. Straus (with A.J. Lincoln). 1990. "Intrafamily Violence and Crime and Violence Outside the Family." In M.A. Straus and R.J. Gelles (eds.), *Physical Violence in American Families: Risk Factors and Adaptations to Violence in 8,145 Families.* New Brunswick: Transaction.

Hough, M. 1985. "The Impact of Victimisation: Findings from the British Crime Survey." *Victimology* 10: 488–97.

Howarth, G., and P. Rock. 2000. "Aftermath and the Construction of Victimisation: 'The Other Victims of Crime.'" *The Howard Journal* 39(1): 58–78.

Howitt, D. 1998. *Crime, the Media and the Law.* New York: Wiley.

Howlett, K. 2000. "Is White-Collar Crime Giving Justice Black Eye?" *The Globe and Mail,* August 14: A1, A6. Used by permission.

Humphries, D. 1981. "Serious Crime, News Coverage, and Ideology: A Content Analysis of Crime Coverage in a Metropolitan Paper." *Crime and Delinquency* 27(2): 191–205.

Hunt, J. 1985. "Police Accounts of Normal Force." *Urban Life* 13(4): 315–41.

Ianni, F.A.J. 1971. "The Mafia and the Web of Kinship." *The Public Interest* 16: 78–100.

Ianni, F.A.J., and E. Reuss-Ianni. 1972. *A Family Business: Kinship and Social Control in Organized Crime.* New York: Russell Sage Foundation.

Innes, C.A., and L.A. Greenfeld. 1990. "Violent State Prisoners and Their Victims." *Bureau of Justice Statistics Special Report.* Washington: U.S. Department of Justice.

Iso-Ahola, S. 1980. *The Social Psychology of Leisure and Recreation.* Dubuque: William C. Brown.

Jackson, P.G. 1990. "Sources of Data." In K.L. Kempf (ed.), *Measurement Issues in Criminology.* New York: Springer-Verlag.

Jackson, P.I. 1989. *Minority Group Threat, Crime, and Policing.* New York: Praeger.

Jacobs, J.B. 1999. *Gotham Unbound: How New York was Liberated from the Grip of Organized Crime.* New York: New York University Press.

Jacobs, N. 1965. "The Phantom Slasher of Taipei: Mass Hysteria in a Non-Western Society." *Social Problems* 12: 318–28.

Janhevich, D.E. 1999. "Violence Committed by Strangers." In the Canadian Centre for Justice Statistics (eds.), *The Juristat Reader: A Statistical Overview of the Canadian Justice System.* Toronto: Thompson. Used by permission.

Janoff-Bulman, R., and I.H. Frieze. 1983. "A Theoretical Perspective for Understanding Reactions to Victimization." *Journal of Social Issues* 39(2): 1–17.

Jeffery, C.R. 1990. *Criminology: An Interdisciplinary Approach.* Englewood Cliffs: Prentice-Hall.

Jenkins, P. 1992. *Intimate Enemies: Moral Panic in Great Britain.* New York: Aldine de Gruyter.

———— 1994. *Using Murder: The Social Construction of Serial Homicide.* New York: Walter de Gruyter.

Jenkins, P., and D. Meier-Katkin. 1992. "Satanism: Myth and Reality in a Contemporary Moral Panic." *Crime, Law and Social Change* 17: 53–75.

Jensen, G.F., and D. Brownfield. 1986. "Gender, Lifestyles, and Victimization: Beyond Routine Activity." *Violence and Victims* 1(2): 85–99.

Johnson, D.M. 1945. "The 'Phantom Anesthetist' of Mattoon: A Field Study of Mass Hysteria." *Journal of Abnormal and Social Psychology* 40: 175–86.

Johnson, G.D., G.J. Palileo, and N.B. Gray. 1992. "Date Rape on a Southern Campus." *Sociology and Social Research* 76(2): 37–41.

Johnson, H. 1996. *Dangerous Domains.* Scarborough: Nelson Canada.

———— 2000. "Violence against Women: A Special Topic Survey." In R.A. Silverman, J.J. Teevan, and V.F. Sacco (eds.), *Crime in Canadian Society,* 6th ed. Toronto: Harcourt Brace.

Johnson, H., and V.P. Bunge. 2001. "Prevalence and Consequence of Spousal Assault in Canada." *Canadian Journal of Criminology* 43(1): 27–35.

Johnson, H., and V. Sacco. 1995. "Researching Violence against Women: Statistics Canada National Survey." *Canadian Journal of Criminology* 37(3): 281–304.

Johnson, I.M., and R.T. Sigler. 2000. "Public Perceptions: The Stability of the Public's Endorsements of the Definition and Criminalization of the Abuse of Women." *Journal of Criminal Justice* 28: 165–79.

Johnson, K.J., and M.P. Ferraro. 2000. "Research on Domestic Violence in the 1990s: Making Distinctions." *Journal of Marriage and the Family* 62: 948–63.

Johnson, S.D., K. Bowers, and A. Hirschfield. 1997. "New Insights into the Spatial and Temporal Distribution of Repeat Victimisation." *British Journal of Criminology* 37: 224–241.

Jones, M. 1994. "Time Use of the Elderly." In *Canadian Social Trends: A Canadian Studies Reader*, pp. 349–51. Toronto: Thompson Educational Publishing.

Junger, M. 1987. "Women's Experiences of Sexual Harassment: Some Implications for Their Fear of Crime." *British Journal of Criminology* 27(4): 358–83.

Junger-Tas, J., and I.H. Marshall. 1999. "The Self-Report Methodology in Crime Research." In M. Tonry (ed.), *Crime and Justice: A Review of Research*, pp. 291–367, Vol. 25. Chicago: University of Chicago Press.

Jupp, V. 1989. *Methods of Criminological Research.* London: Unwin Hyman.

Kantor, G.K., and M.A. Straus. 1987. "The Drunken Bum Theory of Wife Beating." *Social Problems* 34(2): 213–30.

Kapferer, J.N. 1989. "A Mass Poisoning Rumor in Europe." *Public Opinion Quarterly* 53: 467–81.

Kappeler, V.E., M. Blumberg, and G.W. Potter. 2000. *The Mythology of Crime and Criminal Justice,* 3rd ed. Prospect Heights: Waveland Press.

Karmen, A. 2001. *Crime Victims: An Introduction to Victimology.* 4th ed. Belmont: Wadsworth.

Katz, J. 1987. "What Makes Crime 'News.'" *Media, Culture and Society* 9: 47–75.

Katz, J., and W.J. Chambliss. 1995. "Biology and Crime." In J.F. Sheley (ed.), *Criminology.* 2nd ed, pp. 275–304. Belmont: Wadsworth.

Kaufman, P., K.A. Chandler, and M.R. Rand. 1998. *Indicators of School Crime and Safety, 1998.* Washington: Departments of Education and Justice.

Keane, C. 1995. "Victimization and Fear: Assessing the Role of Offender and Offence." *Canadian Journal of Criminology* 37(3): 431–55.

——— 2000. "Corporate Crime." In R.A. Silverman, J.J. Teevan, and V.F. Sacco (eds.), *Crime in Canadian Society,* 6th ed. Toronto: Harcourt Brace.

Keane, C., P.S. Maxim, and J.J. Teevan. 1996. "Testing a General Theory of Crime." In R.A. Silverman, J.J. Teevan, and V.F. Sacco (eds.), *Crime in Canadian Society,* 5th ed. Toronto: Harcourt Brace.

Kellam, S.G. 2000. "Community and Institutional Partnerships for School Violence Prevention." In *Preventing School Violence: Plenary Papers of the*

1999 Conference on Criminal Justice Research and Evaluation—Enhancing Policy and Practice through Research, Volume 2. Washington: Office of Justice Programs, National Institute of Justice.

Kelling, G.L. 1999. "'Broken Windows' and Police Discretion." *National Institute of Justice Research Report.* Washington: Office of Justice Programs, National Institute of Justice.

Kelling, G.L., and C.M. Coles. 1996. *Fixing Broken Windows.* New York: The Free Press.

Kempf, K.L. 1987. "Specialization and the Criminal Career." *Criminology* 25: 399–420.

Kennedy, L.W. 1988. "Going It Alone: Unreported Crime and Individual Self-Help." *Journal of Criminal Justice* 16(5): 403–12.

——— 1991. "Evaluating Community Policing." *Canadian Police College Journal* 15(4): 275–90.

Kennedy, L.W., and S. Baron. 1993. "Routine Activities and a Subculture of Violence: A Study of Violence on the Street." *Journal of Research in Crime and Delinquency* 30(1): 88–112.

Kennedy, L.W., and D.R. Forde. 1990. "Routine Activities and Crime: An Analysis of Victimization in Canada." *Criminology* 28(1): 101–15.

——— 1999. *When Push Comes to Shove: A Routine Conflict Approach to Violence.* Albany: State University of New York Press.

Kennedy, L.W., and V.F. Sacco. 1998. *Crime Victims in Context.* Los Angeles: Roxbury.

Kennedy, L.W., and R.A. Silverman. 1990. "The Elderly Victim of Homicide: An Application of the Routine Activities Approach." *Sociological Quarterly* 31(2): 307–19.

——— 1985. "Significant Others and Fear of Crime among the Elderly." *International Journal of Aging and Human Development* 20(4): 241–56.

Kennedy, L.W., and D. Veitch. 1997. "Why Are the Crime Rates Going Down? A Case Study in Edmonton." *Canadian Journal of Criminology* 39(1): 51–69.

Kershaw, C., T. Budd, G. Kinshott, J. Mattinson, P. Mayhew, and A. Myhill. 2000. *The 2000 British Crime Survey.* London: Home Office.

Kinderlehrer, J. 1983. "Delinquent Diets: Partners in Crime." *Prevention* (October): 141–4.

Kitsuse, K.I. 1962. "Societal Reaction to Deviant Behavior: Problems of Theory and Method." *Social Problems* 9: 247–56.

Klaus, P.A., and M.R. Rand. 1984. *Family Violence.* Washington: Bureau of Justice Statistics.

Kleck, G., and S. Sayles. 1990. "Rape and Resistance." *Social Problems* 37(2): 149–62.

Klockars, C.B. 1985. *The Idea of Police.* Beverly Hills: Sage.

Koenig, D.J. 1991. *Do Police Cause Crime? Police Activity, Police Strength, and Crime Rates.* Ottawa: Canadian Police College.

Kooistra, P.G., and J.S. Mahoney Jr. 1999. "The Historical Roots of Tabloid TV Crime." In J. Ferrell and N. Websdale, *Making Trouble: Cultural Constructions of Crime, Deviance and Control.* New York: Aldine de Gruyter.

Kong, R. 1996. "Criminal Harassment." *Juristat* 16, 12.

Kornhauser, R. 1978. *Social Sources of Delinquency.* Chicago: University of Chicago Press.

Krahn, H., and L.W. Kennedy. 1985. "Producing Personal Safety: The Effects of Crime Rates, Police Force Size, and Fear of Crime." *Criminology* 23(4): 697–710.

Krupat, E., and P. Kubzansky. 1987. "Designing to Deter Crime." *Psychology Today* (October): 58–61.

Kueneman, R. 2000. "The Origins and Role of Law in Society." In R. Linden (ed.), *Criminology: A Canadian Perspective.* 4th ed. Toronto: Harcourt Brace.

Kurz, D. 1987. "Emergency Department Responses to Battered Women: Resistance to Medicalization." *Social Problems* 34(1): 69–81.

Lab, S.P. 1992. *Crime Prevention: Approaches, Practices and Evaluations,* 2nd ed. Cincinnati: Anderson.

LaGrange, R.L., and K.F. Ferraro 1987. "The Elderly's Fear of Crime: A Critical Examination of the Research." *Research on Aging* 9: 372–91.

———— 1989. "Assessing Age and Gender Differences in Perceived Risk and Fear of Crime." *Criminology* 27: 697–719.

LaGrange, R.L., K.F. Ferraro, and M. Supancic. 1992. "Perceived Risk and Fear of Crime: Role of Social and Physical Incivilities." *Journal of Research in Crime and Delinquency* 29: 311–34.

LaGrange, T.C., and R.A. Silverman. 1999. "Low Self-Control and Opportunity: Testing the General Theory of Crime as an Explanation for Gender Differences in Delinquency." *Criminology* 37(1): 41–72.

Langan, P.A. 1983. "Career Patterns in Crime." *Bureau of Justice Statistics: Special Report.* Washington: U.S. Department of Justice.

Lasley, J.R., and J.L. Rosenbaum. 1988. "Routine Activities and Multiple Personal Victimization." *Sociology and Social Research* 73(1): 47–50.

Laub, J.H. 1990. "Patterns of Criminal Victimization in the United States." In A.J. Lurigio, W.G. Skogan, and R.C. Davis (eds.), *Victims of Crime: Problems, Policies and Programs.* Newbury Park: Sage.

Laub, J.H., and R.J. Sampson. 1993. "Turning Points in the Life Course: Why Change Matters to the Study of Crime." *Criminology* 31(3): 301–25.

Lauritsen, J.L., R.J. Sampson, and J.H. Laub. 1991. "The Link between Offending and Victimization among Adolescents." *Criminology* 29(2): 265–92.

Lawson, P.E. 1982. *Solving Somebody Else's Blues.* Latham: University Press of America.

Le Bourdais, C., G. Neill, and P. Turcotte. 2000. "The Changing Face of Conjugal Relationships." *Canadian Social Trends* Spring: 14–17.

Lee, M.R. 2000. "The Social Dimensions of Interpersonal Dispute Resolution: A Test of a General Theoretical Framework with Survey Data." *Sociological Inquiry* 70(2): 137–56.

Lejeune, R., and N. Alex. 1973. "On Being Mugged." *Urban Life and Culture* 2(3): 259–83.

Lemert, E.M. 1951. *Social Pathology.* New York: McGraw-Hill.

Leroux, T.G., and M. Petrunik. 1990. "The Construction of Elder Abuse as a Social Problem: A Canadian Perspective." *International Journal of Health Services* 20(4): 651–63.

Letkemann, P. 1973. *Crime as Work.* Englewood Cliffs: Prentice-Hall.

Levi, K. 1981. "Becoming a Hit Man: Neutralization in a Very Deviant Career." *Urban Life* 10: 47–63.

Lichter, R.S., L.S. Lichter, and S. Rothman. 1994. *Prime Time: How TV Portrays American Culture.* Washington: Regnery Publishers.

Light, I. 1977. "The Ethnic Vice Industry, 1880–1944." *American Sociological Review* 42 (June): 464–79.

Lindner, C., and R.L. Bonn. 1996. "Probation Officer Victimization and Fieldwork Practices: Results of a National Study." *Federal Probation* 60(2): 16–23.

Lindquist, J.H., and J.M. Duke. 1982. "The Elderly Victim at Risk." *Criminology* 20(1): 115–26.

Liska, A.E., and W. Baccaglini. 1990. "Feeling Safe by Comparison: Crime in the Newspapers." *Social Problems* 37(3): 360–74.

Liska, A.E., and B.D. Warner. 1991. "Functions of Crime: A Paradoxical Process." *American Journal of Sociology* 6: 1441–63.

Lizotte, A.J. 1985. "The Uniqueness of Rape: Reporting Assaultive Violence to the Police." *Crime and Delinquency* 31(2): 169–90.

Lloyd, S.A., J.E. Koval, and R.M. Cale. 1989. "Courtship and Violence in Dating Relationships." In M.A. Pirog-Good and J.E. Stets (eds.), *Violence in Dating Relationships.* New York: Praeger.

Locke, D. 2000a. "Family Homocide." *Family Violence in Canada: A Statistical Profile 2000.* Ottawa: Statistics Canada.

——— 2000b. "Violence Against Children and Youth by Family Members." *Family Violence in Canada: A Statistical Profile 2000.* Ottawa: Statistics Canada.

Loeber, R., D.P. Farrington, and D.A. Waschbusch. 1998. "Serious and Violent Juvenile Offenders." In R. Loeber and D.P. Farrington (eds.), *Serious & Violent Juvenile Offenders: Risk Factors and Successful Interventions.* Thousand Oaks: Sage.

Longshore, D. 1998. "Self-Control and Criminal Opportunity: A Prospective Test of the General Theory of Crime." *Social Problems* 45(1): 102–13.

Longshore, D., and S. Turner. 1998. "Self-Control and Criminal Opportunity: Cross-Sectional Test of the General Theory of Crime." *Criminal Justice and Behavior* 25(1): 81–98.

Loseke, D.R. 1989. "'Violence' Is 'Violence' ... or Is It? The Social Construction of 'Wife Abuse' and Public Policy." In J. Best (ed.), *Images of Issues: Typifying Contemporary Social Problems.* New York: Aldine de Gruyter.

——— 2000. *Thinking about Social Problems: An Introduction to Constructionist Perspectives.* Hawthorne: Aldine de Gruyter.

Lowney, K.S., and J. Best. 1995. "Stalking Strangers and Lovers: Changing Media Typifications of a New Crime Problem." In J. Best (ed.), *Images of Issues,* 2nd ed. New York: Aldine de Gruyter.

Luckenbill, D.F. 1977. "Criminal Homicide as a Situated Transaction." *Social Problems* 25(2): 176–86. Used by permission.

——— 1984. "Murder and Assault." In R.F. Meier (ed.), *Major Forms of Crime.* Beverly Hills: Sage.

Luckenbill, D.F., and J. Best. 1981. "Careers in Deviance and Respectability: The Analogy's Limitation." *Social Problems* 29: 197–206. Used by permission.

Lurigio, A.J. 1987. "Are All Victims Alike? The Adverse, Generalized and Differential Impact of Crime." *Crime and Delinquency* 33: 452–67.

Luxton, M. 1988. "Thinking About the Future." *Family Matters: Sociology and Contemporary Canadian Families.* Toronto: Methuen.

Lynch, J.P. 1987. "Routine Activity and Victimization at Work." *Journal of Quantitative Criminology* 3(4): 283–300.

Lynch, J.P., and D. Cantor. 1992. "Ecological and Behavioral Influences on Property Victimization at Home: Implications for Opportunity Theory." *Journal of Research in Crime and Delinquency* 29(3): 335–62.

Lyon, D. 1994. *Electronic Eye: The Rise of Surveillance.* Cambridge: Polity Press.

Macmillan, R. 1995. "Changes in the Structure of Life Courses and the Decline of Social Capital in Canadian Society: A Time Series Analysis of Property Crime Rates." *Canadian Journal of Sociology* 20(1): 51–79.

———— 2000. "Adolescent Victimization and Income Deficits in Adulthood: Rethinking the Costs of Criminal Violence from a Life-Course Perspective." *Criminology* 38(2): 553–88.

Madriz, E. 1996. "The Perception of Risk in the Workplace: A Test of Routine Activity Theory." *Journal of Criminal Justice* 24(5): 407–18.

Maguire, B., D. Sandage, G.A. Weatherby. 2000. "Violence, Morality, and Television Commercials." *Sociological Spectrum* 20: 121–43.

Maguire, M., with T. Bennett. 1982. *Burglary in a Dwelling: The Offence, the Offender and the Victim.* London: Heinemann.

Malamuth, N.M. 1983. "Factors Associated with Rape as Predictors of Laboratory Aggression against Women." *Journal of Personality and Social Psychology* 45: 432–42.

Malamuth, N.M., and E. Donnerstein. 1984. *Pornography and Sexual Aggression.* Orlando: Academic Press.

Martin, R., R.J. Mutchnick, and W.T. Austin. 1990. *Criminological Thought: Pioneers Past and Present.* New York: Macmillan.

Massey, J.L., M.D. Krohn, and L.M. Bonati. 1989. "Property Crime and the Routine Activities of Individuals." *Journal of Research in Crime and Delinquency* 26(4): 378–400.

Mastrofski, S. 1983. "The Police and Noncrime Services." In G. Whitaker and C.D. Phillips (eds.), *Evaluating Performance of Criminal Justice Agencies.* Beverly Hills: Sage.

Mastrofski, S.D., J.B. Snipes, R.B. Parks, and C.D. Maxwell. 2000. "The Helping Hand of the Law: Police Control of Citizens on Request." *Criminology* 38(2): 307–42.

Matza, D., and G.M. Sykes. 1957. "Techniques of Neutralization: A Theory of Delinquency." *American Sociological Review* 5: 1–12.

———— 1961. "Juvenile Delinquency and Subterranean Values." *American Sociological Review* 26: 712–19.

Maxfield, M.G. 1987. "Household Composition, Routine Activity, and Victimization: A Comparative Analysis." *Journal of Quantitative Criminology* 3(4): 301–20.

———— 1990. "Homicide Circumstances, 1976–1985: A Taxonomy Based on Supplementary Homicide Reports." *Criminology* 28: 671–95.

———— 1999. "The National Incident-Based Reporting System: Research and Policy Implications." *Journal of Quantitative Criminology* 15(2): 119–49.

Maxfield, M.G., B.L. Weiler, and C.S. Widom. 2000. "Comparing Self-Reports and Official Records of Arrests." *Journal of Quantitative Criminology* 16(1): 87–110.

Maxwell, S.R., and M.K. Gray. 2000. "Deterrence: Testing the Effects of Perceived Sanction Certainty on Probation Violations." *Sociological Inquiry* 70(2): 117–36.

Maxwell, S.R., and C.D. Maxwell. 2000. "Examining the 'Criminal Careers' of Prostitutes within the Nexus of Drug Use, Drug Selling, and other Illicit Activities." *Criminology* 38(3): 787–809.

May, D.C., and R.G. Dunaway. 2000. "Predictors of Fear of Criminal Victimization at School among Adolescents." *Sociological Spectrum* 20: 149–68.

May, H. 1999. "Who Killed Whom? Victimization and Culpability in the Social Construction of Murder." *British Journal of Sociology* 50(3): 489–506.

Mayhew, P., D. Elliott, and L. Dowds. 1989. *The 1988 British Crime Survey: A Home Office Research and Planning Unit Report.* London: HMSO Books.

Mayhew, P., N. Maung, and C. Mirrlees-Black. 1993. *The 1992 British Crime Survey.* London: HMSO Books.

Mazerolle, P., R. Brame, R. Paternoster, A. Piquero, and C. Dean. 2000. "Onset Age, Persistence, and Offending Versatility: Comparisons Across Gender." *Criminology* 38(4): 1143–72.

McCarthy, B., and J. Hagan. 1991. "Homelessness: A Criminogenic Situation?" *British Journal of Criminology* 31(4): 393–410.

McCarthy, B., J. Hagan, and T.S. Woodward. 1999. "In the Company of Women: Structure and Agency in a Revised Power-Control Theory of Gender and Delinquency." *Criminology* 37(4): 761–88.

McClearly, R.M., B.C. Nienstedt, and J.M. Erven. 1982. "Uniform Crime Reports as Organizational Outcomes: Three Time Series Experiments." *Social Problems* 29(4): 361–72.

McCord, J. 1991. "Family Relationships, Juvenile Delinquency, and Adult Criminality." *Criminology* 29(3): 397–417.

McIntosh, M. 1975. *The Organization of Crime.* London: Macmillan.

Meadows, R.J. 1998. *Understanding Violence and Victimization.* Upper Saddle River, N.J.: Prentice Hall.

Mednick, S., T. Moffitt, and S. Stack. 1987. *The Causes of Crime: New Biological Approaches.* New York: Cambridge University Press.

Meier, R., and G. Geis. 1997. *Victimless Crimes?: Prostitution, Drugs, and Abortion.* Los Angeles: Roxbury.

Meier, R.F., L.W. Kennedy, and V.F. Sacco (eds.). 2001. *The Process and Structure of Crime.* Vol. 9, Advances in Criminological Theory. Piscataway: Transaction.

Melbin, M. 1987. *Night as Frontier.* New York: The Free Press.

Menard, S. 1995. "A Developmental Test of Mertonian Anomie Theory." *Journal of Research in Crime and Delinquency* 32(2): 136–74.

Menard, S., and H.C. Covey. 1988. "UCR and NCS: Comparisons over Space and Time." *Journal of Criminal Justice* 16: 371–84.

Merry, S.E. 1981. *Urban Danger.* Philadelphia: Temple University Press.

Merton, R.K. 1938. "Social Structure and Anomie." *American Sociological Review* 3: 672–82.

Messner, S., and R. Rosenfeld. 1997. *Crime and the American Dream*, 2nd ed. Belmont: Wadsworth.

Messner, S.F., and J.R. Blau. 1987. "Routine Leisure Activities and Rates of Crime: A Macro-Level Analysis." *Social Forces* 65: 1035–51.

Michalowski, R.J., and E.W. Bohlander. 1976. "Repression and Criminal Justice in Capitalist America." *Sociological Inquiry* 46(2): 95–106.

Miethe, T.D. 1982. "Public Consensus on Crime Seriousness: Normative Structure or Methodological Artifact?" *Criminology* 20: 515–26.

——— 1995. "Fear and Withdrawal from Urban Life." *Annals of the American Academy of Political and Social Science* 539: 14–27.

Miethe, T.D., and K.A. Drass. 1999. "Exploring the Social Context of Instrumental and Expressive Homocides." *Journal of Quantitative Criminology* 15(1): 1–21.

Miethe, T.D., and G.R. Lee. 1984. "Fear of Crime among Older People: A Reassessment of the Predictive Power of Crime-Related Factors." *The Sociological Quarterly* 25: 397–415.

Miethe, T.D., and R. McCorkle. 1998. *Crime Profiles: The Anatomy of Dangerous Persons, Places, and Situations.* Los Angeles: Roxbury.

Miethe, T.D., and R.F. Meier. 1994. *Crime and Its Social Context*. Albany: State University of New York Press.

Milan, A. 2000. "One Hundred Years of Families." *Canadian Social Trends* Spring: 2–12.

Miller, G. 1978. *Odd Jobs*. Englewood Cliffs: Prentice-Hall.

Miller, J.L., and A.B. Anderson. 1986. "Updating the Deterrence Doctrine." *Journal of Criminal Law and Criminology* 77(2): 418–38.

Miller, L.J. 1990. "Violent Families and the Rhetoric of Harmony." *British Journal of Sociology* 41(2): 263–88.

Miller, T.R., M.A. Cohen, and B. Wiersema. 1996. *Victim Costs and Consequences: A New Look*. Washington: National Institute of Justice.

Miller, W. 1958. "Lower Class Culture as a Generating Milieu of Gang Delinquency." *Journal of Social Issues* 14: 5–19.

Minor, W.W. 1981. "Techniques of Neutralization: A Reconceptualization and Empirical Examination." *Journal of Research in Crime and Delinquency* 18: 295–318.

Mirrlees-Black, C., T. Budd, S. Partridge, and P. Mayhew. 1998. "The 1998 British Crime Survey." *Home Office Statistical Bulletin* 21.

Mirrlees-Black, C., P. Mayhew, and A. Percy. 1996. *The 1996 British Crime Survey*. London: Home Office.

Moeller, G.L. 1989. "Fear of Criminal Victimization: The Effects of Neighborhood Racial Composition." *Sociological Inquiry* 59: 208–21.

Moffitt, T.E., D.R. Lynam, and P.A. Silva. 1994. "Neuropsychological Tests Predicting Persistent Male Delinquency." *Criminology* 32(2): 277–300.

Monkkonen, E.H. 1983. "The Organized Response to Crime in Nineteenth- and Twentieth-Century America." *Journal of Interdisciplinary History* 14(1): 113–28.

Morin, E. 1971. *Rumor in Orleans*. New York: Pantheon.

Muehlenhard, C.L., and M.A. Linton. 1987. "Date Rape and Sexual Aggression in Dating Situations: Incidence and Risk Factors." *Journal of Counseling Psychology* 34(2): 186–196.

Murphy, C. 1993. "The Development, Impact, and Implications of Community Policing in Canada." In J. Chacko and S.E. Nancoo (eds.), *Community Policing in Canada*, pp. 13–26. Toronto: Canadian Scholar's Press.

Murray, C., and R. Herrnstein. 1994. *The Bell Curve*. New York: The Free Press.

Nagin, D.S., and R. Paternoster. 1993. "Enduring Individual Differences and Rational Choices of Crime." *Law and Society Review* 27(3): 467–96.

Nakhaie, M.R., R.A. Silverman and T.C. LaGrange, 2000. "Self Control and Social Control." *Canadian Journal of Sociology* 25(1): 35–59.

National Crime Prevention Centre. 2000. *Policy Framework for Addressing Crime Prevention and Youth Ages 12 to 18.* Ottawa: National Crime Prevention Centre.

———— N.D. *Jack's Troubled Career.* Ottawa: National Crime Prevention Centre.

National Crime Prevention Institute. 1986. *Understanding Crime Prevention.* Boston: Butterworths.

Nelson, B. 1984. *Making an Issue of Child Abuse.* Chicago: University of Chicago Press.

Nettler, G. 1984. *Explaining Crime.* New York: McGraw-Hill.

Newman, G.R. 1990. "Popular Culture and Criminal Justice: A Preliminary Analysis." *Journal of Criminal Justice* 18: 261–74.

Newman, O. 1972. *Defensible Space: Crime Prevention through Urban Design.* New York: Macmillan.

Normandeau, A. 1987. "Crime on the Montreal Metro." *Sociology and Social Research* 71(4): 289–92.

Normandeau, A., and B. Leighton. 1993. "A Growing Canadian Consensus: Community Policing." In J. Chacko and S.E. Nancoo (eds.), *Community Policing in Canada.* Toronto: Canadian Scholar's Press.

Obeidallah, D., and F.J. Earls. 1999. *Adolescent Girls: The Role of Depression in the Development of Delinquency.* Washington: Office of Justice Programs, U.S. Department of Justice. Used by permission.

O'Brien, R.M. 1985. *Crime and Victimization Data,* Vol. 4. Law and Criminal Justice Series. Beverly Hills: Sage.

———— 1986. "Rare Events, Sample Sizes and Statistical Problems in the Analysis of the NCS City Surveys." *Journal of Criminal Justice* 14: 441–48.

O'Grady, B. 1989. "Crime Violence and Victimization: A Newfoundland Case." *Canadian Criminology Forum* 10: 1–16.

O'Grady, W., M. Asbridge, and T. Abernathy. 2000. "Illegal Tobacco Sales to Youth." *Canadian Journal of Criminology* 42(1): 1–20.

O'Kane, J.M. 1992. *Crooked Ladder: Gangsters, Ethnicity and the American Dream.* New Brunswick: Transaction Books.

O'Keefe, G.J. 1984. "Public Views on Crime: Television Exposure and Media Credibility." In R.N. Bostrom (ed.), *Communication Yearbook 8.* Beverly Hills: Sage.

Osgood, D.W., and J.M. Chambers. 2000. "Social Disorganization Outside the Metropolis: An Analysis of Rural Youth Violence." *Criminology* 38(1): 81–115.

Osgood, D.W., J.K. Wilson, P.M. O'Malley, J.G. Bachman, and L.D. Johnston. 1996. "Routine Activities and Individual Deviant Behaviour." *American Sociological Review* 61: 635–55.

Packer, H.L. 1969. *The Limits of the Criminal Sanction.* Stanford: Stanford University Press.

Pagelow, M.D. 1989. "The Incidence and Prevalence of Criminal Abuse of Other Family Members." In L. Ohlin and M. Tonry (eds.), *Family Violence.* Chicago: University of Chicago Press.

Palenski, J.E. 1984. "The Use of Mediation by Police." *Mediation Quarterly* 5: 31–8.

Papadopoulos, C. 1997. *A Comparison of Crime in the U.S. and Canada.* Unpublished MA thesis. Edmonton: University of Alberta.

Parks, G. 2000. "The High/Scope Perry Preschool Project." *OJJDP Juvenile Justice Bulletin.* Washington, D.C.: Office of Justice Programs, U.S. Department of Justice.

Parsons, T. 1951. *The Social System.* Glencoe: Free Press.

Paternoster, R., and R. Brame. 1997. "Multiple Routes to Delinquency? A Test of Developmental and General Theories of Crimes." *Criminology* 35(1): 49–84.

Paternoster, R., and P. Mazerolle. 1994. "General Strain Theory and Delinquency: A Replication and Extension." *Journal of Research in Crime and Delinquency* 31(3): 235–63.

Patterson, G.R., and T.J. Dishion. 1985. "Contributions of Families and Peers to Delinquency." *Criminology* 23: 63–79.

Pease, K., and G. Laycock. 1996. *Revictimization: Reducing the Heat on Hot Victims.* Washington: National Institute of Justice.

Pepinsky, H., and P. Jesilow. 1984. *Myths That Cause Crime.* Cabin John: Seven Locks Press.

Peterson, R.D., L.J. Krivo, and M.A. Harris. 2000. "Disadvantage and Neighborhood Violent Crime: Do Local Institutions Matter?" *Journal of Research in Crime and Delinquency* 37(1): 31–63.

Pfohl, S. 1977. "The Discovery of Child Abuse." *Social Problems* 24(3): 315–21.

Pfuhl, E.H. 1986. *The Deviance Process,* 2nd ed. Belmont: Wadsworth.

Phelps, T.G. 1983. "The Criminal as Hero in American Fiction." *Wisconsin Law Review* 6: 1427–54.

Phillips, D.P. 1983. "The Impact of Mass Media Violence on U.S. Homicides." *American Sociological Review* 48 (August): 560–68.

Pillemer, K.A., and D. Finkelhor. 1988. "The Prevalence of Elder Abuse: A Random Sample Survey." *The Gerontologist* 28(1): 51–7.

Pipes, D. 1997. *Conspiracy: How the Paranoid Style Flourishes and Where it Comes From.* New York: Free Press.

Piquero A., and R. Paternoster. 1998. "An Application of Stafford and Warr's Reconceptualization of Deterrence to Drinking and Driving." *Journal of Research in Crime and Delinquency* 35(1): 3–39.

Piquero, A.R., R. MacIntosh, and M. Hickman. 2000. "Does Self-Control Affect Survey Response? Applying Exploratory Confirmatory, and Item Response Theory Analysis to Grasmick et al.'s Self-Control Scale." *Criminology* 38(3): 897–929.

Potter, R.H., and L.E. Saltzman. 2000. "Violence Prevention and Corrections-related Activities of the Centers for Disease Control and Prevention." *The Criminologist* 25(2): 1, 4–6.

Pound, R. 1943. "A Survey of Social Interests." *Harvard Law Review* 53: 1–39.

Pratt, T.C. and F.T. Cullen. 2000. "The Empirical Status of Gottfredson and Hirschi's General Theory of Crime: A Meta-Analysis." *Criminology* 38(3): 931–64.

Provenzo, E.F. 1991. *Video Kids: Making Sense of Nintendo.* Cambridge: Harvard University Press.

Quinn, M.J., and S.K. Tomita. 1986. *Elder Abuse and Neglect: Causes, Diagnosis and Intervention Strategies.* New York: Springer-Verlag.

Quinney, R., and J. Wildeman. 1991. *The Problem of Crime: A Peace and Social Justice Perspective.* Mountain View: Mayfield.

Ramos, Reyes. 1998. "Anatomy of a Drive-By: What Can We Learn from an Unexpected Death?" *The Sociological Quarterly* 39(2): 271–88.

Randall, D.M., L. Lee-Sammons, and P.H. Hagner. 1988. "Common versus Elite Crime Coverage in Network News." *Social Science Quarterly* 69(4): 910–29.

Rankin, J.H., and L.E. Wells. 1990. "The Effect of Parental Attachments and Direct Controls on Delinquency." *Journal of Research in Crime and Delinquency* 27(2): 140–65.

Reasons, C.E., L. Ross, and C. Paterson. 1981. *Assault on the Worker: Occupational Health and Safety in Canada.* Toronto: Butterworths.

Reckless, W. 1967. *The Crime Problem,* 4th ed. New York: Meredith.

Reiman, J.H. 1998. *The Rich Get Richer and the Poor Get Prison,* 5th ed. New York: Macmillan.

Reiss, A.J. Jr. 1984. "Consequences of Compliance and Deterrence Models of Law Enforcement for the Exercise of Police Discretion." *Law and Contemporary Problems* 47(4): 83–122.

———— 1986. "Official and Survey Crime Statistics." In E.A. Fattah (ed.), *From Crime Policy to Victim Policy–Reorienting the Justice System.* London: Macmillan.

Reinarman, C., and H.G. Levine. 1989. "The Crack Attack: Politics and Media in America's Latest Drug Scare." In J. Best (ed.), *Images of Issues.* New York: Aldine de Gruyter.

Reppetto, T. 1974. *A Residential Crime.* Cambridge: Ballinger.

Resick, P.A. 1987. "Psychological Effects of Victimization: Implications for the Criminal Justice System." *Crime and Delinquency* 33: 468–78.

Reuter, P. 1984a. "The (Continued) Vitality of Mythical Numbers." *Public Interest* 75: 135–47.

———— 1984b. "Social Control in Illegal Markets." In D. Black (ed.), *Toward a General Theory of Social Control, Volume 2: Selected Problems.* Orlando: Academic Press.

———— 1995. "The Decline of the American Mafia." *The Public Interest* 120: 88–9.

Rice, T.W., and C.R. Goldman. 1994. "Another Look at the Subculture of Violence Thesis: Who Murders Whom under What Circumstances?" *Sociological Spectrum* 14: 371–84.

Richardson, J.T., J. Best, and D.G. Bromley. 1991. *The Satanism Scare.* New York: Aldine de Gruyter.

Richie, B.E. 2000. "Exploring the Link Between Violence Against Women and Women's Involvement in Illegal Activity." *Research on Women and Girls in the Justice System,* Vol. 3. Washington: Office of Justice Programs, National Institute of Justice.

Riley, D. 1987. "Time and Crime: The Link between Teenager Lifestyle and Delinquency." *Journal of Quantitative Criminology* 3(4): 339–54.

Roberts, D. 1999a. "Insanity Rulings Blasted after Killings in Winnipeg." *Globe and Mail,* January 5: A1, A7.

———— 1999b. "Man Gets Two Life Sentences in Killings." *Globe and Mail,* December 4: A2.

Roberts, K. 1983. *Youth and Leisure.* London: George Allen & Unwin.

Robinson, M.B., and B.H. Zaitzow. 1999. "Criminologists: Are We What We Study? A National Self-Report Study of Crime Experts." *The Criminologist* 24(2): 1, 4, 17–19.

Rodgers, K., and G. Roberts. 1995. "Women's Non-Spousal Multiple Victimization: A Test of the Routine Activities Theory." *Canadian Journal of Criminology* 37(3): 363–91.

Roncek, D.W., and P.A. Maier. 1991. "Bars, Blocks and Crimes Revisited: Linking the Theory of Routine Activities to the Empiricism of 'Hot Spots.'" *Criminology* 29(4): 725–53.

Roncek, D.W., and M.A. Pravatiner. 1989. "Additional Evidence That Taverns Enhance Nearby Crime." *Sociology and Social Research* 73(4): 185–8.

Rosenbaum, D.P. 1987. "The Theory and Research behind Neighborhood Watch: Is It a Sound Fear and Crime Reduction Strategy?" *Crime and Delinquency* 33(1): 103–34. Used by permission of Sage Publications Inc.

———— 1988. "Community Crime Prevention: A Review and Synthesis of the Literature." *Justice Quarterly* 5(3): 323-95.

———— 1998. "The Changing Role of the Police: Assessing the Current Transition to Community Policing." In J-P. Brodeur (ed.), *How to Recognize Good Policing: Problems and Issues*. Thousand Oaks: Sage.

Rosnow, R.L. 1988. "Rumour as Communication: A Contextual Approach." *Journal of Communication* 38(1): 12–28.

Rosnow, R.L., and G.A. Fine. 1976. *Rumor and Gossip*. New York: Elsevier.

Ross, R., and G.L. Staines. 1972. "The Politics of Analyzing Social Problems." *Social Problems* 20(1): 18–40.

Rossmo, D. K. 2000. *Geographic Profiling*. Boca Raton, FL: CRC Press.

Rountree, P.W. 2000. "Weapons at School: Are the Predictors Generalizable Across Context?" *Sociological Spectrum* 20: 291–324.

Rountree, P.W., and K.C. Land. 1996. "Burglary Victimization, Perceptions of Crime Risk, and Routine Activities: A Multilevel Analysis across Seattle Neighbourhoods and Census Tracts." *Journal of Research in Crime and Delinquency* 33(2): 147–80.

Rubington, C., and M.S. Weinberg. 1987. *Deviance: The Interactionist Perspective*. New York: Macmillan.

Rush, G. 1994. *The Dictionary of Criminal Justice*, 4th ed. Guilford: Dushkin.

Sacco, V.F. 1990. "Gender, Fear and Victimization: A Preliminary Application of Power-Control Theory." *Sociological Spectrum* 10: 485–506.

——— 1995. "Media Constructions of Crime." *The Annals of the American Academy of Political and Social Science* 539: 141–54.

——— 1998. "Evaluating Satisfaction." In J-P. Brodeur (ed.), *How to Recognize Good Policing: Problems and Issues*, pp. 123–37. Thousand Oaks: Sage.

——— 2000. "News that Counts: Newspaper Images of Crime and Victimization Statistics." *Criminologie* 33(1): 203–23.

Sacco, V.F., and B.J. Fair. 1988. "Images of Legal Control: Crime News and the Process of Organizational Legitimation." *Canadian Journal of Communication* 13: 113–22.

Sacco, V.F., and H. Johnson. 1990. *Patterns of Criminal Victimization in Canada*. Ottawa: Minister of Supply and Services.

Sacco, V.F., H. Johnson, and R. Arnold. 1993. "Urban–Rural Residence and Criminal Victimization." *Canadian Journal of Sociology* 18(4): 431–51.

Sacco, V.F., and R.A. Silverman. 1982. "Crime Prevention through Mass Media: Prospects and Problems." *Journal of Criminal Justice* 10: 257–69.

Sacco, V.F., and E. Zureik. 1990. "Correlates of Computer Misuses: Data from a Self-Reporting Sample." *Behaviour and Information Technology* 9(5): 353–69.

Sagarin, E. 1975. *Deviants and Deviance*. New York: Praeger.

Sagrestano, L.M., C.L. Heavey, and A. Christensen. 1999. "Perceived Power and Physical Violence in Marital Conflict." *Journal of Social Issues* 55(1): 65–79.

St. John, C., and T. Heald-Moore. 1996. "Racial Prejudice and Fear of Criminal Victimization by Strangers in Public Settings." *Sociological Inquiry* 66(3): 267–84.

Sales, E., M. Baum, and B. Shore. 1984. "Victim Readjustment Following Assault." *Journal of Social Issues* 40(1): 117–36.

Salinger, L.R., P. Jesilow, H.N. Pontell, and G. Geis. 1993. "Assaults against Airline Flight Attendants: A Victimization Study." In H.N. Pontell (ed.), *Social Deviance*. Englewood Cliffs: Prentice-Hall.

Sampson, R.J. 1985. "Race and Criminal Violence: A Demographically Disaggregated Analysis of Urban Homicide." *Crime and Delinquency* 31(1): 47–82.

——— 1987. "Urban Black Violence: The Effect of Male Joblessness and Family Disruption." *American Journal of Sociology* 93(2): 348–82.

Sampson, R.J., and W.B. Groves. 1989. "Community Structure and Crime: Testing Social Disorganization Theory." *American Journal of Sociology* 94: 774–802.

Sampson, R.J., and J.H. Laub. 1990. "Crime and Deviance over the Life Course: The Salience of Adult Social Bonds." *American Sociological Review* 55: 609–27.

Sampson, R.J., and J.L. Lauritsen. 1990. "Deviant Lifestyles, Proximity Crime, and the Offender-Victim Link in Personal Violence." *Journal of Research in Crime and Delinquency* 27(2): 110–39.

Sampson, R.J., S. Raudenbush, and F.J. Earls. 1997. "Neighborhoods and Violent Crime: A Multilevel Study of Collective Efficacy." *Science* 277: 918–24.

Sanger, D.E. 1993. "How to Visit America and Get Out Alive." *Globe and Mail*, June 18: A9.

Sasson, T. 1995. *Crime Talks.* New York: Aldine de Gruyter.

Savitz, L.D. 1978. "Official Police Statistics and Their Limitations." In L.D. Savitz and N.Johnston (eds.), *Crime in Society.* New York: John Wiley.

Scheingold, S.A. 1984. *The Politics of Law and Order: Street Crime and Public Policy.* New York: Longman.

Schelling, T.C. 1967. "Economic Analysis of Organized Crime." In *President's Commission on Law Enforcement and Administration of Justice Task Force Report: Organized Crime, Annotations and Consultant's Papers,* 114–26. Washington: U.S. Government Printing Office.

Scheppele, K.L., and P.B. Bart. 1983. "Through Women's Eyes: Defining Danger in the Wake of Sexual Assault." *Journal of Social Issues* 39: 63–81.

Schissel, B. 1992. "The Influence of Economic Factors and Social Control Policy on Crime Rate Changes in Canada, 1962–1988." *Canadian Journal of Sociology* 17(4): 405–28.

Schissel, B., and K. Fedec. 1999. "The Selling of Innocence." *Canadian Journal of Criminology* 41(1): 33–56.

Schlesinger, P., R.E. Dobash, R.P. Dobash, and C.K. Weaver. 1992. *Women Viewing Violence.* London: BFI.

Schneider, V.W., and B. Wiersema. 1990. "Limits and Use of the Uniform Crime Reports." In D.L. MacKenzie, P.J. Baunach, and R.R. Roberg (eds.), *Measuring Crime: Large-Scale, Long-Range Efforts.* Albany: State University of New York Press.

Schur, E.M. 1965. *Crimes without Victims.* Englewood Cliffs: Prentice-Hall.

Scott, M., and S. Lyman. 1968. "Accounts." *American Sociological Review* 33: 42–62.

Scully, D., and J. Marolla. 1984. "Convicted Rapists' Vocabulary of Motive: Excuses and Justifications." *Social Problems* 31(5): 530–44.

Sellin, T. 1938. "Culture Conflict and Crime." A Report of the Subcommittee on Delinquency of the Committee on Personality and Culture. *Social Science Research Council Bulletin* 41.

Shaffer, E.B. 1980. *Community Policing.* London: Croom Helm.

Shaw, C.R., and H.D. McKay. 1942. *Juvenile Delinquency in Urban Areas.* Chicago: University of Chicago Press.

Sheldon, W.H. 1949. *Varieties of Delinquent Youth: An Introduction to Constitutional Psychiatry.* New York: Harper and Brothers.

Sheley, J.F. 1991. "Conflict in Criminal Law." In J.F. Sheley (ed.), *Criminology: A Contemporary Handbook.* Belmont: Wadsworth.

Sheley, J.F., and J.D. Wright. 1998. "High School Youths, Weapons, and Violence: A National Survey." *National Institute of Justice Research in Brief.* Washington: Office of Justice Programs, National Institute of Justice.

Sherman, L. 1992. *Policing Domestic Violence: Experiments and Dilemmas.* New York: The Free Press.

Sherman, L., and R. Berk. 1984. "The Specific Deterrent Effects of Arrest for Domestic Assault." *American Sociological Review* 49: 261–72.

Sherman, L., P.R. Gartin, and M.E. Buerger. 1989. "Routine Activities and the Criminology of Place." *Criminology* 27(1): 27–55.

Sherman, L., D.C. Gottfredson, D.L. MacKenzie, J. Eck, P. Reuter, and S.D. Bushway. 1998. "Preventing Crime: What Works, What Doesn't, What's Promising." *National Institute of Justice Research in Brief.* Washington: Office of Justice Programs, U.S. Department of Justice.

Sherrill, R. 1997. "A Year in Corporate Crime." *The Nation* April 7: 11–12, 14, 16–20.

Shibutani, T. 1966. *Improvised News: A Sociological Study of Rumor.* Indianapolis: Bobbs-Merrill.

Shotland, R.L. 1976. "Spontaneous Vigilantism: A Bystander Response to Criminal Behavior." In H.J. Rosenbaum and P.C. Sederberg (eds.), *Vigilante Politics.* Philadelphia: University of Pennsylvania Press.

Shotland, R.L., and L.I. Goodstein. 1984. "The Role of Bystanders in Crime Control." *Journal of Social Issues* 40(1): 9–26.

Shotland, R.L., and M.K. Straw. 1976. "Bystander Response to an Assault: When a Man Attacks a Woman." *Journal of Personality and Social Psychology* 34: 990–9.

Shover, N. 1973. "The Social Organization of Burglary." *Social Problems* 201 (Spring): 499–513.

——— 1983. "The Later Stages of Ordinary Property Offender Careers." *Social Problems* 30: 208–18.

Silverman, R.A., and L.W. Kennedy. 1993. *Deadly Deeds: Murder in Canada.* Scarborough: Nelson Canada.

Silverman, R.A., and M.O. Nielsen. 1992. *Aboriginal Peoples and Canadian Criminal Justice.* Toronto: Butterworths.

Silverman, R.A., J.J. Teevan, and V.F. Sacco (eds.). 2000. *Crime in Canadian Society*, 6th ed. Toronto: Harcourt Brace.

Simon, D.R. 1996. *Elite Deviance*, 5th ed. Boston: Allyn & Bacon.

Simon, D.R., and D.S. Eitzen. 1993. *Elite Deviance,* 4th ed. Boston: Allyn & Bacon.

Simourd, L., and D.A. Andrews. 2000. "Correlates of Delinquency: A Look at Gender Differences." In R.A. Silverman, J.J. Teevan, and V.F. Sacco (eds.), *Crime in Canadian Society*, 6th ed. Toronto: Harcourt Brace.

Simpson, S.C., and C.S. Koper. 1992. "Deterring Corporate Crime." *Criminology* 30(3): 347–75.

Simpson, S.S. 1989. "Feminist Theory, Crime and Justice." *Criminology* 27(4): 605–31.

Singer, S.I., and M. Levine. 1988. "Power-Control Theory, Gender and Delinquency: A Partial Replication with Additional Evidence on the Effect of Peers." *Criminology* 26: 627–47.

Skaret, D., and C. Wilgosh. 1989. "Learning Disabilities and Juvenile Delinquency: A Causal Relationship." *International Journal for the Advancement of Counselling* 12: 113–23.

Skipper, J.K. 1985. "Nicknames of Notorious American Twentieth Century Deviants: The Decline of the Folk Hero Syndrome." *Deviant Behavior* 6: 99–114.

Skogan, W.G. 1976. "Citizen Reporting of Crime: Some National Panel Data." *Criminology* 13(4): 535–49.

——— 1977. "Dimensions of the Dark Figure of Unreported Crime." *Crime and Delinquency* 23: 41–50.

——— 1981. "On Attitudes and Behavior." In D.A. Lewis (ed.), *Reactions to Crime.* Beverly Hills: Sage.

——— 1986. "Methodological Issues in the Study of Victimization." In E.A. Fattah (ed.), *From Crime Policy to Victim Policy—Reorienting the Justice System.* London: Macmillan.

———— 1987. "The Impact of Victimization on Fear." *Crime and Delinquency* 33: 135–54.

———— 1990a. "The National Crime Survey Redesign." *Public Opinion Quarterly* 54: 256–72.

———— 1990b. *Disorder and Decline.* New York: The Free Press.

———— 1993. "The Various Meanings of Fear." In W. Bilsky, C. Pfeiffer, and P. Wetzels (eds.), *Fear of Crime and Criminal Victimization.* Stuttgart: Ferdinand Enke Verlag.

Skogan, W.G., and M.G. Maxfield. 1981. *Coping with Crime: Individual and Neighborhood Reactions.* Beverly Hills: Sage.

Skogan, W.G., and M.A. Wycoff. 1987. "Some Unexpected Effects of a Police Service for Victims." *Crime and Delinquency* 33: 490–501.

Skolnick, J. 1966. *Justice without Trial.* New York: John Wiley.

Smith, D. 1975. *The Mafia Mystique.* New York: Basic Books.

Smith, D.A. 1987. "Police Response to Interpersonal Violence: Defining the Parameters of Legal Control." *Social Forces* 65(3): 767–82.

Smith, D.A., and G.R. Jarjoura. 1989. "Household Characteristics, Neighborhood Composition and Victimization Risk." *Social Forces* 68(2): 621–40.

Smith, L.N., and G.D. Hill. 1991. "Victimization and Fear of Crime." *Criminal Justice and Behavior* 18: 217–39.

Smith, R.S., S.G. Frazee, and E.L. Davison. 2000. "Furthering the Integration of Routine Activity and Social Disorganization Theories: Small Units of Analysis and the Study of Street Robbery as a Diffusion Process." *Criminology* 38(2): 489–524.

Snider, L. 1992. "Commercial Crime." In V.F. Sacco (ed.), *Deviance: Conformity and Control in Canadian Society,* 2nd ed. Scarborough: Prentice-Hall.

———— 1993. *Bad Business: Corporate Crime in Canada.* Scarborough: Nelson Canada.

Solicitor General of Canada. 1983. *Canadian Urban Victimization Survey Bulletin 1: Victims of Crime.* Ottawa: Programs Branch/Research and Statistics Group.

———— 1984. *Canadian Urban Victimization Survey Bulletin 3: Crime Prevention Awareness and Practice.* Ottawa: Programs Branch/Research and Statistics Group.

———— 1998. *The Organized Crime Impact Study.* Ottawa: Solicitor General of Canada.

Sorenson, A.M., and D. Brownfield. 1995. "Adolescent Drug Use and a General Theory of Crime: An Analysis of Theoretical Integration." *Canadian Journal of Criminology* 37(1): 19–37.

Sparks, R. 1992. *Television and the Drama of Crime.* Buckingham: Open University Press.

Spector, M., and J.I. Kitsuse. 1977. *Constructing Social Problems.* Menlo Park: Cummings.

Sprott, J.B., and A.N. Doob. 2000. "Bad, Sad, and Rejected: The Lives of Aggressive Children." *Canadian Journal of Criminology* 42(2): 123–34.

Stafford, M.C., and O.R. Galle. 1984. "Victimization Rates, Exposure to Risk, and Fear of Crime." *Criminology* 22(2): 173–85.

Stafford, M.C., and J.P. Gibbs. 1980. "Crime Rates in an Ecological Context: Extension of a Proposition." *Social Science Quarterly* 61(3–4): 653–65.

Stafford, M.C., and M. Warr. 1993. "A Reconceptualization of General and Specific Deterrence." *Journal of Research in Crime and Delinquency* 30(2): 123–35.

Standing Committee on Justice and the Solicitor General. 1993. *Crime Prevention in Canada: Toward a National Strategy.* Ottawa: Queen's Printer.

Stanko, E. 1985. *Intimate Intrusions: Women's Experience of Male Violence.* London: Routledge & Kegan Paul.

——— 1995. "Women, Crime, and Fear." *Annals of the Academy of Political and Social Science* 539: 46–58.

Steffensmeier, D., and E. Allan. 1995. "Criminal Behaviour: Gender and Crime." In J.F. Sheley (ed.), *Criminology: A Contemporary Handbook*, 2nd ed. Belmont: Wadsworth.

Steffensmeier, D.J., and R.H. Steffensmeier. 1977. "Who Reports Shoplifters?: Research Continuities and Further Developments." *International Journal of Criminology and Penology* 3: 79–95.

Steinmetz, S. 1977-78. "The Battered Husband Syndrome." *Victimology: An International Journal* 2: 499–509.

Stevenson, K., J. Tufts, D. Hendrick, and M. Kowalski. 1998. *A Profile of Youth in Canada.* Ottawa: Minister of Industry.

Stone, S.D. 1993. "Getting the Message Out: Feminists, the Press and Violence against Women." *Canadian Review of Sociology and Anthropology* 30(3): 377–400.

Straus, M.A. 1990. "Social Stress and Marital Violence in a National Sample of American Families." In M.A. Straus and R.J. Gelles (eds.), *Physical Violence in American Families: Risk Factors and Adaptations to Violence in 8,145 Families.* New Brunswick: Transaction.

————— 1991. "Discipline and Deviance: Physical Punishment of Children and Violence and Other Forms of Crime in Adulthood." *Social Problems* 38(2): 133–52.

Straus, M.A., and C. Smith. 1990. "Family Patterns and Child Abuse." In M.A. Straus and R.J. Gelles (eds.), *Physical Violence in American Families: Risk Factors and Adaptations to Violence in 8,145 Families.* New Brunswick: Transaction.

Strike, C. 1995. "Women Assaulted by Strangers." *Canadian Social Trends* 36: 2–6.

Sugarman, D.B., and G.T. Hotaling. 1989. "Dating Violence: Prevalence, Context and Risk Markers." In M.A. Pirog-Good and J.E. Stets (eds.), *Violence in Dating Relationships.* New York: Praeger.

Sumser, J. 1996. *Morality and Social Order in Television Crime Drama.* Jefferson: McFarland and Co.

Surette, R. 1992. *Media, Crime, and Criminal Justice: Images and Realities.* Pacific Grove: Brooks/Cole.

Sutherland, E.H. 1940. "White-Collar Criminality." *American Sociological Review* 5: 1–12.

————— 1947. *Principles of Criminology,* 4th ed. Chicago: Lippincott.

————— 1961. *White Collar Crime.* New York: Holt, Rinehart & Winston.

Tanner, J. 1992. "Youthful Deviance." In V.F. Sacco (ed.), *Deviance: Control and Conformity in Canadian Society,* 2nd ed. Scarborough: Prentice-Hall.

————— 2001. *Teenage Troubles.* 2nd ed. Scarborough: Nelson Canada.

Tate, E.D. 1998. "The Ontario Royal Commission on Violence in the Communications Industry: Twenty Years Later." *British Journal of Communication Studies* 13(1): 148–63.

Taylor, R.B., and S. Gottfredson. 1986. "Environmental Design and Prevention: An Examination of Community Dynamics." In A.J. Reiss, Jr., and M. Tonry (eds.), *Communities and Crime.* Chicago: University of Chicago Press.

Taylor, R.B., and A.V. Harrell. 1996. *Physical Environment and Crime.* Washington: U.S. Department of Justice.

Taylor, S.E., J.V. Wood, and R.R. Lichtman. 1983. "It Could Be Worse: Selective Evaluation as a Response to Victimization." *Journal of Social Issues* 39: 19–40.

Teevan, J.J., and H.B. Dryburgh. 2000. "First Person Accounts and Sociological Explanations of Delinquency." *Canadian Review of Sociology and Anthropology* 37(1): 77–93.

Thornberry, T.P. 1987. "Toward an Interactional Theory of Delinquency." *Criminology* 25(4): 863–92.

Thornberry, T.P., A.J. Lizotte, M.D. Krohn, M. Farnworth, and S.J. Jang. 1991. "Testing Interactional Theory: An Examination of Reciprocal Causal Relationships Among Family, School, and Delinquency." *Journal of Criminal Law and Criminology* 82(1): 3–33.

Tibbetts, S.G., and D.C. Herz. 1996. "Gender Differences in Factors of Social Control and Rational Choice." *Deviant Behavior: An Interdisciplinary Journal* 17: 183–208.

Tierney, K. 1982. "The Battered Women Movement and the Creation of the Wife Beating Problem." *Social Problems* 29: 207–20.

Timmer, D.A., and W.H. Norman. 1984. "The Ideology of Victim Precipitation." *Criminal Justice Review* 9: 63–8.

Tjaden, P., and N. Thoennes. 1998a. "Prevalence, Incidence, and Consequences of Violence Against Women: Findings from the National Violence Against Women Survey." *National Institute of Justice Centers for Disease Control and Prevention*. Washington: U.S. Department of Justice.

——— 1998b. "Stalking in America: Findings from the National Violence Against Women Survey." *National Institute of Justice Centers for Disease Control and Prevention*. Washington: U.S. Department of Justice.

Toby, J. 1974. "The Socialization and Control of Deviant Motivation." In Daniel Glaser (ed.), *Handbook of Criminology*. Chicago: Rand McNally.

Toby, Jackson. 1995. "The Schools." In J.Q. Wilson and J. Peterson (eds.), *Crime: Twenty-eight Leading Experts Look at the Most Pressing Problem of our Time*. San Francisco: Institute for Contemporary Studies Press.

Tracy, P.E., and J.A. Fox. 1989. "A Field Experiment on Insurance Fraud in Auto Body Repair." *Criminology* 27: 509–603.

Traub, S.H., and C.B. Little (eds.). 1980. *Theories of Deviance*, 2nd ed. Itasca: F.E. Peacock.

Tremblay, M., and P. Tremblay. 1998. "Social Structure, Integration Opportunities, and the Direction of Violent Offenses." *Journal of Research in Crime and Delinquency* 35(3): 295–315.

Tremblay, S. 1999. "Crime Statistics in Canada, 1998." *Juristat* 19(9).

——— 2000. "Crime Statistics in Canada, 1999." *Juristat* 20(5).

Tufts, Jennifer. 2000. "Public Attitudes Towards the Criminal Justice System." *Juristat* 20(12).

Tunnell, K.D. 1992. *Choosing Crime: The Criminal Calculus of Property Offenders.* Chicago: Nelson-Hall.

———— 1998. "Reflections on Crime, Criminals, and Control in Newsmagazine Television Programs." In F. Bailey and D. Hale (eds.), *Popular Culture, Crime and Justice.* Belmont: West/Wadsworth.

Turk, A. 1976. "Law as a Weapon in Social Conflict." *Social Problems* 23: 276–92.

Turner, P.A. 1993. *I Heard It Through the Grapevine.* Berkeley: University of California Press.

Tyler, T. 1990. *Why People Obey the Law.* Chicago: University of Chicago Press.

Uggen, C. 2000. "Class, Gender, and Arrest: An Intergenerational Analysis of Workplace Power and Control." *Criminology* 38(3): 835–62.

U.S. Department of Justice. 1988. *Report to the Nation on Crime and Justice,* 2nd ed. Washington: Bureau of Justice Statistics.

Van Brunschot, E. 2000. "Assault Stories." In R.A. Silverman, J.T. Teevan, and V.F. Sacco (eds.), *Crime in Canadian Society,* 6th ed. Toronto: Harcourt Brace.

Van den Haag, E. 1975. *Punishing Criminals: Concerning a Very Old and Painful Question.* New York: Basic Books.

van Dijk, J.J.M., and J. de Waard. 1991. "A Two-Dimensional Typology of Crime Prevention Projects with a Bibliography." *Criminal Justice Abstracts* (September).

van Wormer, K.S., and C. Batollos. 2000. *Women and the Criminal Justice System.* Boston: Allyn & Bacon.

Venkatesh, S.A. 1997. "The Social Organization of Street Gang Activity in an Urban Ghetto." *American Journal of Sociology* 103(1): 82–111.

Veysey, B.M., and S.T. Messner. 1999. "Further Testing of Social Disorganization Theory: An Elaboration of Sampson and Grove's 'Community Structure and Crime.'" *Journal of Research in Crime and Delinquency* 36(2): 156–74.

Victor, J.S. 1993. *Satanic Panic.* Chicago: Open Court.

Visher, C.A. 1991. "Career Offenders and Selective Incapacitation." In J.F. Sheley (ed.), *Criminology: A Contemporary Handbook.* Belmont: Wadsworth.

Vogel, R.E., and M.J. Himlein. 1995. "Dating and Sexual Victimization: An Analysis of Risk Factors among Precollege Women." *Journal of Criminal Justice* 23(2): 153–62.

Vold, G.B., T.J. Bernard, and J.B. Snipes. 1998. *Theoretical Criminology*, 4th ed. New York: Oxford University Press.

Voumvakis, S.E., and R.V. Ericson. 1984. *News Accounts of Attacks on Women: A Comparison of Three Toronto Newspapers.* Toronto: Centre of Criminology, University of Toronto.

Vowell, P.R., and D.C. May. 2000. "Another Look at Classic Strain Theory." *Sociological Inquiry* 70(1): 42–60.

Wachs, E. 1988. *Crime-Victim Stories: New York City's Urban Folklore.* Bloomington and Indianapolis: Indiana University Press.

Wagner, D. 1997. *The New Temperance: The American Obsession with Sin and Vice.* Boulder: Westview Press.

Walby, S., and A. Myhill, *Reducing Domestic Violence…What Works?* London: Home Office Research.

Walker, S.G., and C.R. Walker. 1993. "The Victoria Community Police Stations: An Exercise in Innovation." In J. Chacko and S.E. Nancoo (eds.), *Community Policing in Canada*, pp. 47–89. Toronto: Canadian Scholar's Press.

Walklate, S. 1989. *Victimology: The Victim and the Criminal Justice System.* London: Unwin Hyman.

Waller, I. 1982. "Victimization Studies as Guides to Action: Some Cautions and Suggestions." In H.J. Schneider (ed.), *The Victim in International Perspective.* New York: Aldine de Gruyter.

——— 1989. *Current Trends in European Crime Prevention: Implications for Canada.* Ottawa: Department of Justice Canada.

Waller, I., and N. Okihiro. 1978. *Burglary: The Victim and the Public.* Toronto: University of Toronto Press.

Waller, I., and R. Weiler. 1984. *Crime Prevention through Social Development.* Ottawa: Canadian Council on Social Development.

Walters, G.D., and T.W. White. 1989. "Heredity and Crime: Bad Genes or Bad Research." *Criminology* 27(3): 455–8.

Warchol, G. 1998. *Bureau of Justice Statistics Special Report, National Crime Survey, Workplace Violence.* Washington: U.S. Department of Justice.

Warr, M. 1985. "Fear of Rape among Urban Women." *Social Problems* 32: 238–50.

——— 1988. "Rape, Burglary, and Opportunity." *Journal of Quantitative Criminology* 4(3): 275–88.

————— 1989. "What Is the Perceived Seriousness of Crime?" *Criminology* 27: 795–821.

————— 1990. "Dangerous Situations: Social Control and Fear of Victimization." *Social Forces* 68(3): 891–907.

————— 1991. "America's Perceptions of Crime and Punishment." In J.F. Sheley (ed.), *Criminology: A Contemporary Handbook.* Belmont: Wadsworth.

————— 1998. "Life-Course Transitions and Desistance from Crime." *Criminology* 36(2): 183–215.

Warr, M., and M.C. Stafford. 1983. "Fear of Victimization: A Look at Proximate Causes." *Social Forces* 61: 1033–43.

Webb, V.J., and I.H. Marshall. 1989. "Response to Criminal Victimization by Older Americans." *Criminal Justice and Behavior* 16(2): 239–58.

Weed, F. 1995. *Certainty of Justice: Reforms in the Crime Victim Movement.* New York: Aldine de Gruyter.

Weeks, E.L., J.M. Boles, A.P. Garbin, and J. Blount. 1986. "The Transformation of Sexual Harassment from a Private Trouble to a Public Issue." *Sociological Inquiry* 56: 432–55.

Weis, J.G. 1989. "Family Violence Research Methodology and Design." In L. Ohlin and M. Tonry (eds.), *Family Violence, Crime and Justice—A Review of Research,* vol. 11. Chicago: University of Chicago Press.

Welch, D. 2000. "News into the Next Century: Introduction." *Historical Journal of Film, Radio and Television* 20(1): 5–13.

Wellford, C. 1975. "Labelling Theory and Criminology: An Assessment." *Social Problems* 22: 332–45.

Wellford, C.F. 1997. "Victimization Rates for Domestic Travelers." *Journal of Criminal Justice* 3: 205–10.

Wells, L.E., and J.H. Rankin. 1986. "The Broken Homes Model of Delinquency: Analytical Issues." *Journal of Research in Crime and Delinquency* 23(1): 68–93.

————— 1988. "Direct Parental Controls and Delinquency." *Criminology* 26: 263–85.

————— 1991. "Families and Delinquency: A Meta-Analysis of the Impact of Broken Homes." *Social Problems* 38(1): 71–93.

Whitaker, C.J., and L.D. Bastian. 1991. *Teenage Victims.* A National Crime Survey Report. Washington: U.S. Department of Justice.

White, R. and F. Hanes. 2000. *Crime and Criminology,* 2nd ed. Oxford: Oxford University Press.

Widom, C.S. 1995. "Victimization of Childhood Sexual Abuse—Later Criminal Consequences." Washington: U.S. Department of Justice.

Will, J.A., and J.H. McGrath 1995. "Crime, Neighborhood Perceptions, and the Underclass: The Relationship between Fear of Crime and Class Position." *Journal of Criminal Justice* 23(2): 163–76.

Williams, K.R., and R.L. Flewelling. 1988. "The Social Production of Criminal Homicide: A Comparative Study of Disaggregated Rates in American Cities." *American Sociological Review* 53: 421–31.

Williams, K.R., and R. Hawkins. 1986. "Perceptual Research on General Deterrence: A Critical Review." *Law and Society Review* 20: 545–72.

Wilson, J. 1980. "Sociology of Leisure." *Annual Review of Sociology* 6: 21–40.

Wilson, J.Q. 1983. *Thinking About Crime.* New York: Vintage.

Wilson, J.Q., and R.J. Herrnstein. 1985. *Crime and Human Nature.* New York: Simon & Schuster.

Wilson, J.Q., and G.L. Kelling. 1982. "Broken Windows." *Atlantic Monthly* (March): 29–38.

Wilson, W.J. 1987. *The Truly Disadvantaged: The Inner City, the Underclass, and Public Policy.* Chicago: University of Chicago Press.

Wirth, L. 1938. "Urbanism as a Way of Life." *American Journal of Sociology* 44: 3–24.

Wittebrood, K., and P. Nieuwbeerta. 2000. "Criminal Victimization During One's Life Course: The Effects of Previous Victimization and Patterns of Routine Activities." *Journal of Research in Crime and Delinquency* 37(1): 91–122.

Wolf, L. 1991. "Drug Crimes." *Canadian Social Trends* 20: 27–9.

Wolfgang, M. 1958. *Patterns in Criminal Homicide.* Philadelphia: University of Pennsylvania Press.

Wolfgang, M., and F. Ferracuti. 1967. *The Subculture of Violence: Towards an Integrated Theory in Criminology.* Beverly Hills: Sage.

Wolfgang, M., R.M. Figlio, and T. Sellin. 1972. *Delinquency in a Birth Cohort.* Chicago: University of Chicago Press.

Wood, C. 2000. "Why Do Men Do It?" *Maclean's,* August 7: 34–7.

Wood, D.S., and C.T. Griffiths. 2000. "Patterns of Aboriginal Crime." In R.A. Silverman, J.T. Teevan, and V.F. Sacco (eds.), *Crime in Canadian Society,* 6th ed. Toronto: Harcourt Brace.

Wortley, S. 1999. "A Northern Taboo: Research on Race, Crime, and Criminal Justice in Canada." *Canadian Journal of Criminology* April 1999 41(2): 261–74.

Wright, J.D., and P. Rossi. 1986. *Armed and Considered Dangerous: A Survey of Felons and Their Firearms*. Hawthorne: Aldine de Gruyter.

Wright, J.P., and F.T. Cullen. 2000. "Juvenile Involvement in Occupational Delinquency." *Criminology* 38(3): 863–96.

Wright, R., and T. Bennett. 1990. "Exploring the Offender's Perspective: Observing and Interviewing Criminals." In K.L. Kempf (ed.), *Measurement Issues in Criminology*. New York: Springer-Verlag.

Wright R., and S.H. Decker. 1994. *Burglars on the Job: Streetlife and Residential Break-Ins*. Boston: Northeastern University Press.

Wright, R., R.H. Logie, and S.H. Decker. 1995. "Criminal Expertise and Offender Decision Making: An Experimental Study of the Target Selection Process in Residential Burglary." *Journal of Research in Crime and Delinquency* 32(1): 39–53.

Wright, R.A., and J.M. Miller. 1998. "Taboo Until Today: The Coverage of Biological Arguments in Criminology Textbooks, 1961 to 1970 and 1987 to 1996." *Journal of Criminal Justice* 26(1): 1–19.

Yin, P. 1980. "Fear of Crime among the Elderly: Some Issues and Suggestions." *Social Problems* 27: 492–504.

——— 1982. "Fear of Crime as a Problem for the Elderly." *Social Problems* 30: 240–5.

Zawitz, M.W., P.A. Klaus, R. Bachman, L.D. Bastian, M.M. DeBerry, Jr., M.R. Rand, and B.M. Tayler. 1993. *Highlights from 20 Years of Surveying Crime Victims*. Washington: Bureau of Justice Statistics.

Ziegenhagen, E.A., and D. Brosnan. 1985. "Victims' Responses to Robbery and Crime Control Policy." *Criminology* 23: 675–95.

NAME INDEX

SUBJECT INDEX